Fodor's 2001

Vancouver and British Columbia

The complete guide, thoroughly up-to-date

Packed with details that will make your trip

The must-see sights, off and on the beaten path

What to see, what to skip

Vacation itineraries, walking tours, day trips

Smart lodging and dining options

Essential local do's and taboos

Transportation tips

Key contacts, savvy travel advice

When to go, what to pack

Clear, accurate, easy-to-use maps

Excerpted from *Fodor's Canada 2001*

...vel Publications

...ors.com

Fodor's Vancouver and British Columbia

EDITOR: Christine Swiac

Editorial Contributors: Shannon Kelly, Sue Kernaghan
Editorial Production: Linda K. Schmidt
Maps: David Lindroth, *cartographer*; Rebecca Baer and Robert Blake, *map editors*
Design: Fabrizio La Rocca, *creative director*; Guido Caroti, *art director*; Jolie Novak, *senior picture editor*
Cover Design: Pentagram
Production/Manufacturing: Angela McLean
Cover Photograph: Paul A. Souders/Corbis

Copyright

ISBN 0–679–00729–6

ISSN 1531–3425

Special Sales

Important Tip

Although all prices, opening times, and other details in this book are based on information supplied to us at press time, changes occur all the time in the travel world, and Fodor's cannot accept responsibility for facts that become outdated or for inadvertent errors or omissions. So **always confirm information when it matters,** especially if you're making a detour to visit a specific place.

CONTENTS

On the Road with Fodor's   v

Don't Forget to Write *v*

Smart Travel Tips A to Z   x

1   Destination: Vancouver and British Columbia   1

The Beauty and the Buzz *2*
New and Noteworthy *3*
What's Where *4*
Fodor's Choice *4*
Books and Videos *6*
Festivals and Seasonal Events *8*

2   Vancouver   10

Exploring Vancouver *14*
CLOSE-UP: *Rainy Days 25*
CLOSE-UP: *Urban Safari 28*
Dining *39*
Lodging *53*
Nightlife and the Arts *61*
Outdoor Activities and Sports *65*
Shopping *69*
Vancouver A to Z *71*

3   Victoria and Vancouver Island   78

Victoria *82*
Vancouver Island *99*

4   British Columbia   121

Coast Mountain Circle *125*
Sunshine Coast *138*
The Gulf Islands *143*
North Coast *150*
The Cariboo and the North *154*
The High Country and the Okanagan Valley *157*
The Kootenays *165*
British Columbia A to Z *167*

Index   173

IV

Contents

Maps

Canada *vi–vii*
Southern British Columbia
 vii–ix
Greater Vancouver *12–13*
Downtown Vancouver *17*
Stanley Park *24*
Granville Island *29*
Downtown Vancouver
 Dining *40*

Greater Vancouver Dining *49*
Vancouver Lodging *55*
Vancouver Island *81*
Downtown Victoria *84*
Southern British Columbia
 126–127
Salt Spring Island *147*

ON THE ROAD WITH FODOR'S

EVERY TRIP is significant, so we've pulled out all the stops in preparing *Fodor's Vancouver and British Columbia 2001*. To guide you in putting together your Pacific Northwest experience, we've created multiday itineraries and neighborhood walks. Our writer has seen all corners of Vancouver and British Columbia and will direct you to the places that are truly worth your time and money.

Vancouver-born freelance writer **Sue Kernaghan,** now a resident of Salt Spring Island, enjoyed getting reacquainted with her hometown for this book. A fourth-generation British Columbian, Sue has pestered elderly relatives for historical insights and covered a lot of dirt roads, open water, and country pubs while researching the places covered in this book.

Don't Forget to Write

We love feedback—positive and negative—and follow up on all suggestions. So contact the Vancouver and British Columbia editor at editors@fodors.com or c/o Fodor's, 280 Park Avenue, New York, New York 10017. Have a wonderful trip!

Karen Cure
Editorial Director

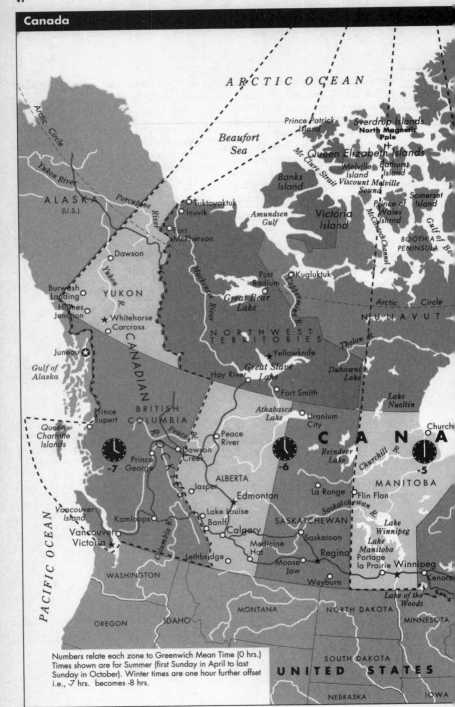

ARCTIC OCEAN

Prince Patrick Island

Sverdrup Islands
North Magnetic Pole

Beaufort Sea

Queen Elizabeth Islands

Mc Clure Strait

Melville Island

Bathurst Island

Viscount Melville Sound

Banks Island

Prince of Wales Island

McClintock Channel

Somerset Island

Amundsen Gulf

Victoria Island

BOOTHIA PENINSULA

Gulf of Bo

Arctic Circle

Yukon River

Porcupine River

Tuktoyaktuk

Inuvik

Fort McPherson

ALASKA (U.S.)

Dawson

Yukon R.

Mackenzie River

Port Radium

Kugluktuk

Coppermine R.

Great Bear Lake

Arctic Circle

NUNAVUT

Burwash Landing

Haines Junction

YUKON

Whitehorse

Carcross

NORTHWEST TERRITORIES

Thelon R.

Yellowknife

Juneau

CANADIAN

Great Slave Lake

Dubawnt Lake

Lake Nueltin

Gulf of Alaska

Hay River

Fort Smith

Prince Rupert

Queen Charlotte Islands

BRITISH COLUMBIA

Athabasca Lake

Uranium City

C A N A D A

Lake Nueltin

Peace R.

Peace River

Reindeer Lake

Churchill R.

Church

Prince George

-7

Dawson Creek

-6

-5

Vancouver Island

ALBERTA

Jasper

La Ronge

Flin Flon

MANITOBA

Saskatchewan R.

PACIFIC OCEAN

Kamloops

Edmonton

Lake Louise

Banff

Columbia R.

SASKATCHEWAN

Saskatoon

Lake Winnipeg

Vancouver

Victoria

Calgary

Medicine Hat

Regina

Lake Manitoba

Portage la Prairie

Winnipeg

Lethbridge

Moose Jaw

Kenora

WASHINGTON

Weyburn

Lake of the Woods

OREGON

IDAHO

MONTANA

NORTH DAKOTA

MINNESOTA

Numbers relate each zone to Greenwich Mean Time (0 hrs.)
Times shown are for Summer (first Sunday in April to last
Sunday in October). Winter times are one hour further offset
i.e., -7 hrs. becomes -8 hrs.

SOUTH DAKOTA

U N I T E D   S T A T E S

NEBRASKA

IOWA

ICELAND

Denmark Strait

GREENLAND
(Denmark)

Ellesmere Island

Devon
Island

Lancaster Sound

*Baffin
Bay*

*Davis
Strait*

Baffin Island

Prince
Charles
Island

*Foxe
Basin*

Sothia

Lake Amadjuak

Iqaluit ★
Lake Harbour ○

Hudson Strait

Cape Chidley

Ivujivik ○

*Southampton
Island*

*Ungava
Bay*

*Labrador
Sea*

Nain ●

Battle
Harbour

Coats
Island

Mansel
Island

🕐 2:30

*Hudson
Bay*

Belcher
Islands

🕐 -4

Schefferville ○

LABRADOR

Goose Bay ○

Gander ○

D   A

Fort Severn ○

Labrador City ○

St. John's

Severn R.

Fort George ○

QUÉBEC

Sept-Iles ○

🕐 -3

*James
Bay*

*Lake
Mistassini*

Anticosti Island

ST. PIERRE AND
MIQUELON
(France)

Moosonee ○

*GASPÉ
PENINSULA*

Rimouski ○

ONTARIO

Chicoutimi ○

St. Lawrence River

PRINCE
EDWARD
ISLAND

Sydney

*Lake
Nipigon*

Cochrane ○

Ste. Agathe-
Des-Monts ○

Québec
City ★

NEW
BRUNSWICK

Charlottetown

Timmins ○

Trois-
Rivières ○

Fredericton ★

NOVA
SCOTIA

Thunder
Bay ○

Sault
Ste. Marie ○

North
Bay ○

Montréal ●

Saint John ●

Halifax ★

Lake Superior

Sudbury ○

Ottawa ★

MAINE

*Bay of
Fundy*

*Lake
Huron*

Toronto ●

*Lake
Ontario*

VT.

N.H.

ATLANTIC
OCEAN

WISCONSIN

Lake Michigan

Niagara
Falls

Lake Erie

NEW YORK

MASSACHUSETTS

R.I.

N

MICHIGAN

CONN.

ILLINOIS

INDIANA

OHIO

PENNSYLVANIA

N.J.

| 0 | | 400 miles |
| 0 | | 600 km |

Southern British Columbia

ALASKA (USA)

Takla Lake

Hazelton

Babine Lake

Stuart Lake

Nisga'a Memorial Lava Bed Park

Terrace

Skeena River

NAIKOON PROVINCIAL PARK

Masset

Prince Rupert

Port Edward

Kitimat

Douglas Channel

Ootsa Lake

Eutsuk Lake

TWEEDSMUIR PARK

Hecate Strait

Tlell

Graham Island

Skidegate

Queen Charlotte

Queen Charlotte Islands (Haida Gwaii)

Moresby Island

Grenville Channel

Finlayson Channel

Bella Coola

GWAII HAANAS NATIONAL PARK RESERVE

Bella Bella

Discovery Coast Passage

Fitz Hugh Sound

COAST

MOUNTAIN

Queen Charlotte Strait

Cape Scott

Port Hardy

PACIFIC OCEAN

VANCOUVER ISLAND

Campbell River

Courte

STRATHCONA PROVINCIAL PARK

Tofino

KEY

— Rail Lines

🛥 Ferry

🍁 Trans-Canada Hwy.

N

0   100 miles

0   140 km

SMART TRAVEL TIPS A TO Z

Basic Information on Traveling in British Columbia, Savvy Tips to Make Your Trip a Breeze, and Companies and Organizations to Contact

AIR TRAVEL

BOOKING

When you book **look for nonstop flights** and **remember that "direct" flights stop at least once.** Try to avoid connecting flights, which require a change of plane.

CARRIERS

When flying internationally, you must usually choose between a domestic carrier, the national flag carrier of the country you are visiting, and a foreign carrier from a third country. You may, for example, choose to fly Air Canada to Canada. National flag carriers have the greatest number of nonstops. Domestic carriers may have better connections to your hometown and serve a greater number of gateway cities. Third-party carriers may have a price advantage.

Within Canada, regularly scheduled flights to every major city and to most smaller cities are available on one of the country's two major airlines—Air Canada or Canadian Airlines International—and the regional feeder airlines associated with them. At press time, Air Canada was in the process of merging its operations with the smaller, financially troubled Canadian Airlines, but was promising to maintain it as a separate brand. The smaller regional airlines can also be contacted through Air Canada's toll-free numbers or at local numbers within each of the many cities they serve.

For regulations and for the locations of air bases that allow private flights, you should check with the regional tourist agencies for charter companies and with the District Controller of Air Services in the territorial (and provincial) capitals. Private pilots should obtain information from the Canada Map Office.

➤ MAJOR AIRLINES: **Air Canada** (☎ 888/247–2262); **American** (☎ 800/433–7300); **Delta** (☎ 800/241–4141); **Northwest** (☎ 800/225–2525); **United** (☎ 800/241–6522);

➤ SMALLER AIRLINES: **Alaska Airlines** (☎ 800/426–0333) from many western U.S. cities. **Horizon Air** (☎ 800/547–9308). ☞ Within Canada, *below.*

➤ FROM THE U.K.: **Air Canada** (☎ 0870/524–7226). **British Airways** (☎ 0845/722–2111).

➤ WITHIN CANADA: **Air Canada** (☎ 604/688–5515 in Vancouver; 888/247–2262 in U.S. and Canada). **Canadian Airlines International** (☎ 800/426–7000) provides coast-to-coast service. **Canadian Regional** (☎ 604/688–5515 or 604/279–6611) serves British Columbia with extended service out of Portland and Seattle. **Canada 3000 Airlines** (☎ 877/973–3000), **Royal Airlines** (☎ 877/769–2524), and **Air Transat** (800/470–1011) fly between many major Canadian cities and may offer lower rates. **WestJet Airlines** (☎ 800/538–5696) serves destinations throughout western Canada with good rates.

➤ INFORMATION FOR PRIVATE PILOTS: The **Canada Map Office** (✉ 130 Bentley Ave., Nepean, ON K1A 0E9, ☎ 800/465–6277) has the "Canada Flight Supplement" (lists of airports with Canada Customs services) as well as aeronautical charts.

CHECK-IN & BOARDING

Assuming that not everyone with a ticket will show up, airlines routinely overbook planes. When everyone does, airlines ask for volunteers to give up their seats. In return, these volunteers usually get a certificate for a free flight and are rebooked on the next flight out. If there are not enough volunteers, the airline must choose who will be denied boarding. The first to get bumped are passengers who checked in late and those flying on discounted tickets, so **get to the gate and check in as early as possible,** especially during peak periods.

Always **bring a government-issued photo ID to the airport** (a passport is best). You will be asked to show it before you are allowed to check in. U.S. Customs and Immigration maintains an office at Vancouver International Airport; U.S.-bound passengers should arrive early enough to clear customs before their flight.

Security measures at Canadian airports are similar to those in the United States. Be sure you're not carrying anything that could be construed as a weapon: a letter opener, Swiss Army knife, or a toy weapon, for example. Arriving passengers from overseas flights might find a beagle in a green coat sniffing their luggage; he's looking for forbidden agricultural products.

Departing passengers in Vancouver must pay a $10 airport-improvement fee before they can board their plane.

CUTTING COSTS

The least expensive airfares to Vancouver must usually be purchased in advance and are nonrefundable. It's smart to **call a number of airlines, and when you are quoted a good price, book it on the spot**—the same fare may not be available the next day. Always **check different routings** and look into using different airports. Travel agents, especially low-fare specialists (☞ Discounts & Deals, *below*), are helpful.

Consolidators are another good source. They buy tickets for scheduled international flights at reduced rates from the airlines, then sell them at prices that beat the best fare available directly from the airlines, usually without restrictions. Sometimes you can even get your money back if you need to return the ticket. Carefully read the fine print detailing penalties for changes and cancellations, and **confirm your consolidator reservation with the airline.**

When you **fly as a courier,** you trade your checked-luggage space for a ticket deeply subsidized by a courier service. There are restrictions on when you can book and how long you can stay.

➤ CONSOLIDATORS: **Cheap Tickets** (☎ 800/377–1000). **Discount Airline Ticket Service** (☎ 800/576–1600). **Unitravel** (☎ 800/325–2222). **Up & Away Travel** (☎ 212/889–2345). **World Travel Network** (☎ 800/409–6753).

ENJOYING THE FLIGHT

For more legroom, **request an emergency-aisle seat.** Don't sit in the row in front of the emergency aisle or in front of a bulkhead, where seats may not recline. If you have dietary concerns, **ask for special meals when booking.** These can be vegetarian, low-cholesterol, or kosher, for example. On long flights, try to maintain a normal routine, to help fight jet lag. At night, **get some sleep.** By day, **eat light meals, drink water** (not alcohol), and **move around the cabin** to stretch your legs.

None of the major airlines or charter lines permit smoking.

FLYING TIMES

Flights from New York to Vancouver take about 5½ hours nonstop; from Chicago, about 4½ hours nonstop; and from Los Angeles, about 3 hours nonstop.

HOW TO COMPLAIN

If your baggage goes astray or your flight goes awry, complain right away. Most carriers require that you **file a claim immediately.**

➤ AIRLINE COMPLAINTS: **U.S. Department of Transportation Aviation Consumer Protection Division** (✉ C-75, Room 4107, Washington, DC 20590, ☎ 202/366–2220, airconsumer@ost.dot.gov, www.dot.gov/airconsumer). **Federal Aviation Administration Consumer Hotline** (☎ 800/322–7873).

AIRPORTS

The major gateway is **Vancouver International Airport.** For further information about airport transfers, *see* the A to Z section at the end of Chapters 2, 3, and 4.

➤ AIRPORT INFORMATION: **Vancouver International Airport** (Grant Mc-Conachie Way, Richmond, ☎ 604/ 276–6101).

BIKE TRAVEL

Despite Canada's harsh climate and demanding landscape, bicycle travel has become very popular in the past 20 years. Long-distance bicycle travel is popular along the Pacific Coast. Some terrain in this area is steep and hilly, but it's always varied and interesting. One of the most spectacular trails in Western Canada follows the abandoned 600-km-long (370-mi-long) Kettle Valley Railway through the mountains of British Columbia.

In many areas, some of the prettiest roads have dirt or gravel surfaces, which make a hybrid bike more practical than a road bike. Bicycle rentals are readily available in all major cities, in recreational areas, and in resort towns.

➤ BIKE MAPS: For maps and information on bicycle routes, consult the regional tourism information offices.

➤ BIKE RENTALS: Many hotels, inns, and bed-and-breakfasts either have bikes available for their guests or can arrange to rent them. Prices vary from $20 a day to $50 or $60. There are usually reduced rates for long-term rentals. In all cases, a deposit is required—usually $150 to $130, depending on the value of the bicycle—which can be made with a credit card. Always ask if the rate includes insurance against theft or damage.

BIKES IN FLIGHT

Most airlines accommodate bikes as luggage, provided they are dismantled and boxed. For bike boxes, often free at bike shops, you'll pay about $5 from airlines (at least $100 for bike bags). International travelers can sometimes substitute a bike for a piece of checked luggage at no charge; otherwise, the cost is about $100. Domestic and Canadian airlines charge $25–$50.

BOAT & FERRY TRAVEL

Ferries play an important part in the transportation network of British Columbia. In some areas, ferries provide the only form of access into and out of communities. In other places, ferries transport thousands of commuters a day to and from work in the cities. For visitors, ferries are one of the best ways to get a feel for the region and its ties to the sea.

Ferries operate between the state of Washington and British Columbia's Vancouver Island. Individual chapters in the book have additional information about these.

➤ BOAT & FERRY INFORMATION: On the west coast, **British Columbia (BC) Ferry Corporation** (✉ 1112 Fort St., Victoria, BC V8V 4V2, ☎ 250/386–3431) has 42 ports of call.

BUS TRAVEL

The bus is an essential form of transportation in Canada, especially if you want to visit out-of-the-way towns that do not have airports or rail lines.

FARES & SCHEDULES

Bus terminals in major cities and even in many smaller ones are usually efficient operations with service all week and plenty of agents on hand to handle ticket sales. In villages and some smaller towns, the bus station is simply a counter in a local convenience store, gas station, or snack bar. Getting information on schedules beyond the local ones is sometimes difficult in these places.

➤ BUS INFORMATION: **Greyhound Lines** (✉ 877 Greyhound Way SW, Calgary, AB T3C 3V8, ☎ 800/661–8747 in Canada, 800/231–2222 in the U.S.) **Gray Line** (☎ 604/879–3363 in Vancouver, 250/388–5248 in Victoria, 800/667–0882 elsewhere). **Pacific Coach Lines** (☎ 640/662–8074 in Vancouver, 250/385–4411 in Victoria, 800/661–1725 elsewhere). **Quick Shuttle** (☎ 604/940–4428; 800/665–2122 in the U.S.). In the United Kingdom, contact **Greyhound International** (✉ Sussex House, London Rd., E. Grinstead, East Sussex RHI9 1LD, UK, (☎ 01342/ 317317).

PAYING

In major bus terminals, most bus lines accept at least some of the major credit cards. Some smaller lines require cash or take only Visa or MasterCard. All accept travelers' checks in U.S. or Canadian currency with suitable identification, but it's advisable to exchange foreign currency (including U.S. currency) at a bank or exchange office. To buy a ticket in really small centers, it's best to use cash or a bank card.

RESERVATIONS

Most bus lines do not accept reservations. You should plan on picking up your tickets at least 45 minutes before the bus's scheduled departure time.

BUSINESS HOURS

BANKS & OFFICES

Most banks in Canada are open Monday through Thursday 10–3 and Friday 10–5 or 6. Some banks are open longer hours and also on Saturday morning. All banks are closed on national holidays.

GAS STATIONS

Most highway and city gas stations in Canada are open seven days a week (although there's rarely a mechanic on duty Sunday) and some are open around the clock. In small towns, gas stations are often closed on Sunday, although they may take turns staying open.

MUSEUMS

Museum hours vary, but most open at 10 or 11 and close in the evening. Some smaller museums close for lunch. Many museums are closed on Monday; some make up for it by staying open late on Wednesday, often free.

SHOPS

Stores, shops, and supermarkets tend to be open Monday through Saturday 9–6, although in major cities supermarkets are often open 7:30 AM–9 PM. Blue laws are in effect in much of Canada, but a growing number of provinces have stores with limited Sunday hours, usually noon–5 (shops in areas highly frequented by tourists are usually open Sunday). Retail stores often stay open Thursday and Friday evenings, most shopping malls until 9 PM. Drugstores in the bigger cities are often open until 11 PM, and convenience stores usually are open 24 hours a day, seven days a week.

CAMERAS & PHOTOGRAPHY

The natural splendor of British Columbia will vie for the attention of your camera lens. The water and islands, along with the urban centers and small villages, are all worthy of your attention. Seize the sunny times of day for the clearest shots.

➤ PHOTO HELP: **Kodak Information Center** (☎ 800/242–2424). *Kodak Guide to Shooting Great Travel Pictures,* available in bookstores or from Fodor's Travel Publications (☎ 800/533–6478; US$16.50 plus US$5.50 shipping).

EQUIPMENT PRECAUTIONS

Always **keep your film and tape out of the sun.** Carry an extra supply of batteries, and **be prepared to turn on your camera or camcorder** to prove to security personnel that the device is real. Always **ask for hand inspection of film,** which becomes clouded after repeated exposure to airport X-ray machines, and **keep videotapes away from metal detectors.**

CAR RENTAL

➤ MAJOR AGENCIES: **Alamo** (☎ 800/522–9696; 020/8759–6200 in the U.K.). **Avis** (☎ 800/331–1212; 800/879–2847 in Canada; 02/9353–9000 in Australia; 09/525–1982 in New Zealand; 0870/606–0100 in the U.K.). **Budget** (☎ 800/527–0700; 0870/607–5000 in the U.K., through affiliate Europcar). **Dollar** (☎ 800/800–6000; 0124/622–0111 in the U.K., through affiliate Sixt Kenning; 02/9223–1444 in Australia). **Hertz** (☎ 800/654–3001; 800/263–0600 in Canada; 020/8897–2072 in the U.K.; 02/9669–2444 in Australia; 09/256–8690 in New Zealand) **National Car Rental** (☎ 800/227–7368; 020/8680–4800 in the U.K., where it is known as National Europe). **National Inter-Rent** (☎ 800/227–7368).

THE GOLD GUIDE / SMART TRAVEL TIPS

CUTTING COSTS

To get the best deal, **book through a travel agent who will shop around.** Also **price local car-rental companies,** although the service and maintenance may not be as good as those of a major player. Remember to ask about required deposits, cancellation penalties, and drop-off charges if you're planning to pick up the car in one city and leave it in another. If you're traveling during a holiday period, also make sure that a confirmed reservation guarantees you a car.

Do **look into wholesalers,** companies that do not own fleets but rent in bulk from those that do and often offer better rates than traditional car-rental operations.

➤ WHOLESALERS: **Auto Europe** (☎ 207/842–2000 or 800/223–5555, FAX 800–235–6321, www. autoeurope.com).

INSURANCE

When driving a rented car you are generally responsible for any damage to or loss of the vehicle as well as for any property damage or personal injury that you may cause. Before you rent, see what coverage your personal auto-insurance policy and credit cards already provide.

REQUIREMENTS & RESTRICTIONS

In British Columbia your own driver's license is acceptable, children six and under must use a child seat, and car rentals incur both a 14% sales tax and a $1.50 per day social services tax.

SURCHARGES

Before you pick up a car in one city and leave it in another, **ask about drop-off charges or one-way service fees,** which can be substantial. Note, too, that some rental agencies charge extra if you return the car before the time specified in your contract. To avoid a hefty refueling fee, **fill the tank just before you turn in the car,** but be aware that gas stations near the rental outlet may overcharge.

CAR TRAVEL

Canada's highway system is excellent. It includes the Trans-Canada High-

way, which uses several different numbers and is the longest highway in the world—running about 8,000 km (5,000 mi) from Victoria, British Columbia, to St. John's, Newfoundland, using ferries to bridge coastal waters at each end. The second-longest Canadian highway, the Yellowhead Highway (Highway 16), follows a route from the Pacific Coast and over the Rockies to the prairies. North of the population centers, roads become fewer and less developed.

FROM THE U.S.

Drivers must carry owner registration and proof of insurance coverage, which is compulsory in Canada. The Canadian Non-Resident Inter-Provincial Motor Vehicle Liability Insurance Card, available from any U.S. insurance company, is accepted as evidence of financial responsibility in Canada. The minimum liability coverage in British Columbia is $200,000. If you are driving a car that is not registered in your name, carry a letter from the owner that authorizes your use of the vehicle.

The U.S. interstate highway network provides quick and easy access to Western Canada in spite of imposing mountain barriers. From the south, Interstate 5 (I–5) runs from the U.S.-Mexican border through California, into Oregon and Washington, and ends at the U.S.-Canadian border. Most of the region's population lives along this corridor.

The main entry point into Canada by car is on I–5 at Blaine, Washington, 30 mi south of Vancouver. Three highways enter British Columbia from the east: Highway 1, or the Trans-Canada Highway (the longest highway in the world, running more than 5,000 mi from St. John's, Newfoundland, to Victoria, British Columbia), Highway 3, or the Crowsnest Highway, which crosses southern British Columbia, and Highway 16, the Yellowhead Highway, which runs through northern British Columbia from the Rocky Mountains to Prince Rupert.

Border-crossing procedures are usually quick and simple (☞ Passports and Visas, *below*). Every British Columbia border crossing (except the one at Aldergrove, which closes at midnight) is open 24 hours. The I–5 border crossing at Blaine, Washington, (also known as the Douglas, or Peace Arch, border crossing) is one of the busiest border crossings between the United States and Canada. The peak traffic time at the border northbound into Canada is daily at 4 PM. Southbound, delays can be expected evenings and weekend mornings. Try to plan on reaching the border at off-peak times.

➤ INSURANCE INFORMATION: **Superintendent of Financial Institutions** (✉ 1900–1050 W. Pender St., Vancouver, BC V6E3S7, ☎ 604/660–2947).

GASOLINE

Gasoline costs from 44¢ to 80¢ a liter. (There are 3.8 liters in a U.S. gallon.) Distances are always shown in kilometers, and gasoline is always sold in liters.

RULES OF THE ROAD

By law, you are required to wear seat belts (and to use infant seats). Some provinces have a statutory requirement to drive with vehicle headlights on for extended periods after dawn and before sunset.

Speed limits, given in kilometers, vary from province to province, but they are usually within the 90–100 kph (50–60 mph) range outside the cities.

WINTER DRIVING

In coastal areas, the mild, damp climate contributes to roadways that are frequently wet. Winter snowfalls are not common (generally only once or twice a year), but when snow does fall, traffic grinds to a halt and the roadways become treacherous and stay that way until the snow melts.

Tire chains, studs, or snow tires are essential equipment for winter travel in mountain areas such as Whistler. If you're planning to drive into high elevations, be sure to check the weather forecast beforehand. Even the main highway mountain passes can be forced to close because of snow conditions. During the winter

months, provincial highway departments operate snow advisory telephone lines that give pass conditions.

CHILDREN IN BRITISH COLUMBIA

Travelers crossing the border with children should **carry identification for them** similar to that required by adults (i.e., passport or birth certificate). Children traveling with one parent or other adult should **bring a letter of permission** from the other parent, parents, or legal guardian. Divorced parents with shared custody rights should **carry legal documents establishing their status.** If you are renting a car, don't forget to **arrange for a car seat** when you reserve.

FLYING

If your children are two or older, **ask about children's airfares.** As a general rule, infants under two not occupying a seat fly at greatly reduced fares or even for free. When booking, **confirm carry-on allowances** if you're traveling with infants. In general, for babies charged 10% of the adult fare you are allowed one carry-on bag and a collapsible stroller; if the flight is full, the stroller may have to be checked or you may be limited to less.

Experts agree that it's a good idea to use safety seats aloft for children weighing less than 40 pounds. Airlines set their own policies: U.S. carriers usually require that the child be ticketed, even if he or she is young enough to ride free, since the safety seats must be strapped into regular seats. Do **check your airline's policy about using safety seats during take-off and landing.** And since safety seats are not allowed just everywhere in the plane, get your seat assignments early.

When reserving, **request children's meals or a freestanding bassinet** if you need them. But note that bulkhead seats, where you must sit to use the bassinet, may lack an overhead bin or storage space on the floor.

LODGING

Most hotels in British Columbia allow children under a certain age to stay in their parents' room at no extra charge, but others charge for them as extra adults; be sure to **find out the cutoff age for children's discounts.**

SIGHTS & ATTRACTIONS

Places that are especially appealing to children are indicated by a rubber-duckie icon in the margin.

CONCIERGES

Concierges, found in many city hotels, can help you with theater tickets and dinner reservations: a good one with connections may be able to get you prime-time dinner reservations at the restaurant of the moment. You can also turn to your hotel's concierge for help with travel arrangements, sightseeing plans, services ranging from aromatherapy to zipper repair, and emergencies. Always, **always tip** a concierge who has been of assistance.

CONSUMER PROTECTION

Whenever shopping or buying travel services in British Columbia, **pay with a major credit card** so you can cancel payment or get reimbursed if there's a problem. If you're doing business with a particular company for the first time, **contact the Better Business Bureau and the attorney general's offices** in your own state as well as in the company's home area. Have any complaints been filed? Finally, if you're buying a package or tour, always **consider travel insurance** that includes default coverage (☞ Insurance, *below*).

➤ BBBs: **Council of Better Business Bureaus** (✉ 4200 Wilson Blvd., Suite 800, Arlington, VA 22203, ☎ 703/276–0100, ℻ 703/525–8277 www.bbb.org). **British Columbia Better Business Bureaus** (✉ BC, Vancouver V6B 2M1 ☎ 604/682–2711 for mainland British Columbia; ✉ 1005 Langley St., Room 201, Victoria V8W 1V7, ☎ 250/386–6348 for Vancouver Island).

CUSTOMS & DUTIES

When shopping, **keep receipts** for all purchases. Upon reentering the country, **be ready to show customs officials what you've bought.** If you feel a duty is incorrect or object to the way your clearance was handled, note the inspector's badge number and ask to see a supervisor. If the problem isn't resolved, write to the appropriate authorities, beginning with the port director at your point of entry.

U.S. Customs and Immigration has preclearance services at Vancouver International Airport. This allows U.S.-bound air passengers to depart their airplane directly on arrival at their U.S. destination without further inspection and delays.

IN CANADA

American and British visitors may bring in the following items duty-free: 200 cigarettes, 50 cigars, and 7 ounces of tobacco; 1 bottle (1.1 liters or 40 imperial ounces) of liquor or wine, or 24 355-ml (12-ounce) bottles or cans of beer for personal consumption. Any alcohol and tobacco products in excess of these amounts is subject to duty, provincial fees, and taxes. You must be 19 or over to bring alcohol or tobacco into British Columbia. You can also bring in gifts up to the value of $60 (Canadian) per gift.

A deposit is sometimes required for trailers (refunded upon return). Cats and dogs must have a certificate issued by a licensed veterinarian that clearly identifies the animal and certifies that it has been vaccinated against rabies during the preceding 36 months. Seeing-eye dogs are allowed into Canada without restriction. Plant material must be declared and inspected. There may be restrictions on some live plants, bulbs, and seeds. With certain restrictions or prohibitions on some fruits and vegetables, visitors may bring food with them for their own use, providing the quantity is consistent with the duration of the visit.

Canada's firearms laws are significantly stricter than those in the U.S. All handguns and semiautomatic and fully automatic weapons are prohibited and cannot be brought into the country. Sporting rifles and shotguns may be imported provided they are to be used for sporting, hunting, or competition while in Canada. All firearms must be declared to Canada Customs at the first point of entry.

Failure to declare firearms will result in their seizure, and criminal charges may be made. From January 1, 2001, new regulations require visitors to have a confirmed "Firearms Declaration" to bring any guns into Canada. A fee of $50 will apply and will be good for a one-year period. For more information, contact the Canadian Firearms Centre.

➤ INFORMATION: **Revenue Canada** (✉ 2265 St. Laurent Blvd. S, Ottawa, ON K1G 4K3, ☎ 613/993–0534; 800/461–9999 in Canada). **Canadian Firearms Centre** (☎ 800/731–4000).

IN AUSTRALIA

Australian residents who are 18 or older may bring home $A400 worth of souvenirs and gifts (including jewelry), 250 cigarettes or 250 grams of tobacco, and 1,125 ml of alcohol (including wine, beer, and spirits). Residents under 18 may bring back $A200 worth of goods. Prohibited items include meat products. Seeds, plants, and fruits need to be declared upon arrival.

➤ INFORMATION: **Australian Customs Service** (Regional Director, ✉ Box 8, Sydney, NSW 2001, ☎ 02/9213–2000, ℻ 02/9213–4000).

IN NEW ZEALAND

Homeward-bound residents 17 or older may bring back NZ$700 worth of souvenirs and gifts. Your duty-free allowance also includes 4.5 liters of wine or beer; one 1,125-ml bottle of spirits; and either 200 cigarettes, 250 grams of tobacco, 50 cigars, or a combination of the three up to 250 grams. Prohibited items include meat products, seeds, plants, and fruits.

➤ INFORMATION: **New Zealand Customs** (Custom House, ✉ 50 Anzac Ave., Box 29, Auckland, New Zealand, ☎ 09/359–6655, ℻ 09/359–6732).

IN THE U.K.

From countries outside the European Union, including Canada, U.K. residents may bring home, duty-free, 200 cigarettes or 50 cigars; 1 liter of spirits or 2 liters of fortified or sparkling wine or liqueurs; 2 liters of still table wine; 60 ml of perfume; 250 ml of toilet water; plus £136 worth of other goods, including gifts and souvenirs. If returning from outside the EU, prohibited items include meat products, seeds, plants, and fruits.

➤ INFORMATION: **HM Customs and Excise** (✉ Dorset House, Stamford St., Bromley, Kent BR1 1XX, ☎ 020/7202–4227).

IN THE U.S.

U.S. residents who have been out of the country for at least 48 hours (and who have not used the US$400 allowance or any part of it in the past 30 days) may bring home US$400 worth of foreign goods duty-free. U.S. residents 21 and older may bring back 1 liter of alcohol duty-free. In addition, regardless of your age, you are allowed 200 cigarettes and 100 non-Cuban cigars. Antiques, which the U.S. Customs Service defines as objects more than 100 years old, enter duty-free, as do original works of art done entirely by hand, including paintings, drawings, and sculptures.

You may also send packages home duty-free: up to US$200 worth of goods for personal use, with a limit of one parcel per addressee per day (except alcohol or tobacco products or perfume worth more than US$5); label the package PERSONAL USE and attach a list of its contents and their retail value. Do not label the package UNSOLICITED GIFT or your duty-free exemption will drop to US$100. Mailed items do not affect your duty-free allowance on your return.

➤ INFORMATION: **U.S. Customs Service** (✉ 1300 Pennsylvania Ave. NW, Washington, DC 20229, www.customs.gov; inquiries ☎ 202/354–1000; complaints c/o ✉ Office of Regulations and Rulings; registration of equipment c/o ✉ Resource Management, ☎ 202/927–0540).

DINING

The restaurants we list are the cream of the crop in each price category. Properties indicated by an ✕🏠 are lodging establishments whose restaurant warrants a special trip. For

SMART TRAVEL TIPS / THE GOLD GUIDE

information about dining, including a price chart, *see* Dining *in* Pleasures and Pastimes at the beginning of each chapter.

RESERVATIONS & DRESS

Reservations are always a good idea: we mention them only when they're essential or not accepted. Book as far ahead as you can, and reconfirm as soon as you arrive. We mention dress only when men are required to wear a jacket or a jacket and tie.

DISABILITIES & ACCESSIBILITY

Travelers with disabilities do not have the same blanket legal protection in Canada that they have in the United States. Indeed, some facilities—city buses, for example—aren't easy to use in a wheelchair. However, thanks to increased awareness and government-incentive programs, most major attractions—museums, churches, theaters—are equipped with ramps and lifts to handle wheelchairs. National and provincial institutions—parks, public monuments, and government buildings—are particularly accessible.

➤ LOCAL RESOURCES: If you drop by the **Vancouver Tourist Info Centre** (✉ 200 Burrard St., ☎ 604/683–2000), you can look in its General Information binder for a list of area attractions that are wheelchair-accessible. You can also call 800/435–5622 for a free copy of the *Super Natural British Columbia's Accommodations Guide,* which notes the accessibility of lodgings in the province.

RESERVATIONS

When discussing accessibility with an operator or reservations agent, **ask hard questions.** Are there any stairs, inside *or* out? Are there grab bars next to the toilet *and* in the shower/tub? How wide is the doorway to the room? To the bathroom? For the most extensive facilities meeting the latest legal specifications, **opt for newer accommodations.**

➤ COMPLAINTS: **Disability Rights Section** (✉ U.S. Department of Justice, Civil Rights Division, Box 66738, Washington, DC 20035-6738, ☎ 202/514–0301 or 800/514–0301; TTY 202/514–0301 or 800/514–

0301, FAX 202/307–1198) for general complaints. **Aviation Consumer Protection Division** (☞ Air Travel, *above*) for airline-related problems. **Civil Rights Office** (✉ U.S. Department of Transportation, Departmental Office of Civil Rights, S-30, 400 7th St. SW, Room 10215, Washington, DC 20590, ☎ 202/366–4648, FAX 202/366–9371) for problems with surface transportation.

In Canada, contact the **Council of Canadians with Disabilities** (✉ 294 Portage Ave., Suite 926, Winnipeg, MN R3C 0B9, ☎ 204/947–0303, FAX 204/942–4625). To file a complaint about transportation obstacles at Canadian airports (including flights), railroads, or ferries, contact the Director, **Accessible Transportation Directorate** (☎ 819/997–6828 or 800/883–1813), at the Canadian Transportation Agency.

TRAVEL AGENCIES

In the United States, the Americans with Disabilities Act requires that travel firms serve the needs of all travelers. Some agencies specialize in working with people with disabilities.

➤ TRAVELERS WITH MOBILITY PROBLEMS: **Access Adventures** (✉ 206 Chestnut Ridge Rd., Rochester, NY 14624, ☎ 716/889–9096, dltravel@prodigy.net), run by a former physical-rehabilitation counselor. **CareVacations** (✉ 5-5110 50th Ave., Leduc, Alberta T9E 6V4, ☎ 780/986–6404 or 877/478–7827, FAX 780/986–8332, www.carevacations.com), for group tours and cruise vacations. **Flying Wheels Travel** (✉ 143 W. Bridge St., Box 382, Owatonna, MN 55060, ☎ 507/451–5005 or 800/535–6790, FAX 507/451–1685, thq@ll.net, www.flyingwheels.com).

➤ TRAVELERS WITH DEVELOPMENTAL DISABILITIES: **Sprout** (✉ 893 Amsterdam Ave., New York, NY 10025, ☎ 212/222–9575 or 888/222–9575, FAX 212/222–9768, sprout@interport.net, www.gosprout.org).

DISCOUNTS & DEALS

Be a smart shopper and **compare all your options** before making decisions. A plane ticket bought with a promotional coupon from travel clubs, coupon books, and direct-mail offers may not be cheaper than the least expensive fare from a discount ticket agency. And always keep in mind that what you get is just as important as what you save.

DISCOUNT RESERVATIONS

To save money, **look into discount reservations services** with toll-free numbers, which use their buying power to get a better price on hotels, airline tickets, even car rentals. When booking a room, always **call the hotel's local toll-free number** (if one is available) rather than the central reservations number—you'll often get a better price. Always ask about special packages or corporate rates.

When shopping for the best deal on hotels and car rentals, **look for guaranteed exchange rates,** which protect you against a falling U.S. dollar. With your rate locked in, you won't pay more, even if the price goes up in the local currency.

➤ AIRLINE TICKETS: ☎ 800/FLY–4–LESS. ☎ 800/FLY–ASAP.

➤ HOTEL ROOMS: **Hotel Reservations Network** (☎ 800/964–6835, www.hoteldiscounts.com). **RMC Travel** (☎ 800/245–5738, www.rmcwebtravel.com). **Steigenberger Reservation Service** (☎ 800/223–5652, www.srs-worldhotels.com).

PACKAGE DEALS

Don't confuse packages and guided tours. When you buy a package, you travel on your own, just as though you had planned the trip yourself. Fly/drive packages, which combine airfare and car rental, are often a good deal.

ECOTOURISM

British Columbia's rugged wilderness areas often have very delicate ecosystems. Travelers should stick to marked trails and avoid disturbing the local flora. Sand dunes in western Canada, important nesting grounds for sea birds, often are protected.

GAY & LESBIAN TRAVEL

Canada is generally a fairly tolerant country, and same-sex couples will face few problems in the major metropolitan areas. Vancouver has a large, visible, and very active gay and lesbian community.

The epicenter of Vancouver's gay scene is the stretch of Davie Street between Burrard and Jervis streets—a cluster of cafés, casual eating places, and shops offering designer T-shirts and sleek housewares. Pride, held the first weekend of August, features parties, tea dances, and cruises, and culminates in a parade on Sunday.

Same-sex couples might not get as warm and open a welcome in rural areas as they do in the big cities. Much of the British Columbia interior harbors more conservative views.

➤ GAY- & LESBIAN-FRIENDLY TRAVEL AGENCIES: **Different Roads Travel** (✉ 8383 Wilshire Blvd., Suite 902, Beverly Hills, CA 90211, ☎ 323/651–5557 or 800/429–8747). **Kennedy Travel** (✉ 314 Jericho Turnpike, Floral Park, NY 11001, ☎ 516/352–4888 or 800/237–7433, www.kennedytravel.com). **Now Voyager** (✉ 4406 18th St., San Francisco, CA 94114, ☎ 415/626–1169 or 800/255–6951, www.nowvoyager.com). **Skylink Travel and Tour** (✉ 1006 Mendocino Ave., Santa Rosa, CA 95401, ☎ 707/546–9888 or 800/225–5759, FAX 707/546–9891, www.skylinktravel.com), serving lesbian travelers.

HOLIDAYS

NATIONAL HOLIDAYS

Canadian national holidays for 2001 are as follows: New Year's Day, Good Friday (April 21), Easter Monday (April 24), Victoria Day (May 22), Canada Day (July 1), Labour Day (September 4), Thanksgiving (October 9), Remembrance Day (November 11), Christmas, and Boxing Day (December 26).

British Columbia Day (August 7) is a provincial holiday.

INSURANCE

The most useful travel-insurance plan is a comprehensive policy that includes coverage for trip cancellation and interruption, default, trip delay, and medical expenses (with a waiver for preexisting conditions).

Without insurance you will lose all or most of your money if you cancel your trip, regardless of the reason. Default insurance covers you if your tour operator, airline, or cruise line goes out of business. Trip-delay covers expenses that arise because of bad weather or mechanical delays. Study the fine print when comparing policies.British and Australian citizens need extra medical coverage when traveling overseas.

Always **buy travel policies directly from the insurance company**; if you buy them from a cruise line, airline, or tour operator that goes out of business you probably will not be covered for the agency or operator's default, a major risk. Before making any purchase, **review your existing health and home-owner's policies** to find what they cover away from home.

➤ TRAVEL INSURERS: In the U.S.: **Access America** (⊠ 6600 W. Broad St., Richmond, VA 23230, ☎ 804/285–3300 or 800/284–8300, ℻ 804/673–1583, www.previewtravel.com), **Travel Guard International** (⊠ 1145 Clark St., Stevens Point, WI 54481, ☎ 715/345–0505 or 800/826–1300, ℻ 800/955–8785, www.noelgroup.com). In Canada: **Voyager Insurance** (⊠ 44 Peel Center Dr., Brampton, Ontario L6T 4M8, ☎ 905/791–8700; 800/668–4342 in Canada).

➤ INSURANCE INFORMATION: In the U.K.: **Association of British Insurers** (⊠ 51–55 Gresham St., London EC2V 7HQ, ☎ 020/7600–3333, ℻ 020/7696–8999, info@abi.org.uk, www.abi.org.uk). In Australia: **Insurance Council of Australia** (☎ 03/9614–1077, ℻ 03/9614–7924).

LODGING

British Columbia hosts a range of accommodations. In the cities you'll have a choice of luxury hotels, moderately priced modern properties, and smaller older hotels with perhaps fewer conveniences but more charm. Options in smaller towns and in the country include large, full-service resorts; small, privately owned hotels; roadside mo-

tels; and bed-and-breakfasts. Even here you'll need to make reservations at least on the day on which you're planning to pull into town.

There is no national government rating system for hotels. In British Columbia, a blue Approved Accommodation decal on the window or door of a hotel or motel indicates that it has met provincial hotel-association standards for courtesy, comfort, and cleanliness.

Expect accommodations to cost more in summer than in the off-season (except for places such as ski resorts, where winter is high season). When making reservations, **ask about special deals and packages.** Big-city hotels that cater to business travelers often offer weekend packages, and many city hotels offer rooms at up to 50% off in winter. If you're planning to visit a major city or resort area in high season, **book well in advance.** Also be aware of any special events or festivals that may coincide with your visit and fill every room for miles around. For resorts and lodges, consider the winter ski-season high as well and plan accordingly.

The lodgings we list are the cream of the crop in each price category. We always list the facilities that are available—but we don't specify whether they cost extra: when pricing accommodations, always ask what's included and what costs extra. Properties indicated by an ✕▥ are lodging establishments whose restaurant warrants a special trip.

Assume that hotels operate on the European Plan (EP, with no meals) unless we specify that they use the Continental Plan (CP, with a Continental breakfast daily), Modified American Plan (MAP, with breakfast and dinner daily), or the Full American Plan (FAP, with all meals).

APARTMENT & VILLA RENTALS

If you want a home base that's roomy enough for a family and comes with cooking facilities, **consider a furnished rental.** These can save you money, especially if you're traveling with a group. Home-exchange directories sometimes list rentals as well as exchanges.

➤ INTERNATIONAL AGENTS: **Hideaways International** (✉ 767 Islington St., Portsmouth, NH 03801, ☎ 603/430–4433 or 800/843–4433, FAX 603/430–4444, info@hideaways.com, www.hideaways.com; membership $99).

B&BS

Bed-and-breakfasts can be found in both the country and the cities. For assistance in booking these, **contact the appropriate provincial tourist board,** which either has a listing of B&Bs or can refer you to an association that will help you secure reservations. Be sure to **check out the B&B's Web site,** which may have useful information, although you should also find out how up-to-date it is. Room quality varies from house to house as well, so you can **ask to see a room before making a choice.**

CAMPING

Campgrounds range from rustic woodland settings far from the nearest paved road to facility-packed open fields full of sleek motorhomes next to major highways. Some of the best sites are in national and provincial parks—well cared for, well equipped, and close to plenty of nature and activity programs for both children and adults. Campers tend to be working- or middle-class families with a fair sprinkling of seniors, but their tastes and practices are as varied as the campsites they favor. Some see camping simply as a way to get practical, low-cost lodgings on a road trip, while other, more sedentary campers will move into one campground with as much elaborate equipment as they can and set up for a long stay. Wilderness camping for hikers and canoeists is available in national and provincial parks.

HOME EXCHANGES

If you would like to exchange your home for someone else's, **join a home-exchange organization,** which will send you its updated listings of available exchanges for a year and will include your own listing in at least

one of them. It's up to you to make specific arrangements.

➤ EXCHANGE CLUBS: **HomeLink International** (✉ Box 650, Key West, FL 33041, ☎ 305/294–7766 or 800/638–3841, FAX 305/294–1448, usa@homelink.org, www.homelink.org; $98 per year). **Intervac U.S.** (✉ Box 590504, San Francisco, CA 94159, ☎ 800/756–4663, FAX 415/435–7440, www.intervac.com; $89 per year includes two catalogues).

HOSTELS

No matter what your age, you can **save on lodging costs by staying at hostels.** In some 5,000 locations in more than 70 countries around the world, Hostelling International (HI), the umbrella group for a number of national youth-hostel associations, offers single-sex, dorm-style beds and, at many hostels, rooms for couples and family accommodations. Membership in any HI national hostel association, open to travelers of all ages, allows you to stay in HI-affiliated hostels at member rates; one-year membership is about US$25 for adults (C$26.75 in Canada, £9.30 in the U.K., A$30 in Australia, and NZ$30 in New Zealand); hostels run about US$10–$25 per night. Members have priority if the hostel is full; they're also eligible for discounts around the world, even on rail and bus travel in some countries.

➤ ORGANIZATIONS: **Hostelling International—American Youth Hostels** (✉ 733 15th St. NW, Suite 840, Washington, DC 20005, ☎ 202/783–6161, FAX 202/783–6171, www.hiayh.org). **Hostelling International—Canada** (✉ 400–205 Catherine St., Ottawa, Ontario K2P 1C3, ☎ 613/237–7884, FAX 613/237–7868, www.hostellingintl.ca). **Youth Hostel Association of England and Wales** (✉ Trevelyan House, 8 St. Stephen's Hill, St. Albans, Hertfordshire AL1 2DY, ☎ 01727/855215 or 01727/845047, FAX 01727/844126, www.yha.uk). **Australian Youth Hostel Association** (✉ 10 Mallett St., Camperdown, NSW 2050, ☎ 02/9565–1699, FAX 02/9565–1325, www.yha.com.au). **Youth Hostels Association of New**

Zealand (✉ Box 436, Christchurch,, ☎ 03/379–9970, FAX 03/365–4476, www.yha.org.nz).

HOTELS

All hotels listed have private bath unless otherwise noted.

➤ TOLL-FREE NUMBERS: **Best Western** (☎ 800/528–1234, www.bestwestern. com). **Choice** (☎ 800/221–2222, www.hotelchoice.com). **Clarion** (☎ 800/252–7466, www.choicehotels. com). **Coast Hotels** (☎ 800/663–1144). **Comfort** (☎ 800/228–5150, www.comfortinn.com). **Days Inn** (☎ 800/325–2525. www.daysinn.com). **Fairmont Hotels & Resorts** (☎ 800/441–1414; 0800/898852 in the U.K.). **Four Seasons** (☎ 800/332–3442, www.fourseasons.com). **Hilton** (☎ 800/445–8667, www.hilton.com). **Holiday Inn** (☎ 800/465–4329, www.holiday-inn.com). **Howard Johnson** (☎ 800/654–4656, www. hojo.com). **Hyatt Hotels & Resorts** (☎ 800/233–1234, www.hyatt.com). **Marriott** (☎ 800/228–9290, www. marriott.com). **Quality Inn** (☎ 800/228–5151, www.qualityinn.com). **Radisson** (☎ 800/333–3333, www. radisson.com). **Ramada** (☎ 800/228–2828. www.ramada.com). **Relais & Châteaux** (☎ 800/735–2478). **Renaissance Hotels & Resorts** (☎ 800/468–3571, www.renaissancehotels. com). **Sheraton** (☎ 800/325–3535, www.sheraton.com). **Sleep Inn** (☎ 800/753–3746, www.sleepinn.com). **Westin Hotels & Resorts** (☎ 800/228–3000, www.starwood.com). **Wyndham Hotels & Resorts** (☎ 800/822-4200, www.wyndham.com).

MAIL & SHIPPING

In Canada you can **buy stamps at the post office or from automatic vending machines** in most hotel lobbies, railway stations, airports, bus terminals, many retail outlets, and some newsstands. If you're sending mail to Canada, **be sure to include the postal code** (six digits and letters). Note that the suite number often appears before the street number in an address, followed by a hyphen.

The postal abbreviation for British Columbia is BC.

POSTAL RATES

Within Canada, postcards and letters up to 30 grams cost 46¢; between 31 grams and 50 grams, the cost is 73¢; and between 51 grams and 100 grams, the cost is 92¢. Letters and postcards to the United States cost 55¢ for up to 30 grams, 80¢ for between 31 and 50 grams, and $1.25 for up to 100 grams. Prices include GST (Goods and Services Tax).

International mail and postcards run 95¢ for up to 20 grams, $1.45 for between 21 and 50 grams, and $2.35 for between 51 and 100 grams.

RECEIVING MAIL

Visitors may have mail sent to them c/o General Delivery in the town they are visiting, for pickup in person within 15 days, after which it will be returned to the sender.

MEDIA

NEWSPAPERS & MAGAZINES

Maclean's (published weekly) and Saturday Night (published monthly) are Canada's two main general-interest magazines. Both cover arts and culture as well as politics. The two major daily newspapers in British Columbia are the Vancouver Sun and The Province. Canada has two national newspapers, The National Post and The Globe and Mail—both are published in Toronto and both are available at newsstands in major foreign cities. The arts-and-entertainment sections of both papers have advance news of major events and exhibitions across the country. Both also have Web sites with limited information on cultural events. Southam, the biggest newspaper chain in Canada, owns the National Post, and its Web site (www.southam.com) has links to daily newspapers in most other Canadian cities.

RADIO & TELEVISION

U.S. television dominates Canada's airwaves. In border areas—where most Canadians live—American networks, including Fox and PBS, as well as NBC, CBS, and ABC, are readily available. Canada's two major networks—the state-owned Canadian Broadcasting Corp. (CBC) and the private CTV—and the smaller Global Network broadcast a steady diet of U.S. sitcoms and dramas in prime time with only a scattering of Canadian-produced dramas and comedies. The selection of Canadian-produced current-affairs programs, however, is much wider. The CBC also has a parallel French-language network. Canadian cable subscribers have the usual vast menu of specialty channels to choose from, including the all-news outlets operated by CTV and CBC.

The CBC operates the country's only truly national radio network. In fact, it operates four of them, two in English and two in French. Its Radio 1 network, usually broadcast on the AM band, has a daily schedule rich in news, current-affairs, and discussion programs. One of the most popular shows, "As It Happens," takes a quirky and highly entertaining look at national, world, and weird events every evening at 6. Radio 2, usually broadcast on FM, emphasizes music and often features live classical concerts by some of Canada's best orchestras, opera companies, and choral groups. The two French-language networks more or less follow the same pattern.

MONEY MATTERS

Prices throughout this guide are given for adults. Substantially reduced fees are almost always available for children, students, and senior citizens. For information on taxes, *see* Taxes, *below*.

ATMS

ATMs are available in most bank, trust-company, and credit-union branches across the country, as well as in many convenience stores, malls, and gas stations.

CREDIT CARDS

Throughout this guide, the following abbreviations are used: AE, American Express; D, Discover; DC, Diner's Club; MC, MasterCard; and V, Visa.

➤ REPORTING LOST CARDS: **American Express** (☎ 800/528–4800). **Diners Club** (☎ 800/234–6377). **Discover** (☎ 800/347–2683). **MasterCard** (☎ 800/ 307–7309). **Visa** (☎ 800/336–8472).

CURRENCY

U.S. dollars are accepted in much of British Columbia (especially in communities near the border). However, to get the most favorable exchange rate, **exchange at least some of your money into Canadian funds at a bank or other financial institution.** Traveler's checks (some are available in Canadian dollars) and major U.S. credit cards are accepted in most areas.

The units of currency in Canada are the Canadian dollar (C$) and the cent, in almost the same denominations as U.S. currency ($5, $10, $20, 1¢, 5¢, 10¢, 25¢, etc.). The $1 and $2 bill are no longer used; they have been replaced by $1 and $2 coins (known as a "loonie," because of the loon that appears on the coin, and a "toonie," respectively). At press time the exchange rate was US$1 to C$1.49, £1 to C$2.22, C$1 to A$1.16, and C$1 to NZ$1.47.

Throughout this book, unless otherwise stated, all prices, including dining and lodging, are given in Canadian dollars.

CURRENCY EXCHANGE

For the most favorable rates, **change money through banks.** Although ATM transaction fees may be higher abroad than at home, ATM rates are excellent because they are based on wholesale rates offered only by major banks. You won't do as well at exchange booths in airports or rail or bus stations, in hotels, in restaurants, or in stores. To avoid lines at airport exchange booths, **get a bit of local currency before you leave home.**

➤ EXCHANGE SERVICES: **International Currency Express** (☎ 888/278–6628 for orders, www.foreignmoney.com). **Thomas Cook Currency Services** (☎ 800/287–7362 for telephone orders and retail locations, www.us. thomascook.com).

NATIONAL PARKS

If you plan to visit several parks in British Columbia, you may be able to **save money on park fees by buying a multipark pass,** including the Western Canada Annual Pass, available

THE GOLD GUIDE / SMART TRAVEL TIPS

through Parks Canada to Canadians and non-Canadians. As Parks Canada is decentralized, it's best to contact the park you plan to visit for information. You can buy passes at the parks covered by the pass.

➤ PARK PASSES: **Parks Canada national office** (⊠ 25 Eddy St., Hull, PQ K1A 0M5, ☎ 800/213–7275, www.parkscanada.pch.gc.ca).

OUTDOORS & SPORTS

BICYCLING

➤ ASSOCIATION: **Canadian Cycling Association** (⊠ 1600 James Naismith Dr., Gloucester, ON K1B 5N4, ☎ 613/748–5629).

CANOEING AND KAYAKING

British Columbia tourist offices can be of assistance, especially in locating an outfitter to suit your needs.

➤ ASSOCIATION: **Canadian Recreational Canoeing Association** (⊠ Box 398, Merrickville, ON K0G 1N0, ☎ 613/269–2910, www.crca.ca).

CLIMBING/MOUNTAINEERING

➤ ASSOCIATION: **Alpine Club of Canada** (⊠ Box 8040, Canmore, AB T1W 2T8, ☎ 403/678–3200, www.AlpineClubofCanada.ca).

FISHING

➤ INFORMATION/LICENSES: **Department of Fisheries and Oceans** (⊠ Recreational Fisheries Division, 555 W. Hastings St., Suite 400, Vancouver, BC V6B 5G3, ☎ 604/666–2828) for saltwater fishing. **British Columbia Department of Environment and Lands** (⊠ 10470–152nd St., Surrey, BC V3R 0Y3, ☎ 604/582–5200) for freshwater fishing.

GOLF

➤ ASSOCIATION: **Royal Canadian Golf Association** (⊠ 1333 Dorval Dr., Oakville, ON L6J 4Z3, ☎ 905/849–9700, www.rcga.org).

SCUBA DIVING

➤ ASSOCIATION: **Canadian Amateur Diving Association** (⊠ 1600 James Naismith Dr., Suite 705, Gloucester, ON K1B 5N4, ☎ 613/748–5631, www.diving.ca).

SKIING

British Columbia has more than 40 downhill and cross-country ski resorts, including the top-rated **Whistler** resort near Vancouver. Contact Whistler Ski Corp. (☎ 604/664–5614) or a regional tourism office for more information.

TENNIS

➤ ASSOCIATION: **Tennis Canada** (⊠ 3111 Steeles Ave. W, Downsview, ON M3J 3H2, ☎ 416/665–9777, www.tenniscanada.com).

PACKING

Summer days in British Columbia are warm, but evenings can cool off substantially. Your best bet is to **dress in layers**—sweatshirts, sweaters, and jackets are removed or put on as the day progresses. Chances are **you'll need rain gear**, too, especially if you're visiting in the winter. If you plan to explore the region's cities on foot, or if you choose to hike along mountain trails or beaches, bring comfortable walking shoes. Dining out is usually an informal affair, although some restaurants prefer a jacket and tie for men and dresses for women.

If you plan on camping or hiking in the deep woods in summer, particularly in northern British Columbia, **always carry insect repellent**, especially in June, which is blackfly season.

In your carry-on luggage, **pack an extra pair of eyeglasses or contact lenses** and **enough of any medication you take** to last the entire trip. You may also ask your doctor to write a spare prescription using the drug's generic name, since brand names may vary from country to country. In luggage to be checked, **never pack prescription drugs or valuables.** To avoid customs delays, carry medications in their original packaging. And don't forget to carry with you the addresses of offices that handle refunds of lost traveler's checks.

CHECKING LUGGAGE

How many carry-on bags you can bring with you is up to the airline. Most allow two, but not always, so make sure that everything you carry aboard will fit under your seat or in the overhead bin, and get to the gate early. Note that if you have a seat at the back of the plane, you'll probably board first, while the overhead bins are still empty.

If you are flying internationally, note that baggage allowances may be determined not by piece but by weight—generally 88 pounds (40 kilograms) in first class, 66 pounds (30 kilograms) in business class, and 44 pounds (20 kilograms) in economy.

Airline liability for baggage is limited to $1,250 per person on flights within the United States. On international flights it amounts to $9.07 per pound or $20 per kilogram for checked baggage (roughly $640 per 70-pound bag) and $400 per passenger for unchecked baggage. You can buy additional coverage at check-in for about $10 per $1,000 of coverage, but it excludes a rather extensive list of items, shown on your airline ticket.

Before departure, **itemize your bags' contents** and their worth, and label the bags with your name, address, and phone number. (If you use your home address, cover it so potential thieves can't see it readily.) Inside each bag, **pack a copy of your itinerary.** At check-in, **make sure that each bag is correctly tagged** with the destination airport's three-letter code. If your bags arrive damaged or fail to arrive at all, file a written report with the airline before leaving the airport.

PASSPORTS & VISAS

When traveling internationally, **carry your passport even if you don't need one** (it's always the best form of I.D.) and **make two photocopies of the data page** (one for someone at home and another for you, carried separately from your passport). If you lose your passport, promptly call the nearest embassy or consulate and the local police.

ENTERING CANADA

Citizens and legal residents of the United States do not need a passport or a visa to enter Canada, but proof of citizenship (a birth certificate or valid passport) and some form of photo identification will be requested. Naturalized U.S. residents should carry their naturalization certificate. Permanent residents who are not citizens should carry their "green card." U.S. residents entering Canada from a third country must have a valid passport, naturalization certificate, or "green card."

Citizens of the United Kingdom need only a valid passport to enter Canada for stays of up to six months.

PASSPORT OFFICES

The best time to apply for a passport or to renew is in fall and winter. Before any trip, check your passport's expiration date, and, if necessary, renew it as soon as possible.

➤ AUSTRALIAN CITIZENS: **Australian Passport Office** (☎ 131–232, www.dfat.gov.au/passports).

➤ NEW ZEALAND CITIZENS: **New Zealand Passport Office** (☎ 04/494–0700, www.passports.govt.nz).

➤ U.K. CITIZENS: **London Passport Office** (☎ 0870/521–0410) for fees and documentation requirements and to request an emergency passport.

SENIOR-CITIZEN TRAVEL

To qualify for age-related discounts, **mention your senior-citizen status up front** when booking hotel reservations (not when checking out) and before you're seated in restaurants (not when paying the bill). When renting a car, ask about promotional car-rental discounts, which can be cheaper than senior-citizen rates.

➤ EDUCATIONAL PROGRAMS: **Elderhostel** (✉ 75 Federal St., 3rd floor, Boston, MA 02110, ☎ 877/426–8056, FAX 877/426–2166, www.elderhostel.org). **Interhostel** (✉ University of New Hampshire, 6 Garrison Ave., Durham, NH 03824, ☎ 603/862–1147 or 800/733–9753, FAX 603/862–1113, www.learn.unh.edu).

STUDENTS IN CANADA

Persons under 18 years of age who are not accompanied by their parents should **bring a letter from a parent or** guardian giving them permission to travel to Canada.

➤ I.D.s &Services: **Council Travel** (CIEE; ✉ 205 E. 42nd St., 14th floor, New York, NY 10017, ☎ 212/822–2700 or 888/268–6245, FAX 212/822–2699, info@councilexchanges.org, www.councilexchanges.org) for mail orders only, in the U.S. **Travel Cuts** (✉ 187 College St., Toronto, Ontario M5T 1P7, ☎ 416/979–2406 or 800/667–2887, www.travelcuts.com) in Canada.

TAXES

A goods and services tax (GST) of 7% applies on virtually every transaction in Canada except for the purchase of basic groceries.

In addition to imposing the GST, in British Columbia consumers pay a 7% sales tax. This tax does not apply to food, ferries, or accommodations. Taxes of 10% are, however, levied on accommodations and alcoholic beverages sold in bars and restaurants.

GST REFUNDS

You can **get a GST refund on purchases taken out of the country and on short-term accommodations of less than one month** (but not on food, drink, tobacco, car or motor home rentals, or transportation); rebate forms, which must be submitted within 60 days of leaving Canada, may be obtained from certain retailers, duty-free shops, customs officials, or from Revenue Canada. Instant cash rebates up to a maximum of $500 are provided by some duty-free shops when leaving Canada, and most vendors do not charge GST on goods that are shipped directly to the purchaser's home. Always **save your original receipts** from stores and hotels (not just credit-card receipts), and **be sure the name and address of the establishment is shown on the receipt.** Original receipts are not returned. To be eligible for a refund, receipts must total at least $200, and each individual receipt must show a minimum purchase of $50.

➤ INFORMATION: **Revenue Canada** (✉ Visitor Rebate Program, Summerside Tax Centre, 275 Pope Rd., Suite 104,

Summerside, PE C1N 6C6, ☎ 902/432–5608; 800/668–4748 in Canada).

TIPPING

Tips and service charges are not usually added to a bill in Canada. In general, tip 15% of the total bill. This goes for waiters, waitresses, barbers and hairdressers, and taxi drivers. Porters and doormen should get about $1 a bag (or more in a luxury hotel). For maid service, leave at least $2 a day ($3 in luxury hotels).

TOURS & PACKAGES

Because everything is prearranged on a prepackaged tour or independent vacation, you'll spend less time planning—and often get it all at a good price.

BOOKING WITH AN AGENT

Travel agents are excellent resources. But it's a good idea to collect brochures from several agencies as some agents' suggestions may be influenced by relationships with tour and package firms that reward them for volume sales. If you have a special interest, **find an agent with expertise in that area**; ASTA (☞ Travel Agencies, *below*) has a database of specialists worldwide.

Make sure your travel agent knows the accommodations and other services of the place they're recommending. Ask about the hotel's location, room size, beds, and whether it has a pool, room service, or programs for children, if you care about these. Has your agent been there in person or sent others whom you can contact?

Do some homework on your own, too: local tourism boards can provide information about lesser-known and small-niche operators, some of which may sell only direct.

BUYER BEWARE

Each year consumers are stranded or lose their money when tour operators—even large ones with excellent reputations—go out of business. So **check out the operator.** Ask several travel agents about its reputation, and try to **book with a company that has a consumer-protection program.**

(Look for information in the company's brochure.) In the United States, members of the National Tour Association and the United States Tour Operators Association are required to set aside funds to cover your payments and travel arrangements in the event that the company defaults. It's also a good idea to choose a company that participates in the American Society of Travel Agents' Tour Operator Program (TOP); ASTA will act as mediator in any disputes between you and your tour operator.

Remember that the more your package or tour includes the better you can predict the ultimate cost of your vacation. Make sure you know exactly what is covered, and **beware of hidden costs.** Are taxes, tips, and transfers included? Entertainment and excursions? These can add up.

➤ TOUR-OPERATOR RECOMMENDATIONS: **American Society of Travel Agents** (☞ Travel Agencies, *below*). **National Tour Association** (NTA; ✉ 546 E. Main St., Lexington, KY 40508, ☎ 606/226–4444 or 800/682–8886, www.ntaonline.com). **United States Tour Operators Association** (USTOA; ✉ 342 Madison Ave., Suite 1522, New York, NY 10173, ☎ 212/599–6599 or 800/468–7862, FAX 212/599–6744, ustoa@aol.com, www.ustoa.com).

THEME TRIPS

The companies listed below provide multiday tours in British Columbia. Additional local or regionally based companies that have different-length trips with these themes are listed in each chapter, either with information about the town or in the A to Z section that concludes the chapter.

➤ ADVENTURE: **American Wilderness Experience** (✉ Box 1486, Boulder, CO 80306, ☎ 303/444–2622 or 800/444–0099, FAX 303/635–0658). **Ecosummer Expeditions** (✉ Box 1765, Clearwater, BC V0E 1N0, ☎ 250/674–0102 or 800/465–8884, FAX 250/674–2187). **Mountain Travel-Sobek** (✉ 6420 Fairmount Ave., El Cerrito, CA 94530, ☎ 510/527–8100 or 888/687–6235, FAX 510/525–7710).

O.A.R.S. (✉ Box 67, Angels Camp, CA 95222, ☎ 209/736–4677 or 800/346–6277, FAX 209/736–2902). **Trek America** (✉ Box 189, Rockaway, NJ 07866, ☎ 973/983–1144 or 800/221–0596, FAX 973/983–8551).

➤ BICYCLING: **Backroads** (✉ 801 Cedar St., Berkeley, CA 94710-1800, ☎ 510/527–1555 or 800/462–2848, FAX 510/527–1444). **Bicycle Adventures** (✉ Box 11219, Olympia, WA 98508, ☎ 360/786–0989 or 800/443–6060, FAX 360/786–9661). **Bike Rider Tours** (✉ Box 130254, Boston, MA 02113, ☎ 617/723–2354 or 800/473–7040, FAX 617/723–2355). **Butterfield & Robinson** (✉ 70 Bond St., Toronto, ON M5B 1X3, ☎ 416/864–1354 or 800/678–1147, FAX 416/864–0541). **Easy Rider Tours** (✉ Box 228, Newburyport, MA 01950, ☎ 978/463–6955 or 800/488–8332, FAX 978/463–6988). **Imagine Tours** (✉ Box 475, Davis, CA 95617, ☎ 530/758–8782 or 888/592–8687, FAX 530/758–8778). **Rocky Mountain Worldwide Cycle Tours** (✉ Box 268, Garibaldi Highlands, Squamish, BC V0N 1T0, ☎ 604/898–8488 or 800/661–2453, FAX 604/898–8489). **Timberline Adventures** (✉ 7975 E. Harvard, Suite J, Denver, CO 80231, ☎ 303/759–3804 or 800/417–2453, FAX 303/368–1651). **Vermont Bicycle Touring** (✉ Box 711, Bristol, VT 05443-0711, ☎ 800/245–3868 or 802/453–4811, FAX 802/453–4806). **Les Voyages du Tour de l'Île,** (✉ 1251 rue Rache Est, Montréal, PQ H2J 2J9, ☎ 514/521–8356 or 888/899–1111, FAX 514/512–5711).

➤ DUDE RANCHES: **American Wilderness Experience** (☞ Adventure, *above*).

➤ FISHING: **Cutting Loose Expeditions** (✉ Box 447, Winter Park, FL 32790-0447, ☎ 407/629–4700 or 800/533–4746, FAX 407/740–7816). **Fishing International** (✉ Box 2132, Santa Rosa, CA 95405, ☎ 707/542–4242 or 800/950–4242, FAX 707/526–3474). **Rod & Reel Adventures** (✉ 566 Thomson La., Copperopolis, CA 95228, ☎ 209/785–0444 or 800/356–6982, FAX 209/785–0447).

➤ PHOTOGRAPHY: **Joseph Van Os Photo Safaris** (✉ Box 655, Vashon,

WA 98070, ☎ 206/463–5383, FAX 206/463–5484).

➤ SKIING: **Canadian Mountain Holidays** (✉ 217 Bear St., Banff, AB T0L 0C0, ☎ 403/762–7100 or 800/661–0252, FAX 403/762–5879). **Selkirk Tangiers Helicopter Skiing** (✉ Box 139, Revelstoke, BC V0E 2S0, ☎ 250/837–5378 or 800/663–7080, FAX 250/837–5766). **Skican** (✉ 443 Mt. Pleasant Rd., Toronto, ON M4S 2L8, ☎ 416/488–1169 or 888/475–4226, FAX 416/488–7620). **Whistler Heli-Skiing** (✉ Box 894, Whistler, BC V0N 1B0, ☎ 604/932–7007 or 888/435–4754, FAX 604/932–9992).

➤ SPAS: **Spa-Finders** (✉ 91 5th Ave., Suite 600, New York, NY 10003-3039, ☎ 212/924–6800 or 800/255–7727).

➤ WALKING/HIKING: **Backroads** (☞ Bicycling, *above*). **Butterfield & Robinson** (☞ Bicycling, *above*). **Canadian Mountain Holidays** (☞ Skiing, *above*). **Country Walkers** (✉ Box 180, Waterbury, VT 05676-0180, ☎ 802/244–1387 or 800/464–9255, FAX 802/244–5661) **New England Hiking Holidays** (✉ Box 1648, North Conway, NH 03860, ☎ 603/356–9696 or 800/869–0949). **Timberline Adventures** (☞ Bicycling, *above*). **Walking the World** (✉ Box 1186, Fort Collins, CO 80522, ☎ 970/498–0500 or 800/340–9255, FAX 970/498–9100) specializes in tours for ages 50 and older.

TRAIN TRAVEL

Amtrak, the U.S. passenger rail system has the *Mt. Baker International* line, which takes a highly scenic coastal route from Seattle to Vancouver once daily. High-speed train service between Eugene, Oregon, and Vancouver, with stops in Portland, Seattle, and elsewhere, was scheduled to begin by 2001.

Canada's passenger service, **VIA Rail Canada,** operates transcontinental routes on the *Canadian* three times weekly in each direction between eastern Canada and Vancouver.

➤ TRAIN INFORMATION: **Amtrak** (☎ 800/872–7245). **VIA Rail Canada** (☎ 800/561–3949 in the U.S.; 800/561–8630 in Canada).

WITHIN BRITISH COLUMBIA

British Columbia has a number of scenic train routes in addition to those operated by Amtrak and VIA Rail Canada. The **Rocky Mountaineer** is a two-day all-daylight rail cruise that runs from May through October between Vancouver and the Canadian Rockies. There are two routes—one to Banff/Calgary and the other to Jasper—through landscapes considered to be the most spectacular in the world. An overnight hotel stop is made in Kamloops.

On Vancouver Island, **VIA Rail** runs the *E&N Railway* daily in summer and six times a week in winter from Victoria north to Courtenay. **BC Rail** operates daily service from its North Vancouver terminal to Whistler and thrice-weekly service to the town of Prince George. At Prince George it is possible to connect with VIA Rail's *Skeena* service east to Jasper and Alberta or west to Prince Rupert. BC Rail also operates two summertime (May–October) excursion trains along scenic Howe Sound: the *Royal Hudson* steam train and the *Pacific Starlight Dinner Train.*

➤ RAIL COMPANIES: **Rocky Mountaineer** (✉ Great Canadian Railtour Co., Ltd., 1150 Station St., 1st floor, Vancouver, BC V6A 2X7, ☎ 604/606–7245 in Vancouver; 800/665–7245 in the U.S.; 800/663–8238 in the U.S. and elsewhere in Canada). **BC Rail** (✉ 1311 W. 1st St., North Vancouver, BC V7P 1A6, ☎ 604/984–5500 in Vancouver; 800/663–8238 in the U.S. and elsewhere in Canada). **VIA Rail** (☎ 800/561–8630 in Canada; 800/561–3949 in the U.S.).

CUTTING COSTS

If you're planning to travel a lot by train, **look into the Canrail pass.** It allows 12 days of coach-class travel within a 30-day period; sleeping cars are available, but they sell out very early and must be reserved at least a month in advance during the high season (June–mid-October), when the pass is C$589 for adults age 25–60, C$529 for travelers under 25 or over 60. Low-season rates (October 16–May) are C$379 for adults and C$345 for youths and senior citizens. The pass is not valid during the

Christmas period (December 15–
January 5). For more information and
reservations, contact a travel agent in
the U.S. or Long-Haul Leisurail in the
United Kingdom (☞ *below*).

Train travelers can **check out the new
30-day North American RailPass**
offered by Amtrak and VIA Rail. It
allows unlimited coach/economy
travel in the U.S. and Canada. You
must indicate the itinerary when
purchasing the pass. The cost is $645
June–October 15, $450 at other
times.

FARES & SCHEDULES

➤ TRAIN INFORMATION: **Amtrak** (☎
800/872–7245). **Great Canadian Rail
Tour Co.** (☎ 800/665–7245). **VIA
Rail Canada** (☎ 800/561–3949). In
the U.K., **Long-Haul Leisurail** (✉ Box
113, Peterborough, PE3 8HY UK, ☎
01733/335599) represents both VIA
Rail and Rocky Mountaineer Railtours.

TRAVEL AGENCIES

A good travel agent puts your needs
first. Look for an agency that has
been in business at least five years,
emphasizes customer service, and has
someone on staff who specializes in
your destination. In addition, **make
sure the agency belongs to a professional trade organization.** The American Society of Travel Agents (ASTA),
with 27,000 agents in some 170
countries, is the largest and most
influential in the field. Operating
under the motto "Integrity in Travel,"
maintains and enforces a strict code
of ethics and will step in to help
mediate any agent-client disputes if
necessary. ASTA also maintains a
Web site that includes a directory of
agents. (If a travel agency is also
acting as your tour operator, *see*
Buyer Beware *in* Tours & Packages,
above.)

➤ LOCAL AGENT REFERRALS: **American Society of Travel Agents** (ASTA;
☎ 800/965–2782 24-hr hot line, FAX
703/684–8319, www.astanet.com).
Association of British Travel Agents
(✉ 68–71 Newman St., London W1P
4AH, ☎ 0171/637–2444, FAX 0171/
637–0713, information@abta.co.uk,

www.abtanet.com). **Association of
Canadian Travel Agents** (✉ 1729
Bank St., Suite 201, Ottawa, Ontario
K1V 7Z5, ☎ 613/521–0474, FAX 613/
521–0805, acta.ntl@sympatico.ca).
**Australian Federation of Travel
Agents** (✉ Level 3, 309 Pitt St.,
Sydney 2000, ☎ 02/9264–3299, FAX
02/9264–1085, www.afta.com.au).
**Travel Agents' Association of New
Zealand** (✉ Box 1888, Wellington
10033, ☎ 04/499–0104, FAX 04/499–
0827, taanz@tiasnet.co.nz).

VISITOR INFORMATION

➤ TOURIST INFORMATION: For
Canada, **Canadian Tourism Commis-
sion** (☎ 613/946–1000, www.
canadatourism.com); in British
Columbia, **Tourism B.C** (✉ Plaza
Level, 200 Burrard St., Vancouver,
V6C 3L6, ☎ 800/663–6000).

➤ IN THE U.K.: **Visit Canada Center**
(✉ 62–65 Trafalgar Sq., London,
WC2 5DY, ☎ 0891/715–000). Calls
to the Visit Canada Center cost 50p
per minute peak rate and 45p per
minute cheap rate.

WEB SITES

Do check out the World Wide Web
when you're planning. You'll find
everything from current weather
forecasts to virtual tours of famous
cities. Fodor's Web site, www.fodors.
com, is a great place to start your on-
line travels. When you see a 🔄 in this
book, go to www.fodors.com/urls for
an up-to-date link to that destination's site.There are also many sites
with information specifically on
Canada, a few of which follow.

➤ CANADIAN WEB SITES: For Canadian festivals, www.festivalseeker.
com; for British Columbia, www.
travel.bc.ca; for Vancouver, www.
tourism-vancouver.org.

WHEN TO GO

For more information on when to
visit, *see* the When to Tour section at
the beginning of each chapter.

CLIMATE

The following are average daily
maximum and minimum temperatures for Vancouver.

VANCOUVER

Jan.	42F	6C	May	60F	16C	Sept.	65F	18C
	33	1		47	8		52	11
Feb.	45F	7C	June	65F	18C	Oct.	56F	13C
	36	2		52	11		45	7
Mar.	48F	9C	July	70F	21C	Nov.	48F	9C
	37	3		55	13		39	4
Apr.	54F	12C	Aug.	70F	21C	Dec.	43F	6C
	41	5		55	13		35	2

➤ Forecasts: **Weather Channel Connection** (☎ 900/932–8437), 95¢ per minute from a Touch-Tone phone.

1 DESTINATION: VANCOUVER AND BRITISH COLUMBIA

THE BEAUTY AND THE BUZZ

LIVE ON AN island, a pretty piece of rock called Salt Spring off the coast of British Columbia, and every few weeks I leave this island to go into town to admire the bright lights of Vancouver. The sailing, usually on BC Ferries' venerable *Queen of Nanaimo,* takes three hours (even though I can see the mainland from a hill near my home), but the journey is always a pleasure. In the winter, soft rains tap against the cabin windows; in the summer, I make like a backpacker and stretch out in the sun across the life-jacket boxes on deck.

We sail through a maze of green-backed islands, dotted with lighthouses and summer homes perched on precipitous slopes. I usually pass the time with someone—a student from Japan, another islander, or a family on vacation from Australia, Alaska, or Arizona—and I always hope, for their sake, that the captain will come on the loudspeaker and announce: "Attention passengers, we have a pod of orcas off the starboard bow." I remember once chatting to a crew member who'd worked the same sailing for twenty years. "Do you ever get bored?" I asked. "Are you kidding," he replied, gesturing at the islands passing by the window. "Look at it!"

You can't help but look at it. It's fair to say that British Columbia, from the fjord-cut coast to the forests, lakes, and mountains inland, to the wilderness of the north, is one of the most beautiful places on earth. Even the metropolis of Vancouver, with two million people and counting, enjoys a dramatic natural setting, with the sea at its toes and the mountains as a backdrop.

The scenery of course, has always been here (and much of the environmentally conscious population is working hard to keep it that way), but what's new is the buzz. Every time I come to town, there are four new fashionable restaurants in Yaletown, another Rodeo Drive transplant on Robson Street, a recently inaugurated music festival, another theater, or even a whole new downtown neighborhood. Vancouver isn't getting bigger exactly (there's not much room left on the downtown peninsula), but it is becoming more interesting, with the fusty, the provincial, and the dull being replaced with the trendy, the urban, and the vibrant.

It wasn't always like this. In 1886, when a small town-site on Burrard Inlet was incorporated as the City of Vancouver, it amounted to little more than a sawmill, a few saloons, and enough shacks for about 400 frontier-types. Vancouver was a rough town in those days. Saloons outnumbered churches, and city fathers, unwilling to tax one another, filled their coffers by fining the local prostitutes. It was a good place to make money, though, especially if you turned your hand to lumbering, whiskey sales, or land speculation.

THE NEXT 100 years or so were a bit, well, dull. For most of the 20th century Vancouver was a staid, provincial little place, its multiculturalism buried under a cloak of British colonial propriety; Vancouverites looked to the old country (be that England or Ontario) for new fashions and ideas, turned some of their best waterfront property over to warehouses, industry, and railyards, and had so little regard for their early history that at one point there were plans (happily scuppered) to build a freeway through the oldest part of the city.

Things lightened up a bit in the 1960s, when thousands of young Canadians—and Americans—flocked to the West Coast under the misguided notion that it was an easygoing place. It wasn't, but by sheer weight of numbers they made it so. Vancouver's hippie legacy is manifest in funky shops along Fourth Avenue and Commercial Drive, a popular nude beach, the Vancouver Folk Music Festival and other long-running events, and a deep-seated reputation for flakiness.

The biggest change happened in the mid-1980s, when the city cleaned up a section of its old industrial waterfront and invited the planet to Expo '86, the World's Fair. The event was uncommonly profitable and, as I recall, a lot of fun, but few envisioned the watershed in Vancouver's history that it would become. To this day people here define Vancouver as two different cities: pre- and post-'86. "Expo changed everything," they'll say, often with mixed emotions.

What happened? The fair opened up a good stretch of waterfront to public use, and left the city a number of other people-friendly legacies, including the cruise-ship terminal and convention center at Canada Place, and the SkyTrain, a rapid-transit link. It also showed millions of visitors something that they, and many locals, had overlooked: that Vancouver is one of the most beautifully situated cities anywhere.

As growing numbers of tourists were discovering Vancouver during the 1980s and '90s, so were thousands of newcomers from Asia. The wave of immigration, led by relatively well-off people from Hong Kong and Taiwan, boosted property values, dramatically improved the culinary scene, and added an element of urban sophistication that was new to Canada's West Coast. The Vancouver of 2001 is a modern metropolis, with one foot in Asia, the other in the Pacific Northwest, and better access than ever before to the surrounding wilderness—nothing like the sleepy backwater I grew up in.

OF COURSE ONE can pine for the pre-1986 days, when traffic was lighter and that famous laid-back West Coast attitude more evident. For that, though, there's Victoria, British Columbia's capital, at the tip of Vancouver Island. Worth the trip for the ferry ride alone, Victoria, a virtually industry-free government town, has always been a looker. Its Inner Harbour, bobbing with sailboats, lined with hanging flower baskets and stately Victorian brick edifices, and backed with the mountain peaks of the mainland, has impressed visitors from the early days.

When James Douglas, British Columbia's first governor, arrived in 1842, he wrote: "The place appears a perfect Eden in the midst of the dreary wilderness of the Northwest Coast, and so different is its general aspect . . . that one might be pardoned for supposing it had dropped from the clouds." Yes, Victoria is a pretty town,

but I take exception to his assessment of the surrounding wilds. This wilderness has been occupied for at least 10,000 years by native peoples who, thanks in part to the wealth of forest and sea, were able to create one of the richest cultures in North America. Their legacy is in evidence in British Columbia's two leading museums—the Royal British Columbia Museum in Victoria and the Museum of Anthropology in Vancouver—as well as in villages throughout the province.

Fortunately, much of British Columbia's hinterland is intact, in provincial and national parks and in areas such as the roadless fjords of the northern coast and the forests of the far north, which have never had much population. British Columbia boasts some of the last remaining true wilderness in North America and, despite the pleasures of the cities, a chance to experience this wild, from a kayak, sailboat, floatplane, or hiking path—lodging at a luxury resort or a simple campsite—is the main attraction for many visitors to the province.

The sheer size of the province means that even long-term residents find they have to pick and choose their experiences: the old-growth rainforest and Pacific surf of Vancouver Island, the hiking trails and ski resorts of the interior mountains, the Okanagan wine country and the high-country guest ranches, the pure wilderness of the northern coast. Chances are no one has ever seen it all.

–Sue Kernaghan

NEW AND NOTEWORTHY

Whether you're planning to visit British Columbia's great outdoors, its beautiful Pacific coast, or its metropolitan areas, it's good to know that your dollar will stretch further (even with higher Canadian taxes), making the province a great travel value. Following the trend of the past few years, the exchange rate (summer 2000) is about US$1 to C$1.49, and £1 to C$2.23.

Many of the province's historic railway lines came back to life in 2000, offering several new train excursions. In addition to the long-established Starlight Dinner Train and the Royal Hudson Steam Train traveling into the mountains north of **Vancouver,** the century-old tramcars of the Downtown Historic Railway now take passengers around False Creek. Elsewhere in the province, the Pacific Wilderness Railway Company operates a vintage train from Victoria to the mountainous **Malahat,** a 1929 Baldwin steam locomotive takes passengers along the waterfront in **Port Alberni,** and the Okanagan Valley Wine Train travels a vintage line between **Penticton** and **Kelowna.**

WHAT'S WHERE

Vancouver

The spectacular setting of cosmopolitan Vancouver has inspired people from around the world to settle here. The Pacific Ocean and the mountains of the North Shore form a dramatic backdrop to the gleaming towers of commerce downtown and make it easy to pursue outdoor pleasures. You can trace the city's history in **Gastown** and **Chinatown,** savor the wilderness only blocks from the city center in **Stanley Park,** or dine on superb ethnic or Pacific Northwest cuisine before you sample the city's nightlife. People from every corner of the world create a vibrant atmosphere.

Museums and buildings of architectural and historical significance are the primary draw in **downtown Vancouver.** There's also plenty of fine shopping to provide breaks along the way. Vancouver is a new city when compared to others, but one that's rich in culture and diversity.

You can steal away from the hubbub of Vancouver in minutes, to Pacific beaches, rugged mountains, and forested islands. Opportunities for whale- and nature-watching, as well as year-round skiing and superb fishing and kayaking, abound.

Victoria and Vancouver Island

The Anglophile provincial capital of **Victoria** has a climate like that of Devon in Great Britain, with glorious, flower- and sunshine-filled springs. The city is home to half the population of **Vancouver Island,** the largest Pacific coastal island. Vistors to the island can travel from Victoria to the many

nearby coastal and island towns in the east or explore the largely uninhabited mountains, forests, and beaches in the west.

British Columbia

British Columbia is clearly a world apart. In the Lower Mainland, in and around Vancouver, it appears a brash young province with a population that sees its future on the Pacific Rim. Pardoxically, in the north are ancient rainforests, untamed wilderness, and First Nations peoples who have lived on the land for more than 10,000 years.

British Columbia's natural beauty and prospects of outdoor adventure draw growing numbers of vacationers every year. Only two hours north of Vancouver is the popular resort town of Whistler, with North America's two biggest ski mountains. The Okanagan Valley in the east, replete with lakes and vineyards, is famous for its wines. Near Vancouver lies the Sunshine Coast, with secluded fjords and the Gulf Islands, popular vacation spots for B.C. residents. To the extreme north are the Cariboo and the North Coast, vast areas of mountainous and forrested terrain. Visitors find ghost towns abandoned after the gold- and silver-rush eras, the foothills of the Rockies, and plenty of opportunities for activities that include fishing, boating, hiking, and skiing.

FODOR'S CHOICE

Sights and Attractions

★ **Chesterman Beach, Tofino.** The open Pacific Ocean meets old-growth forest at Canada's western edge. The beauty of winter storms has made even harsh weather an attraction.

★ **Dr. Sun Yat-Sen Classical Chinese Garden, Vancouver.** The first authentic Ming Dynasty–style garden outside of China, this garden was built in 1986 by 52 artisans from Suzhou, the Garden City of the People's Republic.

★ **Granville Island, Vancouver.** This small sandbar was a derelict factory district, but its industrial buildings and tin sheds, painted in upbeat primary colors, now house restaurants, a public market, marine activities, and artists' studios.

★ **Museum of Anthropology, Vancouver.** Vancouver's most spectacular museum displays aboriginal art from the Pacific Northwest and around the world—dramatic totem poles and canoes; exquisite carvings of gold, silver, and argillite; and masks, tools, and textiles from many cultures.

Parks and Gardens

★ **Stanley Park, Vancouver.** An afternoon in this 1,000-acre wilderness park, only blocks from downtown, can include beaches, the ocean, the harbor, Douglas fir and cedar forests, and a good look at the North Shore mountains.

★ **Butchart Gardens, Victoria.** Stunning display gardens exhibit more than 700 varieties of flowers and have Italian, Japanese, and English rose gardens.

★ **Pacific Rim National Park Reserve, Vancouver Island.** This park on Canada's far west coast comprises a hard-packed white-sand beach, a group of islands, and a demanding coastal hiking trail with panoramic views of the sea and the rain forest.

Dining

★ **C, Vancouver.** The name and decor are minimalist, but the innovative seafood and the stunning marina-side location overlooking False Creek make this one of Vancouver's most exciting restaurants. $$$$

★ **Bacchus, Vancouver.** Low lighting, velvet drapes, and Venetian glass lamps create a mildly decadent feel at this seriously sensuous Italian restaurant inside the Wedgewood Hotel. $$–$$$$

★ **Cafe Brio, Victoria.** "Fresh" is the word at this café, in a building that resembles an Italian villa. The restaurant works with local organic farms and serves produce the day it's harvested. $$–$$$$

★ **Il Giardino di Umberto, Vancouver.** Tuscan favorites are served in this little yellow house at the end of Hornby Street. The vine-draped courtyard with a wood-burning oven is especially romantic. $$–$$$$

★ **Liliget Feast House, Vancouver.** This intimate downstairs longhouse near English Bay is one of the few places in the world serving original Northwest Coast native cuisine. $$–$$$$

★ **Tojo's, Vancouver.** Hidekazu Tojo is a sushi-making legend, with more than 2,000 preparations tucked away in his creative mind. $$$

★ **Imperial Chinese Seafood, Vancouver.** This Cantonese restaurant in the Art Deco Marine Building has two-story floor-to-ceiling windows with stupendous views of Stanley Park and the North Shore mountains across Burrard Inlet. $$–$$$

★ **Vij's, Vancouver.** Vikram Vij, who calls his elegant South Granville restaurant a "curry art gallery," brings together the best of the subcontinent and the Pacific Northwest for exciting new interpretations of Indian cuisine. $$

Lodging

★ **Hotel Vancouver, Vancouver.** The copper roof of this grand château-style hotel dominates Vancouver's skyline. The hotel itself, opened in 1939 by the Canadian National Railway, commands a regal position in the center of town. $$$$

★ **Pan Pacific Hotel, Vancouver.** A centerpiece of Vancouver's Trade and Convention Centre and a cruise-ship terminal, the luxurious Pan Pacific has a dramatic three-story atrium lobby and expansive views of the harbor and mountains. $$$$

★ **Sooke Harbour House, Sooke, Vancouver Island.** West of Victoria, this light and airy oceanfront inn looks like the home of a discerning art collector; the restaurant is one of Canada's finest. $$$$

★ **Listel Vancouver, Vancouver.** This Robson Street hotel doubles as an art gallery, with about half of its guest rooms displaying the works of well-known contemporary artists. $$$–$$$$

★ **Sutton Place, Vancouver.** The feeling here is more of an exclusive European guest house than a large modern hotel. Guest rooms are furnished with rich, dark woods reminiscent of 19th-century France, and the service is gracious and attentive. $$$–$$$$

★ **English Bay Inn, Vancouver.** In this renovated 1930s Tudor house a block from the ocean and Stanley Park, the guest rooms have wonderful sleigh beds with matching armoires. $$–$$$

★ **West End Guest House, Vancouver.** From its gracious front parlor, cozy fireplace, and early 1900s furniture to its bright-pink exterior, this lovely Victorian house built in 1906 is a true "painted lady." *$$–$$$*

⭐ **River Run, Ladner.** This unique bed-and-breakfast is part of a small houseboat community 30 minutes south of Vancouver. The accommodations include a floating house, a net loft, and two river's-edge cottages. *$$*

BOOKS AND VIDEOS

Pauline Johnson's *Legends of Vancouver* is a colorful compilation of regional native myths. Longtime Vancouver resident George Bowering wrote the lively *British Columbia: A Swashbuckling History of the Province.* Lois Simmie's children's book *Mister Got-to-Go* takes place in the Sylvia Hotel. Annette, the protagonist of Margaret A. Robinson's *A Woman of Her Tribe,* leaves her village to study in Victoria but feels alienated upon her return.

Photographer Morton Beebe's beautiful *Cascadia: A Tale of Two Cities, Seattle and Vancouver, B.C.* explores the cultural and natural wonders of Seattle, Vancouver, and the regions surrounding each city. Chuck Davis's *Greater Vancouver Book* is a comprehensive look at Vancouver's past and present.

Denise Chong's *The Concubine's Children,* and Wayson Joy's *The Jade Peony* are novels about immigrant life in Vancouver's Chinatown.

Michael Kluckner's *Heritage Walks Around Vancouver,* Robin Ward's *Vancouver,* and Rhodri Windsor Liscombe's *The New Spirit: Modern Architecture in Vancouver 1938–1963* explore the city's architectural heritage. Gerald B. Straley's *Trees of Vancouver* is a good survey of the major and less-common varieties. Straley's book is one of many titles published by the press of University of British Columbia about Canada's far west.

Film and television production is a big business in British Columbia—C$808 million was spent in 1998 making it the third largest production area in North America, after Los Angeles and New York.

Vancouver often stands in for other urban areas—including New York City in *Rumble in the Bronx* (1994) and *Friday the 13th: Jason Takes Manhattan* (1989)—but occasionally plays itself. The 1995 Canadian feature *The War Between Us* re-creates 1940s Vancouver as it explores the fate of a well-to-do family of Japanese descent whose members are interned in a camp in interior British Columbia following the outbreak of World War II. *Once in a Blue Moon* (1995), another period piece shot in British Columbia, concerns a 10-year-old boy who comes of age in the suburbs of Vancouver in the late 1960s. For a peek at Vancouver's 1990s slacker culture, check out *Live Bait,* a 1995 homage to Woody Allen. The sometimes goofy sci-fi flick *Cyberjack* (1995) conjures up a Vancouver of the 21st century, complete with flying SeaBuses.

The last decade has been the heyday of British Columbia film production, but the area's cinematic roots go back more than a half century. Estelle Taylor, Thomas Meighan, and Anna May Wong starred in *The Alaskan,* a 1924 Paramount drama about a man who rescues Alaska from the clutches of corrupt robber barons. The 1945 *Son of Lassie* is not one of the lovable collie's best pictures, but does contain scenes shot in British Columbia. Rugged Sterling Hayden starred in *Timberjack,* a 1954 offering from Republic Pictures. Oliver Reed starred in the 1966 film *The Trap,* about a 19th-century trapper and his wife in British Columbia.

Robert Altman shot scenes in British Columbia for two of his early films, *That Cold Day in the Park* and *McCabe and Mrs. Miller.* The 1976 remake of the Orson Welles thriller *Journey Into Fear,* starring Vincent Price, Shelley Winters, and Sam Waterston, was shot in and around Vancouver, as was the 1980 *The Grey Fox,* based on the life of an early 1900s stagecoach bandit. *Klondike Fever,* a 1979 picture starring Rod Steiger, concerns the 1897–98 gold rush.

Among the productions filmed wholly or partly in British Columbia in the past decade or so are *Roxanne, Stakeout, The Accused,* the *Look Who's Talking* movies, the Jean Claude Van Damme action picture *Time Cop, The Crush, Cousins, This Boy's Life, Stay Tuned, Jennifer Eight,* the Robin Williams fantasy *Jumanji,* the

Adam Sandler comedy *Happy Gilmore*, the remake of *Little Women*, *Cyberteens in Love* (check your local video store for this curious Canadian production), *Bounty Hunters II*, *Mr. Magoo*, *Deep Rising*, *Seven Years in Tibet*, and *Kundun*.

The TV series *21 Jump Street*, which made Johnny Depp a star, was one of several 1980s television series filmed in Vancou-ver. Since then, production has increased greatly. Other small-screen shows shot here include *Poltergeist*, *Highlanders*, *Millennium*, and *The X-Files*. *Neon Rider*, *Northwood*, *The Odyssey*, and *Mom P.I.* are among the Canadian series produced in Vancouver or elsewhere in British Columbia in the 1990s.

FESTIVALS AND SEASONAL EVENTS

British Columbia: Skiing competitions take place at most alpine ski resorts throughout British Columbia (through February).

➤ DECEMBER: **Vancouver:** The **Carol Ships,** sailboats full of carolers and decorated with colored lights, ply Vancouver harbor.

➤ JANUARY: **Sun Peaks, Okanagan Valley:** The annual **Okanagan Icewine Festival** is held in alpine Sun Peaks Village. The event showcases British Columbian icewine, a sweet wine made from grapes frozen on the vine. Contact Okanagan Wine Festivals (☎ 250/861–6654) for more information.

Victoria and Vancouver: The **Polar Bear Swims** on New Year's Day in Vancouver and Victoria are said to bring good luck all year.

SPRING

➤ MARCH: **Vancouver Island:** The **Pacific Rim Whale Festival** on Vancouver Island celebrates the spring migration of gray whales with guided tours by whale experts and music and dancing.

➤ APRIL: **Vancouver:** Sip the best vintages at the **Vancouver Playhouse International Wine Festival**

(☎ 604/872–6622), which attracts wineries from around the world.

Victoria: The **TerrifVic Jazz Party** has top international bands.

➤ MAY: **Vancouver:** The **Vancouver International Children's Festival,** said to be the largest event of its kind in the world, presents dozens of free open-air stage performances in mime, puppetry, music, and theater.

Victoria: Swiftsure International draws more than 300 competitors to Victoria's harbor for an international yachting event.

➤ LATE MAY: **Victoria: Victoria Day,** on the second-to-last weekend in May, is a holiday throughout Canada, but Victoria celebrates in earnest, with picnics and a parade.

SUMMER

➤ JUNE: **Vancouver:** The **Canadian International Dragon Boat Festival** in late June features races between long, slender boats decorated with huge dragon heads, an event based on a Chinese "awakening the dragons" ritual. The festival also includes community and children's activities, dance performances, and arts exhibits. The **Du Maurier International Jazz Festival,** also in late June, celebrates a broad spectrum of jazz, blues, and related improvised music, with more than 200 perfor-

mances in venues around Vancouver.

➤ JUNE–SEPT.: **Vancouver: Bard on the Beach** is a series of Shakespearean plays performed under a huge seaside tent at Vanier Park. **Whistler Summer Festivals** present street entertainment and a variety of music at Whistler Resort.

➤ JULY 1: **British Columbia: Canada Day** inspires celebrations around the province in honor of Canada's birthday.

Vancouver: Canada Place hosts an entire day of free outdoor concerts followed by a fireworks display in the harbor.

Victoria: The daylong **Great Canadian Family Picnic** is hosted in Beacon Hill Park. The event usually includes children's games, bands, food booths, and fireworks.

➤ JULY: **Vancouver:** People travel from all over Canada to attend the **Folk Music Festival.** The **Symphony of Fire,** an international musical fireworks competition, blasts off over four evenings from a barge in English Bay. **Vancouver:** The **Vancouver International Comedy Festival** presents all manner of silliness (much of it free) on Granville Island.

➤ AUGUST: **Squamish:** The **Squamish Days Loggers Sports Festival** is a four-day event that draws loggers from around the world to compete in tree climbing, ax throwing, speed chopping, and birling (log rolling). Contact the Squamish Chamber of Commerce

(☎ 604/892–9244) for information.

AUTUMN

➤ SEPTEMBER: **Vancouver:** The **Vancouver Fringe Festival** attracts cutting-edge theater to the city's smaller stages.

➤ LATE SEPT.–EARLY OCT.: **Vancouver:** The **Vancouver International Film Festival** showcases lesser-known international filmmakers.

➤ OCTOBER: **Okanagan Valley:** The annual **Okanagan Fall Wine Festival** takes place over 10 days, with more than 110 events. There is also an annual wine festival in the spring. Contact Okanagan Wine Festivals (☎ 250/861–6654) for more information.

Vancouver: Pop and highbrow authors read, sign books, and speak at the **Vancouver International Writers Festival.**

2 VANCOUVER

The spectacular setting of cosmopolitan
Vancouver has drawn people from around
the world to settle here. The ocean and
mountains form a dramatic backdrop to
downtown's gleaming towers of commerce
and make it easy to pursue all kinds of
outdoor pleasures. You can trace the city's
history in Gastown and Chinatown, savor
the wilderness only blocks from the city
center in Stanley Park, or dine on superb
ethnic or Pacific Northwest cuisine before
you sample the city's nightlife.

By Sue
Kernaghan

VANCOUVER IS A YOUNG CITY, even by North American standards. It was not yet a town when British Columbia became part of the Canadian confederation in 1871. The city's history, such as it is, remains visible to the naked eye: eras are stacked east to west along the waterfront, from cobblestone late-Victorian Gastown to shiny postmodern glass cathedrals of commerce.

The Chinese, among the first to recognize the possibilities of Vancouver's setting, came to British Columbia during the 1850s seeking the gold that inspired them to name the province Gum-shan, or Gold Mountain. As laborers they built the Canadian Pacific Railway, giving Vancouver a purpose—one beyond the natural splendor that Royal Navy captain George Vancouver admired during his cruise around its harbor on June 13, 1792. The Canadian transcontinental railway, along with the city's Great White Fleet of clipper ships, gave Vancouver a full week's edge over the California ports in shipping tea and silk to New York at the end of the 19th century.

For its original inhabitants, the Coast Salish peoples, Vancouver was the sacred spot where the mythical Thunderbird and Killer Whale flung wind and rain all about the heavens during their epic battles. How else to explain the coast's fits of meteorological temper? Devotees of a later religious tradition might worship in the groves of Stanley Park or in the fir and cedar interior of Christ Church Cathedral, the city's oldest church.

These days, Vancouver, with a metropolitan-area population of 2 million, is booming. Many Asians have migrated here, mainly from Hong Kong, but other regions are represented as well. The mild climate, exquisite natural scenery, and relaxed, outdoor lifestyle are attracting new residents to British Columbia's business center, and the number of visitors is increasing for the same reasons. Many people get their first glimpse of Vancouver when catching an Alaskan cruise, and many return at some point to spend more time here.

Pleasures and Pastimes

Dining
Downtown bistros, waterfront seafood palaces, and upscale pan-Asian restaurants are among Vancouver's diverse gastronomical offerings. Several cutting-edge establishments are perfecting and defining Pacific Northwest fare, which incorporates regional seafood—notably salmon—and locally grown produce, often accompanied by British Columbian wines.

The Great Outdoors
Nature has truly blessed this city, surrounding it with verdant forests, towering mountains, coves, inlets, rivers, and the wide sea. Biking, hiking, skiing, snowboarding, and sailing are among the many outdoor activities possible in or near the city. Whether you prefer to relax on a beach by yourself or join a kayaking tour with an outfitter, Vancouver has plenty to offer.

Nightlife and the Arts
Vancouver residents support the arts enthusiastically, especially during the city's film, jazz, folk, and theater festivals, most of which take place between June and October. The opera, ballet, and symphonic companies are thriving. And the city boasts a range of live-music venues, pubs, and nightclubs, though the province's peculiar liquor laws can be baffling (you can, for example, play darts, but not Scrabble, in a

12

B.C. Golf
Museum **42**

B.C. Sports
Hall of Fame
and Museum **50**

Capilano River
Regional Park **53**

Capilano Suspension
Bridge and Park **52**

Grouse Mountain . . .**54**

Hastings Mill
Museum **41**

H.R. MacMillan
Space Centre **38**

Kitsilano Beach **40**

Library Square **48**

Museum of
Anthropology **43**

Nitobe Memorial
Garden **44**

Queen Elizabeth
Park **47**

Roundhouse **49**

Science World **51**

University of B.C.
Botanical Garden . . .**45**

Vancouver Martime
Museum **39**

Vancouver Museum . .**37**

VanDusen
Botanical Garden . . .**46**

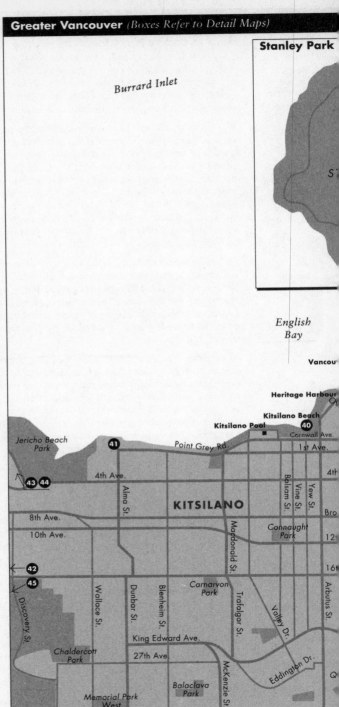

Greater Vancouver *(Boxes Refer to Detail Maps)*

Stanley Park

Burrard Inlet

*English
Bay*

Vancou

Heritage Harbour

Kitsilano Beach
40

Kitsilano Pool   Cornwall Ave.

Point Grey Rd.   1st Ave.

*Jericho Beach
Park*   **41**

4th Ave.   4th

43 **44**

Alma St.   Balsam St.   Vine St.   Yew St.   Bro

KITSILANO

8th Ave.   *Connaught
Park*   12

10th Ave.   Macdonald St.   16

42   *Carnarvon
Park*   Arbutus St.

45   Wallace St.   Dunbar St.   Blenheim St.   Trafalgar St.   Valley Dr.

Discovery St.   King Edward Ave.   McKenzie St.   Eddington Dr.

*Chaldercott
Park*   27th Ave   Q

*Balaclava
Park*

*Memorial Park
West*

52
53
54

1A
99A

Lions Gate Br.

NORTH
VANCOUVER

NLEY PARK

Burrard Inlet

N

0 _____ 1 mile
0 _____ 1 km

Denman St.

Downtown Vancouver

W. Pender St.
W. Georgia St.
Robson St.
Haro St.
Thurlow St.
Burrard St.
Hornby St.
Howe St.
Dunsmuir St.
Seymour St.
Homer St.
Cambie St.
W. Hastings St.

**Ford Centre for
the Performing Arts**

Cordova St.

Centennial

Powell St.

Hastings St.

7A

Powell St.

Dunley Ave.

Strathcona
Park

Clark

quatic Centre

48

50

38 37

Burrard
Br.

Pacific Blvd.

Granville St.

Richards St.

Davie St.

Ave.

Vanier
Park

Burrard St.

Granville

Granville
Island

**Granville
Island**

False Creek

Cambie Br.

2nd Ave.

Quebec St.

51

Terminal Ave.

49

Broadway

7

Cedar
Cottage
Park

Granville St.

Hemlock St.

Oak St.

Heather St.

12th Ave.

16th Ave.

Cambie St.

Manitoba St.

Main St.

Fraser St.

Windsor St.

Shaughnessy
Park

Matthews   Ave.

99

28th Ave.

King Edward

1A

46

↓

47

33rd Ave.

bar). Many pubs operate with a restaurant license, which requires patrons to order food with their drink. A bylaw introduced in 2000 bans smoking indoors in all public places in British Columbia, including pubs and bars, though observance is uneven.

EXPLORING VANCOUVER

The heart of Vancouver—which includes downtown, Stanley Park, Yaletown, and the West End—sits on a peninsula bordered by English Bay and the Pacific Ocean to the west; by False Creek, the inlet home to Granville Island, to the south; and by Burrard Inlet, the city's working port, to the north, past which loom the North Shore mountains. The oldest parts of the city—Gastown and Chinatown—lie at the edge of Burrard Inlet, around Main Street, which runs north–south and is roughly the dividing line between the east and west sides. All the avenues, which are numbered, have east and west designations. One note about printed Vancouver street addresses: suite numbers often appear *before* the street number, followed by a hyphen.

You'll find places of interest elsewhere in the city, either on the North Shore across Burrard Inlet, south of downtown in the Kitsilano area across English Bay, or in the Granville Island area across False Creek.

Great Itineraries

IF YOU HAVE 1 OR 2 DAYS

If you have only one day in Vancouver, start with an early morning walk, bike, or shuttle ride through Stanley Park to see the Vancouver Aquarium Marine Science Centre and the views from Prospect Point and take a stroll along the seawall. Head northeast from the park on Denman Street to Robson Street for lunch and meander on foot through the trendy shops between Denman and Burrard Street, and then walk northeast on Burrard to view the many buildings of architectural interest. Stop along the way at the Vancouver Art Gallery, the Canadian Craft Museum, and the Pacific Mineral Museum. On Day 2 take a leisurely walking tour of the shops, eateries, and cobblestone streets of Gastown, Chinatown, and Yaletown.

IF YOU HAVE 3 OR 4 DAYS

If you have another day to tour Vancouver and have followed the itinerary above, head to the south side of False Creek and English Bay on Day 3 to delve into the public market and the many boutiques, eateries, and theaters of Granville Island. Buses and ferries provide easy transit, and touring the island is best accomplished on foot. (If you drive, parking is available, but traffic to get on the island can be congested, especially on weekends.)

On Day 4, tour the sights beyond downtown Vancouver. Make time for the Museum of Anthropology on the campus of the University of British Columbia. Also visit the Vancouver Museum, the H.R. MacMillan Space Centre, and the Vancouver Maritime Museum, all in the Kitsilano area. If you'd rather play outside, head to the North Shore mountains, where you can swing high above the Capilano River on a suspension bridge or take in the panoramic city views as you ride the Skyride to the top of Grouse Mountain.

Robson to the Waterfront

Numbers in the text correspond to numbers in the margin and on the Downtown Vancouver map.

Museums and buildings of architectural and historical significance are the primary draw in downtown Vancouver, but there's also plenty of fine shopping.

A Good Walk

Begin at the northwest end of **Robson Street** ①, at Bute or Thurlow street. Follow Robson southeast to Hornby Street to reach landscaped **Robson Square** ②, which will be on your right. The **Vancouver Art Gallery** ③ will be on your left. Head northeast on Hornby Street to get to the **Hotel Vancouver** ④, a city landmark.

At Georgia and Hornby streets, catercorner to the Hotel Vancouver, is the **Hong Kong Bank of Canada Building.** The three-story-high public lobby atrium has a café, regularly changing art exhibitions, and one of the city's more intriguing public-art installations; *Pendulum,* by B.C. artist Alan Storey, is a 90-ft-long hollow aluminum sculpture that arcs hypnotically overhead. The 1991 **Cathedral Place** office tower, on the other side of Hornby Street, is one of Vancouver's most attractive postmodern buildings. The three large sculptures of nurses at the corners of the building are replicas of the statues that adorned the Georgia Medical–Dental Building, the Art Deco structure that previously occupied this site; the faux copper roof mimics that of the Hotel Vancouver. Step into the lobby to see another interesting sculpture, Robert Studer's *Navigational Device,* suspended from high on the north wall.

The north exit of Cathedral Place (cut through the café) will lead you to a peaceful green courtyard, off of which is the **Canadian Craft Museum** ⑤. Farther to the west of Cathedral Place is the Gothic-style **Christ Church Cathedral** ⑥. About three blocks north (toward the water) on the left side of Burrard Street is the Art Deco **Marine Building** ⑦.

Facing the water, make a right onto Hastings Street and follow it east less than a half block for a look at the exterior of the exclusive Vancouver Club. In the tiny public park next door is *Working Landscape* by Daniel Laskarin, an art installation that consists of three revolving wooden platforms. The Vancouver Club marks the start of the old financial district, which runs southeast along Hastings. The district's older temple-style banks, investment houses, and businesspeople's clubs are the surviving legacy of the city's sophisticated pre-World War I architecture.

On the south side of Hastings just past Hornby Street is the **Pacific Mineral Museum** ⑧, which opened in 2000. Continue along Hastings to **Sinclair Centre** ⑨, between Howe and Granville streets. The magnificently restored complex of government buildings houses offices and retail shops. At 698 W. Hastings St., near Granville Street, the jewelry store Birks now occupies the Roman-influenced former headquarters of the **Canadian Imperial Bank of Commerce** (CIBC). The 1907 cast-iron clock that stands outside was, at its previous location at Granville and Georgia streets, a favorite rendezvous point for generations of Vancouverites. The imposing 1931 **Royal Bank** building stands directly across the street. At Hastings and Seymour streets, about a block southeast of here, is the elevator to the **Lookout at Harbour Centre** ⑩.

On Seymour, head toward Burrard Inlet to the **Waterfront Station** ⑪. Take a peek at the murals inside the 19th-century structure, then take the west staircase (to your left, with your back to the entrance) up to Granville Square Plaza, from which you can see the working harbor to your right. Walk straight across the plaza to the SkyTrain station, turn right, and you'll face the soaring canopies of **Canada Place** ⑫, where you can stroll around the cruise-ship–style decks for great ocean and mountain views or catch a film at the IMAX theater. Across Canada

Place Way (next door to the Waterfront Centre Hotel) is the **Vancou-ver Tourist Info Centre.**

TIMING

This tour takes about an hour to walk, not counting stops along the way. The Canadian Craft Museum, Pacific Mineral Museum, and the Vancouver Art Gallery each warrant an hour or more, depending on the exhibits.

Sights to See

⑫ Canada Place. When Vancouver hosted the Expo '86 world's fair, a former cargo pier was transformed into the off-site Canadian pavilion. The complex, which now encompasses the luxurious **Pan Pacific Hotel** (☞ Lodging, *below*), the **Vancouver Convention and Exhibition Centre,** and the city's main **cruise-ship terminal,** mimics the style, and size, of a luxury ocean liner. Visitors can stroll its exterior promenade to admire views of Burrard Inlet, Stanley Park, and the North Shore mountains. At the prow (the north end) are the **CN IMAX Theatre** (☎ 604/682–4629) and an outdoor performance space. The roof, shaped like five sails, has become a landmark of Vancouver's skyline. ⊠ *999 Canada Place Way,* ☎ *604/775–8687.* ⚊ *IMAX $9.50.*

⑤ Canadian Craft Museum. One of Vancouver's most interesting cultural facilities, the craft museum displays functional and decorative modern and historical crafts in an attractive, two-tiered postmodern building. Exhibits change throughout the year, so there's always something new to see. The gift shop has an excellent selection of one-of-a-kind Canadian crafts, and the courtyard is a quiet place to take a break. ⊠ *Cathedral Place Courtyard, 639 Hornby St. (also accessible from 925 W. Georgia St.),* ☎ *604/687–8266.* ⚊ *$5, donation Thurs. 5–9.* ☉ *May–Aug., Mon.–Wed. and Fri.–Sat. 10–5, Thurs. 10–9, Sun. noon–5; Sept.–Apr., Mon., Wed., Fri., and Sat. 10–5, Thurs. 10–9, Sun. noon–5.*

⑥ Christ Church Cathedral. The oldest church in Vancouver was built in 1889–95. Constructed in the Gothic style, it looks like the parish church of an English village from the outside—though underneath its sandstone-clad exterior, it's made of Douglas fir from what is now South Vancouver. The 32 stained-glass windows depict Old and New Testament scenes, often set against Vancouver landmarks (St. Nicholas presiding over the Lions Gate Bridge, for example). The building's excellent acoustics enhance the choral evensong, carols, and Gregorian chants frequently sung here. ⊠ *690 Burrard St.,* ☎ *604/682–3848.* ☉ *Weekdays 10–4. Services Sun. 8 AM, 10:30 AM, 9:30 PM; weekdays 12:10 PM.*

④ Hotel Vancouver. One of the last railway-built hotels in Canada, the Hotel Vancouver (☞ Lodging, *below*) was designed in the château style, its architectural details reminiscent of a medieval French castle. Construction began in 1928, but the hotel was barely finished in time for the 1939 visit of King George VI of England. The exterior of the building, one of the most recognizable in Vancouver's skyline, has carvings of malevolent-looking gargoyles at the corners, native chiefs on the Hornby Street side, and an assortment of grotesque mythological figures. ⊠ *900 W. Georgia St.,* ☎ *604/684–3131.*

⑩ Lookout at Harbour Centre. The lookout looks like a flying saucer stuck atop a high-rise. At 167 m (553 ft) high, it affords one of the best views of Vancouver. A glass elevator whizzes you up 50 stories to the circular observation deck, where knowledgeable guides point out the sights. On a clear day you can see Vancouver Island. Tickets are good all day, so you can visit in daytime and return for another peek after dark. The top-floor restaurant makes one complete revolution per hour; the elevator ride up

Downtown Vancouver

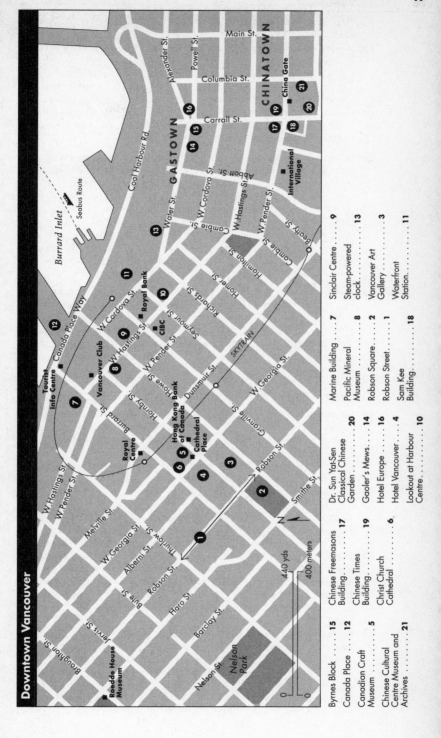

Byrnes Block **15**
Canada Place **12**
Canadian Craft Museum **5**
Chinese Cultural Centre Museum and Archives **21**

Chinese Freemasons Building **17**
Chinese Times Building **19**
Christ Church Cathedral **6**

Dr. Sun Yat-Sen Classical Chinese Garden **20**
Gaoler's Mews . . . **14**
Hotel Europe . . . **16**
Hotel Vancouver . . . **4**
Lookout at Harbour Centre **10**

Marine Building **7**
Pacific Mineral Museum **8**
Robson Square . . . **2**
Robson Street . . . **1**
Sam Kee Building **18**

Sinclair Centre **9**
Steam-powered clock **13**
Vancouver Art Gallery **3**
Waterfront Station **11**

is free for diners. ⊠ *555 W. Hastings St.,* ☎ *604/689–0421.* 🎫 *$9.* ☉ *May–Aug., daily 8:30 AM–10:30 PM; Sept.–Apr., daily 9–9.*

❼ Marine Building. Terra-cotta bas-reliefs depicting the history of transportation—airships, steamships, locomotives, and submarines—as well as Maya and Egyptian motifs and images of marine life adorn this Art Deco structure erected in 1930. These motifs were considered radical at the time because most architects were still applying classical or Gothic ornamentation. Step inside for a look at the beautifully restored interior, and then walk to the corner of Hastings and Hornby streets for the best view of the building. ⊠ *355 Burrard St.*

❽ Pacific Mineral Museum. Vancouver's newest museum, in a renovated 1921 building, opened in early 2000. Launched partly to house and display the University of B.C.'s mineral collection, the museum's Main and Discovery galleries illustrate the role of minerals in our lives—as art, as essential to our way of life, and as part of the universe. The Vault Gallery looks at their role as objects of desire, showcasing stunning examples of gold, silver, platinum, and gems. The museum shop sells collectors' specimens as well as gifts and souvenirs. ⊠ *848 W. Hastings St.,* ☎ *604/689– 8700.* 🎫 *$4.* ☉ *Mid-May–early Sept., weekdays 10–5, weekends 10–6; early Sept.–mid-May, Tues.–Fri. 10–5, weekends 10–6.*

❷ Robson Square. Architect Arthur Erickson designed this plaza, which was completed in 1979, to be *the* gathering place of downtown Vancouver. Landscaped walkways connect the **Vancouver Art Gallery** (☞ *below*), government offices, a convention center, and law courts. An ice-skating rink (used for ballroom dancing in summer) and restaurants occupy the level below the street. Political protests and impromptu demonstrations take place on the gallery stairs, a tradition that dates from the days when the building was a courthouse. ⊠ *Bordered by Howe, Hornby, Robson, and Smithe streets.*

❶ Robson Street. Ultrachic Robson Street is often called Vancouver's Rodeo Drive because of its many see-and-be-seen sidewalk cafés and high-end boutiques. The street, which links downtown and the West End, is particularly lively between Jervis and Burrard streets. The shops (☞ Shopping, *below*) may be like those elsewhere, but the people-watching, café-lounging, window-shopping scene draws crowds day and night.

OFF THE
BEATEN PATH

ROEDDE HOUSE MUSEUM – Two short blocks south of the fast pace of Robson Street—and a century away—is the Roedde (pronounced "roady") House Museum, an 1893 mansion in the Queen Anne revival style, set among Victorian-style gardens. Though the gardens (free)are worth a visit anytime, the only way to see the restored, antique-furnished interior is to catch one of the guided tours. ⊠ *1415 Barclay St. between Broughton and Nicola,* ☎ *604/684–7040.* 🎫 *$4; $5 Sun., including tea.* ☉ *Tours: Tues.–Fri. 2 PM; call for Sun. schedule.*

❾ Sinclair Centre. The outstanding Vancouver architect Richard Henriquez knitted four government office buildings into Sinclair Centre, an office–retail complex. The two Hastings Street buildings—the 1910 **Post Office**, which has an elegant clock tower, and the 1911 **Winch Building**—are linked with the 1937 **Post Office Extension** and the 1913 **Customs Examining Warehouse** to the north. As part of a meticulous $37 million restoration in the mid-1980s, the post-office facade was moved to the Granville Street side of the complex. The original clockwork from the old clock tower is on display inside, on the upper level of the arcade. ⊠ *757 W. Hastings St.*

❸ **Vancouver Art Gallery.** Painter Emily Carr's haunting evocations of the British Columbian hinterland are the biggest attraction at the city's main art gallery. Carr (1871–1945), a grocer's daughter from Victoria, fell in love with the wilderness around her and shocked middle-class Victorian society by running off to paint it. Her work accentuates the mysticism and the danger of B.C.'s wilderness—no pretty landscapes here—and records the passing of native cultures. The gallery, which also hosts touring exhibits of varying quality, is housed in a 1911 courthouse that Arthur Erickson redesigned in the early 1980s. Lions guard the majestic front steps, and columns and domes are among the original Classical architectural elements. The Gallery Café has a fine terrace, and the gallery's shop has a noteworthy selection of prints and cards. You can visit the café and shop without an admission ticket. ⊠ *750 Hornby St.,* ☎ *604/662–4719.* ⊡ *$10, donation Thurs. 5–9.* ☉ *Easter–mid-Oct., Mon.–Wed. and Fri.–Sun. 10–5:30, Thurs. 10–9; closed Mon. mid-Oct.–Easter.*

Vancouver Tourist Info Centre. Here you'll find brochures and personnel to answer questions, book tours, and reserve accommodations—and a nice view to boot. ⊠ *200 Burrard St.,* ☎ *604/683–2000.* ☉ *Sept.–late May, weekdays 8:30–5, Sat. 9–5; late May–Aug., daily 8–6.*

⓫ **Waterfront Station.** This former Canadian Pacific Railway passenger terminal was built between 1912 and 1914 as the western terminus for Canada's transcontinental railway. After Canada's railways merged, the station became obsolete, but a 1978 renovation turned it into an office–retail complex and depot for SkyTrain, SeaBus, and West Coast Express passengers. In the waiting rooms, panels near the ceiling depict the scenery travelers once saw on journeys across Canada. Here you can catch a 13-minute SeaBus trip across the harbor to the waterfront public market at Lonsdale Quay in North Vancouver. ⊠ *601 W. Cordova St.,* ☎ *604/521–0400 for SeaBus and SkyTrain; 604/683–7245 for West Coast Express.*

Gastown and Chinatown

Gastown is where Vancouver originated after "Gassy" Jack Deighton canoed into Burrard Inlet in 1867 with his wife, some whiskey, and a few amenities. The smooth-talking Deighton convinced local mill workers into building him a saloon in exchange for a barrel of whiskey. (It didn't take much convincing. His saloon was on the edge of lumber-company land, where alcohol was forbidden.) In 1885, when the Canadian Pacific Railway announced that Burrard Inlet would be the terminus for the new transcontinental railway, the little town—called Granville Townsite at the time—saw it s population grow fivefold over a few months. But on June 13, 1886, two short months after Granville's incorporation as the City of Vancouver, a clearing fire got out of hand and burned down the entire town. It was rebuilt by the time the first transcontinental train arrived, in May 1887, and Vancouver became a transfer point for trade with the Far East and soon was crowded with hotels, warehouses, brothels, and saloons. The Klondike gold rush encouraged further development that lasted until 1912, when the so-called Golden Years ended. From the 1930s to the 1950s, hotels were converted into rooming houses, and the warehouse district shifted elsewhere. The neglected area gradually became run down. These days, Gastown, which along with Chinatown was declared a historic district in 1971 and has been revitalized, is home to boutiques, cafés, loft apartments, and souvenir shops.

Chinatown has some of the city's oldest buildings and is the third-largest such area in North America. A sizable Chinese community was already here because of the 1858 Cariboo gold rush in central British Columbia, but the greatest influx from China came during construction of the Canadian Pacific Railway in the 1880s, when more than 10,000 laborers were recruited. Though they were performing the valuable and hazardous task of blasting the rail bed through the Rocky Mountains, the Chinese were discriminated against. The Anti-Asiatic Riots of 1907 stopped population growth in Chinatown for 50 years, and immigration from China was discouraged by increasingly restrictive policies that climaxed in a $500-per-head tax during the 1920s. In the 1960s the city council planned bulldozer urban renewal for Strathcona, the residential part of Chinatown, as well as freeway connections through the most historic blocks of the district. Fortunately the project was halted, and today Chinatown is an expanding, vital neighborhood fueled by the investments of immigrants from Hong Kong and elsewhere. The style of architecture in Vancouver's Chinatown is patterned on that of Guangzhou (Canton).

Numbers in the text correspond to numbers in the margin and on the Downtown Vancouver map.

A Good Walk

Start at **The Landing,** a former warehouse at the corner of Water and Richards streets, downtown. Built in 1905 with Gold Rush money, it was renovated in 1988 to include upscale shops, a brew pub, and a restaurant. The window at the rear of the lobby offers good views of Burrard Inlet and the North Shore mountains. A block east, at the corner of Water and Cambie streets, you can see and hear the world's first **steam-powered clock** ⑬. About two blocks east on the other side of the street, tucked behind 12 Water Street, is **Gaoler's Mews** ⑭. Two buildings of historical and architectural note are the **Byrnes Block** ⑮, on the corner of Water and Carrall streets, and the **Hotel Europe** ⑯, at Powell and Alexander streets. A statue of Gassy Jack Deighton stands on the west side of Maple Tree Square, at the intersection of Water, Powell, Alexander, and Carrall streets, where he built his first saloon.

From Maple Tree Square it's only three blocks south on Carrall Street to Pender Street, where Chinatown begins. **Note:** This route passes through a rough part of town, however, so it's much safer to backtrack two blocks on Water Street through Gastown to Cambie Street, then head south (left) to Pender Street and east (left again) to Carrall Street. If you're interested in law and order, though, you might take a detour to the **Vancouver Police Centennial Museum** at Cordova and Gore streets, just east of Main Street.

If you come along Pender Street, you'll pass International Village, an Asian-oriented shopping and cinema development. Old Chinatown starts at the corner of Carrall and Pender streets. The **Chinese Freemasons Building** ⑰ and the **Sam Kee Building** ⑱ are here, and directly across Carrall Street is the **Chinese Times Building** ⑲. About a half block east and across Pender, tucked into a courtyard behind the brightly painted China Gate—a four-column entranceway originally built for the Chinese Pavilion at Expo '86—is the **Dr. Sun Yat-Sen Classical Chinese Garden** ⑳. Next to the garden is the free, public Dr. Sun Yat-Sen Park. A short path through the park will take you out to Columbia Street, where, to your left, you'll find the entrance to the **Chinese Cultural Centre Museum and Archives** ㉑ (not to be confused with the Chinese Cultural Centre that fronts Pender Street). At press time, plans were in place to construct a seven-story pagoda with an observatory, cultural displays, and a tearoom at 599 Columbia Street, next to the museum.

Finish your tour of Chinatown by poking around in the open-front markets, bakeries, herbalists, and import shops that line several blocks of Pender and Keefer streets running east. **Kuen Way Martial Arts Supplies,** at 28 E. Pender, has intriguing displays of swords, dragon costumes, and ceremonial drums. **Ming Wo Cookware,** at 23 E. Pender, has a great selection of Eastern and Western culinary supplies. **Ten Ren Tea and Ginseng Company,** at 550 Main, and **Ten Lee Hong Tea and Ginseng,** at 500 Main, carry every kind of tea imaginable. For art, ceramics, and rosewood furniture, have a look at **Yeu Hua Handicraft Ltd.,** at 173 E. Pender. If you're in the area in summer on a Friday, Saturday, or Sunday, check out the bustling **Night Market,** for which the 200 blocks of Keefer and East Pender are closed to traffic 6:30 to 11.

TIMING

The walk takes about an hour. Allow extra time for a guided tour of the Dr. Sun Yat-Sen Classical Chinese Garden. This tour is best done by day, though shops and restaurants are open into the night in both areas.

Sights to See

⑮ Byrnes Block. George Byrnes constructed Vancouver's oldest brick building on the site of Gassy Jack Deighton's second saloon after the 1886 Great Fire, which wiped out most of the fledgling settlement of Vancouver. For a while this building was Vancouver's top luxury hotel, the Alhambra Hotel, charging a dollar a night. The site of Deighton's original saloon, just east of the Byrnes Block where his statue now stands, is the zero point from which all Vancouver street addresses start. ⊠ *2 Water St.*

㉑ Chinese Cultural Centre Museum and Archives. The first museum in Canada dedicated to preserving and promoting Chinese–Canadian history and culture opened in 1998. The art gallery on the main floor exhibits the works of Chinese and Chinese-Canadian artists. The museum on the second floor has an intriguing collection of historical photos. ⊠ *555 Columbia St.,* ☎ *604/687–0282.* ▧ *$3.* ☉ *Tues.–Sun. 11–5.*

⑰ Chinese Freemasons Building. Two completely different facades distinguish this structure on the northwest corner of Pender and Carrall streets. The side facing Pender represents a fine example of Cantonese recessed balconies. The Carrall Street side displays the standard Victorian style common throughout the British Empire. Dr. Sun Yat-Sen hid for months in this building from agents of the Manchu dynasty while he raised funds for its overthrow, which he accomplished in 1911. ⊠ *3 W. Pender St.*

⑲ Chinese Times Building. Police officers during the early 20th century could hear the clicking sounds of clandestine mah-jongg games played after sunset on the hidden mezzanine floor of this 1902 structure. But attempts by vice squads to enforce restrictive policies against the Chinese gamblers proved fruitless because police were unable to find the players. The office building isn't open to the public. ⊠ *1 E. Pender St.*

★ **⑳ Dr. Sun Yat-Sen Classical Chinese Garden.** The first authentic Ming Dynasty–style garden outside China, this garden was built in 1986 by 52 artisans from Suzhou, the Garden City of the People's Republic. It incorporates design elements and traditional materials from several of that city's centuries-old private gardens. No power tools, screws, or nails were used in the construction. Forty-five-minute guided tours, included in the ticket price, are offered throughout the day; they are valuable in understanding the philosophy and symbolism that are central to the garden's design. (Call ahead for times.) Friday evenings from mid-June through September, musicians perform traditional Chinese music in the garden. The free public park next door is also designed as a traditional Chinese garden. ⊠ *578 Carrall St.*, ☎ *604/689–7133.* ⬚ *$7.50.* ⊘ *May–June 14 and Sept., daily 10–6; June 15–Aug., daily 9:30–7; Oct.–Apr., daily 10–4:30.* ⌁

⑭ **Gaoler's Mews.** Once the site of the city's first civic buildings—the constable's cabin and customs house, and a two-cell log jail—this atmospheric cobblestone courtyard today is home to cafés and architectural offices. ⊠ *Behind 12 Water St.*

⑯ **Hotel Europe.** Once billed as the best hotel in the city, this 1908 flat-iron building is one of the world's best examples of this style of triangular architecture. Now used for government-subsidized housing and not open to the public, the hotel still has its original Italian tile work and leaded glass windows. The glass tiles in the sidewalk on Alexander Street once provided light for an underground saloon. ⊠ *43 Powell St.*

⑱ **Sam Kee Building.** *Ripley's Believe It or Not!* recognizes this 6-ft-wide structure as the narrowest office building in the world. In 1913, after the city confiscated most of the then-owner's land to widen Pender Street, he built a store on what was left in protest. Customers had to be served through the windows. These days the building houses an insurance agency, whose employees make do within the 4-ft-10-inch-wide interior. The glass panes in the sidewalk on Pender Street once provided light for Chinatown's public baths, which, in the early 20th century, were in the basement here. The presence of this and other underground sites has fueled rumors that Chinatown and Gastown were connected by tunnels that enabled residents of the latter to anonymously enjoy the vices of the former. Tunnels haven't been found, however. ⊠ *8 W. Pender St.*

⑬ **Steam-powered clock.** An underground steam system, which also heats many local buildings, powers the world's first steam clock—possibly Vancouver's most-photographed attraction. The whistle blows every quarter hour, and on the hour a huge cloud of steam spews from the apparatus. The clock, based on an 1870s design, was built in 1977 by Ray Saunders of Landmark Clocks (at 123 Cambie St.) to commemorate the community effort that saved Gastown from demolition. ⊠ *Water and Cambie Sts.*

OFF THE   **VANCOUVER POLICE CENTENNIAL MUSEUM** – It's not in the best of neigh-
BEATEN PATH   borhoods, and its morgue and autopsy areas will be off-putting to some, but this museum provides an intriguing glimpse into the history of the Vancouver police. Firearms and counterfeit money are on exhibit, as are clues from some of the city's unsolved crimes. ⊠ *240 E. Cordova St.*, ☎ *604/665–3346.* ⬚ *$5.* ⊘ *May–Aug., weekdays 9–3, Sat. 10–3; Sept.–Apr., weekdays 9–3.*

Stanley Park

A 1,000-acre wilderness park only blocks from the downtown section of a major city is both a rarity and a treasure. In the 1860s, because of a threat of American invasion, the area that is now Stanley Park was designated a military reserve—though it was never needed. When the city of Vancouver was incorporated in 1886, the council's first act was to request that the land be set aside as a park. In 1888 permission was granted and the grounds were named Stanley Park after Lord Stanley, then governor general of Canada.

If you're driving to Stanley Park, head northwest on Georgia Street from downtown. If you're taking public transit, catch any bus labeled STAN-

LEY PARK at the corner of Hastings and Granville streets downtown. You can also catch North Vancouver Bus 240 or 246 from anywhere on West Georgia Street to the park entrance at Georgia and Chilco streets, or a Robson Bus 5 to Robson and Denman streets, where you'll find a number of bicycle-rental outlets.

To reach Stanley Park's main attractions, you can bike, walk, drive, or take the park shuttle. The seawall path, a 9-km (5½-mi) paved shoreline route popular with walkers, cyclists, and rollerbladers, is one of several car-free zones within the park. If you have the time (about a half day) and the energy, strolling the entire seawall is an exhilarating experience. Cyclists (☞ Biking, *below*, for information about rentals) must ride in a counterclockwise direction and stay on their side of the path.

The **Stanley Park Shuttle** (☎ 604/257–8400) operates mid-May to mid-September, providing frequent (15-minute intervals) transportation between 14 major park sights. You can pick it up on Pipeline Road, near the Georgia Street park entrance, or at any of the stops in the park. At press time, the shuttle was expected to remain free and operate 10 to 6:30 daily, but a small fare was being considered.

From mid-September to mid-May, the traffic in Stanley Park is lighter than at other times of the year and there's little competition for parking. Lots are available at or near all the major attractions; a $5 ticket allows you to park all day and to move between lots. Another way to see the park is on one of the **Stanley Park Horse Drawn Tours** (☞ Guided Tours *in* Vancouver A to Z, *below*).

Numbers in the text correspond to numbers in the margin and on the Stanley Park map.

A Good Tour

If you're walking or cycling, start at the foot of Alberni Street, beside Lost Lagoon. Go through the underpass and veer right, following the cycle-path markings, to the seawall. If you're driving, enter the park at the foot of Georgia Street; be sure to stay in the right lane, or you'll have to go over the Lions Gate Bridge. Keep to your right and you'll go beneath an underpass. This will put you on scenic Stanley Park Drive, which circles the park.

Whether you're on the seawall or Stanley Park Drive, the old wooden structure that you pass on your right is the Vancouver Rowing Club, a private athletic club established in 1903. Just ahead and to your left is a parking lot, an information booth (staffed daily from March 15 through October) and the turnoff to the **Vancouver Aquarium Marine Science Centre** ㉒, the **Miniature Railway and Children's Farmyard** ㉓, and **Painters' Corner,** where artists sell their work.

You'll next pass the Royal Vancouver Yacht Club. About ½ km (⅓ mi) farther is the causeway to **Deadman's Island,** a former burial ground for the local Salish people and the early settlers. It's now a small naval installation, HMCS *Discovery,* and isn't open to the public. The **totem poles** ㉔, which are a bit farther down Stanley Park Drive and slightly inland on your left, are a popular photo stop. Ahead at the water's edge is the **Nine O'Clock Gun** ㉕. To the north is Brockton Point and its small lighthouse and foghorn.

Inland on your left is Brockton Oval, where rugby is played, and a cricket pitch, where you may see a game on summer weekends. Next, on the water side, watch for **Girl in a Wetsuit,** a sculpture on a rock just offshore that mimics Copenhagen's Little Mermaid. A little farther along the seashore,

Stanley Park

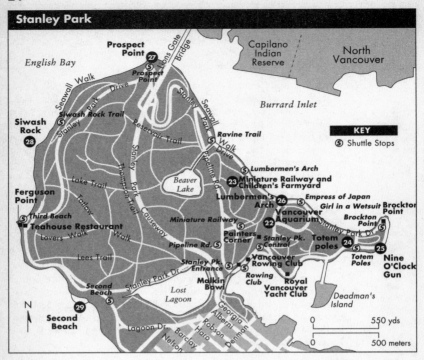

you'll see a replica of the dragon-shape figurehead from the *S.S. Empress of Japan,* which plied these waters between 1891 and 1922.

At Km 3 (Mi 2) of the drive is **Lumbermen's Arch** ㉖, a log archway. There are a picnic area, a snack bar, and a small beach here. The **Children's Water Park,** across the road, is a big draw throughout the summer. Cyclists and walkers can turn off here for a shortcut back to the aquarium, the Miniature Railway and the Children's Farmyard, and the park entrance.

About 2 km (1 mi) farther along the seawall or Stanley Park Drive is the Lions Gate Bridge. Here drivers and cyclists part company. Cyclists ride under the bridge and past the cormorants' nests tucked beneath **Prospect Point** ㉗. Drivers pass over the bridge and reach a viewpoint and café at the top of Prospect Point. Both routes then continue around to the English Bay side of the park and the beginning of sandy beaches. The imposing monolith offshore is **Siwash Rock** ㉘, the focus of a native legend. Farther along you'll reach the swimming area and snack bar at Third Beach.

The next attraction along the seawall is the large heated pool at **Second Beach** ㉙. If you're walking or cycling, you can take a shortcut from here back to Lost Lagoon by taking the perpendicular pathway behind the pool that cuts into the park. The wood footbridge that's ahead will lead you to a path along the south side of the lagoon to your starting point at the foot of Alberni or Georgia streets. If you continue along the seawall from Second Beach, you will emerge from the park into a residential neighborhood of high-rises, the West End. You can walk back to Alberni Street along Denman Street, where there are places to stop for coffee, a drink, or ice cream. **Mum's Gelato,** at 855 Denman Street, serves delicious ice cream.

RAINY DAYS

IT'S NO SECRET that it rains in Vancouver. Easterners call it the Wet Coast, film types call it Brollywood, and those courtesy umbrellas distributed by some hotels are not meant to shield you from the sun. The secret is that some people quite like it.

For many it's the atmosphere. Bobbing among the harbor freighters on the SeaBus or taking a rare solitary stroll on the **Stanley Park Seawall** (☞ Stanley Park) gain a certain nautical cachet in bad weather. The **Museum of Anthropology** (☞ Greater Vancouver) is best seen on a wet day, when dark skies and streaming windows evoke the storm-lashed northern rain forest from which the artifacts came. It's not cheerful, sunny art; it's mystical, spiritual, and so elemental that it's best seen on a gray and stormy day. The weather sets the mood.

If denial is more your thing, you can escape to the tropics in the conservatory at **Queen Elizabeth Park** (☞ Greater Vancouver) or into the wet but warm rain-forest display at the **Vancouver Aquarium** (☞ Stanley Park).

The best thing about rain, though, is that it forces many normally frenetic Vancouverites to slow down. This is probably why the city has so embraced the coffeehouse culture—sipping a cappuc-cino is the only way to look even marginally cool while a puddle forms at your feet. Favorite places to let your umbrella drip include **Delaney's,** quite the social center, and **Bojangles,** a cozy place near Stanley Park. The wraparound windows at Granville Island's **Blue Parrot Café** (☞ Coffeehouses *in* Nightlife and the Arts, *above*) afford views of people and boats. Vancouver's two Chapters mega-bookstores (☞ Shopping, *above*) have their own in-house **Starbucks.** The one at Robson Street has a fireplace and great views over the Vancouver Art Gallery. If you must have an urban-outdoorsy ambience, try the concourse at Library Square, which holds Vancouver's only indoor-outdoor sidewalk café.

Or you could take tea—that's proper tea, with cakes and sandwiches and none of those silly modern tea bags. If you're uncertain of the proper etiquette, simply observe the other guests and follow their lead. The **Empress Hotel** (☞ Victoria *in* Chapter 3) in Victoria is an institution, but tea can be taken (if a little tongue in cheek) in Vancouver as well. Try **Bacchus,** in the Wedgewood Hotel; the **900 West** lounge; **Griffin's,** in the Hotel Vancouver; or **La Promenade,** in the Sutton Place Hotel (☞ Lodging, *above*). You don't have to wear hats and gloves, and you don't have to discuss the weather.

TIMING

The driving tour takes about an hour. You'll find parking near most of the sights in the park. Your biking time will depend on your speed, but with stops to see the sights, expect the ride to take several hours. It takes at least two hours to see the aquarium thoroughly. If you're going to walk the park and take in most of the sights, plan on spending the day. The seawall can get crowded on summer weekends, but inside the park is a 28-km (17-mi) network of peaceful, usually deserted, walking and cycling paths through old- and second-growth forest. Take a map—they're available at park concession stands—and don't go into the woods alone or after dusk.

Sights to See

🚸 26 **Lumbermen's Arch.** Made of one massive log, this archway, erected in 1947, is dedicated to the workers in Vancouver's first industry. Beside the arch is an asphalt path that leads back to Lost Lagoon and the Vancouver Aquarium.

🚸 23 **Miniature Railway and Children's Farmyard.** A child-size steam train takes kids and adults on a ride through the woods. Next door there's a farmyard full of critters, including goats, rabbits, and guinea pigs. At Christmastime, an elaborate light display illuminates the route. ✉ *Off Pipeline Rd.,* 🕾 *604/257–8530.* 🎫 *$2.50 for railway, $2.50 for farmyard, higher fees during Christmas season.* ☉ *June–Sept., daily 11– 4; Oct.–Dec. 4 and Jan. 4–Apr. 1, weekends 11–4 (weather permitting); early Dec. to early Jan., daily 3–10.*

25 **Nine O'Clock Gun.** This cannonlike apparatus by the water was installed in 1890 to alert fishermen to a curfew ending weekend fishing. Now it signals 9 o'clock every night and ships set their chronometers by it.

27 **Prospect Point.** Cormorants build their seaweed nests along the cliff ledges here. The large black diving birds are distinguished by their long necks and beaks. When not nesting, they often perch atop floating logs or boulders. Another remarkable bird found along the park's shore is the beautiful great blue heron. Herons prey on fish. The oldest heron rookery in British Columbia is in the trees near the aquarium, where the birds like to horn in during feeding time for the whales. Prospect Point offers striking views of the North Shore and Burrard Inlet. There's also a souvenir shop, a snack bar, and a restaurant here.

NEED A BREAK?

At the top of Prospect Point is the **Prospect Point Café** (🕾 604/669– 2737), with a deck overlooking the Lions Gate Bridge. It specializes in all manner of salmon dishes and makes a good lunch or dinner stop—if you can squeeze in among the tour groups.

🚸 29 **Second Beach.** In summer a draw is the 50-m pool, which has lifeguards and water slides. The shallow end fills up on hot days, but the lap-swimming end is usually deserted. The sandy beach also has a playground and covered picnic areas. 🕾 *604/257–8371.* 🎫 *Beach free, pool $3.90.* ☉ *Pool late May–mid-June, weekdays noon–9, weekends 10–9; mid-June–mid-Aug., daily 10–9; mid-Aug.–Labor Day, daily 10–8.*

28 **Siwash Rock.** Legend tells of a young First Nations man who, about to become a father, bathed persistently to wash his sins away so that his son could be born pure. For his devotion he was blessed by the gods and immortalized in the shape of Siwash Rock, just offshore. Two small rocks, said to be his wife and child, are on the cliff above the site.

24 **Totem poles.** Totem poles were not made in the Vancouver area; these eight poles, carved of Western red cedar by the Kwakiutl and Haida peoples, were brought to the park in the 1920s from the north coast

of British Columbia. The carvings of animals, fish, birds, and mythological creatures are like family coats-of-arms or crests.

★ ☾ ㉒ **Vancouver Aquarium Marine Science Centre.** This excellent research and educational facility is a delight for children and natural-history buffs. In the Amazon rain-forest gallery you can walk through a jungle setting populated with piranhas, caimans, and tropical birds and vegetation. Other displays, many with hands-on features for kids, show the underwater life of coastal British Columbia, the Canadian Arctic, and the tropics. Huge tanks have large windows for underwater viewing of beluga whales and playful sea otters. Whale shows are held several times a day. You can even hear whale sounds on radio station ORCA FM, which picks up the wild calls with an underwater microphone off Vancouver Island. A listening post is downstairs by the whale pool. A Pacific Canada Pavilion, built in 1999, looks at the aquatic life in the waters of British Columbia, and a demonstration salmon stream flows through Stanley Park from Burrard Inlet to the aquarium. There's also a café and a gift shop. Be prepared for lines on weekends and school holidays. ☎ 604/659–3474. ⌦ $12.95. ☉ July–Labor Day, daily 9:30–7; Labor Day–June, daily 10–5:30. ◈

Granville Island

One of North America's most successful urban-redevelopment schemes was just a sandbar until World War I, when the federal government dredged False Creek for access to the sawmills that lined the shore. The sludge from the creek was heaped onto the sandbar to create the island. It was used to house much-needed industrial and logging-equipment plants, but the businesses had begun to deteriorate by the 1960s. In the early '70s, the federal government came up with a creative plan to redevelop the island with a public market, marine activities, and artisans' studios but to retain the architecture's industrial character. The refurbished Granville Island opened to the public in 1979 and was an immediate hit with locals and visitors alike.

Besides the popular public market, the island is home to a marina, an art college, three theaters, several restaurants and pubs, park space, playgrounds, and dozens of craft shops and artisans studios. It's also among the venues for Vancouver's comedy, jazz, and fringe-theater festivals (☞ Nightlife and the Arts, *below*), and a great place to catch top-quality street entertainment.

Though the island is now technically a peninsula—connected years ago, by landfill, to the south shore of False Creek—its distinct atmosphere sets it apart from the rest of the city.

Numbers in the text correspond to numbers in the margin and on the Granville Island map.

A Good Walk

To reach Granville Island on foot, make the 15-minute walk from downtown Vancouver to the south end of Hornby Street. Aquabus Ferries depart from here and deliver passengers across False Creek at the **Granville Island Public Market** ㉚. False Creek Ferries leave every five minutes for Granville Island from a dock behind the Vancouver Aquatic Centre, on Beach Avenue. Still another option is to take a 20-minute ride on a TransLink bus; from Waterfront Station or stops on Granville Street, take a False Creek South Bus 50 to the edge of the island. Or, from Granville Street and Broadway, catch Granville Island Bus 51 for direct service to Granville Island. If you drive, parking is free for one to three hours, and paid parking is available in garages on the island.

URBAN SAFARI

DURING WORLD WAR II, the Canadian military set up watchtowers along Vancouver's Point Grey so soldiers could detect signs of a Japanese invasion. The lookouts called the alarm once, when they spotted a large, submerged object making its way into Burrard Inlet. Tension mounted, but Japanese subs rarely sport blow holes, so the innocent whale was left alone. You won't see many whales in Vancouver's harbor these days—they're across the way, off Vancouver Island—but in and near this city on the edge of a rain forest you do have a better chance of spotting wildlife than in almost any other urban area.

A good place to start is **Stanley Park** (☞ *above*), a 1,000-acre forest abutting the downtown core. Here cormorants nest in the cliffs under Prospect Point, blue herons stroll the public beaches, and outgoing (though hardly tame) raccoons and squirrels pose for photos. Skunks and coyotes are more withdrawn but they also live here and, like the others, they sometimes amble into the West End, a high-rise residential neighborhood bordering the park.

The 850-acre **George C. Reifel Migratory Bird Sanctuary** (✉ 5191 Robertson Rd., Delta, ☎ 604/946–6980 for directions), on Westham Island about an hour's drive south of Vancouver, is a stopping-off point for at least 240 species of migratory birds traveling along North America's Pacific Flyway. The sanctuary and the marshlands of nearby **Boundary Bay** host Canada geese, snow geese, and one of the largest populations of waterfowl to winter anywhere in Canada. Bird lovers won't want to miss these spots.

One species is the focus of the **Brackendale Eagle Reserve.** About an hour's drive north of Vancouver, the reserve is 7 km (4 mi) north of Squamish in the town of Brackendale (follow signs from Highway 99). Every January since time immemorial, eagles (2,607 in 2000) from all over North America have gathered here to feed on spawning salmon. Each January eaglewatchers attend the **Brackendale Winter Eagle Festival and Count,** sponsored by the Brackendale Art Gallery (✉ 41950 Government Rd., ☎ 604/898–3333); it started simply as a bird count and has since blossomed into a month-long music, arts, and social event.

Less common, but all the more heartstopping should you run into one on a trail, are the big mammals—the cougars, black bears, and other animals that once had the run of this territory. Most of the 3,000 or so cougars and 140,000 black bears in British Columbia avoid humans, but sightings have increased in recent years as urban development encroaches on their habitats. Cougars have been spotted in suburban North Vancouver, and in downtown Victoria (one, famously, at the Empress Hotel and another in a basement suite near the Parliament buildings). From May through October in Whistler (☞ Chapter 4) it's not unusual to see bears near, or even in, the village, so it's important to follow a few rules. Don't leave food or garbage lying about. If you see a bear, don't approach it; back away slowly and speak in a calm voice.

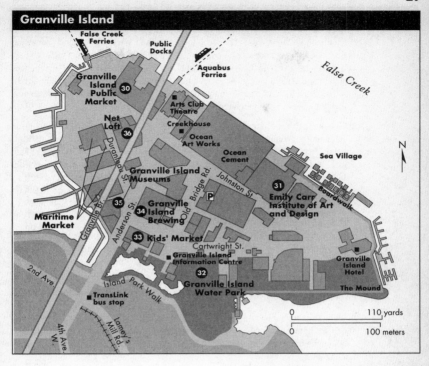

Granville Island

Another way to travel is to hop the Downtown Historic Railway (☎ 604/665–3903), two early 20th-century electric trams that on summer weekend afternoons run from Science World (☞ Yaletown and False Creek, *below*) to Granville Island. (☞ Getting Around *in* Vancouver A to Z, *below*).

The Granville Island Public Market, which has a slew of food and other stalls, is a short walk from the bus, ferry, or tram stop.

From the market, to start a clockwise tour of the island, walk south on Johnston Street or take the waterside boardwalk behind the Arts Club Theatre. Either way, just past the shops and studios in the Creekhouse building, you'll reach **Ocean Art Works,** an open space where you can watch First Nations artists at work. Just before you get to the **Emily Carr Institute of Art and Design** ③, you'll pass Ocean Cement, one of the last of the island's industries (its lease does not expire until 2004). Follow a walkway along the south side of the art school to Sea Village, one of the only houseboat communities in Vancouver. Then take the boardwalk that starts at the houseboats and continues partway around the island. Just past the Granville Island Hotel is a small hill called The Mound, a natural amphitheater for outdoor performances.

Turn right onto **Cartwright Street.** This end of the island is home to a mix of crafts galleries, studios, and workshops, and is a great place to watch artisans at work. You can see wooden boats being built at the Alder Bay Boat Company and view printmakers in action at New Leaf Editions, for instance. The Federation of Canadian Artists Gallery, the Crafts Association of B.C. Crafthouse, and the Gallery of BC Ceramics all showcase local works. At New-Small Glass Studio, around the corner, at 1440 Old Bridge Road, you can watch glassblowers at work.

Back on Cartwright Street, you can pick up maps and find out about special events, including the festivals, outdoor concerts, and dance performances often held on the island, at the **Granville Island Information Centre** (open daily 9–6). The **Granville Island Water Park** ㉜, just before the information center, and the **Kids' Market** ㉝, a bit farther down the street, will make any child's visit to Granville Island a thrill. Adults can head for the microbrewery tour at **Granville Island Brewing** ㉞, across the street from the Kids' Market.

Cross Anderson Street and walk north on Duranleau Street. On your left are the **Granville Island Museums** ㉟, with fishing, train, and model-boat displays. Next are the sea-oriented shops of the Maritime Market. The last place to explore is the upscale **Net Loft** ㊱ shopping arcade. Once you have come full circle, you can either take the ferry back to downtown Vancouver or stay for dinner and catch a play at the Arts Club or the Waterfront Theatre (☞ Nightlife and the Arts, *below*).

TIMING

If your schedule is tight, you can tour Granville Island in three to four hours. If you like to shop, or if there's a festival in progress, you'll likely need a full day.

Sights to See

㉛ **Emily Carr Institute of Art and Design.** The institute's three main buildings—tin-plated structures formerly used for industrial purposes—were renovated in the 1970s. The **Charles H. Scott Gallery,** to the right of the main entrance, hosts contemporary exhibitions in various media. ⊠ *1399 Johnston St.,* ☎ *604/844–3811.* ☞ *Free.* ☼ *Weekdays noon–5, weekends 10–5.*

㉞ **Granville Island Brewing.** Tours of Canada's first modern microbrewery last about a half hour and include a souvenir glass and a taste of four brews, including some that aren't on the market yet. Kids are welcome—they get a taste of root beer. ⊠ *1441 Cartwright St.,* ☎ *604/ 687–2739.* ☞ *$7.* ☼ *Sun.–Thurs. 9:30–7, Fri. and Sat. 9:30–8 (call for tour times).*

㉟ **Granville Island Museums.** Here you'll find three museums under one roof. The **Sport Fishing Museum** houses one of North America's leading collections of angling artifacts, including the world's biggest collection of Hardy reels and fly plates, and a mounted replica of the largest salmon ever caught with a rod and reel. You can also try your luck against the virtual 35-lb salmon that inhabits the video fish-fighting simulator. The collection of the **Model Ships Museum** includes exquisitely detailed early-20th-century military and working vessels, as well as a cast-bronze replica of the HMS *Hood,* the British Royal Navy ship that dealt the final blows to sink the German warship the *Bismarck* in 1941, and several submarine models that have starred in TV's *The X-Files.* The **Model Trains Museum,** the world's largest toy-train collection on public display, includes a diorama of the Fraser Canyon that involves 1,000 ft of track. Hobbyists will find goodies in the gift shop. ⊠ *1502 Duranleau St.,* ☎ *604/683–1939.* ☞ *$6 for all three museums.* ☼ *Daily 10–5:30.*

★ ㉚ **Granville Island Public Market.** Because no chain stores are allowed in this 50,000-square-ft building, each outlet here is unique. Dozens of stalls sell locally grown produce direct from the farm; others offer crafts, wine, chocolates, cheeses, fish, meat, flowers, and exotic foods. In summer, market gardeners sell fruit and vegetables from trucks outside. At the north end of the market you can pick up a snack, espresso, or fixings for lunch on the wharf. The Market Courtyard, on the water side, is a good place to catch street entertainers. Weekends can get madly busy here. ☒ *1689 Johnston St.,* ☎ *604/666–6477.* ☉ *Daily 9–6.* ☜

☺ ㉜ **Granville Island Water Park.** This kids' paradise has slides, pipes, and sprinklers for children to shower one another. Parents can keep an eye on things from the patio of the **Cat's Meow** café next door. ☒ *1318 Cartwright St.,* ☎ *604/257–8195.* ☒ *Free.* ☉ *Late May–late June, call for hrs; July–Aug., daily 10–6.*

☺ ㉝ **Kids' Market.** A slice of kids' heaven on Granville Island, the Kids' Market has two floors of small shops that sell all kinds of toys, arts-and-crafts materials, CDs and tapes, chemistry sets, and other fun stuff. ☒ *1496 Cartwright St.,* ☎ *604/689–8447.* ☉ *Daily 10–6.*

㊱ **Net Loft.** This blue-and-red building includes a bookstore, a café, and a collection of high-quality boutiques selling imported and locally made crafts, exotic fabrics, handmade paper, and First Nations art. ☒ *1666 Johnston St., across from Public Market,* ☎ *no phone.* ☉ *Daily 10–6.*

Kitsilano

The beachfront district of Kitsilano (popularly known as Kits), south of downtown Vancouver, is among the trendiest of Canadian neighborhoods. Originally inhabited by the Squamish people, whose Chief Khahtsahlanough gave the area its name, Kitsilano began to attract day-trippers from Vancouver in the early part of this century. Some stayed and built lavish waterfront mansions; others built simpler Craftsman-style houses farther up the slope. After a period of decline in the mid-20th century, Kits, which contains many restored wood-frame Craftsman houses, is once again chic.

Kitsilano is home to three museums, some fashionable shops, and popular pubs and cafés. Kits has hidden treasures, too: rare boats moored at Heritage Harbour, stately mansions on forested lots, and, all along the waterfront, quiet coves and shady paths within a stone's throw of Canada's liveliest beach.

Numbers in the text correspond to numbers in the margin and on the Greater Vancouver map.

A Good Walk

Vanier Park, the grassy beachside setting for three museums and the best kite-flying venue in Vancouver, is the logical gateway to Kits. The most enjoyable way to get here is by False Creek Ferries, from Granville Island or from behind the Vancouver Aquatic Centre, on Beach Avenue. The ferries dock at Heritage Harbour behind the Vancouver Maritime Museum. You can also walk or cycle about 1 km (½ mi) along the waterfront pathway from Granville Island (leave the island by Anderson Street and keep to your right along the waterfront). If you prefer to come by road, drive over the Burrard Street Bridge, turn right at Chestnut Street, and park in either of the museum parking lots, or take Bus 2 or 22 from Burrard Street downtown, get off at Cypress Street and Cornwall Avenue, and walk over to the park.

Vancouver Museum ㊲, which showcases the city's natural and cultural history, shares a building with the **H.R. MacMillan Space Centre** ㊳, a high-tech museum focusing on outer space. To the west and toward the water is the **Vancouver Maritime Museum** ㊴, which traces the maritime history of the West Coast. Each museum has hands-on exhibits that appeal to kids.

Behind the Maritime Museum, where you'll dock if you come in by ferry, is Heritage Harbour, home to a rotating series of boats of historical interest, including *BCP 45,* the picturesque fishing boat that used to appear on Canada's $5 bill. In summer the big tent set up in Vanier Park is the venue for the Bard on the Beach Shakespeare series (☞ Nightlife and the Arts, *below*).

West of the Maritime Museum is a quiet, grassy beach. A staircase leads up from the beach to a paved walkway. Take a moment to look at the 100-ft-tall replica Kwakiutl totem pole in front of the museum, and then follow the walkway west to popular **Kitsilano Beach** ⑩. Across the water you can see Stanley Park, and behind you is Vancouver's downtown core. Continue past the pool, keeping to the water, and you'll enter a shady pathway lined with blackberry bushes that runs behind the Kitsilano Yacht Club. Soon the lane opens up to a viewpoint and gives access to another sandy cove.

About ½ km (¼ mi) from the yacht club, the path ends at a wooden staircase. This leads up to a viewpoint and a park on Point Grey Road. Across the street from the top of the staircase, at 2590 Point Grey Road, is an Edwardian-era mansion that was built by a member of Kitsilano's early elite. Double back the way you came—heading east toward Kits Beach—but this time follow Point Grey Road for a look at the front of the homes you could see from the beach path. The 1909 Logan House, at 2530 Point Grey Rd., is an ivory-color Edwardian dream home with a curved balcony.

Follow Point Grey Road as it curves to the right, and cross Cornwall Avenue at Balsam Street. Turn left on either York or 1st Avenue and walk two blocks to Yew Street, where in summer you'll find one of the biggest concentrations of sidewalk pubs and cafés in Greater Vancouver. Alternatively, you can hike up the hill to 4th Avenue, once the heart of the hippie district, and explore the shops between Balsam and Burrard streets. You can catch a bus back to downtown Vancouver on Cornwall or 4th Avenue, or cut across Kits Beach Park back to Vanier Park.

TIMING

The walk alone will take about 1½ hours. Add two hours to see the MacMillan Space Centre and an hour for each of the other museums. With time out for shopping or swimming, a visit to Kitsilano could easily fill a whole day.

Sights to See

🅱 ⑩ **Kitsilano Beach.** Picnic sites, a playground, Vancouver's biggest outdoor pool, and some fine people-watching can all be found at Kits Beach (☞ Outdoor Activities and Sports, *below*). Inland from the pool, the **Kitsilano Showboat** hosts free performances, mostly of the children's dancing variety, during summer. ⊠ *Off Cornwall Ave.,* ☎ *604/738–8535 for beach information, 604/731–0011 for pool (both summer only).* 🎟 *Beach free, pool $3.90.* ☉ Pool: late May–mid-June, weekdays noon–9, weekends 10–9; mid-June–mid-Aug., daily 10–9; mid-Aug.–Labor Day, daily 10–8.

🅱 ㊳ **H.R. MacMillan Space Centre.** The interactive exhibits and high-tech learning systems at this museum include a Virtual Voyages ride, where visitors can take a simulated space journey (definitely not for those afraid of flying); Ground Station Canada, showcasing Canada's achievements in space; and the Cosmic Courtyard, full of hands-on space-oriented exhibits. During the day catch the astronomy show at the **H.R. MacMillan Star Theatre.** When the sky is clear, the half-meter telescope at the **Gordon MacMillan Southam Observatory** (☎ 604/738–2855) is focused on whatever stars or planets are worth watching that night. Admission to the observatory is free, and it's open in the evening, weather permitting (call for hours). ⊠ *Vanier Park, 1100 Chestnut St.,* ☎ *604/738–7827.* ⛉ *$12.50.* ⊙ *July–Aug., daily 10–5; Sept.–June, Tues.–Sun. 10–5.*

⛉ ㊈ **Vancouver Maritime Museum.** About a third of the museum has been turned over to kids, with touchable displays that provide a chance to drive a tug, build an underwater robot, or dress up as a seafarer. Toddlers and school-age children will appreciate the hands-on displays in Pirates' Cove and the Children's Maritime Discovery Centre. The museum also has an extensive collection of model ships and is the last moorage for the *St. Roch,* the first ship to sail in both directions through the treacherous Northwest Passage. Historic boats are moored at **Heritage Harbour,** behind the museum, and a huge replica of a Kwakiutl totem pole stands out front. ⊠ *Vanier Park, 1905 Ogden Ave., north end of Cypress St.,* ☎ *604/257–8300.* ⛉ *Museum $6, Heritage Harbour free.* ⊙ *Mid-May–Aug., daily 10–5; Sept.–mid-May, Tues.–Sat. 10–5, Sun. noon–5.*

⛉ ㊇ **Vancouver Museum.** Life-size replicas of a trading post, the sleeping quarters of an immigrant ship, a Victorian parlor, a 1910 kitchen, and an 19th-century Canadian Pacific Railway passenger car are the highlights of this museum that focuses on the city's history, from early European exploration to the Edwardian era. An orientation gallery includes examples of First Nations art and artifacts. ⊠ *Vanier Park, 1100 Chestnut St.,* ☎ *604/736–4431.* ⛉ *$8.* ⊙ *Fri.–Wed. 10–5; Thurs. 10–9.*

Greater Vancouver

Some of Vancouver's best gardens, natural sights, and museums, including the renowned Museum of Anthropology, are south of downtown, on the campus of the University of British Columbia and in the city's southern residential districts. Individual attractions are easily reached by TransLink buses (☞ Getting Around *in* Vancouver A to Z, *below*), but you'll need a car to see them all comfortably in a day.

Numbers in the text correspond to numbers in the margin and on the Greater Vancouver map.

A Good Drive

From downtown Vancouver, cross the **Burrard Street Bridge** and follow the marked scenic route. This will take you along Cornwall Avenue, which becomes Point Grey Road and follows the waterfront to Alma Street. The little wooden structure at the corner of Point Grey Road and Alma Street is the **Hastings Mill Museum** ㊶, which was Vancouver's first retail shop. If you're golf fan, you might take a detour to the **British Columbia Golf Museum** ㊷, on Blanca Street at the edge of the University Golf Course.

The scenic route continues south on Alma Street and then west (to the right) on 4th Avenue. Take the right fork onto **Northwest Marine Drive,** which winds past Jericho, Locarno, and Spanish Banks beaches and up to the University of British Columbia (UBC). Here you'll find the **Museum of Anthropology** ㊸ (opposite Gate 4), which houses one of the world's best collections of Pacific Northwest First Nations artifacts, and, just across Marine Drive, **Nitobe Memorial Garden** ㊹, a Japanese-style strolling garden. There is limited and expensive metered parking at the Museum of Anthropology. A better option, if you want time to explore the garden as well, is to park in the Fraser River Parkade. To find it, turn left off Northwest Marine Drive at University Gate 4 or 6, then follow the signs. Both the Museum of Anthropology and the Nitobe Memorial Garden are a short walk from the parking lot.

Three kilometers (2 miles) farther along Marine Drive is the **University of British Columbia Botanical Garden** ㊺, which has plenty of parking. For more gardens, follow Marine Drive through the university grounds and take the left fork onto 41st Avenue. Turn left again onto Oak Street to reach the entrance of the **VanDusen Botanical Garden** ㊻, on your left. The complex is planted with an English-style maze, water and herb gardens, and more. Return to 41st Avenue, continue farther east (turn left), and then turn left again on Cambie Street to reach **Queen Elizabeth Park** ㊼, which overlooks the city. To get back downtown, continue north on Cambie Street and over the Cambie Street Bridge.

TIMING

Except during rush hour, it takes about 30 minutes to drive from downtown to the University of British Columbia. You should add another 30 to 45 minutes of driving time for the rest of the tour, and about two hours to visit each of the main attractions.

Sights to See

㊷ **British Columbia Golf Museum.** This offbeat museum at the edge of the University Golf Club is a treat for those who can't get enough of the game. Housed in a 1930 colonial bungalow that once served as the course clubhouse, the museum has a fine collection of historic photos, trophies, antique clubs, and other golfing memorabilia. The exhibits are arranged like a golf course in 18 sections, or holes, with a theme for each. ⊠ *2545 Blanca St.,* ☎ *604/222–4653.* ⊞ *Free.* ☉ *Tues.–Sun. noon–4.*

㊶ **Hastings Mill Museum.** Vancouver's first store was built in 1865 at the foot of Dunlevy Street in Gastown and moved to this seaside spot in 1930. The only building to predate the 1886 Great Fire, the site is a museum, with displays of First Nations artifacts and pioneer household goods. ⊠ *1575 Alma St.,* ☎ *604/734–1212.* ⊞ *Donation.* ☉ *mid-June–mid-Sept., Tues.–Sun. 11–4; mid-Sept.–Nov. and Feb.–mid-June, weekends 11–4. Closed Dec.–Jan.*

★ ㊸ **Museum of Anthropology.** Part of the University of British Columbia's Department of Anthropology, the MOA has one of the world's leading collections of Pacific Northwest First Nations Art. The Great Hall displays dramatic cedar poles, bentwood boxes, and dugout canoes adorned with images from First Nations mythology. On clear days, the gallery's 50-ft-tall windows provide a striking backdrop of mountains and sea. Another highlight is the work of the late Bill Reid, one of Canada's most respected Haida carvers. His *The Raven and the First Men* (1980), carved in yellow cedar, tells the Haida story of creation. Reid's gold and silver jewelry work is also on display, as are exquisite carvings of gold, silver, and argillite (a black shale found in the Queen Charlotte Islands) by other First Nations artists and thousands of examples of tools, textiles, masks, and other artifacts from around the world. The experience is like poking around the attic of a Victorian explorer. The Koerner Ceramics Gallery contains several hundred pieces from 15th- to 19th-century Europe. Behind the museum are two Haida houses, set on the cliff over the water. This otherwise excellent museum lacks detailed labeling, but the free guided tours—given twice daily, usually at 11 and 2 (call to confirm times)—are very informative. Another option is to visit the museum as part of a First Nations culture tour (☞ Guided Tours in Vancouver A to Z, *below*). Arthur Erickson designed the award-winning cliff-top structure that houses the MOA, which also has a good book and souvenir shop and a summertime café. To reach the museum by transit, take a UBC Bus 4 or 10 from Granville Street downtown to the university loop, which is a 10-minute walk from the museum. ⊠ *University of British Columbia,*

6393 N.W. Marine Dr., ☎ *604/822–3825.* 🎟 *$7, free Tues. 5–9.* ☉ *Memorial Day–Labor Day, Tues. 10–9, Mon. and Wed.–Sun. 10–5; Labor Day–Memorial Day, Tues. 11–9, Wed.–Sun. 11–5.*☜

④④ **Nitobe Memorial Garden.** Opened in 1960 in memory of Japanese scholar and diplomat Dr. Inazo Nitobe (1862–1933), this 2½-acre walled garden, which includes a pond and a ceremonial tea house, is considered one of the most authentic Japanese tea and strolling gardens outside Japan. Designed by Professor Kannosuke Mori of Japan's Chiba University, the garden incorporates many native British Columbia trees and shrubs, pruned and trained in the Japanese fashion and interplanted with Japanese maples and flowering shrubs. The circular path around the park symbolizes the cycle of life and provides a tranquil view from every direction. Cherry blossoms are the highlight in April and May, and in June the irises are magnificent. ⊠ *University of British Columbia, 1903 West Mall,* ☎ *604/822–9666.* 🎟 *Mid-Mar.–mid-Oct. $2.50, mid-Oct.–mid-Mar. by donation.* ☉ *Mid-Mar.–mid-Oct., daily 10–6; mid-Oct.–mid-Mar., weekdays 10–2:30.*

④⑦ **Queen Elizabeth Park.** Besides views of downtown, the park has lavish sunken gardens brimming with roses and other flowers and an abundance of grassy picnicking spots. Other park facilities include 20 tennis courts, pitch and putt, and a restaurant. In the **Bloedel Conservatory** you can see tropical and desert plants and 60 species of free-flying tropical birds in a glass geodesic dome. To reach the park by public transportation, take a Cambie Bus 15 from the corner of Robson and Burrard streets downtown to 33rd Avenue. ⊠ *Cambie St. and 33rd Ave.,* ☎ *604/257–8570.* 🎟 *Conservatory $3.50.* ☉ *Apr.–Sept., weekdays 9–8, weekends 10–9; Oct.–Mar., daily 10–5.*

④⑤ **University of British Columbia Botanical Garden.** Ten thousand trees, shrubs, and rare plants from around the world thrive on this 70-acre research site on the university campus. The complex includes an Asian garden, a garden of medicinal plants, and an Alpine garden with some of the world's rarest plants. Guided tours, by donation, are given Wednesday and Saturday at 1 in the summer (call to confirm). The extensive shop is a paradise for gardeners. ⊠ *6804 S.W. Marine Dr.,* ☎ *604/822–9666.* 🎟 *Summer $4.50, winter free.* ☉ *Mid-Mar.–mid-Oct., daily 10–6; mid-Oct.–mid-Mar., daily 10–2:30.*

④⑥ **VanDusen Botanical Garden.** On what was a 55-acre golf course grows one of Canada's largest botanical gardens. Displays from every continent include an Elizabethan maze, five lakes, an Asian medicinal garden, a North American native medicinal garden with a medicine wheel of standing stones, and a Sino-Himalayan garden. There's also a shop, a library, and a restaurant. The first weekend in June the garden produces North America's largest (in terms of attendance and area)outdoor flower and garden show. Mid-December to early January, a big draw is the festival of lights (5–9 PM daily). The gardens are wheelchair accessible. An Oak Bus 17 will get you here from downtown. Queen Elizabeth Park is a ½-mi walk away, on 37th Avenue. ⊠ *5251 Oak St., at 37th Ave.,* ☎ *604/878–9274 for garden, 604/261–0011 for restaurant.* 🎟 *$5.50 Apr.–Sept., $2.25 Oct.–Mar.* ☉ *June–mid-Aug., daily 10–9; call for off-season hrs.*

Yaletown and False Creek

In 1985–86, the provincial government cleared up a derelict industrial site on the north shore of False Creek, built a world's fair, and invited the world. Twenty million people showed up at Expo '86. Now the site of the fair has become one of the largest urban-redevelopment projects in North America, creating—and, in some cases, reclaiming—a whole new downtown district.

Tucked in among the forest of green-glass, high-rise condo towers is the old warehouse district of Yaletown. First settled by railroad workers who had followed the newly laid tracks from the town of Yale in the Fraser Canyon, Yaletown in the 1880s and '90s was probably the most lawless place in Canada; the Royal Canadian Mounted Police complained it was too far through the forest for them to police it. It's now one of the city's most fashionable neighborhoods, and the Victorian brick loading docks have become terraces for cappuccino bars. The area—which also has restaurants, brew pubs, retail and wholesale fashion outlets, and galleries that sell art and unusual home decor—makes the most of its waterfront location, with a seaside walk and cycle path that runs completely around the shore of False Creek. Parking is tight in Yaletown, though there is a lot at Library Square. It's easier to walk, come by False Creek Ferry, or catch a Yaletown Bus 2 on Burrard or Pender Street.

Numbers in the text correspond to numbers in the margin and on the Greater Vancouver map.

A Good Walk

Start at **Library Square** ㊽ at Homer and Georgia streets. Leave by the Robson Street (east) exit, cross Robson, and continue south on Hamilton Street. On your right you'll see a row of Victorian frame houses built between 1895 and 1900, all painted in candy colors and looking completely out of place among the surrounding high-rises. In 1995 these historic homes were plucked from the West End and moved here to protect them from the onslaught of development.

Cross Smithe Street, and continue down Mainland Street to Nelson Street—you're now in the heart of Yaletown. Stop for a coffee at one of Yaletown's loading-dock cafés or poke around the shops on Hamilton and Homer streets.

From the foot of Mainland Street, turn left on Davie Street and cross Pacific Boulevard. This takes you to the **Roundhouse** ㊾, a former turnaround point for trains that is now a showcase for local arts groups. Behind the Roundhouse is **David Lam Park,** Yaletown's waterfront green space. Continue to the **waterfront** at the foot of Davie Street. Here you'll find an intriguing iron and concrete sculpture with panels that display archival images of events around False Creek. Also at the foot of Davie Street is the Yaletown dock for Aquabus Ferries (☎ 604/689–5858), where you can catch a boat to Granville Island, Science World, Hornby Street, or Stamp's Landing. At press time plans were in place for a marina and restaurant development here as well.

From here you can access Vancouver's seaside path, a car-free, bike, in-line skating, and pedestrian pathway that, with a few detours around construction sites, continues all the way around False Creek. A right turn will take you, in about 3 km (2 mi), to the West End and Stanley Park. To continue this tour, turn left. After about 1 km (½ mi), you'll reach the **Plaza of Nations,** the heart of the old Expo site. Cross the plaza toward Pacific Boulevard and take the pedestrian overpass to B.C. Place Stadium. Walk around to Gate A, where you'll find the **B.C. Sports Hall of Fame and Museum** ㊿. To your left as you leave the museum you'll see the Terry Fox Memorial. This archway at the foot of Robson Street was built in honor of Terry Fox (1958–81), a local student whose cross-Canada run raised millions of dollars for cancer research. From here, you can continue a block west to return to Library Square. To continue the tour, walk two blocks north on Beatty Street and take the SkyTrain one stop east, or retrace your steps to the waterfront and walk another 1 km (½ mi) east to **Science World** ⑤₁, a hands-on museum. From Science World, the SkyTrain will take you back downtown, or you can catch a ferry back to Yaletown or to other stops on False Creek. If you're here on a summer weekend, you can catch the Downtown Historic Railway (☞ Getting Around, *in* A to Z, *below*) to Granville Island.

TIMING

It takes about 1½ hours to walk around all the sights. Allow about an hour for the B.C. Sports Hall of Fame and museum and two hours for Science World.

Sights to See

☝ ⑤₀ **B.C. Sports Hall of Fame and Museum.** Inside the B.C. Place Stadium complex, this museum celebrates the province's sports achievers. You can test your sprinting, rowing, climbing, and throwing prowess in the high-tech participation gallery. ⊠ *B.C. Place, 777 Pacific Blvd. S, Gate A,* ☎ *604/687–5520.* ☞ *$6.* ☉ *Daily 10–5.*

⑧₈ **Library Square.** The spiraling library building, open plazas, and shaded atriums of Library Square, which was completed in the mid-1990s, were built to evoke images of the Colosseum in Rome. A high-tech library is the core of the structure; the outer edge of the spiral houses cafés and boutiques. ⊠ *350 W. Georgia St.,* ☎ *604/331–3600.* ☉ *Mon.–Thurs. 10–8, Fri.–Sat. 10–5, Sun. 1–5.*

Plaza of Nations. The centerpiece of Expo '86 is one of the World's Fair's least used legacies. Now home to a casino and a comedy club (☞ Nightlife and the Arts, *below*), it's at its liveliest in the evening, though a café and a pub with outdoor seating are open during the day, as is a virtual-sports emporium (☞ Sports and Outdoor Activities, *below*). ⊠ *700 block of Pacific Blvd.*

⑨₉ **Roundhouse.** This round brick structure was built in 1888 as the turnaround point for transcontinental trains reaching the end of the line at Vancouver. A spirited local campaign helped to create a home here (in a glass pavilion on the Davie Street side) for **Engine 374,** which pulled the first passenger train into Vancouver on May 23, 1887. Now a community center, the Roundhouse hosts festivals and exhibitions. ⊠ *181 Roundhouse Mews,* ☎ *604/713–1800.* ☞ *Free; admission may be charged to some events.* ☉ *Weekdays 9 AM–10 PM, weekends 9–5.*

NEED A BREAK? Across from the Roundhouse, **Urban Fare** (⊠ 177 Davie St., ☎ 604/ 975–7550) supplies, among other things, truffles, foie gras, and bread air-freighted from France to Yaletown's Francophiles and foodies. It's open daily 7–midnight. You can sample the wares at the café.

☝ ⑤₁ **Science World.** In a gigantic, shiny dome built over an Omnimax Theater, this hands-on museum encourages children to participate in interactive exhibits and demonstrations. Exhibits change throughout the year, so there's always something new to see. ⊠ *1455 Quebec St.,* ☎ *604/443–7443.* ☞ *Science World $11.75, Omnimax $10, combination ticket $14.75.* ☉ *July–Aug., daily 10–6; Sept.–June, weekdays 10–5, weekends and holidays 10–6.*

North Vancouver

The mountains that form a stunning backdrop to Vancouver lie in the district of North Vancouver, a bridge or SeaBus ride away on the North Shore of Burrard Inlet. Although the area is part suburb, the mountainous terrain has kept large parts of North Vancouver forested. This is where Vancouverites and visitors go for easily accessible hiking, skiing, and views of the city lights.

Numbers in the text correspond to numbers in the margin and on the Greater Vancouver map.

A Good Drive

From downtown, drive west down Georgia Street to Stanley Park and across the Lions Gate Bridge to North Vancouver. Stay in the right lane, take the North Vancouver exit, then turn left onto Capilano Road. In about 2 km (1 mi), you'll come to the **Capilano Suspension Bridge and Park** ㉒. A few hundred yards up Capilano Road, on the left, is the entrance to the Capilano Salmon Hatchery, which is part of **Capilano River Regional Park** ㉓. Just north of the Salmon Hatchery and also part of the park is Cleveland Dam, where you can stop for great views of the mountains. As you continue north, Capilano Road becomes Nancy Greene Way, which ends at the base of **Grouse Mountain** ㉔. From here, a cable car to the summit gives you great city views.

Alternatively, you can take the SeaBus from Waterfront Station to Lonsdale Quay and then catch a Grouse Mountain Bus 236. This stops at the Capilano Suspension Bridge and near the Salmon Hatchery on its way to the base of Grouse Mountain.

TIMING

You'll need a half day to see the sights, a full day if you want to hike at Grouse Mountain or Capilano River Regional Park. You'll save a lot of time if you avoid crossing the Lions Gate Bridge during weekday rush hours (about 7–9 AM and 3–6 PM).

Sights to See

㉓ **Capilano River Regional Park.** The park contains hiking trails and footbridges over the Capilano River where it cuts through a dramatic gorge. At the park's **Capilano Salmon Hatchery** (4500 Capilano Park Rd., ☎ 604/666–1790), viewing areas and exhibits illustrate the life cycle of the salmon. The best time of year to see the salmon run is between July and November. At the north end of the park is the **Cleveland Dam** (✉ Capilano Rd., about 2 km, or 1 mi, past main park entrance), which was built in 1954 and named for Dr. E. A. Cleveland, a former chief commissioner of the Greater Vancouver Water District. It dams Capilano River to create the 5½-km-long (3½-mi-long) Capilano Reservoir. A hundred yards from the parking lot, you can walk across the top of the dam to enjoy striking views of the reservoir and mountains behind it. The two sharp peaks to the west are the Lions, for which the Lions Gate Bridge is named. ✉ *Capilano Rd., North Vancouver,* ☎ *604/224–5739.* ☞ *Free.* ☉ *Park daily 8 AM–dusk; hatchery June–Aug., daily 8–8 (call for off-season hrs).*

㉒ **Capilano Suspension Bridge and Park.** At Vancouver's oldest tourist attraction (the original bridge was built in 1889), you can get a taste of the mountains and test your mettle on the swaying, 450-ft cedar-plank suspension bridge that hangs 230 ft above the rushing Capilano River. The park also has viewing decks, nature trails, a totem park and carving center (where you can watch First Nations carvers at work), history and forestry exhibits, a massive gift shop in the original 1911 teahouse, and a restaurant. Most of the attractions are on the near side of the bridge, so you don't have to cross it to enjoy the site. May through October (when park admission is higher than in the other months), guides in 19th-century costumes offer free tours throughout the day. ✉ *3735 Capilano Rd., North Vancouver,* ☎ *604/985–7474.* ☞ *$8.95–$10.75 (plus $2 for parking).* ☉ *Apr.–Oct., daily 8:30–dusk; Nov.–Mar., daily 9–5.*

★ **54** **Grouse Mountain.** North America's largest aerial tramway, the **Skyride** is a great way to take in the city, sea, and mountain vistas (be sure to pick a clear day or evening), and there's plenty to do when you arrive at the top of Grouse Mountain. The Skyride makes the 1-mi climb up to the peak every 15 minutes. A Skyride ticket includes a half-hour video presentation at the Theatre in the Sky. Other mountaintop activities include loggers' sports shows, chairlift rides, walking and mountain-bike tours, hiking, tandem paragliding, helicopter tours, and, in winter, snowshoeing, snowboarding, downhill and cross-country skiing, ice-skating, and Sno-Cat-drawn sleigh rides (☞ Outdoor Activities and Sports, *below*). The mountaintop, which has a café, bistro, and restaurant, is also a popular festival venue, with occasional summer concerts. The **híwus Feast House** (☎ 604/980–9311) presents a traditional First Nations feast and entertainment in a mountaintop longhouse. It's open May through October, and reservations are essential. ⊠ *6400 Nancy Greene Way, North Vancouver,* ☎ *604/980–9311.* ☑ *Skyride and most activities $17.50 (excluding skiing and snowboarding).* ⊙ *Daily 9 AM–10 PM.* ✎

OFF THE BEATEN PATH

LYNN CANYON PARK – With a steep canyon landscape, a temperate rain forest complete with waterfalls, and a suspension bridge 165 ft above raging Lynn Creek, this park provides thrills to go with its scenic views. In summer, guided walks depart from the Ecology Centre, which distributes maps of area hiking trails and has information about the flora and fauna. To get to the park, take the Lions Gate Bridge and Capilano Road, go east on Highway 1, take the Lynn Valley Road exit, and follow the signs. You can also take the SeaBus to Lonsdale Quay and Westlynn Bus 229 to the corner of Peters and Duval streets. A snack bar is open in the summer. ⊠ *3663 Park Rd., North Vancouver,* ☎ *604/981– 3103.* ☑ *Ecology Centre by donation; suspension bridge free.* ⊙ *Apr.– Sept., daily 10–5; Oct.–Mar., weekdays 10–5, weekends noon–4.*

DINING

Vancouver dining is fairly informal. Casual but neat dress is appropriate everywhere. Smoking is prohibited by law in all Vancouver restaurants (indoors). A 15% tip is expected. A 10% liquor tax is charged on wine, beer, and spirits. Some restaurants build this into the price of the beverage, but others add it to the bill. *See* the Downtown Vancouver Dining map to locate downtown restaurants and the Greater Vancouver Dining map to locate restaurants in Kitsilano, Granville Island, and other neighborhoods.

CATEGORY	COST*
$$$$	over $40
$$$	$30–$40
$$	$20–$30
$	under $20

per person, for a three-course meal, excluding drinks, service, and sales tax

Downtown Vancouver

Cafés

$–$$$ ✕ **Bread Garden Bakery, Café & Espresso Bar.** Salads, quiches, elaborate cakes and pies, giant muffins, and fine cappuccinos draw a steady stream of hungry locals to the many branches of this growing, Vancouver-based chain. (It has a few Greater Vancouver locations, too.) Most of the outlets open at 6 AM and stay open at least until midnight. The Yaletown outlet, which is open until 9 PM, shares space with Mile-

40

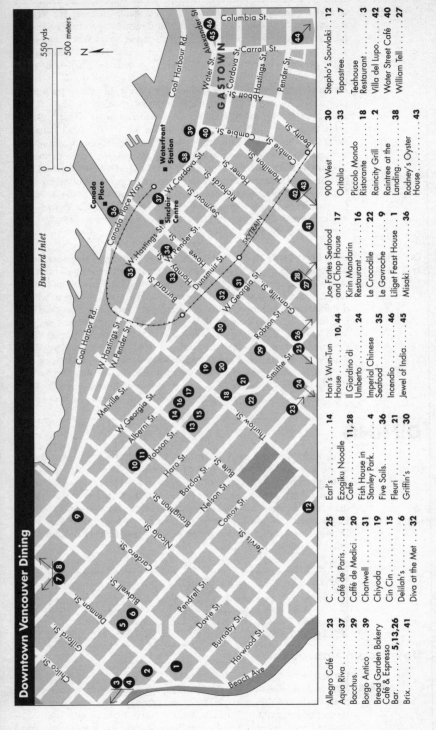

Downtown Vancouver Dining

Allegro Café **23**
Aqua Riva **37**
Bacchus. **29**
Borgo Antico **39**
Bread Garden Bakery
Café & Espresso
Bar. **5,13,26**
Brix **41**

C. **25**
Café de Paris **8**
Caffé de Medici . . **20**
Chartwell **31**
Chiyoda **19**
Cin Cin **15**
Delilah's **6**
Diva at the Met . . . **32**

Earl's **14**
Ezogiku Noodle
Cafe **11,28**
Fish House in
Stanley Park **4**
Five Sails **36**
Fleuri **21**
Griffin's **30**

Hon's Wun-Tun
House **10,44**
Il Giardino di
Umberto **24**
Imperial Chinese
Seafood **35**
Incendio **46**
Jewel of India **45**

Joe Fortes Seafood
and Chop House . . **17**
Kirin Mandarin
Restaurant **16**
Le Crocodile **22**
Le Gavroche **9**
Liliget Feast House . . **1**
Misaki **36**

Piccolo Mondo
Ristorante **18**
Raincity Grill **2**
Raintree at the
Landing. **38**
Rodney's Oyster
House. **43**

900 West **30**
Oritalia **33**

Stepho's Souvlaki . . **12**
Tapastree **7**
Teahouse
Restaurant **3**
Villa del Lupo **42**
Water Street Café . . **40**
William Tell **27**

stones, a popular burger bar. ✉ *812 Bute St., at Robson St.,* ☎ *604/ 688–3213;* ✉ *1040 Denman St.,* ☎ *604/685–2996;* ✉ *1109 Hamilton St.,* ☎ *604/689–9500;* ✉ *101–889 West Pender St.,* ☎ *604/638– 3982. West Pender St. branch closed weekends. AE, DC, MC, V.*

Casual

$–$$$ ✗ **Earl's.** This locally grown chain is a favorite among Vancouverites looking for a lively place to go with a group. Big rooms, cheery decor, cozy booths, upbeat music, chipper service, and consistently good burgers, soups, sandwiches, and vegetarian options keep people coming back. Food and drink is served all day until midnight. ✉ *1185 Robson St.,* ☎ *604/669–0020. AE, MC, V.*

Chinese

$$–$$$$ ✗ **Imperial Chinese Seafood.** The two-story floor-to-ceiling windows
★ at this Cantonese restaurant in the Art Deco Marine Building have stupendous views of Stanley Park and the North Shore mountains across Coal Harbour. Any dish with lobster, crab, or shrimp from the live tanks is recommended, as is the dim sum, served 11 AM to 2:30 PM. ✉ *355 Burrard St.,* ☎ *604/688–8191. Reservations essential. DC, MC, V.*

$$–$$$$ ✗ **Kirin Mandarin Restaurant.** A striking silver mural of a *kirin,* a mythical dragon, presides over this elegant two-tiered restaurant two blocks from most of the major downtown hotels. The specialties here are northern Chinese (Mandarin and Szechuan) dishes, which tend to be richer and spicier than the Cantonese cuisine served at Kirin's other locations (☞ Greater Vancouver, *below*). Dishes include Peking duck and Szechuan hot-and-spicy scallops. ✉ *1166 Alberni St.,* ☎ *604/682– 8833. Reservations essential. AE, DC, MC, V.*

$ ✗ **Hon's Wun-Tun House.** Mr. Hon has been keeping Vancouver residents in Chinese comfort food since the '70s. The best bets on the 300-item menu (nothing is over $10) are the pot stickers (dumplings), the wonton and noodle dishes, and anything with barbecued beef. The Robson Street outlet has a separate kitchen for vegetarians and an army of fast-moving waitresses. The original Keefer Street location is in the heart of Chinatown. ✉ *1339 Robson St.,* ☎ *604/685–0871;* ✉ *268 Keefer St.,* ☎ *604/688–0871. Reservations not accepted. MC, V at Robson St. branch; no credit cards at Keefer St. location.*

Contemporary

$$$$ ✗ **Five Sails.** This special-occasion restaurant at the Pan Pacific Hotel (☞ Lodging, *below*) commands a sweeping view of Canada Place, Lions Gate Bridge, and the lights of the North Shore. The broad-reaching, seasonally changing menu emphasizes fresh fish and seafood and takes its inspiration from all around the Pacific Rim. Highlights have included such dishes as orange-crusted sea bass, and filet mignon with cherry-infused red-wine sauce. ✉ *Pan Pacific Hotel, 300–999 Canada Pl.,* ☎ *604/891–2892 or 604/662–8111. AE, DC, MC, V. No lunch.*

$$$–$$$$ ✗ **Chartwell.** Named after Sir Winston Churchill's country home (a painting of which hangs over one of this elegant restaurant's two fireplaces), the flagship dining room at the Four Seasons hotel (☞ Lodging, *below*) has rich wood paneling, plush banquettes, and deep leather chairs, and is gaining a reputation for its innovative contemporary cuisine. Chef Douglas Anderson's seasonally changing menu makes the most of British Columbia's regional bounty. Highlights include braised Salt Spring Island lamb shoulder served with truffled flageolet cassoulet, and poached lobster with grapefruit risotto. ✉ *791 W. Georgia St.,* ☎ *604/689–9333. Reservations essential. AE, D, DC, MC, V. No lunch Sat.*

$$$–$$$$ ✗ **Diva at the Met.** At this multitiered restaurant in the Metropolitan Hotel (☞ Lodging, *below*), the presentation of the innovative contemporary cuisine is as appealing as the art deco decor. The menu changes seasonally, but top creations from the open kitchen have included smoked Alaska black cod and thyme-roasted venison with black truffled rutabaga *jus* (juice). The after-theater crowd heads here for late-evening snacks and desserts. The creative breakfasts and weekend brunches are also popular. ⊠ *645 Howe St.,* ☎ *604/602–7788. AE, D, DC, MC, V.*

$$$–$$$$ ✕ **Fleuri.** Floral tablecloths, molded ceilings, damask wall coverings, and lush garden scenes depicted in original artwork create an elegant, springlike feel at this spacious restaurant in the Sutton Place hotel (☞ Lodging, *below*). Classical French and Continental cuisines take on Pacific Northwest and subtle Asian influences in such dishes as black-truffle-and-foie-gras flan; tea-steamed sea bass; rack of lamb with lavender and grapefruit crust; and cassoulet of lobster and veal. The dessert cart is tempting but, for ultimate decadence, try the Chocoholic Bar, a 20-item buffet with chocolate fondues, cakes, pies, crepes, and more served Thursday through Sunday evenings. ⊠ *Sutton Place Hotel, 845 Burrard St.,* ☎ *604/642–2900. Reservations essential. AE, D, DC, MC, V.*

$$$–$$$$ ✕ **900 West.** Half of this lofty room in the Hotel Vancouver (☞ Lodging, *below*) is the city's most fashionable (and, to be fair, its only) wine bar; the other half is an elegant dining room serving innovative contemporary cuisine. Using European techniques, fresh British Columbia ingredients, and ideas from around the globe, chef Dino Renaerts's creations are inventive, sometimes complex, and very West Coast. The evolving menu has included veal medallions with prawns, halibut marinated in miso and sake, and—the signature starter—a rare ahi tuna tower. The extensive wine list includes 75 varieties by the glass. ⊠ *Hotel Vancouver, 900 W. Georgia St.,* ☎ *604/669–9378. AE, D, DC, MC, V. No lunch weekends.*

$$$ ✕ **Raincity Grill.** The sophisticated candlelit room and views of English Bay at this West End hot spot play second fiddle to a creative menu that highlights regional seafood, game, meats, and produce. Grilled romaine spears give the Caesar salad a delightful smoky flavor. Varying preparations of salmon and duck are usually available, as is at least one vegetarian selection. The exclusively Pacific Northwest and Californian wine list offers about 100 choices by the glass. Weekend brunches are a local favorite. ⊠ *1193 Denman St.,* ☎ *604/685–7337. AE, DC, MC, V.*

$$$ ✕ **Teahouse Restaurant.** The former officers' mess in Stanley Park is perfectly poised for watching sunsets over the water, especially if you're in the glassed-in wing, which resembles a conservatory. In summer you can dine on the patio. The West Coast menu includes roasted pear salad, morel-stuffed chicken, and rack of lamb with Dijon cream. ⊠ *7501 Stanley Park Dr., Ferguson Point,* ☎ *604/669–3281. Reservations essential. AE, MC, V.*

$$–$$$ ✕ **Aqua Riva.** The views over the harbor and the North Shore mountains are stunning from this lofty, lively modern room just yards from the Canada Place cruise-ship terminal. Food from the wood-fired oven, rotisserie, and grill includes thin-crust pizzas with innovative toppings, grilled salmon, and spit-roasted chicken. There's also a good selection of pastas, salads, and sandwiches and a long list of microbrewery beers and martinis. ⊠ *200 Granville St.,* ☎ *604/683–5599. Reservations essential. AE, DC, MC, V.*

$$–$$$ ✕ **Brix.** The pretty courtyard tucked in beside a 1912 Yaletown warehouse (it used to be the carriage turnaround) is a romantic summer dining spot, and if you want to dine here, reservations are a must. Inside, the long narrow room is simple and comfortable, with exposed brick and white tablecloths. The Pacific Northwest cuisine, with Asian and French influences, includes roasted chicken in hoisin marinade, and grilled

ahi tuna with fennel, pimento–parsley mash, and taro-root chips. An all-day tapas menu, more than 40 wines available by the glass, and live jazz on Sunday evening add up to make this a popular hangout year-round. ⊠ *1138 Homer St.,* ☎ *604/915–9463. AE, MC, V. No lunch weekends.*

$$–$$$ ✕ **Delilah's.** Cherubs dance on the ceiling, candles flicker on the tables, and martini glasses clink during toasts at this popular restaurant. The West Coast Continental cuisine prepared by chef Peg Montgomery is innovative and beautifully presented. Her menu, which changes seasonally, is divided into two- or five-course prix-fixe dinners. Try, if you can, the Mexican chorizo, oven-dried tomatoes, and jack-cheese fritters with tomatillo salsa, or the seared orange roughy (a kind of fish) with roasted couscous and a maple–pecan butter sauce. The Szechuan-style rack of lamb is so popular it's always on the menu. Reservations are accepted only for groups of six or larger. ⊠ *1789 Comox St.,* ☎ *604/687–3424. AE, DC, MC, V. No lunch.*

$$–$$$ ✕ **Griffin's.** Squash-yellow walls, bold black and white tiles, an open kitchen, and splashy food art keep things lively at this high-energy bistro in the Hotel Vancouver (☞ Lodging, *below*). The Pacific Northwest buffets—for breakfast, lunch, evening appetizers, and dessert—are the main attractions here. An à la carte menu features burgers, pizza, pasta, and seafood. A traditional afternoon tea, with a pastry buffet, is served 2:30 to 4:30 daily. ⊠ *Hotel Vancouver, 900 W. Georgia St.,* ☎ *604/662–1900. AE, D, DC, MC, V.*

$$–$$$ ✕ **Raintree at the Landing.** In a beautifully renovated historic building in Gastown, Vancouver's original Pacific Northwest restaurant has waterfront views, fireplaces, a local wine list, and cuisine based on fresh, often organic, regional ingredients. The seasonal menus and daily specials feature innovative treatments of such local bounty as Salt Spring Island lamb and smoked-salmon–wrapped halibut, as well as rich soups, breads baked in-house, and at least three vegetarian options. A favorite is the Pacific Northwest salmon bounty, featuring several varieties of smoked salmon. The set menus are a good value, offering three courses for less than $35. ⊠ *375 Water St.,* ☎ *604/688–5570. Reservations essential. AE, DC, MC, V.*

$$–$$$ ✕ **Water Street Café.** The tables at this popular Gastown café spill out onto the sidewalk for front-row views of the steam clock across the street. Inside, the slate-blue-and-white decor with tall windows overlooking bustling Water Street creates a cheerful, casual lunch or dinner atmosphere. It's tempting to pick one of the 14 varieties of pasta, but the crab, corn, and sweet-potato chowder and the Fanny Bay oysters also are good choices. The breads are baked fresh daily. ⊠ *300 Water St.,* ☎ *604/689–2832. AE, MC, V.*

Continental

$$$–$$$$ ✕ **William Tell.** Silver service plates, embossed linen napkins, and a silver vase on each table set a tone of Swiss luxury at this establishment in the Georgian Court Hotel (☞ Lodging, *below*). Chef Alan Murray prepares excellent sautéed veal sweetbreads with red-onion marmalade and marsala sauce and such Swiss dishes as cheese fondue and thinly sliced veal with mushrooms in a light white-wine sauce. Sunday night there's an all-you-can-eat Swiss buffet. Lunch is served only in the bar-and-bistro area, which caters to a more casual crowd than the main restaurant. ⊠ *765 Beatty St.,* ☎ *604/688–3504. Reservations essential. AE, DC, MC, V. Main dining room closed Mon.*

Eclectic

$$$–$$$$ ✕ **Oritalia.** An offshoot of the San Francisco establishment of the same name, this exciting newcomer features a fusion of Oriental and Mediterranean (Italian, specifically) cuisines—hence the euphonic name. Chef

Julian Bond focuses on seafood; signature dishes include a starter of three tartares (ahi tuna, smoked tout, and sockeye salmon) and such innovative entrées as Szechuan pork chop with a quince tarte Tatin. The 107-seat room, attached to the equally fashionable Sheraton Suites Le Soleil hotel (☞ Lodging, *below*), reflects the East-meets-West theme with rich golds, dark woods, and abstract Asia-inspired wall murals. The tables on the mezzanine offer vertiginous views of the open kitchen and a bird's-eye perspective of the striking handmade golden-glass and wrought-iron chandeliers. ✉ *567 Hornby St.,* ☎ *604/689–8862. Reservations essential. AE, DC, MC, V.*

$–$$ ✕ **Tapastree.** This bistro-style restaurant near Stanley Park was among the first of Vancouver's new tapas-style eateries. It's also where a number of local chefs enjoy after-work snacks. The dishes, all appetizer-size and under $10 each, run the gamut from an Oriental seafood salad with papaya, scallops, and prawns, to Japanese eggplant with pesto and goat cheese or lamb chops with sun-dried tomatoes and gorgonzola. The green and white decor is simple, with small theatrical touches—including splashy paintings and sconces shaped like human arms. An extensive wine list rounds out the evening, which can last until 10:30 on weeknights and midnight on weekends. The small patio, overlooking the quiet end of Robson Street, is a fun place to while away a summer evening. ✉ *1829 Robson St.,* ☎ *604/606–4680. Reservations essential. AE, DC, MC, V. No lunch.*

French

$$$$ ✕ **Bacchus.** Low lighting, velvet drapes, and Venetian glass lamps,
★ presided over by a large canvas of Bacchus, the Greek god of wine and revelry, create a decadent feel at this luxurious restaurant in the Wedgewood Hotel (☞ Lodging, *below*). Chef Robert Sulatycky shines with such French-influenced delicacies as truffle and pistachio–roasted breast of squab, or slow-braised venison with red-currant sauce. ✉ *845 Hornby St.,* ☎ *604/608–5319. Reservations essential. AE, D, DC, MC, V.*

$$$–$$$$ ✕ **Le Crocodile.** Chef and owner Michel Jacob specializes in traditional Alsatian food at this elegant restaurant on Smithe Street off Burrard. Golden yellow walls, café curtains, and burgundy banquettes keep things cozy. Favorite dishes, many of which also appear at lower prices at lunch, include caramel–sweet onion tart, calf's liver with garlic–spinach butter, and venison with chanterelle sauce. ✉ *100–909 Burrard St.,* ☎ *604/669–4298. Reservations essential. AE, DC, MC, V. Closed Sun. No lunch Sat.*

$$$–$$$$ ✕ **Le Gavroche.** Classic French cuisine receives contemporary accents but remains solidly authentic at this restaurant inside a century-old house. The smoked salmon with potato galette is among the simple dishes, but the chefs also prepare more complex fare, such as grilled pork tenderloin with Calvados and Stilton sauce, and rack of lamb with a red-wine sauce and minted gnocchi. The 5,000-label wine cellar stresses Bordeaux and Californian varieties. ✉ *1616 Alberni St.,* ☎ *604/685–3924. Reservations essential. AE, DC, MC, V. No lunch weekends.*

$$–$$$ ✕ **Café de Paris.** Lace café curtains, helpful waiters in aprons and neckties, an old-fashioned dessert cart, and some of the best *pommes frites* (french fries) in town make this long-established West End eatery a favorite among lovers of classic French bistro food—at neighborhood-restaurant prices. Bouillabaisse, cassoulet, mussels steamed in white wine, and steak tartare are all here. The prix-fixe menus, offering three courses for under $20 at lunch and under $30 at dinner, are good values. Regulars book months ahead for the café's special-menu months: watch for the lobster festival in June, couscous in September, and game in October.✉ *751 Denman St.,* ☎ *604/687–1418. Reservations essential. AE, DC, MC, V. No lunch Sat.*

Greek

$ ✕ **Stepho's Souvlaki.** Regulars swear by, and are quite prepared to wait in line for, Stepho's inexpensive and tasty roast lamb, moussaka, and souvlaki, served in a dark and bustling taverna. Its take-out menu is handy for picnics on the beach just down the street. ✉ *1124 Davie St.,* ☎ *604/683–2555. Reservations not accepted. AE, MC, V.*

Indian

$–$$ ✕ **Jewel of India.** Of the numerous Indian restaurants tempting visitors in Gastown, this homey little place just east of Maple Tree Square is a local favorite. Mr. and Mrs. Suri—host and chef, respectively—are originally from the Punjab and offer tandoori specialities slow cooked in a traditional clay oven and vegetarian dishes (favored by rocker Bryan Adams, whose studio is around the corner). Mr. Suri shops for fresh vegetables in Chinatown daily and Mrs. Suri cooks each dish to order, so you can choose the level of spice you prefer. Try the tandoori sampler, with several varieties of meat, or the *chana dahl,* a vegetarian chickpea dish. The blue-and-white decor is standard stuff, but a fireplace on the lower level of this two-tier restaurant and live sitar music Friday and Saturday nights provide plenty of atmosphere. Take-outs and deliveries are also available. ✉ *52 Alexander St. (also accessible from 53 Powell St.),* ☎ *604/687–5665. AE, MC, V. No lunch Sat.*

Italian

$$$–$$$$ ✕ **Caffè de Medici.** This elegant Northern Italian restaurant has ornate
★ molded ceilings, portraits of the Medici family, and a peaceful ambience. Run by the same family (with many of the same customers) since 1980, it is—despite its location on Vancouver's most fashionable street—pleasantly free of attitude. An enticing antipasto table sits in the center of the room, but the grilled giant squid and spinach salad with goat cheese are also recommended starters. Main courses include such consistently good classics as rack of lamb with mustard–rosemary demi-glace, osso buco with saffron risotto, and seafood risotto with a white-wine sauce. The quiet atmosphere and gracious service make this a good choice for business lunches or romantic dinners. ✉ *109–1025 Robson St.,* ☎ *604/669–9322. Reservations essential. AE, DC, MC, V. No lunch weekends.*

$$$–$$$$ ✕ **Cin Cin.** Warm gold walls, high arched windows, and terra-cotta tiles give this fashionable modern Italian restaurant a comfortable, Tuscan air; the heated second-floor terrace, surrounded by trees, feels a long way from busy Robson Street below. The food, from the open kitchen and the wood-fired grill, oven, and rotisserie, reflects chef Romy Prasad's experience cooking in New York City, Italy, Spain, and France. The appetizer platter for two includes house-smoked trout, ahi tuna, eggplant caviar, and wood-grilled baby octopus. Popular main dishes include hot smoked-duck risotto. The upbeat music and the social scene around the hand-carved marble bar make for a lively atmosphere. ✉ *1154 Robson St. (upstairs),* ☎ *604/688–7338. Reservations essential. AE, DC, MC, V. No lunch weekends.*

$$$–$$$$ ✕ **Il Giardino di Umberto.** This little yellow house at the end of Hornby
★ Street hides an attractive jumble of four terra-cotta–tile rooms and a vine-draped courtyard with a wood-burning oven. The Tuscan food features such dishes as smoked salmon with orange, fennel, and leeks; roast reindeer loin with port–peppercorn sauce; and roast ostrich fillet with caramelized shallots. Umberto Menghi, a long-established Vancouver restaurateur, also operates **Circolo** (✉ 1116 Mainland St., ☎ 604/687–1116), a modern Italian restaurant in Yaletown. ✉ *1382 Hornby St.,* ☎ *604/669–2422. Reservations essential. AE, DC, MC, V. Closed Sun. No lunch Sat.*

$$$–$$$$ ✕ **Piccolo Mondo Ristorante.** Soft candlelight, bountiful flower arrangements, and fine European antiques create an intimate feel at this Northern Italian restaurant on a quiet street a block off Robson. Start with an eggplant-and-tuna tart with pecorino cheese and basil oil, and follow it up with the classic osso buco or the linguine tossed with smoked Alaska cod, capers, and red onions. The award-winning wine cellar has more than 4,000 bottles (480 varieties). ⊠ *850 Thurlow St.,* ☎ *604/688–1633. Reservations essential. AE, DC, MC, V. Closed Sun. No lunch Sat.*

$$$–$$$$ ✕ **Villa del Lupo.** Country-house-elegant decor sets a romantic tone at this Victorian house on the edge of trendy Yaletown, home to one of Vancouver's most established Italian restaurants. The contemporary menu takes its inspiration from various regions of Italy. Sea bass wrapped with Parma prosciutto and sage, and osso buco in a sauce of tomatoes, red wine, cinnamon, and lemon are favorites here. The restaurant serves lunch only to groups of 10 or more. ⊠ *869 Hamilton St.,* ☎ *604/688–7436. Reservations essential. AE, DC, MC, V. No lunch.*

$$–$$$$ ✕ **Borgo Antico.** Terra-cotta tiles and graceful archways give this spacious Gastown room a classical feel. A sister restaurant to Il Giardino di Umberto (☞ *above*), Borgo Antico offers such Tuscan dishes as grilled calamari salad, gnocchi with artichokes and sun-dried tomatoes, veal medallions with lemon and capers, and osso buco with risotto. The wine cellar has more than 300 selections. ⊠ *321 Water St.,* ☎ *604/683–8376. Reservations essential. AE, DC, MC, V. Closed Sun. No lunch Sat.*

Japanese

$$–$$$$ ✕ **Misaki.** Local and visiting sushi lovers head for this elegant restaurant in the Pan Pacific Hotel (☞ Lodging, *below*). With its striking black-granite sushi bar and three intimate tatami rooms, Misaki has a relaxing ambience. The chefs here specialize in edomae-style sushi, featuring fresh ingredients from the sea, but the menu also includes such traditional Japanese dishes as miso-broth hot pot, soba noodles, teppan yaki, and lobster and salmon tempura. ⊠ *300–999 Canada Pl.,* ☎ *604/891–2893. AE, DC, MC, V. Closed Sun.*

$$–$$$ ✕ **Chiyoda.** A sushi bar and a *robata* (grill) bar curve through Chiyoda's chic modern main room: on one side are the customers and an array of flat baskets full of the day's offerings; on the other side are the chefs and grills. There are usually more than 35 choices of items to grill, from black cod marinated in miso paste to squid, snapper, oysters, and shiitake mushrooms—all fresh from the market. The kitchen also turns out such specialties as tempura and beef katsu (deep-fried beef). ⊠ *200–1050 Alberni St.,* ☎ *604/688–5050. Reservations essential. AE, DC, MC, V. Closed Sun. No lunch Sat.*

$ ✕ **Ezogiku Noodle Cafe.** Noodles—or, more precisely, Japanese ramen noodles—are the specialty at these cheap and cheerful hole-in-the wall cafés. The two Robson Street locations fill quickly with hungry shoppers and homesick Japanese students. Some say the noodles and soups here are just like those in Tokyo. With nothing over $10, Ezogiku offers one of the best values on this chic shopping strip. ⊠ *270 Robson St., at Hamilton St.,* ☎ *604/685–9466;* ⊠ *1329 Robson St., at Jervis St.,* ☎ *604/685–8606. Reservations not accepted. No credit cards.*

Mediterranean

$$–$$$ ✕ **Allegro Café.** Cushy curved booths, low lighting, friendly staff, and a long martini menu give this downtown place near Robson Square a romantic—even flirtatious—feel. The menu is playful, too, with such rich and offbeat concoctions as pasta bundles with roasted butternut squash and gorgonzola cream, and roast chicken breast with herbs, goat cheese, and peach-and-fig chutney. The rich daily soups and fair prices make this a good weekday lunch stop. ⊠ *888 Nelson St.,* ☎ *604/683–8485. AE, DC, MC, V. No lunch weekends.*

Native American

$$–$$$$ ✕ **Liliget Feast House.** This intimate downstairs room looks like the
★ interior of a longhouse, with wooden walkways across pebble floors, contemporary First Nations art on the walls, and cedar-plank tables with tatami-style benches. Liliget is one of the few places in the world serving the original Northwest Coast First Nations cuisine. A feast or potlatch platter lets you try most of the offerings, which include bannock bread, baked sweet potato with hazelnuts, alder-grilled salmon, toasted seaweed with rice, steamed fern shoots, barbecued venison, oysters, smoked mussels, and oolican oil (prepared from candlefish). ⊠ *1724 Davie St.,* ☎ *604/681–7044. Reservations essential. AE, DC, MC, V. No lunch.*

Pizza

$–$$ ✕ **Incendio.** The thin-crust pizzas, with innovative toppings including Asiago cheese, prosciutto, roasted garlic, and sun-dried tomatoes, and the mix-and-match pastas and sauces (try the hot smoked-duck sausage, artichoke, and tomato combination, or the mango–basil–butter sauce) draw crowds to this Gastown eatery. The room, in a circa 1900 heritage building, with exposed brick, local artwork, and big curved windows, has plenty of atmosphere. ⊠ *103 Columbia St.,* ☎ *604/688–8694. AE, MC, V. No lunch weekends.*

Seafood

$$$$ ✕ **C.** With dishes such as ultrarare grilled ahi tuna served with potato
★ and pea samosa, Dungeness crab and lemon myrtle cake, and octopus–bacon wrapped scallops, C has established itself as Vancouver's most innovative seafood restaurant. In addition to the lunch and dinner menus, C has a raw bar offering sushi, sashimi, oysters, and caviar; an elaborate Sunday brunch; and, at weekday lunch, a West Coast seafood dim sum. The ultramodern interior is done in cool grays (described by some as Captain Nemo meets Zen). The patio, overlooking a marina and well away from traffic, is a pleasant place to spend a summer afternoon. ⊠ *2–1600 Howe St.,* ☎ *604/681–1164. Reservations essential. AE, DC, MC, V. No lunch Sat.*

$$–$$$$ ✕ **Joe Fortes Seafood and Chop House.** This seafood hot spot and chop house just off Robson Street takes in a piano bar, a bistro, an oyster bar, and one of the city's best rooftop patios. Historically something of a singles market, it's been gaining a reputation for its West Coast fusion and seafood menus. Try the cedar-plank salmon, Joe's cioppino (a seafood stew), or the seafood tower—a starter of crab, mussels, clams, scallops, prawns, shrimp, and more, that's meant to be shared. The restaurant, named for a much-loved English Bay lifeguard, is a chop house, too, and it cuts your steaks to order. ⊠ *777 Thurlow St.,* ☎ *604/669–1940. Reservations essential. AE, D, DC, MC, V.*

$$–$$$ ✕ **Fish House in Stanley Park.** Tucked between Stanley Park's tennis courts and putting green, this 1930s former sports pavilion with a conservatory, veranda, and fireplace has a relaxed country-house ambience. Chef Karen Barnaby writes cookbooks, and the titles—*Pacific Passions* and *Screamingly Good Food*—say a lot about the food here, which is hearty, flavorful, and unpretentious. Good choices are the ahi tuna steak Diane or the cornhusk-wrapped salmon with a maple glaze. Before dinner head straight for the oyster bar, or arrive between 5 and 6 to take advantage of the early bird specials. ⊠ *8901 Stanley Park Dr., near Stanley Park's Beach Ave. entrance,* ☎ *604/681–7275. Reservations essential. AE, DC, MC, V.*

\$–\$\$ ✕ **Rodney's Oyster House.** This Yaletown fishing-shack look-alike has the widest selection of oysters in town (up to 18 varieties), from locally harvested bivalves to exotic Japanese kumamotos. You can pick your oysters individually—they're laid out on ice behind the bar and priced at $1.50 to about $3 each—or try the clams, scallops, mussels, periwinkles, and other mollusks from the steamer kettles. Chowders and other hot dishes are on offer as well. ⊠ *1228 Hamilton St.,* ☎ *604/609–0080. AE, DC, MC, V. Closed Sun.*

Greater Vancouver

Cafés

\$–\$\$\$ ✕ **Boleto at Ecco Il Panne.** During the day, this upmarket Italian bakery serves biscotti, baked sweets, and sandwiches made with its own country breads (which you can buy by the loaf); lunch involves frittatas and other light meals. In the evening, the staff puts out tablecloths for a full dinner menu. The decor is very *Roman Holiday,* with potted palms, relief murals, and a scattering of high-backed upholstered chairs. ⊠ *2563 W. Broadway,* ☎ *604/739–1314. Reservations essential for dinner. MC, V. No dinner Sun.–Mon.*

\$ ✕ **Bread Garden Bakery, Café & Espresso Bar.** The Granville Street branch of this local chain (☞ Downtown Vancouver, *above*) is open 24 hours. ⊠ *1880 W. 1st Ave., Kitsilano,* ☎ *604/738–6684;* ⊠ *2996 Granville St.,* ☎ *604/736–6465;* ⊠ *20–601 W. Broadway,* ☎ *604/638–0883. AE, DC, MC, V.*

\$ ✕ **Capers.** These casual cafés, tucked into Vancouver's most lavish health-food stores, sell light organic and vegetarian meals, treats from the in-store bakeries, and good, strong coffee. The West 4th location is a self-serve cafeteria and has a popular courtyard. The West Vancouver store has a full-service restaurant. A third location, at 1675 Robson Street downtown, has outdoor seating and take-out service only. ⊠ *2285 W. 4th Ave.,* ☎ *604/739–6676;* ⊠ *2496 Marine Dr., West Vancouver,* ☎ *604/925–3374. AE, MC, V.*

Casual

\$–\$\$\$ ✕ **Earl's.** The Greater Vancouver offshoots of this local chain have all the features of a popular casual restaurant: wood-fired pizzas, juicy burgers, homemade desserts, comfy booths, chipper staff, and a relaxed atmosphere. ⊠ *901 W. Broadway,* ☎ *604/734–5995;* ⊠ *1601 W. Broadway,* ☎ *604/736–5663. AE, DC, MC, V.*

Chinese

\$\$–\$\$\$\$ ✕ **Grand King Seafood.** In a city noted for its Chinese restaurants, the Grand King is widely considered one of the best. Decorated like most of the city's upmarket Cantonese establishments—with chandelier lighting and round white tables set for large groups—the Grand King emphasizes Cantonese seafood, including lobster with black bean sauce and crab claw in shrimp purée. But the large selection of non-seafood items, like ostrich slices in spicy pepper sauce and sautéed chicken with lily bulbs, is equally exciting. The best bets are the set dinner menus for groups of 2–10. The Grand King also has innovative, popular dim sum, served from the menu rather than on trolleys. ⊠ *705 W. Broadway,* ☎ *604/876–7855. DC, MC, V.*

\$\$–\$\$\$\$ ✕ **Kirin Seafood Restaurant.** The Greater Vancouver outposts of this upscale operation focus on seafood and Cantonese creations, which are milder than the northern Chinese cuisine served at Kirin Mandarin Restaurant (☞ Downtown Vancouver, *above*). ⊠ *555 W. 12th Ave., 2nd floor,* ☎ *604/879–8038;* ⊠ *3 West Centre, Suite 200, 7900 Westminster Hwy., Richmond,* ☎ *604/303–8833. AE, DC, MC, V.*

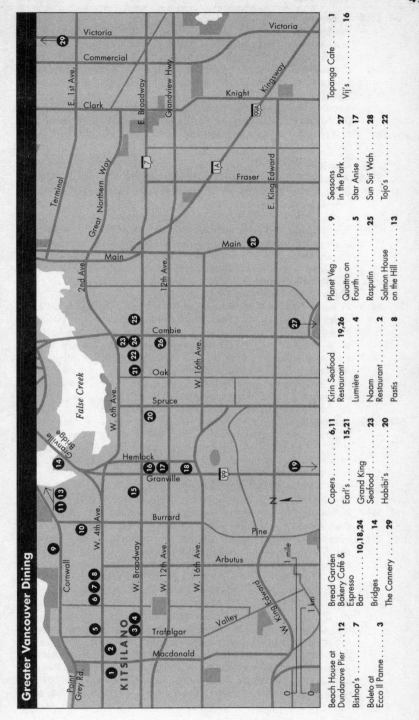

Greater Vancouver Dining

Topanga Cafe **1**
Vij's **16**

Seasons
in the Park **27**
Star Anise **17**
Sun Sui Wah **28**
Tojo's **22**

Planet Veg **9**
Quattro on
Fourth **5**
Rasputin **25**
Salmon House
on the Hill **13**

Kirin Seafood
Restaurant **19,26**
Lumière **4**
Naam
Restaurant **2**
Pastis **8**

Capers **6,11**
Earl's **15,21**
Grand King
Seafood **23**
Habibi's **20**

Bread Garden
Bakery Café &
Espresso
Bar **10,18,24**
Bridges **14**
The Cannery **29**

Beach House at
Dundarave Pier . . **12**
Bishop's **7**
Boleto at
Ecco Il Panne **3**

\$\$–\$\$\$\$ ✕ **Sun Sui Wah.** Sails in the ceiling, reminiscent of Vancouver's land-
★   mark Convention and Exhibition Centre, add a lofty elegance to this
bright and bustling East Side Cantonese restaurant. An offshoot of a
popular Hong Kong establishment, Sun Sui Wah is best known for its
dim sum (served 10:30–3 weekdays, 10–3 on weekends), which ranges
from traditional handmade dumplings to some highly adventurous offerings with Japanese touches. It's worth coming back for dinner for
house specialties such as roasted squab and enormous king crab from
the live tanks. There's another location in Richmond, the suburban heart
of Vancouver's Chinese community. ⊠ *3888 Main St.,* ☎ *604/872–
8822;* ⊠ *4940 No. 3 Rd., Richmond,* ☎ *604/273–8208. AE, MC, V.*

Contemporary

\$\$\$\$ ✕ **Bishop's.** One of Vancouver's most highly regarded restaurants,
★   this refined Kitsilano room serves West Coast cuisine with an emphasis on organic, regional produce. Steamed smoked black cod with a
truffle brandade cake, roast pork tenderloin with shiitake and dried-
pear stuffing, and roast duck breast with candied yams make appear-
ances on the seasonal menu; all are beautifully presented and impeccably
served. The split-level room displays elaborate flower arrangements and
selections from owner John Bishop's extensive art collection. ⊠ *2183
W. 4th Ave.,* ☎ *604/738–2025. Reservations essential. AE, DC, MC,
V. No lunch. Closed 1st wk in Jan.*

\$\$\$–\$\$\$\$ ✕ **Beach House at Dundarave Pier.** It's worth the drive over the Lions
Gate Bridge to West Vancouver for an evening at this 1912 seaside house.
Whether inside the lofty room or outside on the heated beachside
patio, virtually every table has expansive views over Burrard Inlet and
Stanley Park. The Pacific Rim menu changes frequently, but chef
Michael Riley favors updated versions of the classics, with a variety
of innovative game and seafood entrées. After dinner, you can take a
stroll along the pier or the seaside walkway. ⊠ *150–25th St., West Vancouver,* ☎ *604/922–1414. Reservations essential. AE, DC, MC, V.*

\$\$\$–\$\$\$\$ ✕ **Star Anise.** Pacific Northwest cuisine with French flair shines in this
intimate eatery near Granville Street. The menu varies with the sea-
sons, but highlights—creatively and imaginatively prepared by chef
Robert Fortin—have included confit of roast rabbit leg with a Saskatoon berry chutney, braised venison shank with sage spaetzle, and
roast lamb loin filled with figs and hazelnuts. ⊠ *1485 W. 12th Ave.,*
☎ *604/737–1485. AE, DC, MC, V. No lunch.*

\$\$–\$\$\$\$ ✕ **Bridges.** On summer afternoons, locals hang out on the massive outdoor deck of this three-in-one restaurant complex on Granville Island,
near the public market. Overlooking False Creek, the deck serves casual bistro fare, such as burgers, sandwiches, and quesadillas. Indoors
and upstairs, a more formal restaurant serves West Coast cuisine with
an emphasis on seafood. The menu changes frequently, but highlights
have included a timbale of smoked salmon and marinated tuna, grilled
salmon fillet with sorrel cream, arugula, and succotash, as well as seasonally changing sea bass, lobster, and lamb dishes. Exposed beams in
the high ceiling contrast with the elegant rosewood paneling and white
tablecloths. French doors open onto another deck, perched high above
the marina, but the tall windows mean views are good from anywhere
in the room. Bridges also has a cozy pub on the main floor (☞ Nightlife
and the Arts, *below*). ⊠ *1696 Duranleau St.,* ☎ *604/687–4400. Reservations essential for restaurant; bistro reservations not accepted May–
Sept. AE, DC, MC, V. No lunch Mon.–Sat. in the restaurant; restaurant closed Sun. Nov.–Jan.*

Continental

$$–$$$$ ✕ **Seasons in the Park.** Two levels of seating and tall windows allow every table here a commanding view over the gardens in Queen Elizabeth Park, to the city and mountains beyond. Light-wood furnishings and white tablecloths in the comfortable dining room make for an elegant atmosphere that is mirrored in the Continental fare. The menu includes herb-crusted sea bass, confit of Muscovy duck, and other Continental standards. Weekend brunch is popular, and there's a patio for outdoor dining in summer. ✉ *Queen Elizabeth Park, 33rd Ave. and Cambie St.,* ☎ *604/874–8008 or 800/632–9422. Reservations essential. AE, MC, V.*

French

$$$$ ✕ ★**Lumière.** The contemporary French cuisine at this light and airy Kitsilano restaurant isn't so much served as orchestrated, arranged in one of chef Robert Feenie's frequently changing eight-to-twelve-course set menus. A tasting menu may take you from lobster bisque with prawn tempura, to roast venison medallions with kumquat and pineapple chutney, and a Valrhona tart with rum and butter chestnuts. A seafood menu makes the most of what's at the docks that day, and a vegetarian selection, with courses such as wild-mushroom torte and passion-fruit sorbet with hibiscus jus, elevates meatless dining to haute cuisine. ✉ *2551 W. Broadway,* ☎ *604/739–8185. Reservations essential. AE, DC, MC, V. Closed Mon. No lunch.*

$$$–$$$$ ✕ **Pastis.** This tiny 12-table Kitsilano bistro created a stir as soon as it opened in early 1999. The simple decor of brown wicker chairs and white tablecloths belies the elegance of the food. Try the fig and Belgian endive salad with Roquefort and hazelnut vinaigrette; the roasted duck breast and Québec foie gras with Belgian endive, plums, and honey–lime reduction; or the grilled Atlantic salmon fillet with a jus of saffron and pearl onion, layered with peashoots and smoked salmon. ✉ *2153 W. 4th Ave.,* ☎ *604/731–5020. Reservations essential. AE, MC, V. No lunch.*

Indian

$$$–$$$$ ✕ **Vij's.** Vikram Vij, the genial proprietor of Vancouver's most inno-
★ vative Indian restaurant, uses local ingredients and Western ideas to create exciting takes on the cuisines of the subcontinent. Highlights on the brief, seasonally changing menu include cinnamon-spiced buffalo meat with raw sugar masala; tiger prawns with chickpea salad; and rockfish, spot prawns, and scallops in coconut curry. The dishes are far from traditional but are spiced beautifully, allowing exotic flavors such as mango, tamarind, and fenugreek to shine through. The simple room, with bare walls, Indian antiques, and warm lighting from lanterns, doesn't distract from the art on the plate. Reservations aren't accepted, but the inevitable lineups are events in themselves, as the staff serves spicy snacks and tea to waiting diners. ✉ *1480 W. 11th Ave.,* ☎ *604/736–6664. Reservations not accepted. AE, DC, MC, V. No lunch.*

Italian

$$–$$$$ ✕ **Quattro on Fourth.** Healthful (often low-fat and low-sodium) ingredients and uncomplicated seasonings are what you'll find at this Kitsilano restaurant. But the results of the light, simple cooking—dishes such as linguine with prawns, clams, tomato, and white wine, or baked sea bass in a pistachio crust—are still satisfyingly rich. The mosaic floor, mustard-color walls, cherry-stained tables, and a wraparound covered porch enhance the Mediterranean atmosphere. ✉ *2611 W. 4th Ave.,* ☎ *604/734–4444. Reservations essential. AE, DC, MC, V. No lunch.*

Japanese

$$$-$$$$ ✕ **Tojo's.** Hidekazu Tojo is a sushi-making legend in Vancouver, with
★   more than 2,000 special preparations stored in his creative mind. His
handsome tatami rooms, on the second floor of a modern green-glass
tower on West Broadway, provide the proper ambience for intimate
dining, but Tojo's 10-seat sushi bar is a convivial ringside seat for watch-
ing the creation of edible art. Reserve the spot at the end for the best
view. ✉ *202–777 W. Broadway,* ☎ *604/872–8050. Reservations es-
sential. AE, DC, MC, V. Closed Sun. No lunch.*

Middle Eastern

$ ✕ **Habibi's.** The Lebanese home cooking at this family-run café is one
of the area's best values. All the dishes are vegetarian, all are lovingly
prepared, and none is more than $6. Most of the dishes are meze-size
and eaten as dips with warm, homemade pita bread. The idea is to try
several, and experiment with such specialties as *lebneh* (a yogurt cheese
with spices), *balila* (warm chickpeas with garlic and olive oil), and *warak
anab* (rice-stuffed grape leaves). Wooden booths, soft blues music,
and family photos from the old country make a welcome change from
most eateries in this price range. ✉ *1128 W. Broadway,* ☎ *604/732–
7487. Reservations not accepted. No credit cards. Closed Sun.*

Russian

$$-$$$ ✕ **Rasputin.** Don't let the glowering portrait of Rasputin on the wall
put you off—this place is fun, and meals here are, according to the menu
(and Russian tradition), long and joyous occasions. The borscht, served
with sour cream and a garnish of herbs and dill, is rich and flavorful;
the towering appetizer arrangements, featuring salmon caviar with crepes,
smoked salmon, and chopped egg, are meant for sharing; and the
main dishes, including kebabs, cabbage rolls, handmade pierogi, and
trout stuffed with couscous pilaf, are consistently top-notch. The bar
stocks 40 kinds of vodka, and musicians playing balalaikas or Gypsy
violins—often backed up by the regulars in good voice—perform six
nights a week. ✉ *457 W. Broadway,* ☎ *604/879–6675. AE, MC, DC,
V. No lunch.*

Seafood

$$$-$$$$ ✕ **The Cannery.** This long-established East Side favorite has striking
views over the harbor and the mountains beyond. Though the tables
are set with formal white linen and china, the rustic nautical decor—
including a retired fishing boat out front—gives a pretty clear indica-
tion of the specialty here. Vegetarian and meat options are available,
but most diners come for the seafood classics: bouillabaisse, Dun-
geness crab, Nova Scotia lobster, treats from the daily fresh sheet, or
The Cannery's signature salmon Wellington with a pinot-noir sauce.
✉ *2205 Commissioner St. (north foot of Victoria Dr.),* ☎ *604/254–
9606 or 877/254–9606. Reservations essential. AE, D, DC, MC, V.
No lunch weekends.*

$$$-$$$$ ✕ **Salmon House on the Hill.** Perched halfway up a mountain in West
Vancouver, this restaurant has stunning water and city views by day,
and expansive vistas of city lights by night. The chefs here aren't con-
tent to rely on the scenery alone, though; the alder-grilled salmon is
widely regarded as the best in the city. The grilled oysters, British
Columbia prawns, and treats from the daily specials are also tempt-
ing. The Northwest Coast First Nations–theme decor is tastefully
done, though it can hardly compete with what's outside the windows.
The Salmon House is about 30 minutes from Vancouver by car; go over
the Lions Gate Bridge and take the Folkstone Way exit off Highway
1 west. Not every table has a view, so specify when you reserve. ✉ *2229*

Folkstone Way, West Vancouver, ☎ *604/926–3212. Reservations essential. AE, DC, MC, V.*

Tex-Mex

$–$$ ✕ **Topanga Café.** The California-style Mexican food at this 40-seat Kitsilano classic hasn't changed much since 1978, when the Topanga started dishing up fresh salsa and homemade tortilla chips. Quantities are still huge and prices low. Kids can color blank menu covers while waiting for their food; a hundred of their best efforts are framed on the walls. The summer patio is popular. ⊠ *2904 W. 4th Ave.,* ☎ *604/733–3713. Reservations not accepted. MC, V. Closed Sun.*

Vegetarian

$–$$ ✕ **Naam Restaurant.** Vancouver's oldest natural-foods eatery is open 24 hours, so if you need to satisfy a late-night craving for a veggie burger, rest easy. The Naam also serves vegetarian stir-fries, wicked chocolate desserts, and wine, beer, cappuccinos, and fresh juices. Wood tables, an open fireplace, and live blues, folk, and jazz create a homey atmosphere. On warm summer evenings you can sit in the outdoor courtyard. ⊠ *2724 W. 4th Ave.,* ☎ *604/738–7151. AE, MC, V.*

$ ✕ **Planet Veg.** The influences on the fare at this fast-food restaurant range as far afield as India, Mexico, and the Mediterranean. Among the most inspired cheap eats to be found in Kitsilano are the roti rolls—spicy treats in Indian flatbread that are fun, filling, and an excellent value. Eat in, or gather a picnic to take to nearby Kits Beach. ⊠ *1941 Cornwall Ave.,* ☎ *604/734–1001. Reservations not accepted. No credit cards.*

LODGING

Vancouver hotels, especially the more expensive properties downtown, contain fairly comparable facilities. Unless otherwise noted, expect to find the following amenities: minibars, in-room movies, no-smoking rooms and/or floors, room service, massage, baby-sitting, laundry service and dry cleaning, concierge, business services, meeting rooms, and parking (there is usually an additional fee). Lodgings in the inexpensive-to-moderate category generally do not have these amenities. The chart below shows high-season prices, but from mid-October through May, rates throughout the city can drop as much as 50%.

CATEGORY	COST*
$$$$	over $300
$$$	$200–$300
$$	$125–$200
$	under $125

*All prices are for a standard double room, excluding 10% room tax and 7% GST.

✑ *following the text of a review is your signal that the property has a Web site, where you will find details and, usually, images; for a link, visit www.fodors.com/urls.*

$$$$ ▥ **Four Seasons.** This 30-story luxury hotel in downtown Vancouver
★ is famous for pampering guests. The lobby is lavish, with seemingly acres of couches and a fountain in the lounge. Standard rooms, with understated black-and-cream or rust-and-cream color schemes and marble bathroom fixtures, are elegantly furnished, as are the roomier corner rooms with sitting areas. The two opulent split-level suites are handy for putting up visiting royalty. Service at the Four Seasons is top-notch, and the attention to detail is outstanding. The many amenities include free evening limousine service. The formal dining room,

Chartwell (☞ Dining, *above*), is one of the best in the city. ✉ *791 W. Georgia St., V6C 2T4,* ☎ *604/689–9333,* FAX *604/684–4555. 385 rooms, 67 suites. Restaurant, lobby lounge, in-room data ports, indoor-outdoor pool, hot tub, saunas, exercise room, children's programs (ages newborn–12), business services, meeting rooms, parking (fee). AE, D, DC, MC, V.* ✤

$$$$ 🏨 **Hotel Vancouver.** The copper roof of this château-style hotel (☞ Rob-
★   son to the Waterfront *in* Exploring Vancouver, *above*) that opened in 1939 dominates Vancouver's skyline. Even the standard guest rooms have an air of prestige, with high ceilings, mahogany furniture, sitting areas, and down duvets. Rooms on the Entrée Gold floor have extra services and amenities, including a private lounge and their own concierge. A full-service salon and day spa add to the pampering. ✉ *900 W. Georgia St., V6C 2W6,* ☎ *604/684–3131 or 800/441–1414,* FAX *604/662–1929. 555 rooms, 42 suites. 2 restaurants, lobby lounge, in-room data ports, indoor lap pool, wading pool, beauty salon, hot tub, saunas, spa, health club, car rental. AE, D, DC, MC, V.* ✤

$$$$ 🏨 **Metropolitan Hotel.** The structure was built in 1984 as the Man-
darin Oriental Hotel, based on the principles of feng shui, and those precepts have been respected in all renovations since. The spacious rooms are decorated in muted colors, and public areas have Asian art. Business-class rooms come with printers, fax machines, and cordless phones; standard rooms have bathrobes, newspapers, down comforters, and other luxury amenities. The popular junior suites are even bigger and only slightly more expensive than standard rooms. You can catch glimpses of the hotel's restaurant, Diva at the Met (☞ Dining, *above*), through an etched-glass wall in the lobby. ✉ *645 Howe St., V6C 2Y9,* ☎ *604/687–1122 or 800/667–2300,* FAX *604/643–7267. 179 rooms, 18 suites. Restaurant, bar, in-room data ports, indoor lap pool, hot tub, saunas, steam room (men only), exercise room, racquetball. AE, D, DC, MC, V.* ✤

$$$$ 🏨 **Pan Pacific Hotel.** A centerpiece of the waterfront Canada Place, the
★   luxurious Pan Pacific is convenient to the Vancouver Convention and Exhibition Centre and Vancouver's main cruise-ship terminal. Among the dramatic features of the three-story atrium lobby are a totem pole and waterfall. The lounge, restaurant, and café all have huge windows with views of the harbor and mountains. Eighty percent of the rooms have water views, and 30 Global Office rooms have desktop computers and videoconferencing facilities. ✉ *300–999 Canada Pl., V6C 3B5,* ☎ *604/662–8111, 800/663–1515 in Canada, 800/937–1515 in the U.S.,* FAX *604/685–8690. 504 rooms, 39 suites. 3 restaurants, coffee shop, lobby lounge, in-room data ports, in-room safes, pool, beauty salon, hot tubs, outdoor hot tub, saunas, spa, steam rooms, aerobics, health club, indoor track, racquetball, squash, billiards, convention center, business services, travel services. AE, DC, MC, V.* ✤

$$$$ 🏨 **Sheraton Suites Le Soleil.** Cozy and stylish, this boutique hotel,
opened in spring 1999 in the central business district, is popular with independent travelers and businesspeople. Neither tour groups nor conventions book here, and the staff prides itself on attentive, personal service. The golden yellow decor and intimate fireplace in the neoclassical lobby, and the vibrant gold and crimson fabrics in the guest rooms—most of which are small suites—radiate warmth. With lots of luxurious touches, such as 300-thread-count Egyptian cotton sheets, marble bathrooms, and custom-designed Biedermeier-style furniture, Le Soleil is also the first hotel in Canada with Internet TV, offering unlimited Web use. Two penthouse suites have 30-ft ceilings and massive private decks. The hotel doesn't have a pool or fitness facilities, but guests get reduced rates at the YWCA next door. The hotel's restaurant, Oritalia, is highly regarded (☞ Dining, *above*). ✉ *567 Hornby St., V6C 2E8,*

Vancouver Lodging

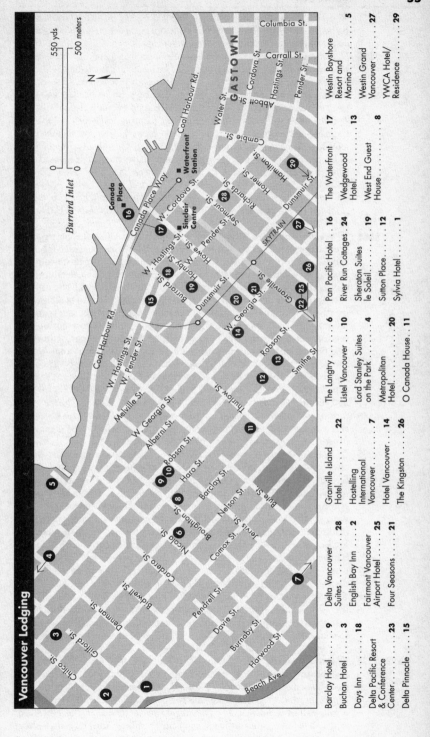

Columbia St.

Carrall St.

GASTOWN

Cordova St.

Hastings St.

Pender St.

Abbott St.

Cambie St.

Cordova St.

Water St.

Hamilton St.

Homer St.

Canada Place

Waterfront Station

Canada Place Way

W. Cordova St.

Sinclair Centre

Richards St.

Seymour St.

Dunsmuir St.

SKYTRAIN

W. Hastings St.

W. Pender St.

Howe St.

Hornby St.

Burrard St.

Dunsmuir St.

Granville St.

W. Georgia St.

Robson St.

Smithe St.

Coal Harbour Rd.

Melville St.

W. Georgia St.

Alberni St.

Robson St.

Haro St.

Barclay St.

Thurlow St.

Nelson St.

Byte St.

Jervis St.

Bidwell St.

Gilford St.

Chilco St.

Denman St.

Cardero St.

Nicola St.

Broughton St.

Comox St.

Pendrell St.

Davie St.

Burnaby St.

Harwood St.

Beach Ave.

Burrard Inlet

N

550 yds
500 meters
0

Barclay Hotel **9**
Buchan Hotel **3**
Days Inn **18**
Delta Pacific Resort & Conference Center **23**
Delta Pinnacle **15**

Delta Vancouver Suites **28**
English Bay Inn **2**
Fairmont Vancouver Airport Hotel **25**
Four Seasons **21**

Granville Island Hotel **22**
Hostelling International Vancouver **7**
Hotel Vancouver **14**
The Kingston **26**

The Langtry **6**
Listel Vancouver **10**
Lord Stanley Suites on the Park **4**
Metropolitan Hotel **20**
O Canada House **11**

Pan Pacific Hotel **16**
River Run Cottages **24**
Sheraton Suites le Soleil **19**
Sutton Place **12**
Sylvia Hotel **1**

The Waterfront **17**
Wedgewood Hotel **13**
West End Guest House **8**

Westin Bayshore Resort and Marina **5**
Westin Grand Vancouver **27**
YWCA Hotel/ Residence **29**

☎ 604/632–3000 or 877/632–3030, 🆁🅰🆇 604/632–3001. *10 rooms, 112 suites. Restaurant, bar, in-room data ports, in-room safes, room service, concierge, business services, meeting rooms. AE, DC, MC, V.* ☜

$$$$ 🏨 **Sutton Place.** The feel here is more of an exclusive European guest
★   house than a large modern hotel. Guest rooms are furnished with rich, dark woods, and the service is gracious and attentive. The hotel's Fleuri restaurant (☞ Dining, *above*), is known for its French and Continental cuisine, Sunday brunch, and weekend evening chocoholic bar. A full European health spa (also open to nonguests) offers Le Stone therapy—a massage using river stones—as well as wraps, facials, manicures, reflexology, and massage therapy. La Grande Residence (part of Sutton Place), an apartment hotel suitable for stays of at least a week, is next door, at 855 Burrard. ✉ *845 Burrard St., V6Z 2K6,* ☎ *604/ 682–5511 or 800/961–7555,* 🆁🅰🆇 *604/682–5513. 350 rooms, 47 suites, 162 apartments. Restaurant, bar, indoor lap pool, hot tub, sauna (women only), spa, steam room (men only), health club. AE, D, DC, MC, V.* ☜

$$$$ 🏨 **Westin Bayshore Resort and Marina.** Perched on the best part of the harbor, adjacent to Stanley Park, the Bayshore has truly fabulous views. The rooms in the tower have balconies and 90° mountain and harbor views; those in the main building feature floor-to-ceiling windows, and many of these rooms also have striking views. The only resort hotel in the downtown area, this is the perfect place to stay in warm weather, especially for families, because of its extensive recreational facilities. A development completed in 2000 added a convention center, marina, and attractive landscaping, including gardens, waterfalls, and ponds. Fishing charters and sightseeing cruises are available from the Bayshore, which is connected to Stanley Park and the Vancouver Convention and Exhibition Centre via seaside walkway. ✉ *1601 Bayshore Dr. (off Cardero St.), V6G 2V4,* ☎ *604/682–3377,* 🆁🅰🆇 *604/ 691–6980. 482 rooms, 28 suites. 2 restaurants, 2 bars, coffee shop, indoor and outdoor pools, hot tub, massage, saunas, steam room, exercise room, boating, fishing, bicycles, children's programs (ages newborn–12), convention center, travel services. AE, DC, MC, V.* ☜

[handwritten margin note: 2-room double bed 259 (CND) #263509 263510]

$$$$ 🏨 **Westin Grand Vancouver.** With its strikingly minimalist decor, cherry-wood and marble lobby, and all-suites layout, the Westin Grand—shaped like a grand piano—is one of the more stylish of the many hotels that have opened in Vancouver since 1999. Most of the compact studio and one-bedroom suites have floor-to-ceiling windows with skyline views, and all units have fully equipped kitchenettes, including microwaves and dishwashers, tucked into armoires. Corner suites are larger and have small balconies. Office suites come with a combination fax–photocopier–printer; all rooms have high-speed Internet access. The hotel is close to Vancouver's main sports and entertainment district and to the fashionable shops and eateries of Yaletown. ✉ *433 Robson St., V6B 6L9,* ☎ *604/602–1999 or 888/680–9393,* 🆁🅰🆇 *604/ 647–2502. 23 rooms, 184 suites. Restaurant, bar, in-room data ports, kitchenettes, outdoor lap pool, outdoor hot tub, sauna, steam room, exercise room, nightclub, piano, children's programs (ages newborn– 12), travel services. AE, DC, MC, V.* ☜

$$$–$$$$ 🏨 **Delta Pinnacle.** The soaring 50-ft-high atrium lobby makes a striking entrance to this 38-story hotel, opened in January 2000 just a block from Vancouver's cruise-ship terminal and central business district. Decorated in modern pale woods and neutral tones, each room has almost a full wall of windows. The rooms on the north side of the 17th floor and above have panoramic views of Burrard Inlet and the North Shore mountains. The hotel's Showcase restaurant and bar serves up West Coast cuisine. ✉ *1128 W. Hastings St., V6E 4R5,* ☎ *604/684–1128,* 🆁🅰🆇 *604/639–4027. 424 rooms, 10 suites. Restaurant, bar, coffee shop,* *in-room data ports, in-room safes, in-room VCRs, minibars, no-smoking floors, room service, indoor lap pool, hot tub, massage, sauna, steam room, exercise room, shops, concierge, concierge floors, business services, meeting rooms, parking (fee). AE, DC, MC, V.* ✧

$$$–$$$$ 🖭 **Delta Vancouver Suites.** Attached to the city's newest conference center (the Morris J. Wosk Centre for Dialogue), this modern luxury hotel is a nice example of early millennial chic. The striking marble and cherry-wood lobby soars four stories. The suites have blonde art deco furnishings, floor-to-ceiling windows, movable work tables, and sliding doors or Japanese screens to close off the bedroom. Slightly pricier Signature Club suites offer a private lounge, Continental breakfast, evening refreshments, and turndown service. The hotel's restaurant, Manhattan, is hidden away from the madding crowd. ⊠ *550 W. Hastings St., V6B 1L6,* ☎ *604/689–8188,* FAX *604/605–8881. 7 rooms, 219 suites. Restaurant, lobby lounge, in-room data ports, indoor pool, hot tub, sauna, exercise room, convention center. AE, D, DC, MC, V.* ✧

$$$–$$$$ 🖭 **Fairmont Vancouver Airport Hotel.** Airport hotels don't get more convenient than this. The Fairmont, opened in October 1999, is built directly on top of the Vancouver International Airport terminal building; the lobby is reached via an overhead walkway from the U.S. departures level. The rooms and public areas are decorated in a minimalist art deco–style, with pale woods, calming neutrals, extensive use of local cedar and slate, and artworks commissioned from local artists. All rooms have soaking tubs, shower stalls, and free high-speed Internet access; they also have floor-to-ceiling windows, the triple-pane construction of which provides near-perfect sound-proofing. Rooms on the north side have mountain views. An extensive health club and day spa is free for guests and is open to nonguests for $15. ⊠ *Vancouver International Airport, Box 23798, Richmond, V7B 1X9,* ☎ *604/207–5200,* FAX *604/ 248–3219. 390 rooms, 2 suites. Restaurant, bar, in-room data ports, in-room safes, indoor lap pool, hot tub, wading pool, massage, saunas, health club, piano, concierge, concierge floor, business services, meeting rooms. AE, DC, MC, V.* ✧

$$$–$$$$ 🖭 **Listel Vancouver.** This hotel on Vancouver's most vibrant shopping
★   street has reinvented itself as something of an art gallery. About half of the guest rooms display the original or limited-edition works of such contemporary artists as Carmelo Sortino, Bernard Cathelin, and Otto Rogers, and each is decorated with antiques or custom-made furniture to complement the art. Gallery-room guests are invited to a reception at the nearby Buschlen Mowatt Gallery (☞ Shopping, *below*) each evening. There's also live jazz in O'Doul's lounge downstairs. ⊠ *1300 Robson St., V6E 1C5,* ☎ *604/684–8461 or 800/663–5491,* FAX *604/684–7092. 119 rooms, 10 suites. Restaurant, lobby lounge, in-room data ports, indoor pool, hot tub, exercise room. AE, D, DC, MC, V.* ✧

$$$–$$$$ 🖭 **The Waterfront.** An underground walkway leads from this striking 23-story glass hotel to Canada Place. Views from the lobby and from 70% of the guest rooms are of Burrard Inlet and Stanley Park. Other rooms look onto a terraced herb garden. The spacious rooms have big picture windows and are attractively furnished with blonde wood furniture and contemporary Canadian artwork. Large corner rooms have the best views. Rooms on the Entrée Gold floor have extra amenities, including in-room safes, a private lounge, and their own concierge. ⊠ *900 Canada Pl. Way, V6C 3L5,* ☎ *604/691–1991 or 800/441–1414,* FAX *604/691– 1999. 489 rooms, 29 suites. Restaurant, lobby lounge, pool, hot tub, sauna, steam room, exercise room, car rental. AE, D, DC, MC, V.* ✧

$$$–$$$$ 🖭 **Wedgewood Hotel.** The small, lavish Wedgewood is run by an
★   owner who cares fervently about her guests. The lobby and guest rooms are decorated in a traditional European style with original artwork and antiques selected by the proprietor on her European trav-

els. Guest rooms are capacious and each has a balcony, a bar, and a desk. The four penthouse suites have fireplaces. All the extra touches are here, too: afternoon ice delivery, dark-out drapes, robes, and a morning newspaper. The turndown service incudes homemade cookies and bottled water. In the lobby is the sensuous Bacchus restaurant and lounge (☞ Dining, *above*). ⊠ *845 Hornby St., V6Z 1V1,* ☎ *604/689–7777 or 800/663–0666,* 𝔉𝔄𝔛 *604/608–5348. 51 rooms, 38 suites. Restaurant, lobby lounge, in-room data ports, in-room safes, sauna, exercise room, meeting rooms. AE, D, DC, MC, V.* 🍂

$$$ 🏨 **Delta Pacific Resort & Conference Center.** The recreational facilities make this 14-acre site a resort: swimming pools (one indoor, with a 225-ft-long water slide), tennis courts with a pro, aqua-exercise classes, outdoor volleyball nets, a play center and summer camps for children, and a playground. The hotel, 15 minutes from the airport and about a 30-minute drive south of downtown Vancouver, is large but casual and friendly. Guest rooms are modern, with contemporary decor; business-class rooms have printers and fax machines. Buses to BC Ferries, Amtrak, and the British Columbia interior all stop at the hotel. ⊠ *10251 St. Edwards Dr., Richmond V6X 2M9,* ☎ *604/278–9611 or 800/ 268–1133,* 𝔉𝔄𝔛 *604/276–1121. 430 rooms, 4 suites. 2 restaurants, coffee bar, lobby lounge, indoor pool, 2 outdoor pools, barbershop, beauty salon, hot tub, saunas, 4 tennis courts, exercise room, squash, bicycles, children's programs (ages 5–12), convention center, car rental, parking (fee). AE, DC, MC, V.* 🍂

$$$ 🏨 **Granville Island Hotel.** Granville Island is one of Vancouver's more entertaining neighborhoods, but unless you've moored up in your own houseboat, the only overnight option is the Granville Island Hotel. The exterior of this modern water's-edge hotel looks like it's made of Lego toy blocks; inside, the decor is more refined, with marble floors and Persian rugs in the lobby and guest rooms. Most rooms have water views, and all have big soaking tubs. Those on the top floor (the third) have small balconies. Step into the corridor and you'll overlook the vats brewing away for the fashionable brew pub and restaurant downstairs. Rooms that don't overlook the pub's summertime patio are the quietest. ⊠ *1253 Johnston St., V6H 3R9,* ☎ *604/683–7373 or 800/ 663–1840,* 𝔉𝔄𝔛 *604/683–3061. 54 rooms. Restaurant, pub, in-room data ports, hot tub, sauna, billiards, meeting rooms. AE, MC, V.* 🍂

$$–$$$$ 🏨 **English Bay Inn.** Antiques furnish these two 1930s Tudor-style
★   houses a block from the ocean and Stanley Park. The main house has an ornate Gothic dining table in the breakfast room, a parlor with wing chairs, a fireplace, a gilt Louis XV clock and candelabra, and a tiny Italianate garden out back. The guest rooms in the main house are equally lavish; three have sleigh beds, one has a romantic four-poster, and the suite has a loft bedroom with its own fireplace. Two rooms and a suite are across the street, in an equally beautiful house that opens onto a small park and has its own sitting and breakfast room. Full breakfast is included, and port and sherry are served each afternoon and evening. ⊠ *1968 Comox St., V6G 1R4,* ☎ *604/683–8002,* 𝔉𝔄𝔛 *604/899–1501. 6 rooms, 2 suites. Free parking. No smoking. AE, MC, V.* 🍂

$$–$$$ 🏨 **O Canada House.** Beautifully restored, this 1897 Victorian within
★   walking distance of downtown is where the first version of O *Canada*, the national anthem, was written, in 1909. Each spacious bedroom is appointed with late-Victorian antiques; modern comforts including in-room TVs, VCRs, phones, and bathrobes, help to make things homey. The top-floor room is enormous, with two double beds and a private sitting area. A separate one-room coach house in the garden is the most romantic option. Full breakfast is included, and guests have the use of a pantry and two parlors, both with fireplaces. ⊠ *1114 Barclay St.,*

V6E 1H1, ☎ *604/688–0555 or 877/688–1114,* FAX *604/488–0556. 7 rooms. Free parking. No smoking. MC, V.* 🐾

$$–$$$ 🛏 **River Run Cottages.** A unique bed-and-breakfast, River Run sits in
★ the serene Fraser River delta in the village of Ladner, a 30-minute drive south of downtown Vancouver, 10 minutes north of the ferry terminal, and near Highway 99 on the way from Seattle. The accommodations include a little gem of a floating house; a loft with a Japanese soaking tub on the deck and a cozy captain's bed; and two river's-edge cottages, each with a fireplace and a deck over the water. A TV and VCR are available on request. Full breakfast and afternoon refreshments are included in the rates at this no-smoking property. ✉ *4551 River Rd. W, Ladner V4K 1R9,* ☎ *604/946–7778,* FAX *604/940–1970. 2 rooms, 2 suites. Refrigerators, bicycles, free parking. MC, V.* 🐾

$–$$$ 🛏 **West End Guest House.** This Victorian house, built in 1906, is a true
★ "painted lady," from its gracious front parlor, cozy fireplace, and early 1900s furniture to its bright pink exterior. Most of the handsome rooms have high brass beds, antiques, and gorgeous linens, as well as TVs and phones; two larger rooms have gas fireplaces. The inn is in a residential neighborhood, a two-minute walk from Robson Street. Room rates include full breakfast. Book by March for summer. ✉ *1362 Haro St., V6E 1G2,* ☎ *604/681–2889,* FAX *604/688–8812. 8 rooms. Bicycles, free parking. No smoking. AE, D, MC, V.* 🐾

$$ 🛏 **Days Inn.** Opened as the Abbotsford in 1920, this six-story hotel is one of the few moderately priced hotels in the business district, and it's conveniently close to the convention center and the U.S. consulate. Rooms are bright, clean, and utilitarian, with phones, TVs, and minirefrigerators. The two-bedroom/one-bathroom units are a good value for groups and families. There is no room service or air-conditioning, but in-room data ports and voice mail are available. ✉ *921 W. Pender St., V6C 1M2,* ☎ *604/681–4335 or 877/681–4335,* FAX *604/681–7808. 80 rooms, 5 suites. Restaurant, lounge, pub, fans, in-room data ports, in-room safes, billiards, coin laundry. AE, D, DC, MC, V.* 🐾

$$ 🛏 **The Langtry.** Inside this rather unremarkable-looking 1939 former apartment building near Robson Street and Stanley Park are four 725-square-ft apartment-size suites furnished with antiques (including a Jacobean sofa and chair in one suite) and equipped with complete kitchens and dining areas and such amenities as feather beds and private phone lines. Host Haike Kingma sets out a beautiful breakfast table (full breakfast is included) in the dining room, or will deliver it to your suite if you prefer. He can also book a range of sightseeing and outdoor adventures around town. The Langtry, named for British stage actress Lily Langtry (1853–1929), is completely no-smoking. ✉ *968 Nicola St., V6G 2C8,* ☎ *604/687–7798,* FAX *604/687–7892. 4 suites. In-room fax, in-room VCRs, coin laundry, travel services, free parking. MC, V.* 🐾

$$ 🛏 **Lord Stanley Suites on the Park.** Here's a secret: these small, attractive, fully equipped suites built in 1998 on the edge of Stanley Park are privately owned and thus charge less than a comparable hotel for a nightly stay (weekly rates are even better). Each suite incorporates an office nook as well as a sitting room, one or two bedrooms, a galley kitchen, and a washer/dryer. Those overlooking busy Georgia Street have an enclosed sunroom; those backing onto quieter Alberni Street have balconies. You'll find many good restaurants on Denman Street, just a block away. A continental breakfast is included. ✉ *1889 Alberni St.,* ☎ *604/688–9299 or 888/767–7829,* FAX *604/688–9297. 103 suites. In-room data ports, in-room VCRs, no-smoking floor, saunas, exercise room, meeting room, parking (fee). AE, DC, MC, V.* 🐾

$–$$ ☎ **Barclay Hotel.** A great location, low rates, and such basic ameni-
ties as in-room phones and TVs (though no elevator) make this three-
story former apartment building one of the city's best-value pension-style
hotels. The guest rooms, with white painted furniture and orange bed-
spreads, are clean if basic, but the 1930s building, with its wide cor-
ridors, skylights, and mahogany staircase, has a certain Old World charm.
The Barclay is steps from the shops and restaurants of Robson Street,
and a 15-minute walk to either the business district or Stanley Park.
Most of the front rooms overlooking Robson Street have mountain views,
but the back rooms are quieter. ✉ *1348 Robson St., V6E 1C5,* ☎ *604/
688–8850,* FAX *604/688–2534. 65 rooms, 20 suites. Restaurant, breakfast room, no-smoking floors, refrigerators (some), concierge, meeting rooms, parking (fee). AE, D, DC, MC, V.*

$ ☎ **Buchan Hotel.** The three-story Buchan, built in the 1930s, sits on a
tree-lined residential street a block from Stanley Park. The hotel's
rooms have basic furnishings (refurbished in 1999), ceiling fans, and color
TVs, but no phones or air-conditioning. The lounge has a fireplace, and
there's storage for bikes and skis. The 35 pension-style rooms with shared
baths may be the most affordable accommodations near downtown. The
Buchan doesn't have an elevator. ✉ *1906 Haro St., V6G 1H7,* ☎ *604/
685–5354 or 800/668–6654,* FAX *604/685–5367. 65 rooms, 30 with bath.
Coin laundry. No smoking. AE, DC, MC, V.* ✒

$ ☎ **Hostelling International Vancouver.** Vancouver has two Hostelling
★ International locations: a big barracklike hostel at Jericho Beach in Kitsilano, and a smaller, downtown hostel near English Bay and Stanley
Park. Each has private rooms for two to four people; bunks in men's,
women's, and coed dorms; a shared kitchen and dining room; and coin
laundry, a TV lounge, bicycle rental, luggage and bike storage, and a
range of low-cost tours and activities. The downtown hostel also has
a meeting room, a games room, and a library, and is accessible to people who use wheelchairs. The Jericho Beach hostel has a café. A free
shuttle bus runs between the hostels and the bus and train station. ✉
Downtown: 1114 Burnaby St., V6E 1P1, ☎ *604/684–4565 or 888/
203–4302,* FAX *604/684–4540. 23 rooms, 44 4-bed dorms;* ✉ *Jericho
Beach: 1515 Discovery St., V6R 4K5,* ☎ *604/224–3208 or 888/203–
4303,* FAX *604/224–4852. 10 rooms, 17- to 14-bed dorms. MC, V.* ✒

$ ☎ **The Kingston.** Convenient to shopping, the Kingston is an old-style
four-story building with no elevator—the type of establishment you'd
find in Europe. Small and immaculate, the spartan rooms all have phones;
some rooms have TVs and private baths. Continental breakfast is included. ✉ *757 Richards St., V6B 3A6,* ☎ *604/684–9024 or 888/713–
3304,* FAX *604/684–9917. 55 rooms, 9 with bath. No-smoking floor,
sauna, coin laundry, parking (fee). AE, MC, V.* ✒

$ ☎ **Sylvia Hotel.** To stay at the Sylvia during the months of June through
August, you'll need to book six months to a year ahead. This ivy-cov-
ered 1912 building is popular because of its low rates and near-perfect
location: about 25 ft from the beach on scenic English Bay, 200 ft from
Stanley Park, and a 20-minute walk from Robson Street. The unadorned
rooms all have private baths, phones, and TVs. Some suites are huge, and
all have kitchens. ✉ *1154 Gilford St., V6G 2P6,* ☎ *604/681–9321,* FAX
*604/682–3551. 97 rooms, 22 suites. Restaurant, bar, room service, dry
cleaning, laundry service, parking (fee). AE, DC, MC, V.* ✒

$ ☎ **YWCA Hotel/Residence.** A secure, 12-story building in the heart of
★ the entertainment district, the YWCA has bright, comfortable rooms—
some big enough to sleep five. All have nightstands and desks, minirefrigerators, phones, sinks, and air-conditioning. Some share a bath down
the hall, some share a bath between two rooms, and others have private baths. The hotel is open to men and women and offers special rates
for seniors, students, and YWCA members; weekly and monthly rates

are available in the off season. Rates include use of the YWCA pool and fitness facility, a 15-minute walk away at 535 Hornby Street. ✉ *733 Beatty St., V6B 2M4,* ☎ *604/895–5830 or 800/663–1424,* FAX *604/ 681–2550. 155 rooms. No-smoking floors, refrigerators, coin laundry, meeting rooms, parking (fee). AE, MC, V.* 🐾

NIGHTLIFE AND THE ARTS

For **events information,** pick up a copy of the free *Georgia Straight* (available at cafés and bookstores around town) or look in the entertainment section of the *Vancouver Sun* (Thursday's paper has listings in the "Queue" section). The **Arts Hotline** (☎ 604/684–2787) has the latest entertainment information. Tickets for many venues can be booked through **Ticketmaster** (☎ 604/280–4444).

The Arts

Dance
The **Scotia Bank Dance Centre** (✉ 1196 Granville St., ☎ 604/606–6400) is the hub of dance in British Columbia; it has performance and rehearsal space and provides information about dance in the province.

Ballet British Columbia (☎ 604/732–5003), based at the Queen Elizabeth Theatre (☞ Theater, *below*), mounts productions and hosts out-of-town companies November through May. A few of the many modern-dance companies in town are Karen Jamieson, DanceArts Vancouver, and JumpStart; among the venues they perform at (besides the Scotia Bank Dance Centre) are the Firehall Arts Centre and the Vancouver East Cultural Centre (☞ Theater, *below*).

Film
Tickets are half price Tuesday at most chain-owned Vancouver movie theaters. The **Vancouver International Film Festival** (☎ 604/685–0260) is held in late September and early October in several theaters around town.

Several movie theaters in Vancouver show foreign and independent films. The **Blinding Light** (✉ 36 Powell St., ☎ 604/684–8288), on the edge of Gastown, showcases locally made short and experimental films, and occasionally invites audience members to bring their own films. Once a month a live band improvises scores to silent movies. For foreign and independent films, try **Fifth Avenue Cinemas** (✉ 2110 Burrard St., ☎ 604/734–7469), the **Park Theater** (✉ 3440 Cambie St., ☎ 604/876–2747), or the **Ridge Theatre** (✉ 3131 Arbutus St., ☎ 604/738–6311). The **Pacific Cinémateque** (✉ 1131 Howe St., ☎ 604/688–8202) shows esoteric and foreign and art films.

Music
CHAMBER MUSIC AND SMALL ENSEMBLES
Early Music Vancouver (☎ 604/732–1610) performs medieval, Renaissance, and Baroque music throughout the year and hosts the Vancouver Early Music Summer Festival in late July to mid-August, at the University of British Columbia. Concerts by the **Friends of Chamber Music** (☎ 604/437–5747) are worth watching for in the local-newspaper entertainment listings. The **Vancouver Recital Society** (☎ 604/602–0363) presents both emerging and well-known classical musicians in recital September–May at the Chan Centre for the Performing Arts and the Vancouver Playhouse (☞ Theater, *below*). In summer the society produces the Vancouver Chamber Music Festival, on the grounds of Crofton House School (✉ 3200 W. 41st Ave.).

CHORAL GROUPS

Choral groups such as the **Bach Choir** (☎ 604/921–8012), the **Vancouver Cantata Singers** (☎ 604/921–8588), and the **Vancouver Chamber Choir** (☎ 604/738–6822) play a major role in Vancouver's classical-music scene.

ORCHESTRAS

The **Vancouver Symphony Orchestra** (☎ 604/876–3434) is the resident company at the Orpheum Theatre (✉ 601 Smithe St.).

Opera

Vancouver Opera (☎ 604/682–2871) stages several productions a year from October through May at the Queen Elizabeth Theatre (☞ Theater, *below*).

Theater

Arts Club Theatre (✉ 1585 Johnston St., ☎ 604/687–1644) operates two stages on Granville Island and presents theatrical performances all year. **Carousel Theatre** (☎ 604/669–3410) performs for children and young people at the Waterfront Theatre (✉ 1411 Cartwright St.) on Granville Island. The **Chan Centre for the Performing Arts** (✉ 6265 Crescent Rd., on the University of British Columbia campus, ☎ 604/822–2697) contains a 1,200-seat concert hall, a theater, and a cinema. The **Firehall Arts Centre** (✉ 280 E. Cordova St., ☎ 604/689–0926) showcases Canadian works in an intimate downtown space. The **Queen Elizabeth Theatre** (✉ 600 Hamilton St., ☎ 604/665–3050) is a major venue for ballet, opera, and other events. An elegant 1930s movie palace, the **Stanley Theatre** (✉ 2750 Granville St., ☎ 604/687–1644) was reopened in 1998 as a live theater. **Vancouver East Cultural Centre** (✉ 1895 Venables St., ☎ 604/254–9578) is a multipurpose performance space. In the same complex as the Queen Elizabeth Theatre, the **Vancouver Playhouse** (✉ 649 Cambie St., ☎ 604/665–3050) is the leading venue in Vancouver for mainstream theatrical shows.

Bard on the Beach (☎ 604/739–0559) is a summer series of Shakespeare's plays performed in tents on the beach at Vanier Park. The **Fringe Vancouver** (☎ 604/257–0350), Vancouver's annual theater festival, is staged in September at various venues in Yaletown and on Granville Island. **Theatre Under the Stars** (☎ 604/687–0174) performs musicals at Malkin Bowl, an outdoor amphitheater in Stanley Park, during July and August.

Nightlife

Bars, Pubs, and Lounges

Unpretentious is the word at the **Atlantic Trap & Gill** (✉ 612 Davie St., ☎ 604/806–6393), a downtown pub designed to help folks from Atlantic Canada (and everyone else) feel at home, with beer kegs for tables, old couches topped with afghans, Atlantic folk music, and goodies such as clam strips on the menu. The **Bacchus Lounge** (✉ 845 Hornby St., ☎ 604/608–5319), in the Wedgewood Hotel, is a relaxing place with plush couches, a fireplace, and a pianist. At **The Bulldog Café** (✉ 510 Nelson St., ☎ 604/688–4438), owner Ray Maigret has re-created a bar like those he remembers from his native Amsterdam: hardwood floors scattered with peanut shells, mugs behind the bar for the regulars, and a menu of Dutch and Indonesian comfort food. Near Stanley Park and attached to the seaside restaurant of the same name, **Cardero's Pub** (✉ 1583 Coal Harbour Quay, ☎ 604/669–7666) has deep leather couches, marina views, and recycled ship timbers and other nautical touches. The pub grub is top-notch. A fountain, greenery, and soft, comfy chairs make the atriumlike **Garden Terrace** (✉ 791 W. Georgia St., ☎ 604/689–9333), in the Four Seasons, a peaceful place to relax over cocktails or a meal. The fireplaces, wing chairs, dark wood, and leather at the **Gerard Lounge** (✉ Sutton Place Hotel, 845 Burrard St., ☎ 604/682–5511) provide a suitably stylish setting for the film-industry types who hang out here. For a pint of properly poured Guinness and live traditional Irish music, try the **Irish Heather** (✉ 217 Carrall St., ☎ 604/688–9779) in Gastown. The **900 West** (✉ 900 W. Georgia St., ☎ 604/669–9378; ☞ Dining, *above*) wine bar at the Hotel Vancouver has 75 wines available by the glass.

There are a couple of choices on Granville Island. The **Backstage Lounge** (✉ 1585 Johnston St., ☎ 604/687–1354) is a good pre- or post-theater spot behind the main stage at the Arts Club Theatre. It has eleven brews on tap, an extensive pub-food menu, live music on weekends, and a waterside patio that fills quickly on warm evenings. **Bridges** (✉ 1696 Duranleau St., ☎ 604/687–4400), near the Public Market, includes a cozy, nautical-theme pub.

Brew Pubs

The Creek (✉ Granville Island Hotel, 1253 Johnston St., ☎ 604/685–7070) is a popular microbrewery lounge with plush velour booths and leather chairs, fireplaces, and pool tables. The in-house vats brew eight varieties of German-style lagers and ales. **Dix Brew Pub** (✉ 871 Beatty St., ☎ 604/682–2739), near Yaletown and B.C. Place Stadium, is a relaxed and good-looking place, with exposed brick and beams, a fireplace, a long mahogany bar, and vats brewing up a variety of lagers. Dix also serves a fine Southern-style barbecue, slow-smoked in-house in an apple or cherry-wood smoker. The brewmasters at **Steamworks** (✉ 375 Water St., ☎ 604/689–2739), on the edge of Gastown, use an age-old steam process and large copper kettles (visible through glass walls in the dining room downstairs) to fashion several brews, including Lions Gate Lager, Coal Porter, and Cascadia Cream Ale. The pub area upstairs has sweeping views of Burrard Inlet and the North Shore mountains. There's also a restaurant downstairs. The **Yaletown Brewing Company** (✉ 1111 Mainland St., ☎ 604/681–2739) occupies a renovated warehouse. The microbrewery turns out eight tasty concoctions and includes a darts and billiards pub and a restaurant.

Casinos

Vancouver has a few casinos; proceeds go to local charities and arts groups. No alcohol is served. The **Great Canadian Casino** (✉ 1133 W. Hastings St., ☎ 604/682–8415) is in the Renaissance Hotel. The **Royal City Star** (✉ Westminster Quay, New Westminster, ☎ 604/878–9999) is a Mississippi riverboat moored on the Fraser River. Its five decks include 30 gaming tables, 300 slot machines, two lounges, and a restaurant. It's open 10 AM–4 AM daily, and takes an hour-long cruise on the river twice a day. Admission is free, though guests must be at least 19 years old. The **Royal Diamond Casino** (✉ 750 Pacific Blvd. S, ☎ 604/685–2340) is in the Plaza of Nations Expo site downtown.

Coffeehouses

A large European population and a shortage of pubs mean that coffeehouses play a big role in Vancouver's social life. The Starbucks invasion is nearly complete—there are blocks in town with two branches—but there are other, more colorful places to have a cappuccino, write that novel, or watch the world go by.

Granville Island has many coffee places, but only the **Blue Parrot Café** (✉ Granville Island Public Market, 1689 Johnston St., ☎ 604/688–5127) provides such sweeping views of the boats on False Creek. Like the public market, the Blue Parrot is madly crowded on weekends.

Blake's on Carrall (✉ 221 Carrall St., ☎ 604/899–3354) is a Gastown hangout.Cushy couches and wholesome goodies make **Bojangles Café** (✉ 785 Denman St., ☎ 604/687–3622) a good place to rest after a walk around Stanley Park. The closest thing in Vancouver to a *La Dolce Vita* set is the **Calabria Café** (✉ 1745 Commercial Dr., ☎ 604/253–7017), with its marble tables, plaster statues, and posters of Italian movie stars. Everyone seems to know everyone else at **Delaney's** (✉ 1105 Denman St., ☎ 604/662–3344), a friendly and often crowded coffee bar near English Bay. Cozy wooden booths and stacks of magazines will tempt you to spend a rainy afternoon here. One cannot live by coffee alone, as proven by the vast selection of teas and related paraphernalia at **Tearoom T** (✉ 1568 W. Broadway, ☎ 604/730–8390).

Comedy Clubs

The **Gastown Comedy Store** (✉ 19 Water St., ☎ 604/682–1727) has stand-up and other comedy acts. The **TheatreSports League** (☎ 604/738–7013), a hilarious improv troupe, performs at the New Review Stage on Granville Island. The **Vancouver International Comedy Festival** (☎ 604/683–0883), held in late July and early August, brings an international collection of improv, stand-up, circus, and other acts to Granville Island. **Yuk Yuks Comedy Club** (✉ 750 Pacific Blvd. S, in the Plaza of Nations Expo site, ☎ 604/687–5233) is a popular stand-up venue.

Gay and Lesbian Nightlife

The multilevel **Celebrities** (✉ 1022 Davie St., ☎ 604/689–3180) is one of Canada's largest gay bars. **Denman Station** (✉ 860 Denman St., ☎ 604/669–3448) is a friendly, low-key pub that's patronized by gay men and women. The **Dufferin** (✉ 900 Seymour St., ☎ 604/683–4251), a downtown pub, has male dancers, female impersonators, and drag karaoke. **Odyssey** (✉ 1251 Howe St., ☎ 604/689–5256) is a dance club with drag shows, go-go boys, and theme nights.

Music

DANCE CLUBS

The **Commodore Ballroom** (✉ 868 Granville St., ☎ 604/739–7469), a 1929 dance hall rich with memories for generations of Vancouverites, reopened in late 1999 after years of closure. Restored to its Art Deco glory, complete with its massive dance floor, the Commodore has done a lot to revitalize the city's live-music scene. Live bands, which have included such major Canadian names as Bryan Adams and Blue Rodeo, play here six nights a week; Tuesday is DJ night. Popular since the 1980s, **Luv-a-Fair** (✉ 1275 Seymour, ☎ 604/685–3288) is still going strong, with DJs spinning the gamut from progressive house to '80s classics. The **Purple Onion Cabaret** (✉ 21 Water St., ☎ 604/602–9442), in Gastown, has both a jazz lounge and a dance club, featuring live and recorded jazz, funk, reggae, and hip hop. **Richard's on Richards** (✉ 1036 Richards St., ☎ 604/687–6794) is one of Vancouver's most established dance clubs, with live bands on weekdays. **Sonar** (✉ 66 Water St., ☎ 604/683–6695), in Gastown, has international dance sounds and frequent touring guest DJs. At the **Stone Temple Cabaret** (✉ 1082 Granville St., ☎ 604/488–1333), DJs play top-40 dance tunes, R&B, and hip hop. **The Wett Bar** (✉ 1320 Richards St., ☎ 604/662–7707) has a huge dance floor, and high-tech sound and light systems.

FOLK

The **Vancouver Folk Music Festival** (☎ 604/602–9798 or 800/883–3655), one of the world's leading folk- and world-music events, takes place at Jericho Beach Park the third weekend of July. For folk and traditional Celtic concerts year-round, call the **Rogue Folk Club** (☎ 604/736–3022).

JAZZ AND SOUL

The hot line of the **Coastal Jazz and Blues Society** (☎ 604/872–5200) has information about concerts and clubs. The society also runs the Vancouver International Jazz Festival, which lights up 40 venues around town every June.

BaBalu (✉ 654 Nelson St., ☎ 604/605–4343) has two house bands that play hip jazz and soul. The funky, brick-lined **Bar None** (✉ 1222 Hamilton St., ☎ 604/689–7000), in Yaletown, has top-40 dance tunes on weekends; on Monday and Tuesday, the nine-piece house band plays jazz, funk, soul, and rock. You can hear live jazz six nights a week at the **Cellar Jazz Café** (✉ 3611 W. Broadway, ☎ 604/738–1959). The cozy, subterranean **Chameleon Urban Lounge** (✉ 801 W. Georgia St., ☎ 604/669–0806), in the basement of the Crowne Plaza Hotel Georgia, is a good place to catch live jazz, R&B, and Latin tunes. At the **Hot Jazz Club** (✉ 2120 Main St., ☎ 604/873–4131), you can dance to live swing, jazz, and salsa bands.

ROCK AND BLUES

The **Rage** (✉ 750 Pacific Blvd. S, ☎ 604/685–5585) hosts touring acts on weeknights and has DJs on weekends. In the early evening, the **Railway Club** (✉ 579 Dunsmuir St., ☎ 604/681–1625) attracts journalists and media types to its pub-style rooms; after 8 it becomes a venue for local rock bands. The **Starfish Room** (✉ 1055 Homer St., ☎ 604/682–4171) showcases local and alternative bands in a nightclub setting. **The Vogue Theatre** (✉ 918 Granville St., ☎ 604/331–7909), a former movie palace, hosts a variety of concerts by visiting performers. Vancouver's most established rhythm-and-blues bar, **The Yale** (✉ 1300 Granville St., ☎ 604/681–9253), has live bands most nights.

Pool Halls

Most of the city's "hot" pool halls are in Yaletown. The loud, industrial-theme **Automotive Billiards Club** (✉ 1095 Homer St., ☎ 604/682–0040) attracts a twenties crowd. **Cutters Billiard** (✉ 1011 Hamilton St., ☎ 604/669–3533) has plenty of tables. The chic **Soho Café & Billiards** (✉ 1144 Homer St., ☎ 604/688–1180) has a few tables tucked in behind a trendy café.

OUTDOOR ACTIVITIES AND SPORTS

Beaches

An almost continuous string of beaches runs from Stanley Park to the University of British Columbia. The water is cool, but the beaches are sandy, edged by grass. All have lifeguards, washrooms, concession stands, and limited parking, unless otherwise noted. Liquor is prohibited in parks and on beaches. For information, call the **Vancouver Board of Parks and Recreation** (☎ 604/738–8535 summer only).

Kitsilano Beach (☞ Kitsilano *in* Exploring Vancouver, *above*), over the Burrard Bridge from downtown, has a lifeguard and is the city's busiest beach—in-line skaters, volleyball games, and sleek young people are ever present. The part of the beach nearest the Vancouver Maritime Museum is the quietest. Facilities include a playground, tennis courts, a heated pool, concession stands, and nearby restaurants and cafés.

The **Point Grey beaches**—Jericho, Locarno, and Spanish Banks—begin at the end of Point Grey Road and offer huge expanses of sand, especially at low tide. The shallow water, warmed slightly by sun and sand, is good for swimming. Farther out, toward Spanish Banks, the beach becomes less crowded. Past Point Grey is Wreck Beach, Vancouver's nude beach.

Among the **West End beaches,** Second Beach and Third Beach, along Beach Drive in Stanley Park, draw families. Second Beach has a guarded pool. A water slide, kayak rentals, street performers, and artists keep things interesting all summer at English Bay Beach, at the foot of Denman Street. Farther along Beach Drive, Sunset Beach is a little too close to the downtown core for clean, safe swimming.

Participant Sports

Biking

One of the best ways to see the city is to cycle along at least part of the **Seaside Bicycle Route.** This 15-km (10-mi), flat, car-free route starts at Canada Place downtown, follows the waterfront around Stanley Park (☞ Stanley Park *in* Exploring Vancouver, *above*), and continues, with a few detours, all the way around False Creek to Spanish Banks Beach.

Rentals are available from a number of places near Stanley Park, including **Bayshore Bicycles** (⊠ 745 Denman St., ☎ 604/688–2453), which is open year-round; the **Westin Bayshore Hotel** (⊠ 1601 W. Georgia St., ☎ 604/689–5071), open March–September; and **Spokes Bicycle Rentals & Espresso Bar** (⊠ 1798 W. Georgia St., ☎ 604/688–5141). Cycling helmets, a legal requirement in Vancouver, come with the rentals.

For guided biking and mountain-bike tours, *see* Bike Tours *in* Contacts and Resources, *below*.

Boating

You can charter motorboats and sailboats from Granville Island through **Blue Pacific Yacht Charters** (⊠ 1519 Foreshore Walk, Granville Island, ☎ 604/682–2161). **Cooper Boating Centre** (⊠ 1620 Duranleau St., Granville Island, ☎ 604/687–4110 or 888/999–6419) has a three-hour introduction to sailing around English Bay, as well as longer cruise-and-learn trips that last from five days to two weeks.

Fishing

You can fish for salmon all year in coastal British Columbia. **Sewell's Marina Horseshoe Bay** (⊠ 6695 Nelson Ave., Horseshoe Bay, ☎ 604/921–3474) offers guided and self-drive salmon fishing charters on Howe Sound. For fly-fishing day trips, contact **Trout Fishing Adventures** (⊠ 985 W. 14th Ave., Suite 201, ☎ 604/838–5873). **Westin Bayshore Yacht Charters** (⊠ 1601 W. Georgia St., ☎ 604/691–6936) operates fishing charters.

Golf

For advance tee-time bookings at any of 60 British Columbia courses, or for a spur of the moment game, call **Last Minute Golf** (☎ 604/878–1833 or 800/684–6344). The company matches golfers and courses, sometimes at substantial green-fee discounts. The half-day packages at **West Coast Golf Shuttle** (☎ 604/878–6800 or 888/599–6800) include the green fee, power cart, and hotel pickup; rental clubs are available.

The challenging 18-hole, par-72 course at **Furry Creek Golf and Country Club** (⊠ Hwy. 99, Furry Creek, ☎ 604/922–9576 or 888/922–9462), a 45-minute drive north of Vancouver, has an $80–$95 green fee and includes a mandatory cart. The course is closed late October to early March. The facilities of the 18-hole, par-71 public **McCleery Golf Course** (⊠ 7188 McDonald St., ☎ 604/257–8191, 604/280–1818 for advance bookings) include a driving range. The green fee is $34–$37; an optional cart costs $25. **Northview Golf and Country Club** (✉ 6857 168th St., Surrey, ☎ 604/576–4653 or 888/574–2211) has two Arnold Palmer–designed 18-hole courses (both par 72) and is the home of the Air Canada Championship (a Professional Golfers' Association, or PGA, tour event). The green fee for the Ridge course (🕑 March–October), where the PGA tour plays, is $75–$85; the fee for the Canal course (open all year) is $55–$65. An optional cart at either course costs $30. At the 18-hole, par-72 course (closed November–March) at the **West-wood Plateau Golf and Country Club** (✉ 3251 Plateau Blvd., Coquit-lam, ☎ 604/552–0777 or 800/580–0785), the green fee, which includes a cart, is $80–$130. The club also has a nine-hole course that's open year-round and a fine restaurant (Galleries on the Plateau).

Health and Fitness Clubs

The **Bentall Centre Athletic Club** (✉ 1055 Dunsmuir St., lower level, ☎ 604/689–4424) has racquetball and squash courts and weight rooms; aerobics classes are also given. The **YMCA** (✉ 955 Burrard St., ☎ 604/689–9622) downtown has daily rates. Facilities include a pool and weight rooms, as well as racquetball, squash, and handball courts, basketball, volleyball, and a boxing room. The **YWCA** (✉ 535 Hornby St., ☎ 604/895–5777) has an ozone pool, weight rooms, fitness classes, a whirlpool, and steam rooms.

Hiking

The weather can change quickly in the mountains, so go prepared and leave word with someone in the city as to your route and when you expect to be back. For **mountain-weather forecasts,** call ☎ 604/664–9021.

Stanley Park (☞ Stanley Park *in* Exploring Vancouver, *above*), the more rugged **Pacific Spirit Park** (✉ 4915 W. 16th Ave., ☎ 604/224–5739), near the University of British Columbia, and the seaside **Lighthouse Park** (✉ Beacon La., off Marine Dr.), in West Vancouver, all have fairly flat, forested trails.

In the mountains of North Vancouver, **Capilano River Regional Park** (☞ North Vancouver *in* Exploring Vancouver, *above*) and the **Lower Seymour Conservation Reserve** (✉ end of Lillooet Rd., North Vancouver, ☎ 604/432–6286) have some easy rain-forest walks. **Mount Seymour** (✉ Mount Seymour Rd. off Seymour Pkwy., North Vancouver, ☎ 604/924–2200) and **Cypress** provincial parks (✉ Cypress Bowl Rd., West Vancouver, ☎ 604/924–2200) offer challenging mountain trails for experienced, well-equipped hikers.

The **Grouse Grind** is a steep (rising 2,800 ft in fewer than 2 mi), grueling trail from the Grouse Mountain (☞ North Vancouver *in* Exploring Vancouver, *above*) parking lot to the top of the mountain; the path is packed with fit Vancouverites most summer afternoons. There are also hiking trails at the top of the mountain, accessed via the Grouse Mountain Skyride.

A number of companies conduct guided walks and hikes in nearby parks and wilderness areas (☞ Walking Tours *in* Contacts and Resources, *below*).

Indoor Sports

Vancouver's wet climate has given rise to two high-tech indoor sports complexes. **Score Virtual Sportsworld** (✉ 770 Pacific Blvd., ☎ 604/602–0513), at the Plaza of Nations downtown, has a climbing wall, a roller-hockey rink, and simulated golf, soccer, baseball, and hockey games.

Jogging

The **Running Room** (⊠ 679 Denman St., ☎ 604/684–9771) is a good source for information about fun runs in the area.

The seawall around **Stanley Park** (☞ Stanley Park *in* Exploring Vancouver, *above*) is 9 km (5½ mi) long; running it provides an excellent minitour of the city. You can take a shorter run of 4 km (2½ mi) in the park around Lost Lagoon.

Skiing

CROSS-COUNTRY

The best cross-country skiing, with 16 km (10 mi) of groomed trails, is at **Cypress Bowl Ski Area** (⊠ Cypress Bowl Ski Area Rd., West Vancouver, Exit 8 off Hwy. 1 westbound, ☎ 604/922–0825). **Grouse Mountain** (☞ *below*) has cross-country trails as well as downhill skiing.

DOWNHILL

Whistler/Blackcomb (☞ Chapter 4), a top-ranked ski destination, is a two-hour drive from Vancouver.

The **North Shore mountains** hold three ski areas. All have rentals, lessons, and night skiing. **Cypress Bowl** (⊠ Cypress Bowl Ski Area Rd., West Vancouver, Exit 8 off Hwy. 1 westbound, ☎ 604/926–5612; 604/419–7669 for snow report) has 25 runs, four chairlifts, and a vertical drop of 1,750 ft. The mountain also has a tobogganing and snow-tubing area. **Grouse Mountain** (⊠ 6400 Nancy Greene Way, ☎ 604/980–9311; 604/986–6262 snow report) has four chairlifts, four surface lifts, a vertical drop of 1,210 ft, extensive night skiing, restaurants, bars, ice-skating, a snowshoeing park, and great city views from the runs. **Mount Seymour** (⊠ 1700 Mt. Seymour Rd., ☎ 604/986–2261; 604/718–7771 snow report) has three chairlifts and a vertical drop of 1,042 ft. The mountain also has a half-pipe for snowboarding, as well as snowshoeing and snow-tubing facilities.

Tennis

There are 180 free public courts around town. Contact the **Vancouver Board of Parks and Recreation** (☎ 604/257–8400) for locations. **Stanley Park** (☞ Stanley Park *in* Exploring Vancouver, *above*) has 18 well-surfaced outdoor courts near English Bay Beach. Some courts charge a fee and can be booked in advance.

Water Sports

KAYAKING

Kayaks are a fun way to explore the waters of False Creek and the shoreline of English Bay. **Ecomarine Ocean Kayak Center** (⊠ 1668 Duranleau St., Granville Island, ☎ 604/689–7575) and **Ocean West Expeditions** (⊠ English Bay Beach, ☎ 800/660–0051) rent kayaks and offer lessons and tours.

For guided kayak trips, *see* Ecology Tours *in* Contacts and Resources, *below.*

RAFTING

The **Canadian Outback Adventure Company** (⊠ ☎ 604/921–7250 or 800/565–8735) runs white-water rafting and scenic (not white-water) floats on day trips from Vancouver.

WINDSURFING

Sailboards and lessons are available during summer at **Windsure Windsurfing School** (⊠ Jericho Beach, ☎ 604/224–0615). The winds aren't very heavy on English Bay, making it a perfect locale for learning the sport. You'll have to travel north to Squamish for more challenging high-wind conditions.

Spectator Sports

Vancouver's professional basketball and hockey teams play at **General Motors Place** (⊠ 800 Griffiths Way, ☎ 604/899–7400). **Ticketmaster** (☎ 604/280–4400) sells tickets to many local sports events.

Basketball
The **Vancouver Grizzlies** (☎ 604/899–7400), a National Basketball Association team, play at General Motors Place.

Football
The **B.C. Lions** (☎ 604/930–5466) Canadian Football League team plays home games at **B.C. Place Stadium** (⊠ 777 Pacific Blvd. S, ☎ 604/661–7373).

Hockey
The **Vancouver Canucks** (☎ 604/899–7400) of the National Hockey League play at General Motors Place.

SHOPPING

Unlike many cities where suburban malls have taken over, Vancouver is full of individual boutiques and specialty shops. Antiques stores, ethnic markets, art galleries, high-fashion outlets, and fine department stores abound. Store hours are generally 9:30 to 6 Monday, Tuesday, Wednesday, and Saturday; 9:30 to 9 Thursday and Friday; and noon to 5 Sunday.

Shopping Districts and Malls

About two dozen high-end art galleries, antiques shops, and Oriental-rug emporiums are packed end to end between 6th and 15th avenues on Granville Street, in an area known as **Gallery Row. Oakridge Shopping Centre** (⊠ 650 W. 41st Ave., at Cambie St., ☎ 604/261–2511) has chic, expensive stores that are fun to browse through. The **Pacific Centre Mall** (⊠ 700 W. Georgia St., ☎ 604/688–7236), on two levels and mostly underground, takes up three city blocks in the heart of downtown. **Robson Street** stretching from Burrard to Bute streets is full of boutiques and cafés. A commercial center has developed around **Sinclair Centre** (⊠ 757 W. Hastings St.), catering to sophisticated and pricey tastes (☞ Robson to the Waterfront *in* Exploring Vancouver, *above*).

Bustling **Chinatown**—centered on Pender and Main streets—is full of restaurants and markets (☞ Gastown and Chinatown *in* Exploring Vancouver, *above*). **Commercial Drive** north of East 1st Avenue is the center of Vancouver's Italian and Latin American communities. You can sip cappuccino in coffee bars, or buy sun-dried tomatoes or an espresso machine. In **Little India,** on Main Street around 50th Avenue, curry houses, sweets shops, grocery stores, discount jewelers, and silk shops abound.

Auction Houses

Love's (⊠ 1635 W. Broadway, ☎ 604/733–1157) holds auctions of household goods, collectibles, and antiques on the last Wednesday and Thursday of each month at noon and 6 PM. **Maynard's** (⊠ 415 W. 2nd Ave., ☎ 604/876–6787) auctions home furnishings every second Wednesday at 7 PM and holds occasional art and antiques auctions.

Department Stores

The Bay (⊠ 674 Granville St., at Georgia St., ☎ 604/681–6211), founded as part of the fur trade in the 17th century, is now a midprice department store downtown. **Eaton's** (⊠ 701 Granville St., ☎ 604/687–1167), once among Vancouver's top department stores, is re-opening under new management as a midprice, fashion-oriented department store. **Holt Renfrew** (✉ 633 Granville St., ☎ 604/681–3121), which focuses on high fashion for men and women, can also be found in many malls.

Specialty Stores

Antiques

Two key antiques hunting grounds are Gallery Row on Granville Street (☞ Shopping Districts, *above*) and the stretch of antiques stores along Main Street from 16th to 25th avenues. **The Vancouver Antique Centre** (✉ 422 Richards St., ☎ 604/669–7444) has 15 antiques and collectibles dealers under one roof.

Treasure hunters enjoy the curio shops clustered along the 300 block of **West Cordova Street,** between Cambie and Richards streets near Gastown.

Art Galleries

Buschlen Mowatt (✉ 1445 W. Georgia St., ☎ 604/682–1234), one of the city's best galleries, exhibits the works of contemporary Canadian and international artists. **Diane Farris** (✉ 1565 W. 7th Ave., ☎ 604/737–2629) often showcases hot new artists. The **Douglas Reynolds Gallery** (✉ 2335 Granville St., ☎ 604/731–9292) has one of the city's finest collections of Northwest-coast First Nations art. The **Inuit Gallery of Vancouver** (✉ 345 Water St., ☎ 604/688–7323) exhibits Northwest-coast and Inuit art. The **Marion Scott Gallery** (✉ 481 Howe St., ☎ 604/685–1934) specializes in Inuit art.

Books

Vancouver's two **Chapters** stores (✉ 788 Robson St., ☎ 604/682–4066; ✉ 2505 Granville St., at Broadway, ☎ 604/731–7822) are enormous, with a café in each location and a series of author readings and other performances. **Duthie Books** (✉ 2239 W. 4th Ave., ☎ 604/732–5344) is a long-established homegrown favorite. The store fell on hard times in 1999 and closed all branches but this one. **MacLeod's Books** (✉ 455 W. Pender St., ☎ 604/681–7654) is one of the city's best antiquarian and used bookstores. **Wanderlust** (✉ 1929 W. 4th Ave., ☎ 604/739–2182) carries thousands of travel books and maps, as well as luggage and travel accessories.

Clothes

For unique women's clothing, try **Dorothy Grant** (✉ 757 W. Hastings St., ☎ 604/681–0201), where traditional Haida designs meld with modern fashion. **Dream** (✉ 311 W. Cordova St., ☎ 604/683–7326) is where up-and-coming local designers sell their wares. **Leone** (✉ 757 W. Hastings St., ☎ 604/683–1133) is an ultrachic boutique, dividing designer collections in themed areas. Handmade Italian suits and other upscale menswear are sold at stylish **Madison Men's Wear** (✉ 1050 W. Pender St., ☎ 604/683–2122). If your tastes are traditional, don't miss **Straith** (✉ 900 W. Georgia St., ☎ 604/685–3301) in the Hotel Vancouver, offering tailored designer fashions for men and women. **Wear Else?** (✉ 2360 W. 4th Ave., ☎ 604/732–3521; ✉ 4401 W. 10th Ave., ☎ 604/221–7755; ✉ Oakridge Shopping Centre, 650 W. 41st Ave., at Cambie St., ☎ 604/266–3613) is a popular womenswear shop with attentive service. At **Versus** (✉ 1008 W. Georgia St., ☎ 604/688–8938) boutique, fashionable shoppers (men and women) sip cappuccino as they browse through stylish Italian designs.

Gifts

Museum and gallery gift shops are among the best places to buy high-quality souvenirs—West Coast native art, books, music, jewelry, and other items. Four noteworthy stores: the **Clamshell Gift Shop** (✉ Vancouver Aquarium Marine Science Centre, ☎ 604/659–3413) in Stanley Park; the **Gallery Shop** (✉ 750 Hornby St., ☎ 604/662–4706) in the Vancouver Art Gallery; the **Museum of Anthropology Gift Shop** (✉ 6393 N.W. Marine Dr., ☎ 604/822–3825) on the University of British Columbia campus; and the **Museum Shop** (✉ 639 Hornby St., ☎ 604/687–8266) in the Canadian Craft Museum.

Hill's Indian Crafts (✉ 165 Water St., ☎ 604/685–4249), in Gastown, has Vancouver's largest selection of First Nations art. **Leona Lattimer Gallery** (✉ 1590 W. 2nd Ave., ☎ 604/732–4556), near Granville Island, is full of native arts and crafts in all price ranges. At the **Salmon Shop** (✉ 1689 Johnston St., ☎ 604/669–3474), in the Granville Island Public Market, you can pick up smoked salmon wrapped for travel.

Jewelry
Vancouver's leading jewelry shops are clustered along Hastings Street. **Birks** (✉ 698 W. Hastings St., ☎ 604/669–3333) takes up the grand lower floor of a neo-classical building that was the former headquarters of the Canadian Imperial Bank of Commerce. **Cartier Jewellers** (✉ 408 Howe St., ☎ 604/683–6878) is the Vancouver outlet of the famous chain. **Palladio** (✉ 855 W. Hastings St., ☎ 604/685–3885) carries modern, high-fashion items

.Outdoor Equipment
Outdoor-oriented Vancouver is a great place to pick up camping and hiking gear. **Coast Mountain Sports** (✉ 2201 W. 4th Ave., ☎ 604/731–6181; ✉ Park Royal Shopping Centre, Marine Dr., West Vancouver, ☎ 604/926–6126) has high-performance (and high-fashion) gear. The massive **Mountain Equipment Co-op** (✉ 130 W. Broadway, ☎ 604/872–7858) is a local institution with a good selection of high-performance and midprice clothing and equipment. A one-time $5 membership is required. **The Three Vets** (✉ 2200 Yukon St., ☎ 604/872–5475), near Cambie Street and Broadway, is an army-surplus–style store with budget-price family camping equipment.

VANCOUVER A TO Z

Arriving and Departing

By Bus
Greyhound Lines (☎ 604/482–8747, 800/661–8747 in Canada, 800/231–2222 in the U.S.) is the largest bus line serving Vancouver. **Pacific Central Station** (✉ 1150 Station St.) is the depot for Greyhound Lines. **Quick Shuttle** (☎ 604/940–4428 or 800/665–2122) bus service runs between downtown Vancouver, Vancouver Airport, Seattle (Seatac) Airport, and downtown Seattle five times a day in winter and up to eight times a day in summer. The **downtown Vancouver depot** (✉ 180 W. Georgia St.) is at the Sandman Hotel.

By Car
Interstate 5 in Washington State becomes **Highway 99** at the U.S.–Canada border. Vancouver is a three-hour drive (226 km, or 140 mi) from Seattle. It's best to avoid border crossings during peak times such as holidays and weekends. Highway 1, the **Trans-Canada Highway,** enters Vancouver from the east. To avoid traffic, arrive after rush hour (8:30 AM).

By Ferry
B.C. Ferries (☎ 250/386–3431, 888/223–3779 in British Columbia) operates two major ferry terminals outside Vancouver. From Tsawwassen to the south (an hour's drive from downtown), ferries sail to Victoria and Nanaimo on Vancouver Island and to the Gulf Islands (the small

islands between the mainland and Vancouver Island). From Horseshoe
Bay (45 minutes north of downtown), ferries sail to the Sunshine Coast
and to Nanaimo on Vancouver Island. Vehicle reservations on Vancouver to Victoria and Nanaimo routes are optional and cost $15 in
addition to the fare.

By Plane

Vancouver International Airport (✉ Grant McConachie Way, Richmond,
☎ 604/276–6101) is on Sea Island, about 23 km (14 mi) south of downtown off Highway 99. An airport-improvement fee is assessed on all
flight departures: $5 for flights within British Columbia or the Yukon,
$10 for other flights within North America, and $15 for overseas
flights. Major credit cards (AE, DC, MC, V), and Canadian and U.S.
currency are accepted. Alaska, America West, American, British Airways, Continental, Northwest, Qantas, Reno, and United serve the airport. The two major domestic carriers are Air Canada and Canadian
Airlines. *See* Air Travel *in* Smart Travel Tips for airline numbers.

Air B.C. (☎ 604/688–5515, 888/247–2262 in British Columbia outside Vancouver and Victoria), operated by Air Canada, serves destinations around the province including the Vancouver airport. **West Coast
Air** (☎ 604/606–6888 or 800/347–2222) and **Harbour Air Seaplanes**
(☎ 604/688–1277 or 800/665–0212) both operate 35-minute harbor-
to-harbor service (downtown Vancouver to downtown Victoria) several times a day. Planes leave from near the Pan Pacific Hotel, which
is at 300–999 Canada Place. **Helijet Airways** (☎ 800/665–4354 or 604/
273–1414) has helicopter service from downtown Vancouver to downtown Seattle and Victoria. The heliport is near Vancouver's Pan Pacific Hotel.

BETWEEN THE AIRPORT AND DOWNTOWN
The drive from the airport to downtown takes 20 to 45 minutes, de-
pending on the time of day. Airport hotels provide free shuttle service
to and from the airport. If you're driving, go over the Arthur Laing
Bridge and north on Granville Street (also signposted as Highway 99).
Signs will direct you to Vancouver City Centre.

The **Vancouver Airporter Service** (☎ 604/946–8866) bus leaves the in-
ternational- and domestic-arrivals levels of the terminal building approximately every half hour, stopping at major downtown hotels. It
operates from 5:23 AM until midnight. The fare is $10 one way and
$17 round-trip.

Taxi stands are in front of the terminal building on domestic- and in-
ternational-arrivals levels. The taxi fare to downtown is about $22.
Area cab companies include **Black Top** (☎ 604/681–2181) and **Yellow**
(☎ 604/681–1111).

Limousine service from **LimoJet Gold** (☎ 604/273–1331) costs about
$34, a bit more than the taxi fare to downtown.

By Train

The **Pacific Central Station** (✉ 1150 Station St.), at Main Street and
Terminal Avenue, near the Main Street SkyTrain station, is the hub for
rail service. **Amtrak** (☎ 800/872–7245) operates the *Mt. Baker International* train between Seattle and Vancouver, and the *Cascades* high-
speed train service between Vancouver and Eugene, Oregon. **VIA Rail**
(☎ 800/561–8630 in Canada, 800/561–3949 in the U.S.) provides
transcontinental service through Jasper to Toronto three times a week.
Passenger trains leave the **BC Rail Station** (✉ 1311 W. 1st St., ☎ 604/
631–3500, 800/339–8752 in British Columbia, 800/663–8238 outside

British Columbia) in North Vancouver for Whistler and the interior of British Columbia.

Getting Around

By Bus

Exact change is needed to ride **TransLink** (☎ 604/521–0400) buses: $1.50 for normal rides or $2.25 for weekday trips to the suburbs, including the SeaBus to the North Shore. Books of 10 tickets are sold at convenience stores and newsstands; look for a red, white, and blue FARE DEALER sign. Day passes, good for unlimited travel all day, cost $6. They are available from fare dealers and at any SeaBus or SkyTrain station. Transfers (ask for one when you board) are valid for 90 minutes, allow travel in both directions, and are good on buses, SkyTrain, and SeaBus. A guide called "Discover Vancouver on Transit" is available free at the Tourist Info Centre (☞ Visitor Information *in* Contacts and Resources, *below*). Buses to West Vancouver (on the North Shore) are operated by West Vancouver Blue Buses (☎ 604/985–7777).

By Car

A car can be handy for touring areas outside the city center, but it isn't essential. On the compact downtown peninsula, however, it's generally easier to get around on foot or by public transport, especially in light of the congestion, limited parking, and many one-way streets. Vancouver's rush-hour traffic, about 7–9 weekday mornings and starting 3 PM weekday afternoons, can be horrendous. The worst bottlenecks outside the city center are the North Shore bridges (especially Lions Gate Bridge), the George Massey Tunnel on Highway 99 south of Vancouver, and Highway 1 through Coquitlam and Surrey. Parking downtown is expensive and tricky to find. Two large underground pay parking garages that usually have space are the **Library Square lot** (⊠ 775 Hamilton St., off Robson St., ☎ 604/669–4183) and the **Pacific Centre lot** (⊠ 700 block of Howe St., east side, ☎ 604/684–9715). Parking fees run about $6 to $10 a day. Don't leave anything in your car, even in the trunk; break-ins are quite common downtown (hotel parking tends to be more secure than public lots). Parking outside the downtown core is an easier proposition.

Right turns are allowed at most red lights after you've come to a full stop.

By Ferry

The **SeaBus** is a 400-passenger commuter ferry that crosses Burrard Inlet from Waterfront Station downtown to the foot of Lonsdale Avenue in North Vancouver. The ride takes 13 minutes and costs the same as the TransLink bus. With a transfer, connection can be made to any TransLink bus or SkyTrain. **Aquabus Ferries** (☎ 604/689–5858) and **False Creek Ferries** (☎ 604/684–7781), which are not part of the TransLink system, connect several stations on False Creek, including Science World, Granville Island, Stamp's Landing, Yaletown, Vanier Park, and the Hornby Street dock. Some Aquabus Ferries can take bicycles. The company also operates a historic 1950s wooden ferry on some runs.

By Rail

Part of an effort to revive streetcar service around False Creek, the volunteer-run **Downtown Historic Railway** (☎ 604/665–3903) operates two restored electric trams (built in 1905 and 1913) along a 5-km (3-mi) track between Science World and Granville Island. The trams, which also stop at First Avenue and Ontario Street and at Leg-in-Boot Square, near Sixth

Avenue and Moberly Street, operate 12:30 to 5 PM weekends and holidays from late May to early October. The adult fare is $2.

By Rapid Transit

A one-line, 25-km (16-mi) rapid-transit system called **SkyTrain** (☎ 604/521–0400) travels underground downtown and is elevated for the rest of its route to New Westminster and Surrey. A new line to Coquitlam was to be completed by 2001. Trains leave about every five minutes. Tickets, sold at each station from machines (correct change is not necessary), must be carried with you as proof of payment. You may use transfers from SkyTrain to SeaBus and TransLink buses (☞ *above*) and vice versa. SkyTrain is convenient for transit between downtown, B.C. Place Stadium, Pacific Central Station, and Science World.

By Taxi

It is difficult to hail a cab in Vancouver. Unless you're near a hotel, you'll have better luck calling a taxi service. Try **Black Top** (☎ 604/681–2181) or **Yellow** (☎ 604/681–1111).

Contacts and Resources

B&B Reservation Agencies

Super, Natural British Columbia (☎ 604/663–6000 or 888/435–5622) can book accommodation anywhere in British Columbia. **Town & Country Bed and Breakfast Reservation Service** (✉ Box 74542, 2803 W. 4th Ave., V6K 1K2, ☎ FAX 604/731–5942) specializes in B&Bs.

Car Rental

Avis (☎ 604/606–2847 or 800/331–1212). **Budget** (☎ 604/668–7000 or 800/527–0700). **Thrifty Car Rental** (☎ 604/606–1666 or 800/367–2277).

Consulates

Australia (✉ 1225-888 Dunsmuir St., ☎ 604/684–1177). **New Zealand** (✉ 1200-888 Dunsmuir St., ☎ 604/684–7388). **United Kingdom** (✉ 800-1111 Melville St., ☎ 604/683–4421). **United States** (✉ 1095 W. Pender St., ☎ 604/685–4311).

Emergencies

Ambulance, fire, police (☎ 911).**Medicentre** (✉ 1055 Dunsmuir St., lower level, ☎ 604/683–8138), a drop-in clinic in the Bentall Centre, is open weekdays. The emergency ward at **St. Paul's Hospital** (✉ 1081 Burrard St., ☎ 604/682–2344), a downtown facility, is open 24 hours.

Guided Tours

Tour prices fluctuate, so inquire about rates when booking. Kids are generally charged half the adult fare.

AIR

You can see Vancouver from the air for about $82 for 30 minutes, or take a 75-minute flight ($167–$188) over nearby mountains and glaciers with **Harbour Air Seaplanes** (☎ 604/688–1277), which leaves from beside the Pan Pacific Hotel. Tour Vancouver, the harbor, or the mountains of the North Shore by helicopter. For $100–$200 per person (minimum of three people), **Vancouver Helicopters** (☎ 604/270–1484) flies from the Harbour Heliport, downtown at 455 Waterfront Road, and the top of Grouse Mountain.

BIKE

By Cycle Tours (☎ 604/936–2453) runs bicycle tours around Vancouver. A unique way to see the heights of the city is on the Grouse Mountain downhill mountain-biking trip operated by **Velo-City Cycle Tours** (☎ 604/924–0288).

BOAT

Aquabus Ferries (☎ 604/689–5858) operates 25-minute minicruises around False Creek for about $6. From May through October, it also offers 45-minute tours of False Creek on a vintage wooden ferry, *The Rainbow Hunter,* for $8. The tours leave hourly from the Aquabus dock on Granville Island. **False Creek Ferries** (☎ 604/684–7781 has a 20-minute False Creek tour for $5, and a 40-minute tour for $8; both leave from Granville Island.

Harbour Cruises (✉ 1 N. Denman St., ☎ 604/688–7246), at the north foot of Denman Street on Coal Harbour, operates a 1¼-hour narrated tour of Burrard Inlet aboard the paddle wheeler MPV *Constitution.* Tours are given from April through October and cost less than $20. Harbour Cruises also offers sunset dinner cruises, four-hour lunch cruises up scenic Indian Arm, and links with the Royal Hudson Steam Train (☞ Train Tours, *below*) to make a daylong boat–train excursion to Howe Sound.

Paddlewheeler River Adventures (✉ 810 Quayside Dr., New Westminster, ☎ 604/525–4465 or 877/825–1302), in the Information Centre at Westminster Quay, will take you out on the Fraser River in an 1800s-style paddle wheeler. Choose from a two-hour Gold Rush–theme tour with a lunch buffet; a Wild West–theme day trip to historic Fort Langley; or a high-tea, Sunday-brunch, or sunset-dinner cruise.

ECOLOGY

In December and January, thousands of bald eagles gather at Brackendale, about an hour north of Vancouver. With **Canadian Outback Adventures** (☎ 604/921–7250 or 800/565–8735), you can watch and photograph the eagles from a slow-moving raft on the river. **Vancouver All-Terrain Adventures** (☎ 604/434–2278 or 888/754–5601) runs four-wheel-drive trips into the mountains near Vancouver, including an eagle-viewing trip.

A number of companies offer sea-kayaking trips out of Vancouver. Most trips offer a good chance of spotting orca whales, and some are suitable for first-timers. **Canadian Outback Adventure Company** (☞ *above*) guides river-rafting and sea-kayaking trips. **Ecosummer Expeditions** (☎ 250/674–0102 or 800/465–8884) offers sailing trips, in addition to sea kayaking. From May through October, **Lotus Land Tours** (☎ 604/684–4922 or 800/528–3531) runs a four-hour sea-kayak trip—including a salmon barbecue lunch—to Twin Island (an uninhabited provincial marine park) to explore marine life in the intertidal zone. Experience is not required; the kayaks are easy for beginners to handle. You can choose to take the same trip by motorboat. **Ocean West Expeditions** (☎ 800/660–0051), on English Bay beach at the foot of Denman Street, offers guided half-day sea-kayaking trips around English Bay and Stanley Park, as well as kayak rentals and multiday trips out of Vancouver.

FIRST NATIONS

West Coast City and Nature Sightseeing (☎ 604/451–1600) gives a daily, four-hour Native Culture tour, with expert guides offering insights into the history and culture of Vancouver-area First Nations peoples. The tours take in the Stanley Park totem poles, the Museum of Anthropology, and two community facilities—the First Nations House of Learning and the Native Education Centre. The $41 fee includes admission to the Museum of Anthropology.

HIKING

Hike B.C. (☎ 604/540–2499) conducts guided hikes and snowshoe trips to the North Shore mountains. **Path of Logic Wilderness Adventures** (☎ 604/802–2082) offers interpretive day hikes around Vancouver.

Guided walks through the rain forests and canyons surrounding the city, including a popular day trip to Bowen Island in Howe Sound, are run by **Rockwood Adventures** (☎ 604/926–7705 or 888/236–6606).

ORIENTATION

Gray Line (☎ 604/879–3363 or 800/667–0882) offers a 3½-hour Grand City bus tour year-round. The tour picks up at all major downtown hotels and includes Stanley Park, Chinatown, Gastown, English Bay, and Queen Elizabeth Park. The fee is about $39. From May through October, Gray Line also has a narrated city tour aboard double-decker buses; passengers can get on and off as they choose and can travel free the next day. Adult fare is about $22. The one-hour **Stanley Park Horse Drawn Tours** (☎ 604/681–5115) operate March 15–October and cost $16.80 per person ($52.30 for a family of four). The tours leave every 20 to 30 minutes from near the information booth on Stanley Park Drive. The **Vancouver Trolley Company** (☎ 604/801–5515 or 888/451–5581) runs old-style trolleys through Vancouver on a two-hour narrated tour of Stanley Park, Gastown, English Bay, Granville Island, and Chinatown, among other sights. A day pass allows you to complete one full circuit, getting off and on as often as you like. Start the trip at any of the 16 sights and buy a ticket ($23) on board. The four-hour City Highlights tour run by **West Coast City and Nature Sightseeing** (☎ 604/451–1600) is about $40. Pickup is available from all major hotels downtown.

North Shore tours usually include any or several of the following: a gondola ride up Grouse Mountain, a walk across the Capilano Suspension Bridge, a stop at a salmon hatchery, a visit to the Lonsdale Quay Market, and a ride back to town on the SeaBus. North Shore tours are offered mid-March–mid-October by **Landsea Tours** (☎ 604/255–7272) and all year by **West Coast City and Nature Sightseeing** (☎ 604/451–1600). The half-day tours are $45 to $55.

PERSONAL GUIDES

Early Motion Tours (☎ 604/687–5088) will pick you up at your hotel for a spin through Vancouver in a 1930 Model-A Ford convertible. **Vancouver All-Terrain Adventures** (☎ 604/434–2278 or 888/754–5601) offers customized city tours in a luxury four-wheel-drive Suburban at $75 an hour for up to seven passengers. Individualized tours in six European languages are available from **VIP Tourguide Services** (☎ 604/214–4677).

TRAIN

You can sample West Coast cuisine in the vintage rail coaches of the **Pacific Starlight Dinner Train** (☎ 604/631–3500, 800/339–8752 in British Columbia, 800/663–8238 outside British Columbia), which leaves the North Vancouver BC Rail station at 6:15 PM, stops at scenic Porteau Cove on Howe Sound, and returns to the station at 10 PM. The train runs Tuesday through Sunday, May through October. Fares, including a three-course meal, are $83.95 for salon seating, $99.95 for the dome car. Reservations are essential.

WALKING

Students from the **Architectural Institute of British Columbia** (☎ 604/683–8588) lead free 90-minute walking tours of the city's top heritage sites July through September. Ninety-minute walking tours of Chinatown leave from the **Chinese Cultural Centre** (✉ 50 E. Pender St., ☎ 604/687–7993). The tours usually are offered May through October (except Sunday) at noon and 2 PM, and cost $5. Call ahead to confirm times. The **Gastown Business Improvement Society** (☎ 604/683–5650) sponsors free 90-minute historical and architectural walking tours daily June through August. Meet the guide at 2 PM at the statue of "Gassy" Jack in Maple Tree Square. **Rockwood Adventures** (☎ 604/926–7705 or 888/236–6606) has guided walks around Vancouver neighborhoods, including Gastown, Granville Island, and Chinatown, and a special walk for art lovers. Guides with **Walkabout Historic Vancouver** (☎ 604/720–0006) take on the costume and the character of early residents for their two-hour historical walking tours around Downtown and Gastown or Granville Island. Tours run all year and cost $18.

Late-Night Pharmacy

Shopper's Drug Mart (✉ 1125 Davie St., ☎ 604/669–2424) is open around the clock.

Road Emergencies

The **British Columbia Automobile Association** (☎ 604/293–2222) provides 24-hour emergency road service for members of the American and the Canadian automobile associations.

Visitor Information

Super, Natural B.C. (☎ 888/435–5622). **Granville Island Information Centre** (✉ 1398 Cartwright St., ☎ 604/666–5784). **Vancouver Tourist Info Centre** (✉ 200 Burrard St., ☎ 604/683–2000).

3 VICTORIA AND VANCOUVER ISLAND

Islands have long held a fascination for travelers, and Vancouver Island, the largest island off North America's West Coast, is no exception. At 320 mi tip to tip, it offers an immense variety of landscapes—from the rolling farmland and protected beaches of the southeast, to the sparsely inhabited forests of the north and the crashing surf on the west. On the southern tip, Victoria, the capital of British Columbia, has shed its tea-cozy image and reemerged as a Pacific Rim metropolis that celebrates its native, Asian, and European roots.

EACHES, WILDERNESS PARKS, mountains, deep temperate rainforests, and a wealth of wildlife have long drawn adventurous
visitors to the West Coast's largest island. These days, however,
a slew of excellent restaurants, country inns, spas, and ecologically sen-
sitive resorts means visitors can enjoy all that beauty in comfort—though
roughing it is still an option.

By Sue
Kernaghan

Despite its growing popularity with visitors, the island rarely feels
crowded. Fewer than a million people live here, and virtually all of them
cluster on the island's sheltered eastern side, between Victoria and Campbell River; half live in Victoria itself. The island's west coast, facing
the open ocean, is wild and often inhospitable, with few roads and only
a handful of small settlements. Nevertheless, the old-growth forests,
magnificent stretch of beach, and challenging trails of the Pacific Rim
National Park Reserve, as well as the chance to see whales offshore,
are major draws for campers, hikers, kayakers, and even surfers.

As rich as Vancouver Island's natural bounty is the cultural heritage
of the Pacific Coast First Nations peoples—the Kwakiutl, Nootka, and
others—who occupied the land for more than 12,000 years before the first
Europeans arrived en masse in the late 19th century. Their art and culture
are on display throughout the island, in totems and petroglyphs, in city
art galleries, and in the striking collections at the Royal British Columbia
Museum in Victoria and the Cowichan Native Village in Duncan.

Pleasures and Pastimes

Dining
Restaurants are generally casual in the region. Smoking is banned in
all public places, including restaurants and bars, in Greater Victoria
and on the Gulf Islands.

CATEGORY	COST*
$$$$	over $35
$$$	$25–$35
$$	$15–$25
$	under $15

*per person, for a three-course meal, excluding drinks, service, and 7% GST

Lodging
Accommodations on Vancouver Island range from bed-and-breakfasts
and country inns to rustic cabins to deluxe ecotourism lodges. Victoria in particular has a great selection of English-style B&Bs. Most small
inns and B&Bs on the island ban smoking indoors, and virtually all
hotels in the area offer no-smoking rooms. Advance reservations are
always a good idea, especially in some of the more isolated towns.

CATEGORY	COST*
$$$$	over $250
$$$	$170–$250
$$	$90–$170
$	under $90

*All prices are for a standard double room, excluding 10% provincial ac-
commodation tax, service charge, and 7% GST.

🕮 *following the text of a review is your signal that the property has
a Web site, where you will find details and, usually, images; for a link,
visit www.fodors.com/urls.*

Outdoor Activities and Sports

CANOEING AND KAYAKING

The island-dotted Strait of Georgia, on the east side of Vancouver Island provides fairly protected sea-going, stunning scenery, and plenty of opportunities to spot orcas, eagles, and other local fauna. The Broken Group Islands, off the island's west coast, draw kayakers from around the world to their protected, wildlife-rich waters. The mountainous Strathcona Provincial Park offers scenic lake and river paddling.

FISHING

Miles of coastline and numerous lakes, rivers, and streams lure anglers to Vancouver Island. Though salmon doesn't run as thickly as it once did, both coasts of the island still provide excellent salmon-fishing opportunities, and many operators offer fishing charters.

HIKING

The West Coast Trail (☞ Pacific Rim National Park Reserve, *below*), one of the world's most famous trails, runs along the western side of Vancouver Island. Other trails also offer plenty of challenge, including the Juan de Fuca Marine Trail and those in Strathcona Provincial Park. But you'll find fine hiking-trail networks in virtually all of the island's many parks.

WHALE-WATCHING

Three resident and several transient pods of orcas (killer whales) travel the island's eastern coastal waters. These, and the gray whales living along the west coast, are the primary focus of the many whale-watching boat tours leaving Victoria, Telegraph Cove, Ucluelet, Bamfield, and Tofino during the spring and summer months. July, August, and September are the best months to see orcas; in March and April, thousands of migrating gray whales pass close to the west coast of Vancouver Island on their way from Baja California to Alaska. Harbor seals, sea lions, porpoises, and marine-bird sightings are a safe bet anytime.

First Nations Culture

Before the arrival of Europeans, the lush landscapes of the Pacific Northwest gave rise to one of the richest and most artistically prolific cultures on the continent. Two of the best places to appreciate it are Victoria's Royal British Columbia Museum and, in Duncan, the Cowichan Native Village, which is run by First Nations people.

Exploring Victoria and Vancouver Island

Vancouver Island, touched by Pacific currents, has the mildest climate in Canada. Temperatures are usually above 32°F in winter and below 80°F in summer, although winter brings frequent rains (especially on the west coast).

When traveling by car, keep in mind that most of Vancouver Island's west coast has very few roads and is accessible mainly by sea or air.

Numbers in the text correspond to numbers in the margin and on the Vancouver Island map.

Great Itineraries

IF YOU HAVE 1–3 DAYS

For a short trip, 🏛 **Victoria** ①–⑯ is a fine place to begin. There's plenty to explore, from the flower-fringed Inner Harbour and the museums and attractions nearby to Market Square and the red gates of Chinatown. World-famous Butchart Gardens is only half an hour away by car, and you might take a full day to explore the beautiful grounds. On Day 3, head west to 🏛 **Sooke** ⑰ or north, over the scenic Mala-

Vancouver Island

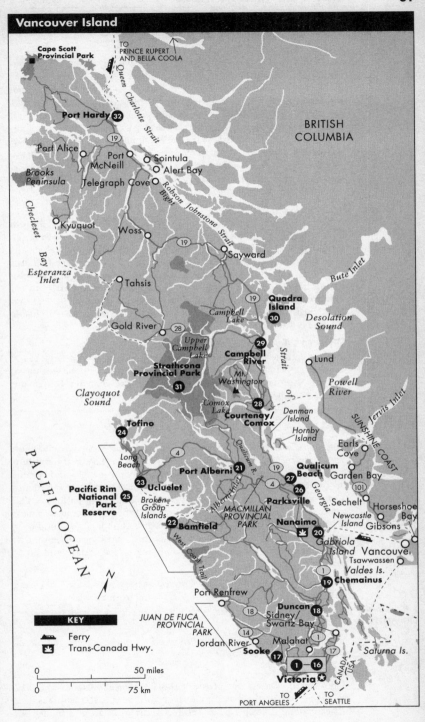

TO PRINCE RUPERT
AND BELLA COOLA

Cape Scott
Provincial Park

**BRITISH
COLUMBIA**

Queen Charlotte Strait

Port Hardy 32

Port Alice

19

Port
McNeill

Sointula

Alert Bay

*Brooks
Peninsula*

Telegraph Cove

Robson Bight

Robson Johnstone Strait

*Checleset
Bay*

Kyuquot

Woss

19

Sayward

*Esperanza
Inlet*

Tahsis

19

Bute Inlet

*Campbell
Lake*

**Quadra
Island** 30

*Desolation
Sound*

Gold River

28

*Upper
Campbell
Lake*

29

**Campbell
River**

Strait

Lund

**Strathcona
Provincial Park** 31

Mt.
Washington

*Powell
River*

*Clayoquot
Sound*

*Comox
Lake*

28

**Courtenay/
Comox**

of

*Denman
Island*

*Hornby
Island*

SUNSHINE COAST

Jervis Inlet

Tofino 24

*Long
Beach*

4

Oualicum R.

19

27

**Qualicum
Beach**

Earls
Cove

Port Alberni 21

Garden Bay

101

Ucluelet 23

25

**Pacific Rim
National
Park
Reserve**

*Broken
Group
Islands*

4

26

Parksville

Georgia

Sechelt

Horseshoe
Bay

*MACMILLAN
PROVINCIAL
PARK*

*Newcastle
Island*

Gibsons

Bamfield 22

Alberni Inlet

Nanaimo

20

*Gabriola
Island*

Vancouver

West Coast Trail

PACIFIC OCEAN

N

19 **Chemainus**

Tsawwassen

Valdes Is.

Port Renfrew

1

Duncan 18

18

*JUAN DE FUCA
PROVINCIAL
PARK*

Sidney/
Swartz Bay

1

Saturna Is.

14

Jordan River

Malahat

1

Sooke 17

17

CANADA
USA

1 — 16

Victoria ★

KEY

⚓ Ferry
🛡 Trans-Canada Hwy.

0   50 miles
0   75 km

TO
PORT ANGELES

TO
SEATTLE

hat region, to **Duncan** ⑱, **Chemainus** ⑲, or **Nanaimo** ⑳, which has ferry service to the mainland.

IF YOU HAVE 4–6 DAYS
A brief stay in ⚑ **Victoria** ①–⑯ can be followed by a tour of Vancouver Island. Follow the itinerary above, heading to **Sooke** ⑰ or **Nanaimo** ⑳ on Day 3. Day 4 allows time to see the Cowichan Native Village in **Duncan** ⑱ and the murals and restored Victorian buildings of ⚑ **Chemainus** ⑲. On Day 5, one alternative is to trek across the island to the scenic west coast to visit ⚑ **Tofino** ㉔ and ⚑ **Ucluelet** ㉓ (pick one for your overnight) and spend some time whale-watching or hiking around **Pacific Rim National Park Reserve** ㉕. Another choice is to continue up the east coast to visit **Strathcona Provincial Park** ㉛ or to do some salmon fishing from ⚑ **Campbell River** ㉙. Spend Day 6 retracing your steps to Victoria or Nanaimo', for ferry service to the mainland.

IF YOU HAVE 7–10 DAYS
A longer trip will allow more time to explore the area in and around the **Pacific Rim National Park Reserve** ㉕, or to visit **Bamfield** ㉒ or the **Broken Group Islands** on the *Lady Rose,* a coastal freighter that sails from **Port Alberni** ㉑. If you're exploring the east coast, you could visit one of the rustic off-shore islands; **Quadra** ㉚, **Denman,** and **Hornby** islands are all easily reached by ferry. Otherwise, head north toward **Port Hardy** ㉜ to see the resident whale pods near Telegraph Cove. From Port Hardy, you can continue a tour of British Columbia on an Inside Passage cruise.

When to Tour Vancouver Island

Though summer is the most popular time to visit, in winter the island has skiing at Mount Washington, near Courtenay, and, off the west coast, dramatic storms that can be fun to watch from a cozy inn. March and April are the best time to see migrating whales off the west coast.

VICTORIA

Originally Fort Victoria, Victoria was the first European settlement on Vancouver Island. It was chosen to be the westernmost trading outpost of the British-owned Hudson's Bay Company in 1843 and became the capital of British Columbia in 1868. Victoria has since evolved into a walkable, livable seaside town of gardens, waterfront pathways, and restored 19th-century architecture. Often described as the country's most British city, these days—except for the odd red phone box, good beer, and well-mannered drivers—Victoria has been working to change that image, preferring to celebrate its combined native, Asian, and European heritage.

The city is 71 km (44 mi), or 1½ hours by ferry plus 1½ hours by car, south of Vancouver, or a 2½-hour ferry ride from Seattle.

Downtown Victoria

Numbers in the text correspond to numbers in the margin and on the Downtown Victoria map.

A Good Walk

Begin on the waterfront at the **Visitors Information Centre,** at 812 Wharf St. Across the way on Government Street is **The Empress** ①, a majestic hotel that opened in 1908. A short walk around the harbor along the Inner Harbour Walk (take any of the staircases from Government Street down to the water level) will take you to the **Royal London Wax Museum** ②. Across Belleville Street is the **Parliament Buildings** ③ complex, seat of the provincial government. Cross Government Street to reach the **Royal British Columbia Museum** ④, one of Canada's most impressive museums. Behind the museum and bordering Douglas Street are the totem poles and ceremonial longhouse of Thunderbird Park; **Helmcken House** ⑤, the oldest house in Victoria; and the tiny 19th-century St. Ann's Schoolhouse. A walk south on Douglas Street leads to the beautiful **Beacon Hill Park** ⑥. A few blocks west of the park on Government Street is the **Emily Carr House** ⑦, the birthplace one of British Columbia's best-known artists. Walk back to Beacon Hill Park, and then proceed north on Douglas Street until you reach Blanshard Street, on your right. Take Blanshard, where just past Academy Close (on the right) you'll see the entrance to **St. Ann's Academy** ⑧, a former convent school with parklike grounds. (There's also a footpath to the academy from Southgate Street.) From St. Ann's, follow Belleville Street west. The next stop, at the corner of Douglas and Belleville streets, is the glass-roofed **Crystal Garden Conservation Centre** ⑨.

From Crystal Garden, head north on Douglas Street to View Street, about five blocks. Turn left at View Street, then right onto Broad Street. A half block up Broad Street you'll see the entrance to Trounce Alley, a pretty pedestrian-only shopping arcade. At the far end of Trounce Alley and across Government Street is the entrance to **Bastion Square** ⑩, with restaurants and small shops. While you're here, you can stop in the **Maritime Museum of British Columbia** ⑪ to learn about an important part of the province's history. Around the corner (to the south) on Wharf Street is the **Victoria Bug Zoo** ⑫, a creepy-crawly attraction popular with kids. North of Bastion Square a few blocks, on Store Street between Johnson Street and Pandora Avenue is **Market Square** ⑬, one of the city's most picturesque shopping districts. Across Pandora Avenue is the entrance to the narrow, shop-lined Fan Tan Alley, which leads to Fisgard Street, the heart of **Chinatown** ⑭.

You can head back south on Government Street until you hit Fort Street. From here, a 25-minute walk or a short drive east will take you to Joan Crescent and lavish **Craigdarroch Castle** ⑮. Down the hill on Moss Street is the **Art Gallery of Greater Victoria** ⑯.

In summer, a ride on Harbour Ferries (☞ Victoria A to Z, *below*) from the Inner Harbour will take you to **Point Ellice House,** a historic waterside home and garden.

TIMING

Many of the attractions in downtown Victoria are within easy walking distance of one another. You can walk this tour in a day, but there's so much to see at the Royal British Columbia Museum and the other museums that you could easily fill two days. This would allow time for some shopping and a visit to Craigdarroch Castle.

Sights to See

⑯ **Art Gallery of Greater Victoria.** This fine museum houses large collections of Chinese and Japanese ceramics and other art and has the only authentic Shinto shrine in North America. A permanent exhibit of British Columbian artist Emily Carr's work is on display. The gallery is a few blocks west of Craigdarroch Castle, off Fort Street. ⌧ *1040 Moss St.,* ☎ *250/384–4101.* ⌧ *$5, Mon. by donation.* ☼ *Mon.–Wed. and Fri.– Sat. 10–5, Thurs. 10–9, Sun. 1–5.*

⑩ **Bastion Square.** James Douglas, the fur trader and former colonial governor for whom Douglas Street was named, chose this spot for the original Fort Victoria and Hudson's Bay Company trading post. Offices, boutiques, and restaurants occupy the old buildings. ⌧ *Off Wharf St. at the end of View St.*

Downtown Victoria

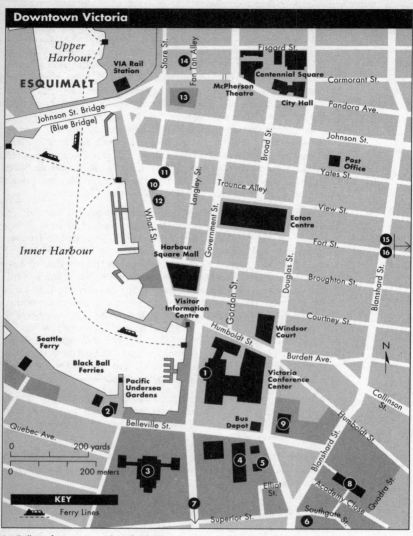

Upper Harbour

ESQUIMALT

VIA Rail Station

Store St.

Fan Tan Alley

14

Fisgard St.

Centennial Square

Cormorant St.

McPherson Theatre

13

City Hall

Pandora Ave.

Johnson St. Bridge (Blue Bridge)

Broad St.

Johnson St.

Post Office

11

10

Langley St.

Trounce Alley

Yates St.

View St.

Eaton Centre

12

Wharf St.

Inner Harbour

Harbour Square Mall

Government St.

Fort St.

15

16

Douglas St.

Broughton St.

Blanshard St.

Visitor Information Centre

Gordon St.

Courtney St.

Humboldt St.

Windsor Court

Seattle Ferry

Burdett Ave.

N

Black Ball Ferries

1

Victoria Conference Center

Pacific Undersea Gardens

2

Belleville St.

Bus Depot

9

Collinson St.

Quebec Ave.

0   200 yards

0   200 meters

3

4

5

Humboldt St.

Blanshard St.

8

Quadra St.

KEY

Elliot St.

Academy Close

Ferry Lines

7

Southgate St.

6

Superior St.

Art Gallery of Greater Victoria . . . **16**

Bastion Square **10**

Beacon Hill Park **6**

Chinatown **14**

Craigdarroch Castle **15**

Crystal Garden Conservation Centre **9**

Emily Carr House . . **7**

The Empress **1**

Helmcken House **5**

Maritime Museum of British Columbia . . . **11**

Market Square **13**

Parliament Buildings **3**

Royal British Columbia Museum **4**

Royal London Wax Museum **2**

St. Ann's Academy **8**

Victoria Bug Zoo . . . **12**

★ ⌚ ❻ **Beacon Hill Park.** The southern lawns of this spacious park have great views of the Olympic Mountains and the Strait of Juan de Fuca. Also here are ponds, jogging and walking paths, abundant flowers and gardens, a petting zoo, and a cricket pitch. The park is also home to Mile Zero of the Trans-Canada Highway. ⊠ *East of Douglas St., south of Southgate St.*

OFF THE
BEATEN PATH

BUTCHART GARDENS – Originally a private estate and still family-run, this stunning 50-acre garden about 21 km (13 mi) north of downtown Victoria has been drawing visitors since it was planted in a limestone quarry in 1904. The site's Japanese, Italian, rose, and sunken gardens grow 700 varieties of flowers in a setting that's beautiful year-round. From mid-June to mid-September, the gardens are illuminated at night, and musicians and other entertainers perform in the afternoons and evenings. In July and August, fireworks light the sky over the gardens on Saturday nights. Bring a picnic if you'd like, or you can eat at one of the restaurants on the premises. There's also a seed and gift shop. ⊠ *800 Benvenuto Ave., Brentwood Bay,* ☎ *250/652–5256, 250/652–4422, 250/652–8222 for dining reservations.* ☲ *June 15–Sept., $16.50; Oct.–Nov. $11.75; Dec.–Jan. 6 $12.25; Jan. 7–Mar. $7.75; Apr.–June 14 $12.75.* ☉ *June 15–Sept. 4, daily 9 AM–10:30 PM; Sept. 5–15, daily 9–9; Sept. 16–June 14, 9 AM–dusk.* ☙

❶❹ **Chinatown.** Chinese immigrants built much of the Canadian Pacific Railway in the 19th century, and their influence still marks the region. Victoria's Chinatown, founded in 1858, is the oldest and most intact such district in Canada. If you enter Chinatown from Government Street, you'll pass under the elaborate **Gate of Harmonious Interest,** made of Taiwanese ceramic tiles and decorative panels. Along Fisgard Street, merchants display paper lanterns, embroidered silks, and produce. Mah-jongg, fan-tan, and dominoes were among the games of chance played on narrow **Fan Tan Alley.** Once the gambling and opium center of Chinatown, it's now lined with offbeat shops. Look for the alley on the south side of Fisgard Street between Nos. 545½ and 549½.

❶❺ **Craigdarroch Castle.** This resplendent mansion was built as the home of one of British Columbia's wealthiest men, coal baron Robert Dunsmuir, who died in 1889, just a few months before the castle's completion. Converted into a museum depicting life in the late 1800s, the castle has ornate Victorian furnishings, stained-glass windows, carved woodwork (precut in Chicago for Dunsmuir and sent by rail), and a beautifully restored ceiling frieze in the drawing room. A winding staircase climbs four floors to a ballroom and a tower overlooking Victoria and the Olympic Mountains. ⊠ *1050 Joan Crescent,* ☎ *250/592–5323.* ☲ *$8.* ☉ *Mid-June–early Sept., daily 9–7; mid-Sept.–mid-June, daily 10–4:30.*

⌚ ❾ **Crystal Garden Conservation Centre.** Opened in 1925 as the largest saltwater swimming pool in the British Empire, this glass-roof building today houses exotic flora and a variety of endangered tropical mammals, reptiles, and birds, including flamingos, tortoises, macaws, lemurs, bats, and butterflies. ⊠ *713 Douglas St.,* ☎ *250/953–8800.* ☲ *$7.50.* ☉ *July–Aug., daily 8:30–8; Sept.–Oct. and Apr.–June, daily 9–6; Nov.–Mar., daily 10–4:30.*

❼ **Emily Carr House.** One of Canada's most celebrated artists and a respected writer, Emily Carr (1871–1945) was born and raised in this very proper wooden Victorian house before abandoning her middle-class life to live in, and paint, the wilds of British Columbia. Carr's own descriptions, from her autobiography *Book of the Small,* were used to restore the house. Occasional exhibitions of her work are also held here. ✉ *207 Government St.,* ☎ *250/383–5843.* 🎫 *$5.* ☉ *Mid-May–mid-Oct., daily 10–5; Dec. 1–24 and Dec. 27–31, daily 11–4. By arrangement rest of the year.*

❶ **The Empress.** A symbol of the city and the Canadian Pacific Railway, the Empress was designed by Francis Rattenbury, who also designed the Parliament Buildings. The elements that made the château-style structure a tourist attraction in the past—Old World architecture, an ornate decor, and a commanding view of the Inner Harbour—are still here. You can stop in for afternoon tea, which is served daily (reservations are recommended, and the dress code calls for smart casual wear). The archives, a historical photo display, are open to the public anytime. **Miniature World** (☎ *250/385–9731*), a display of doll-size dioramas, is on the Humboldt Street side of the complex. ✉ *721 Government St.,* ☎ *250/384–8111.* 🎫 *Free; afternoon tea $39 in peak season; Miniature World $8.*

OFF THE
BEATEN PATH

FORT RODD HILL AND FISGARD LIGHTHOUSE – This 1895 coast artillery fort and the oldest (and still functioning) lighthouse on Canada's west coast are about 15 km (9 mi) west of Victoria, off Highway 1A on the way to Sooke. Next door is **Hatley Castle** (✉ 2005 Sooke Rd., ☎ 250/391–2511). The former estate of coal and railway baron James Dunsmuir, the 1909 castle is set in 650 acres of beautifully landscaped grounds (including Italian, Japanese, and English rose gardens) that are open daily until dusk all year. Garden and castle tours are given daily in summer (call for times). ✉ 603 Fort Rodd Hill Rd., ☎ 250/478–5849. 🎫 $4. ☉ Mar.–Oct., daily 10–5:30; Nov.–Feb., daily 9–4:30.

❺ **Helmcken House.** The oldest house in Victoria was erected in 1852 for pioneer doctor and statesman John Sebastian Helmcken. Audio tours of the house, whose holdings include the family's original early Victorian furnishings and the doctor's 19th-century medical tools, last 20 minutes. Next door are **St. Ann's Schoolhouse,** one of the first schools in British Columbia (you can view the interior through the door), and **Thunderbird Park,** with totem poles and a ceremonial longhouse constructed by Kwakwaka'wakw chief Mungo Martin. ✉ *10 Elliot St., near Douglas and Belleville streets,* ☎ *250/361–0021.* 🎫 *$5.* ☉ *May–Oct., daily 10–5; Nov.–Apr., Thurs.–Mon. noon–4.*

✋ ⓫ **Maritime Museum of British Columbia.** The dugout canoes, model ships, Royal Navy charts, photographs, uniforms, and ship bells at this museum, in Victoria's original courthouse, chronicle the city's seafaring history. A 100-year-old, hand-operated cage elevator, believed to be the oldest in North America, ascends to the third floor, where the original 1888 admiralty courtroom looks set for a court-martial. ✉ *28 Bastion Sq.,* ☎ *250/385–4222.* 🎫 *$5.* ☉ *June–Labor Day, daily 9:30–8:30; Sept.–May, daily 9:30–4:30.*

⓭ **Market Square.** During the late 19th century, this three-level square, built like an old inn courtyard, provided everything a sailor, miner, or lumberjack could want. Restored to its original architectural, if not commercial, character, it's a pedestrian-only, café- and boutique-lined hangout—now, as then, a great spot for people-watching. ✉ *560 Johnson St.,* ☎ *250/386–2441.*

★ ❸ **Parliament Buildings.** These massive stone structures, designed by Francis Rattenbury and completed in 1898, dominate the Inner Harbour. Two statues flank them: one of Sir James Douglas, who chose the site where Victoria was built, and the other of Sir Matthew Baille Begbie, the man in charge of law and order during the gold-rush era.

Atop the central dome is a gilded statue of Capt. George Vancouver, the first European to sail around Vancouver Island. A statue of Queen Victoria reigns over the front of the complex. The Parliament Buildings, which are outlined with more than 3,000 lights at night, typify the rigid symmetry and European elegance of much of the city's architecture. When the legislature is in session, you can sit in the public gallery and watch British Columbia's often polarized democracy at work (custom has the opposing parties sitting 2½ sword lengths apart). Free, informative half-hour tours are obligatory on summer weekends and optional the rest of the time. ⊠ *501 Belleville St.,* ☎ *250/387–3046.* ▨ *Free.* ⊘ *June–Aug., daily 8:30–5; Sept.–May, weekdays 8:30–5.* ⊛

OFF THE
BEATEN PATH

POINT ELLICE HOUSE – The O'Reilly family home, an 1867 Italianate villa overlooking the Upper Harbour, has been restored to its original splendor, with the largest collection of Victorian furnishings in Western Canada. Tea and baked goods are served on the lawn. Visitors can also take an audio tour of the house, stroll in the gardens, or try their hand at croquet. Point Ellice House is a few minutes' drive north of downtown, but it's much more fun to come by sea. Harbour Ferries (☞ Getting Around *in* Victoria A to Z, *below*) leave from a dock in front of The Empress hotel. ⊠ *2616 Pleasant St.,* ☎ *250/380–6506.* ▨ *$5; $17 including tea.* ⊘ *Mid-May–June and Sept. 1–15, daily noon–5; July–Aug., daily 10–5. Tea daily noon–4.*

★ ☙ ❹ **Royal British Columbia Museum.** The museum, easily the best attraction in Victoria, is as much a research and educational center as a draw for the public. The definitive First Peoples exhibit includes a genuine Kwakwaka'wakw longhouse (the builders retain rights to its ceremonial use) and provides insights into the daily life, art, and mythology of both coastal and lesser-known interior peoples, before and after the arrival of Europeans. The Modern History Gallery re-creates most of a frontier town, complete with cobblestone streets, silent movies, and rumbling train sounds. The Natural History Gallery realistically reproduces the sights, sounds, and smells of many of the province's natural habitats, and the Open Ocean mimics, all too realistically, a submarine journey. A 20th Century Gallery, opened in 1999, reviews British Columbia's most recent 100 years; an IMAX theater shows National Geographic films on a six-story-tall screen. ⊠ *675 Belleville St.,* ☎ *250/387–3701 or 800/661–5411.* ▨ *$10.65; IMAX theater $9; combination ticket $17.40.* ⊘ *Museum daily 9–5, theater daily 10–8.* ⊛

❷ **Royal London Wax Museum.** A collection of life-size wax figures resides in this elegant colonnaded building, once Victoria's steamship terminal. The 300-plus characters include members of the British royal family, famous Canadians, Hollywood stars, and some unfortunate souls in a Chamber of Horrors. ⊠ *470 Belleville St.,* ☎ *250/388–4461.* ▨ *$8.* ⊘ *May–Aug., daily 9–7; Sept.–Apr., daily 9:30–5.*

❽ **St. Ann's Academy.** This former convent and school, founded in 1858, played a central role in British Columbia's pioneer life. Closed in 1974, it was carefully restored and reopened as a historic site in 1997. The academy's little chapel—the first Roman Catholic cathedral in Victoria—now looks just as it did in the 1920s. The six acres of grounds, with their fruit trees and herb and flower gardens, are being restored as historic landscapes. ⊠ *835 Humboldt St.,* ☎ *250/953–8828.* ▨ *Free.* ⊘ *July–Aug., daily 10–4; May–June and Sept.–Oct., Wed.–Sun. 10–4. Call for winter hrs.*

☙ ⓬ **Victoria Bug Zoo.** Kids of all ages are drawn to this offbeat, two-room minizoo. Many of the bugs—mostly large tropical varieties, such as stick insects, scorpions, and centipedes—can be held, and staff members are on hand to dispense scientific information. ⊠ *1107 Wharf St.,* ☎ *250/384–2847.* ◳ *$6.* ◷ *July–Aug., daily 9–9; Sept.–June, daily 9:30–5:30.*

Visitor Information Centre. You can get the lowdown on Victoria's tourist and other attractions at this facility near the harbor ferries. The staff here can help you out with maps, theater and concert tickets, accommodation reservations, and outdoor adventure day trips. ⊠ *812 Wharf St.,* ☎ *250/953–2033.* ◷ *July–Aug., daily 8:30–8; May–June and Sept., daily 9–7; Oct.–Apr., daily 9–5.*

Dining

Chinese
$$–$$$$ ✕ **Don Mee's.** A large neon sign invites you inside this traditional Chinese restaurant that's been in business since 1923. The entrées served in the expansive dining room include sweet-and-sour chicken, Peking duck, and ginger fried beef. Dim sum is served at lunchtime. ⊠ *538 Fisgard St.,* ☎ *250/383–1032. AE, DC, MC, V.*

Contemporary
$$$$ ✕ **The Victorian Restaurant.** This small, formal restaurant in the Ocean Pointe Resort Hotel and Spa has striking views over the Inner Harbour. The chef offers such elegantly presented regional dishes as wild mushroom and truffle soup, roast rack of lamb with maple and juniper glaze, and pheasant breast with goat cheese and sun-dried cranberry mousse. The wine list has won a number of awards, including Wine Spectator's Award of Excellence in 1999. ⊠ *Ocean Pointe Resort Hotel and Spa, 45 Songhees Rd. (across the Johnson Street Bridge from downtown Victoria),* ☎ *250/360–5800. Reservations essential. AE, DC, MC, V. Closed Jan. and Mon.–Tues. in Nov.–Apr. No lunch.*

$$$–$$$$ ✕ ★**Camille's.** The menu at quiet and intimate Camille's emphasizes fresh local products and such exotica as ostrich, quail, and emu. These and favorites including the mint-and-mustard-crusted lamb and the roast venison with wild-mushroom polenta are served in a candlelit setting on the lower floor of a historic brick building in Bastion Square. This long-established restaurant has one of Victoria's better wine cellars, and the owners—husband-and-wife team David Mincy and Paige Robinson—often hold wine tastings and seminars. ⊠ *45 Bastion Sq.,* ☎ *250/381–3433. AE, MC, V. No lunch.*

$$$–$$$$ ✕ **Cassis.** This intimate family-run restaurant in Cook Street Village, a few minutes' drive from the Inner Harbour, has the casual elegance of a French neighborhood bistro. The food, however, is creative and contemporary, with a focus on local ingredients. Highlights of the brief, seasonally changing menu include Pacific salmon with shallots, vermouth, fresh sorrel, and cream; and boneless lamb strip loin with ginger, shallots, honey, brandy, and cream. Vegetarian selections, such as a North African vegetable stew and a mushroom, leek, and fennel risotto, are always on offer. The Sunday brunch is popular. ⊠ *253 Cook St.,* ☎ *250/384–1932. Reservations essential. MC, V. Closed Mon. No lunch Tues.–Sat.*

$$$–$$$$ ✕ **Empress Room.** Beautifully presented Pacific Northwest cuisine vies
★   for attention with the elegant setting, where candlelight dances on tapestried walls beneath a carved mahogany ceiling. Fresh local ingredients go into imaginative seasonal dishes such as wild-mushroom-and-chicken terrine, veal tenderloin with a wild rice–herb crust, and Fraser Valley smoked marinated duck breast. The 500-label wine list is excellent, as are the table d'hôte menus. ⊠ *The Empress, 721 Gov-*

ernment St., ☎ *250/389–2727 or 800/644–6611. Reservations essential. AE, D, DC, MC, V. No lunch.*

$$–$$$$ ✕ **Cafe Brio.** A little north of the Inner Harbour, a building resembling
★ an Italian villa is the setting for one of Victoria's most enjoyable restaurants. Candlelight, hardwood floors, lush Modigliani nudes, and rich gold walls create a warm glow. The daily menu depends on what's fresh that day—very fresh. The café works in partnership with local organic farms and serves the produce the same day it's harvested. Favorites have included confit of duck with three-bean, pancetta, and tomato braise; rack of lamb that melts in your mouth; and seared jumbo Alaskan scallops served with preserved lemon and sorrel butter. The vegetarian options are always good, and the extensive wine list goes easy on the markups. ✉ *944 Fort St.,* ☎ *250/383–0009. AE, MC, V. No lunch Sat.–Mon.*

$$–$$$$ ✕ **Herald Street Caffe.** Intriguing combinations are the hallmarks of
★ this art-filled bistro in Victoria's warehouse district. The menu, which changes seasonally, always lists fresh local cuisine, daily fish grills, great pastas, and good vegetarian selections. Try, if available, a starter of East Coast mussels steamed in a lemon Szechuan peppercorn pesto, followed by calamari in tomato–dill ratatouille with crumbled feta, or free-range beef tenderloin stuffed with a wild mushroom–chestnut paté. The wine list is excellent. The restaurant's jazz lounge is open for dinner as well as for late-night snacks until 1:30 AM Thursday to Sunday. ✉ *546 Herald St.,* ☎ *250/381–1441. Reservations essential. AE, DC, MC, V. No lunch Mon.–Tues.*

Eclectic

$$–$$$ ✕ **Süze Lounge and Restaurant.** Gothic candelabras, red velveteen drapes, exposed brick, a vintage mahogany bar, and a long martini list give this friendly, downtown lounge and restaurant a stylish air. The frequently changing menu features pastas, pizzas, risottos, and some creative Asia-influenced dishes. Try, if it's available, the ginger chicken on a sugarcane spear with lemon–sesame drizzle; the duck confit with roasted-garlic mashed potatoes; or the pad Thai—a spicy dish of vegetables with peanut sauce and cilantro. Luscious desserts (the chocolate lava bomb is highly decadent) and a wide range of teas are also specialties. The patio is a popular summer hangout, and dinner is served until midnight Sunday to Wednesday, and until 1 AM the rest of the week. ✉ *515 Yates St.,* ☎ *250/383–2829. AE, DC, MC, V. Reservations essential. No lunch.*

Indian

$$ ✕ **Bengal Lounge.** Buffet lunches and dinners in the elegant Empress hotel include curries with extensive condiment trays of coconut, nuts, cool *raita* (yogurt with mint or cucumber), and chutney. Popular with cabinet ministers and bureaucrats, the curries are almost as much a Victorian tradition as afternoon tea. ✉ *The Empress, 721 Government St.,* ☎ *250/384–8111. AE, D, DC, MC, V. No dinner buffet Fri.–Sat.*

Italian

$$$–$$$$ ✕ **Il Terrazzo.** A charming redbrick terrace edged by potted greenery
★ and warmed by fireplaces and overhead heaters makes Il Terrazzo—tucked away off Waddington Alley near Market Square and not visible from the street—the locals' choice for romantic alfresco dining. Scallops dipped in roasted pistachios and garnished with arugula, Belgian endive, and mango salsa; grilled lamb chops on angel-hair pasta with tomatoes, garlic, mint, and black pepper; and other hearty northern Italian dishes come piping hot from the restaurant's wood oven. ✉ *555 Johnson St., off Waddington Alley (call for directions),* ☎ *250/*

361–0028. Reservations essential. AE, MC, V. No lunch Sun.; no lunch Sat. Oct. –Apr.

Seafood

$$$–$$$$ ✕ **Blue Crab Bar and Grill.** Fresh daily seafood and expansive Inner Harbour views make this modern and airy restaurant a popular lunch and dinner spot. Signature dishes include pan-roasted Pacific salmon fillet with a hazelnut crust, and a West Coast fish pot (like bouillabaisse)in a lemon crab–infused Dungeness crab broth, though the long list of daily specials posted on the blackboard is always tempting. Breads and desserts, made in-house, and a primarily British Columbia and California wine list round out the menu. The attached lounge area, open until 1 AM nightly, has lower priced seafood entrées and equally impressive views. ⊠ *Coast Harbourside Hotel and Marina, 146 Kingston St.,* ☎ *250/480–1999. AE, D, DC, MC, V.*

$$–$$$$ ✕ **The Marina Restaurant.** A prime spot for Sunday brunch, the Marina has a 180° view over Oak Bay. The extensive menu usually lists a variety of pastas, grills, and seafood entrées. There's also a sushi bar. Downstairs is a more casual café-deli with seating on the patio overlooking the marina. ⊠ *1327 Beach Dr.,* ☎ *250/598–8555. AE, DC, MC, V.*

$ ✕ **Barb's Place.** Funky Barb's, a blue-painted take-out shack, sits out where the fishing boats dock, west of the Inner Harbour off Erie Street. Locals consider the authentic fish and chips to be the best in town. You can catch a ferry to Fisherman's Wharf from the Inner Harbour, pick up an order, and take another ferry to Songhees Point for a picnic. ⊠ *Fisherman's Wharf, 310 St. Lawrence St.,* ☎ *250/384–6515. No credit cards. Closed Nov.–Mar.*

Thai

$$–$$$ ✕ **Siam Thai.** The chefs here work wonders with both hot and mild Thai dishes that you can wash down with any of several good beers. The *pad Thai goong* (fried rice noodles with prawns, tofu, peanuts, eggs, bean sprouts, and green onions) and *satay* (grilled, marinated cubes of meat served with a spicy peanut sauce) are good options. ⊠ *512 Fort St.,* ☎ *250/383–9911. AE, DC, MC, V. No lunch Sun.*

Vegetarian

$$ ✕ **Re-Bar Modern Food.** Bright and casual, this kid-friendly café in Bastion Square is *the* place for vegetarians in Victoria; the almond burgers, wild-mushroom ravioli, decadent home-baked goodies, and big breakfasts will keep omnivores happy, too. An extensive tea and fresh-juice selection shares space with espresso, microbrews, and local wines on the drinks list. ⊠ *50 Bastion Sq.,* ☎ *250/361–9223. AE, MC, V. No dinner Sun.–Mon., Oct.–Mar.*

Vietnamese

$$–$$$ ✕ **Le Petit Saigon.** The fare is Vietnamese with French influences at this intimate café-style restaurant. The crab, asparagus, and egg-swirl soup is a specialty, and combination meals are inexpensive and tasty. ⊠ *1010 Langley St.,* ☎ *250/386–1412. AE, MC, V. No lunch Sun.*

Lodging

$$$$ 🏨 **The Aerie.** The million-dollar view of Finlayson Arm and the Gulf ★ Islands persuaded Maria Schuster to build her luxury resort on this scenic hilltop, 30 km (19 mi) north of Victoria. Most of the plush rooms in the Mediterranean-style villa have a patio, a fireplace, and a whirlpool tub; smoking isn't allowed indoors. Chocolate truffles and fresh flowers are just part of the pampering treatment that also includes a full-service Aveda spa. The dining room, with its stunning views over the Gulf Islands, is open to the public for lunch and dinner. The top-notch

Pacific Northwest cuisine relies almost exclusively on local ingredients and incorporates organic products and heritage produce varieties into its à la carte, vegetarian, and multicourse tasting menus. Full breakfast is included. ✉ *600 Ebedora La., Box 108, Malahat V0R 2L0,* ☎ *250/743–7115 or 800/518–1933,* FAX *250/743–4766. 11 rooms, 12 suites. Restaurant, bar, fans, indoor pool, indoor and outdoor hot tubs, sauna, spa, tennis court, hiking, library, meeting room, helipad. AE, DC, MC, V.* 🐢

$$$$ 🏨 **Coast Harbourside Hotel and Marina.** West of the Inner Harbour, the Coast Harbourside has water views but is removed from the traffic on Government Street. From the mahogany-panel lobby and the soothing color schemes in average-size guest rooms to an extensive health club, the hotel is all about relaxation in modern comfort. Fishing and whale-watching charters and the harbor ferries stop at the hotel's marina, and there's a free downtown shuttle. The Blue Crab Bar and Grill (☞ Dining, *above*) is a popular dining spot. ✉ *146 Kingston St., V8V 1V4,* ☎ *250/360–1211 or 800/663–1144,* FAX *250/360–1418. 126 rooms, 6 suites. Restaurant, bar, minibars, no-smoking rooms, room service, indoor-outdoor pool, hot tub, sauna, exercise room, dock, laundry service, business services, meeting rooms, free parking. AE, DC, MC, V.* 🐢

$$$$ 🏨 **The Empress.** For empire builders, movie stars, and a great many
★ others, the exquisitely comfortable Empress is the only place to stay in Victoria. Opened in 1908, this Canadian Pacific château has aged gracefully, with sympathetically restored Edwardian decor, discreet modern amenities, and service standards that recall a more gracious age. A concierge floor, called Entrée Gold, provides boutique-hotel intimacy within the larger hotel. ✉ *721 Government St., V8W 1W5,* ☎ *250/384–8111 or 800/441–1414,* FAX *250/381–4334. 474 rooms, 36 suites. 2 restaurants, lounge, fans, no-smoking rooms, room service, indoor pool, wading pool, hot tub, sauna, spa, exercise room, laundry service, concierge, concierge floor, business services, convention center, parking (fee). AE, D, DC, MC, V.* 🐢

$$$$ 🏨 **Humboldt House.** If you're looking for somewhere to, say, hide an engagement ring in a glass of champagne, Humboldt House should do the trick. This unabashedly romantic hideaway, in a prettily restored Victorian on a quiet side street, has five rooms, each with elaborate boudoir decor, a wood-burning fireplace, down duvets, a CD player, fresh flowers, candles, and a big round whirlpool tub on a platform in the bedroom; though, for romance's sake, rooms don't have phones or TVs. (There's also a pretty two-bedroom cottage about 1 km, or ½ mi, south of the house.)There's sherry in the red velvet parlor and champagne and chocolate truffles to greet you in your room, but the real treat arrives in the morning: a picnic basket loaded with breakfast goodies and delivered to your room by dumbwaiter. ✉ *867 Humboldt St., V8V 2Z6,* ☎ *250/383–0152 or 888/383–0327,* FAX *250/383–6402. 5 rooms, 1 cottage. Refrigerators, free parking. MC, V.* 🐢

$$$$ 🏨 **Ocean Pointe Resort Hotel and Spa.** Across the "blue bridge" (John-
★ son Street Bridge) from downtown Victoria, the waterfront Ocean Pointe has a resort's worth of facilities, including a full spa. The hotel's striking two-story lobby and half of its guest rooms offer romantic views of the Inner Harbour and the lights of the Parliament Buildings across the water. Standard rooms are spacious and airy, and the apartment-size suites have kitchenettes and separate living and dining areas. The Victorian Restaurant (☞ Dining, *above*) serves fine Pacific Northwest cuisine in a scenic setting. ✉ *45 Songhees Rd., V9A 6T3,* ☎ *250/360–2999 or 800/667–4677,* FAX *250/360–5856. 212 rooms, 34 suites. 2 restaurants, bar, wine shop, air-conditioning, in-room data ports, minibars, room service, indoor pool, hot tub, sauna, 2 tennis courts, health*

*club, jogging, racquetball, squash, shops, baby-sitting, laundry service,
concierge, business services, meeting rooms, travel services, parking (fee).
AE, DC, MC, V.* 🖘

$$$–$$$$ ☷ **Abigail's Hotel.** A Tudor-style inn built in 1930, Abigail's is within
   ★   walking distance of downtown. The guest rooms are attractively fur-
nished in an English Arts and Crafts style. Down comforters, together
with whirlpool tubs and fireplaces in many rooms, add to the pam-
pering atmosphere. Six large rooms in the Coach House building are
especially lavish, with whirlpool tubs, four-poster king beds, and wood-
burning fireplaces. All rooms have telephones, but no TVs. Full break-
fast is included. ⊠ *906 McClure St., V8V 3E7,* ☎ *250/388–5363 or
800/561–6565,* 𝐅𝐀𝐗 *250/388–7787. 22 rooms. Breakfast room, library,
laundry service, concierge, free parking. AE, MC, V.* 🖘

$$$–$$$$ ☷ **Beaconsfield Inn.** Built in 1905 and restored in 1984, the Beacons-
   ★   field has retained its Old World charm. Mahogany is used throughout
the house; down comforters and canopy beds adorn some of the rooms,
reinforcing the inn's Edwardian style. Some rooms have fireplaces and whirl-
pool tubs. Added pluses are the guest library and the conservatory–sun-
room. Rates include full breakfast and afternoon tea. The inn is on a quiet
residential street nine blocks from the Inner Harbour. The owners also op-
erate a one-bedroom beach cottage about 10 minutes away. ⊠ *998 Hum-
boldt St., V8V 2Z8,* ☎ *250/384–4044,* 𝐅𝐀𝐗 *250/384–4052. 5 rooms, 4 suites.
Breakfast room, library, free parking. MC, V.* 🖘

$$$–$$$$ ☷ **Clarion Hotel Grand Pacific.** A landscaped courtyard with fountains
and statuary creates a striking entrance to this modern full-service hotel
on the Inner Harbour. Renovated and expanded in 2000, the Clarion
has extensive health-club facilities and is connected to a shopping ar-
cade. It's a short walk to the Parliament Buildings, the Royal British
Columbia Museum, and other central Victoria sights. The guest rooms
are decorated fairly conservatively, with muted colors, and many of
them have great harbor views. ⊠ *450 Quebec St. (main entrance on
Belleville St.), V8V 1W5* ☎ *250/386–0450 or 800/458–6262,* 𝐅𝐀𝐗 *250/
386–8779. 268 rooms, 40 suites. Restaurant, bar, in-room data ports,
in-room safes, no-smoking floor, refrigerators, room service, indoor
lap pool, wading pool, beauty salon, hot tub, massage, sauna, aero-
bics, health club, racquetball, shops, dry cleaning, laundry service, con-
cierge, meeting rooms. AE, D, DC, MC, V.* 🖘

$$$–$$$$ ☷ **A Haterleigh Heritage Inn.** A 1901 Queen Anne-style mansion two
blocks from the Inner Harbour, the Haterleigh was opened as a bed-
and-breakfast after arduous restoration. Leaded- and stained-glass
windows and ornate plasterwork on 11-ft ceilings transport you to a
more gracious time. Several of the Victorian-theme guest rooms have
whirlpool tubs or original claw-foot tubs. The Secret Garden room,
with a balcony and oval whirlpool tub, is a romantic choice, as is the
Day Dreams room on the main floor, with its double whirlpool tub
and private sitting room. Full breakfast and afternoon refreshments
are included in the rates. ⊠ *243 Kingston St., V8V 1V5,* ☎ *250/384–
9995,* 𝐅𝐀𝐗 *250/384–1935. 5 rooms, 1 suite. Free parking. MC, V.* 🖘

$$$–$$$$ ☷ **Laurel Point Inn.** Every room has water views at this modern resort
and convention hotel on a 6-acre peninsula in the Inner Harbour. The
decor, especially in the newer Arthur Erickson–designed suites, is light
and airy, with a strong Asian influence. Chinese art decorates many
public areas, and the Terrace Room lounge looks out over a Japanese
garden. All rooms have balconies, hair dryers, and coffeemakers. ⊠
680 Montreal St., V8V 1Z8, ☎ *250/386–8721 or 800/663–7667,* 𝐅𝐀𝐗
*250/386–9547. 120 rooms, 80 suites. Restaurant, lounge, no-smok-
ing floor, room service, indoor pool, sauna, hot tub, laundry service,
business services, meeting rooms, free parking. AE, DC, MC, V.* 🖘

$$$–$$$$ ⬛ **Oak Bay Beach Hotel & Marine Resort.** This family-run, Tudor-style
★ country inn is beside the ocean in Oak Bay, just 10 minutes from
downtown. Guest rooms are decorated in an 18th-century European
style, with muted tones and sumptuous antiques. Many of the rooms
have striking views over the landscaped gardens and the islands in Haro
Strait; several have balconies, gas fireplaces, and big soaking tubs. An
on-site tour company can arrange just about anything you might like
to do in Victoria, including kayaking, whale watching, golf, and city
tours. The restaurant, Bentley's on the Bay, serves continental cuisine
and an elaborate high tea; the pub has a cozy British ambience. ⊠ *1175
Beach Dr., V8S 2N2,* ☎ *250/598–4556 or 800/668–7758,* FAX *250/598–
6180. 51 rooms. Restaurant, pub, in-room data ports, no-smoking floor,
room service, massage, dock, boating, mountain bikes, piano, baby-
sitting, laundry service, convention center, travel services, free park-
ing. AE, DC, MC, V.* ✑

$$$–$$$$ ⬛ **Prior House Bed & Breakfast Inn.** In a beautifully restored 1912 manor
★ home on a quiet street near Craigdarroch Castle, this B&B has a pretty
garden, a guest library, two parlors, antique furniture, lead-glass win-
dows, and oak paneling. All guest rooms have TVs and fireplaces; some
have whirlpool tubs and private balconies. The Garden Suite, with a
private entrance, two bedrooms, and a full kitchen, is an especially good
value. A chef prepares the lavish breakfasts and afternoon teas, which
are included in the rates. ⊠ *620 St. Charles St., V8S 3N7,* ☎ *250/592–
8847 or 877/924–3300,* FAX *250/592–8223. 5 rooms, 3 suites. Break-
fast room, library, free parking. MC, V.* ✑

$$$–$$$$ ⬛ **Victoria Regent.** Originally built as an apartment building, this
nearly all-suites hotel has an excellent waterfront location, a few min-
utes' walk from the Inner Harbour. The outside is plain, with a glass
facade, but the large apartment-size suites are attractively decorated
with rosewood furniture and contemporary art. Each suite has a
kitchen, living room, dining room, balcony, and one or two bedrooms
with bath, making the Victoria Regent a good choice for families.
Many suites have water views, and the pricier executive suites each in-
clude a fireplace, den, and jet tub. ⊠ *1234 Wharf St., V8W 3H9,* ☎
250/386–2211 or 800/663–7472, FAX *250/386–2622. 10 rooms, 34 suites.
Breakfast room, minibars, meeting rooms, free parking. AE, D, DC,
MC, V. CP.* ✑

$$$ ⬛ **Admiral Motel.** This small, friendly motel along the Inner Harbour
is a good choice for families. About half the rooms have kitchens or
kitchenettes, and all have a balcony or patio. Breakfast is included, and
there's a guest lounge with a fireplace. Small pets are permitted. ⊠ *257
Belleville St., V8V 1X1,* ☎ *888/823–6472,* ☎ FAX *250/388–6267. 22
rooms, 10 suites. Refrigerators, bicycles, coin laundry, free parking.
AE, D, MC, V.* ✑

$$–$$$ ⬛ **Chateau Victoria.** Wonderful views from the upper-floor suites and
rooftop restaurant are a plus at this centrally located 19-story hotel.
All suites have balconies and sitting areas; some have kitchenettes. The
rooms are comfortable and standard in size. ⊠ *740 Burdett Ave.,
V8W 1B2,* ☎ *250/382–4221 or 800/663–5891,* FAX *250/380–1950. 59
rooms, 118 suites. 2 restaurants, 2 lounges, no-smoking floor, in-room
data ports, room service, indoor pool, hot tub, exercise room, baby-
sitting, laundry service, concierge, business services, meeting rooms,
free parking. AE, D, DC, MC, V.* ✑

$$–$$$ ⬛ **Holland House Inn.** This stylish art- and antiques-filled Italian Re-
★ naissance–style home is in a quiet residential neighborhood two blocks
from the Inner Harbour. Guest rooms all have sitting areas, and many
have fireplaces, balconies, and canopied four-poster beds. A 1998 Arts
and Crafts–style addition, linked to the main building through a conservatory, has four large rooms with fireplaces and double soaking tubs.

Full breakfast is included. Smoking isn't allowed. ⊠ *595 Michigan St., V8V 1S7,* ☎ *250/384–6644 or 800/335–3466,* FAX *250/384–6117. 14 rooms. Breakfast room, free parking. AE, MC, V.* ✿

$$–$$$ 🛏 **Mulberry Manor.** The last building designed by Victoria architect Samuel McClure has been restored and decorated to magazine-cover perfection with antiques, luxurious linens, and tile baths. The Jasmine suite includes a wood-burning fireplace and a tub for two. The Tudor-style mansion sits behind a high stone wall on an acre of manicured grounds. The inn is a five-minute drive from the Inner Harbour, among the mansions of the Rockland neighborhood. A full breakfast is included. ⊠ *611 Foul Bay Rd., V8S 1H2,* ☎ *250/370–1918 or 877/370–1918,* FAX *250/370–1968. 2 rooms, 1 suite. Breakfast room, no-smoking rooms, free parking. MC, V.* ✿

$$–$$$ 🛏 **Spinnakers Guest House.** Three delightful houses make up the ac-
★ commodations at this B&B—run by the owner of the popular Spin-nakers Brew Pub—across the Johnson Street Bridge from downtown. A newer Italian villa–style house has three suites that surround an ivy-draped courtyard; all have private entrances and are decorated with Asian antiques, Balinese teak butlers, and other objects gathered during the owner's world travels. Two other houses are beautifully renovated Victorian homes, decorated with original local art and English and Welsh antiques. Most rooms have fireplaces and whirlpool tubs; one of the suites has a kitchen. Full breakfast is included. ⊠ *308 Catherine St., V9A 3S8,* ☎ *250/384–2739 or 877/838–2739. 5 rooms, 5 suites. Restaurant, pub, no-smoking rooms, free parking. AE, D, DC, MC, V.* ✿

$$–$$$ 🛏 **Swans.** Near the waterfront in Victoria's Old Town and within walk-ing distance of most of the major sights, this 1913 former warehouse is one of the city's most attractive boutique hotels. The first floor has a brewery, a bistro, and a pub, and there's a nightclub in the cellar. Large, apartmentlike suites with kitchens, high ceilings, and Pacific Northwest art fill the upper floors. ⊠ *506 Pandora Ave., V8W 1N6,* ☎ *250/361–3310 or 800/668–7926,* FAX *250/361–3491. 29 suites. Restaurant, pub, wine shop, no-smoking rooms, room service, night-club, coin laundry, meeting rooms, parking (fee). AE, DC, MC, V.* ✿

$ 🛏 **The Cherry Bank.** A warren of red wallpapered corridors gives this 1897 Victorian house the look of a wholesome Wild West brothel. No matter: the wacky-looking budget hotel, with a modern restaurant at-tached, is a few blocks from the Inner Harbour and is clean, friendly, and a good value—especially for groups and families. One room has a kitchenette, and another is large enough to sleep six. The rooms don't have phones or TVs, but the rates include a traditional bacon-and-egg breakfast. ⊠ *825 Burdett Ave., V8W 1B3,* ☎ *250/385–5380 or 800/998–6688,* FAX *250/383–0949. 25 rooms, 19 with bath; 1 suite. Restau-rant, pub, free parking. AE, MC, V.* ✿

$ 🛏 **Hostelling International Victoria.** This hostel, in a restored heritage building, is right in the thick of things near the waterfront and Mar-ket Square. The accommodations include private rooms with shared baths as well as beds in men's and women's dorms. Among the ameni-ties: a game room, TV lounge, private lockers, laundry facilities, two shared kitchens, and loads of travel information for your trip. ⊠ *516 Yates St., V8W 1K8,* ☎ *250/385–4511,* FAX *250/385–3232. 110 beds in 10 single-sex and co-ed dorms; 6 private rooms (2–8 people) with-out bath. Coin laundry, travel services. MC, V.* ✿

Nightlife and the Arts

For entertainment listings, pick up a free copy of *Monday Magazine* (it comes out every Thursday), or call the Talking Yellow Pages (☎ 250/953–9000).

The Arts

MUSIC

The **TerriVic Jazz Party** (☎ 250/953–2011) showcases internationally acclaimed musicians every April at seven venues around Victoria. The **Victoria Jazz Society** (☎ 250/388–4423) organizes the annual JazzFest International in late June and the Vancouver Island Blues Bash in Victoria every Labour Day weekend.

The **Victoria Symphony** (☎ 250/385–6515) plays in the Royal Theatre (✉ 805 Broughton St., ☎ 250/386–6121) and at the Farquhar Auditorium at the University of Victoria Centre (✉ Finnerty Rd., ☎ 250/721–8480).

OPERA

Pacific Opera Victoria (☎ 250/385–0222) performs three productions a year at the Royal Theatre.

THEATER

An old church houses the **Belfry Theatre** (✉ 1291 Gladstone Ave., ☎ 250/385–6815), whose resident company specializes in contemporary Canadian dramas. **Langham Court Theatre** (✉ 805 Langham Ct., ☎ 250/384–2142), a small theater in a residential neighborhood, is the home stage of the long-established Victoria Theatre Guild, which stages the works of well-known playwrights. **McPherson Playhouse** (✉ 3 Centennial Sq., ☎ 250/386–6121) hosts touring theater and dance companies. University of Victoria students stage productions on campus at the **Phoenix Theatre** (✉ Finnerty Rd., ☎ 250/721–8000).

Nightlife

BARS AND CLUBS

High-energy dance music draws a young crowd to the **Boom Boom Room** (✉ 1208 Wharf St., ☎ 250/381–2331), on the waterfront. The DJs at **Liquid** (✉ 15 Bastion Sq., ☎ 250/385–2626) play top-40, dance, R&B, and hip-hop tunes. With its cozy Tudor ambience and a waterside deck, the **Snug Pub** (1175 Beach Dr., ☎ 250/598–4556), about 10 minutes from downtown in the Oak Bay Beach Hotel & Marine Resort, is the nearest thing to a traditional English pub in Victoria. **Steamers Public House** (✉ 570 Yates St., ☎ 250/381–4340) has four pool tables and live music every night. The **Strathcona Hotel** (✉ 919 Douglas St., ☎ 250/383–7137) is something of an entertainment complex, with a pub and restaurant, a sports bar, a hillbilly-theme bar, and a nightclub—not to mention beach volleyball, played on the roof in summer. The DJs at the dance club **Sweetwater's** (✉ Market Sq., 27–560 Johnson St., ☎ 250/383–7844) appeal to a wide age group with top-40 dance and country tunes.

BREW PUBS

The deck at the **Harbour Canoe Club** (✉ 450 Swift St., ☎ 250/361–1940), Canada's only marine brew pub, looks over the Gorge and is a delightful place to spend a summer afternoon; you can even rent canoes and kayaks here. Inside, the former power station has been stylishly redone, with high ceilings, exposed brick and beams, a wide range of in-house brews (including one made with maple syrup), top-notch bar snacks, and a restaurant. Chic and arty **Hugo's** (✉ 625 Courtney St., ☎ 250/920–4844) serves lunch, dinner, and four of its own brews. This multipurpose night spot is a pub by day, a lounge in the early evening, and a dance club at night. Across the Johnson Street Bridge from downtown, **Spinnakers Brew Pub** (✉ 308 Catherine St., ☎ 250/386–2739) pours Victoria's most extensive menu of microbrews in an atmospheric setting, with a waterfront patio, a double-sided fireplace, and a multitude of cozy rooms filled with pub paraphernalia. The excellent pub grub and the in-house restaurant make this a popular eatery, too. **Swan's Pub** (⊠ 506 Pandora Ave., ☎ 250/361–3310) serves its own microbrews in a room decorated with Pacific Northwest art; it hosts live jazz and folk acts on weeknights.

Outdoor Activities and Sports

Boating

The quiet upper section of Victoria's harbor, called the Gorge, is a popular boating spot. You can rent a kayak, canoe, motorboat, or rowboat at **Harbour Rentals** (⊠ Heritage Quay, 450 Swift St., ☎ 250/386–2277); guided trips, dinner cruises, and sailboat charters are also available. To rent a powerboat or to book almost any kind of guided marine activity, including seaplane tours, fishing, and kayaking expeditions, contact the **Victoria Marine Adventure Centre** (⊠ 950 Wharf St., ☎ 250/995–2211 or 800/575–6700), on the Inner Harbour near the Visitor Information Centre. You can also rent scooters and bicycles here.

Golf

Several companies in Victoria offer advance tee-time bookings and golf packages (☞ Outdoor Activities and Sports *in* Vancouver Island A to Z, *below*).

The **Cordova Bay Golf Course** (⊠ 5333 Cordova Bay Rd., ☎ 250/658–4444) is an 18-hole, par-72 course with views of Cordova Bay and the San Juan Islands. The green fee is $50. An optional cart costs $30.

Hiking

The **Galloping Goose Regional Trail** (☎ 250/478–3344), an old railroad track that's been reclaimed for walkers, cyclists, and equestrians, runs from downtown Victoria to just north of Sooke. It links with the Peninsula Trail to Sidney to create a continuous 100-km (62-mi) carfree route. **Goldstream Provincial Park** (☎ 250/478–9414), 19 km (12 mi) northwest of Victoria on Highway 1 at Finlayson Arm Road, has an extensive trail system, old-growth forest, waterfalls, a salt marsh, and a river. Park staff lead walks and interpretive programs. Goldstream is a prime site for viewing bald eagles in December and January. **Swan Lake Christmas Hill Nature Sanctuary** (⊠ 3873 Swan Lake Rd., ☎ 250/479–0211), a few miles from downtown, has a 23-acre lake set in 143 acres of fields and wetlands. From the 2½-km (1½-mi) trail and floating boardwalk, birders can spot a variety of waterfowl even in winter, as well as nesting birds in the tall grass. Admission is by donation, sunrise to sunset. The sanctuary's Nature House is open weekdays 8:30–4 and weekends noon–4.

Whale-Watching

To see the pods of orcas that travel in the waters around Vancouver Island, you can take charter boat tours from Victoria May through October. These Zodiac (motor-powered inflatable-boat) excursions cost $75–$80 per person and take about three hours. **Great Pacific Adventures** (☎ 250/386–2277), **Ocean Explorations** (☎ 250/383–6722), and **Seacoast Expeditions** (☎ 250/383–2254) are among the many operators.

Pride of Victoria Cruises and Tours (☎ 250/592–3474 or 800/668–7758) offers whale-watching trips, with a naturalist and lunch, on a 45-ft catamaran. It also offers a range of other wildlife-spotting trips, guided kayak tours, and catamaran cruises. You can book whale-watching trips at the **Victoria Marine Adventure Centre** (☞ Boating, *above*).

Shopping

Shopping Districts and Malls

For a wide selection, head to the larger shopping centers downtown. **Victoria Eaton Centre** (⊠ 1 Victoria Eaton Centre, at Government and Fort Sts., ☎ 250/381–4012), a department store and mall, has about 100 boutiques and restaurants.

Antique Row, on Fort Street between Blanshard and Cook streets, is home to more than 60 antiques, curio, and collectibles shops. **Market Square** (⊠ 560 Johnson St., ☎ 250/386–2441) has everything from fudge, music, and comic books to jewelry, local arts, and New Age accoutrements. High-end fashion boutiques, craft shops, and galleries line **Trounce Alley,** a pedestrian-only lane north of View Street between Broad and Government streets.

Specialty Stores

Shopping in Victoria is easy: Virtually everything can be found in the downtown area on or near Government Street stretching north from The Empress hotel.

At **Artina's** (⊠ 1002 Government St., ☎ 250/386–7000 or 877/386–7700) you can find unusual Canadian art jewelry—mostly handmade, one-of-a-kind pieces. The **Cowichan Trading Co., Ltd.** (⊠ 1328 Government St., ☎ 250/383–0321) sells First Nations jewelry, art, moccasins, and Cowichan Indian sweaters. The **Fran Willis Gallery** (⊠ 1619 Store St., ☎ 250/381–3422) shows contemporary Canadian paintings and sculpture. **Hill's Indian Crafts** (⊠ 1008 Government St., ☎ 250/385–3911) has souvenirs and original West Coast First Nations art. As the name would suggest, **Irish Linen Stores** (⊠ 1019 Government St., ☎ 250/383–6812) stocks fine linen and lace items—hankies, napkins, tablecloths, and place mats. **Munro's Books** (⊠ 1108 Government St., ☎ 250/382–2464), in a restored 1909 building, is one of Canada's prettiest bookstores. If the British spirit of Victoria has you searching for fine teas, head to **Murchie's** (⊠ 1110 Government St., ☎ 250/383–3112) for a choice of 40 varieties, plus blended coffees, tarts, and cakes. Original art and fine Canadian crafts are the focus at the **Northern Passage Gallery** (⊠ 1020 Government St., ☎ 250/381–3380). At **Starfish Glassworks** (⊠ 630 Yates St., ☎ 250/388–7827) you can watch glassblowers create original works.

Victoria A to Z

Arriving and Departing

BY BOAT

BC Ferries (☎ 250/386–3431; 888/223–3779 in British Columbia only) operates daily service between Vancouver and Victoria. The Vancouver terminal is in Tsawwassen, 38 km (24 mi) southwest of downtown at the end of Highway 17. In Victoria, ferries arrive at and depart from the Swartz Bay Terminal at the end of Highway 17 (the Patricia Bay Highway), 32 km (20 mi) north of downtown Victoria. Sailing time is about 1½ hours. Fares cost about $9 per passenger and $32 per vehicle each way. Rates fluctuate depending on the season.

There is daily year-round passenger-only service between Victoria and Seattle on the **Victoria Clipper** (☎ 206/448–5000 in Seattle; 800/888–2535 elsewhere). The round-trip fare is US$115. You'll receive a discount if you order 14-day advance tickets, which have some restrictions.

Washington State Ferries (☎ 250/381–1551; 206/464–6400 in the U.S., 888/808–7977 in WA only) travel daily between Sidney, north of Victoria, and Anacortes, Washington. **Black Ball Transport** (☎ 250/386–

2202, 360/457–4491 in the U.S.) operates ferries daily year-round between Victoria and Port Angeles, Washington.

BY BUS

Pacific Coach Lines (☎ 250/385–4411; 800/661–1725) operates daily,
connecting service between Victoria and Vancouver using BC Ferries.

BY HELICOPTER

Helijet Airways (☎ 800/665–4354, 604/273–1414, or 250/382–6222)
helicopter service is available from downtown Vancouver and downtown Seattle to downtown Victoria.

BY PLANE

Victoria International Airport (✉ Willingdon Rd. off Hwy. 17, Sidney,
☎ 250/953–7500), 25 km (15 mi) from downtown Victoria, is served
by Air B.C., Canadian, Horizon, and WestJet airlines (☞ Air Travel
in Smart Travel Tips for telephone numbers). Air B.C. provides airport-
to-airport service from Vancouver to Victoria at least hourly. Flights
take about 35 minutes.

West Coast Air (☎ 604/606–6888 or 800/347–2222) and **Harbour Air**
(☎ 604/688–1277 or 800/665–0212) provide 35-minute harbor-to-har-
bor service (downtown Vancouver to downtown Victoria) several
times a day. **Kenmore Air Harbour** (☎ 425/486–1257 or 800/543–9595)
operates direct daily floatplane service from Seattle to Victoria's Inner
Harbour.

Airport Transfers: To drive from the airport to downtown, take Highway 17 south. A taxi ride costs between $35 and $40, plus tip. The
Airporter (☎ 250/386–2525) bus service drops off passengers at most
major hotels. The fare is $13 one way, $23 round-trip.

Getting Around

BY BUS

BC Transit (☎ 250/382–6161) serves Victoria and the surrounding
areas. An all-day pass costs $5.50.

BY FERRY

Victoria Harbour Ferries (☎ 250/708–0201) serve the Inner Harbour,
with stops that include The Empress hotel, Chinatown, Point Ellice
House, Ocean Pointe Resort Hotel, and Fisherman's Wharf. Fares
start at $3; harbor tours are $12 to $14. Boats make the rounds every
12 to 20 minutes daily March through October and on sunny weekends the rest of the year. If you're by the Inner Harbour at 9:45 on a
Sunday morning in summer, you can catch the little ferries performing a water ballet—they gather together and do maneuvers set to classical music that's blasted over loudspeakers.

BY TAXI

Taxis are available from **Empress Taxi** (☎ 250/381–2222) and **Victoria Taxi** (☎ 250/383–7111).

Contacts and Resources

CAR RENTAL

Avis (☎ 250/386–8468). **Budget** (☎ 250/953–5300). **Enterprise** (☎ 250/
475–6900). **Island Autos** (☎ 250/384–4881). **National Tilden** (☎ 250/
386–1213).

EMERGENCIES

Ambulance, fire, police (☎ 911).

GUIDED TOURS

The **Ale Trail** (✉ 304–1913 Sooke Rd., ☎ 250/478–9505 or 800/970–
7722) runs tours and beer tastings at Victoria's microbreweries and

When it Comes to Getting Local Currency at an ATM, Same Thing.

Whether you're in Yosemite or Yemen, using your Visa® card or ATM card with the PLUS symbol is the easiest and most convenient way to get local currency. For example, let's say you're in France. When you make a withdrawal, using your secured PIN, it's dispensed in francs, but is debited from your account in U.S. dollars.

This makes it easy to take advantage of favorable exchange rates. And if you need help finding one of Visa's 627,000 ATMs in 127 countries worldwide, visit **visa.com/pd/atm**. We'll make finding an ATM as easy as finding the Eiffel Tower, the Pyramids or even the Grand Canyon.

It's Everywhere You Want To Be.

Pack an easy way to reach the world.

Wherever you travel, the MCI WorldCom Card℠ is the easiest way to stay in touch. You can use it to call to and from more than 125 countries worldwide. And you can earn bonus miles every time you use your card. So go ahead, travel the world. MCI WorldCom℠ makes it even more rewarding. For additional access codes, visit www.wcom.com/worldphone.

EASY TO CALL WORLDWIDE

1. Just dial the WorldPhone® access number of the country you're calling from.

2. Dial or give the operator your MCI WorldCom Card number.

3. Dial or give the number you're calling.

Aruba (A) ⊹	800-888-8
Australia ◆	1-800-881-100
Bahamas ⊹	1-800-888-8000
Barbados (A) ⊹	1-800-888-8000
Bermuda ⊹	1-800-888-8000
British Virgin Islands (A) ⊹	1-800-888-8000
Canada	1-800-888-8000
Costa Rica (A) ◆	0800-012-2222
New Zealand	000-912
Puerto Rico	1-800-888-8000
United States	1-800-888-8000
U.S. Virgin Islands	1-800-888-8000

(A) Calls back to U.S. only.   ⊹ Limited availability.   ◆ Public phones may require deposit of coin or phone card for dial tone.

EARN FREQUENT FLIER MILES

brew pubs. Day tours and packages with accommodation are available. The **Architectural Institute of British Columbia** (☎ 800/667–0753; 604/683–8588 Vancouver office) offers free walking tours of Victoria's historic neighborhoods during July and August. **Gray Line** (☎ 250/388–5248 or 800/667–0882) gives tours on double-decker buses that visit the city center, Chinatown, Antique Row, Oak Bay, and Beacon Hill Park; a combination tour stops at Butchart Gardens as well. The **Pacific Wilderness Railway Company** (☎ 250/381–8600) runs a 2¼-hour round-trip vintage train excursion from Victoria's Pandora Street station to the top of Malahat Mountain, north of Victoria. The trip is made three times a day mid-June to mid-September and on weekends until the end of October. Tickets are $29. **Tally-Ho Horsedrawn Tours** (☎ 250/383–5067) offers a get-acquainted tour of downtown Victoria that includes Beacon Hill Park. **Victoria Carriage Tours** (☎ 250/383–2207) has horse-drawn tours of the city. The best way to see the sights of the Inner Harbour is by **Victoria Harbour Ferries** (☞ Getting Around, *above*).

HOSPITAL

Victoria General Hospital (✉ 1 Hospital Way, off Helmcken Rd., ☎ 250/727–4212).

LATE-NIGHT PHARMACY

London Drugs (✉ 911 Yates St., ☎ 250/381–1113) is open Monday through Saturday until 10 PM.

LODGING RESERVATION SERVICES

Reservations for lodging can be made through **Super, Natural British Columbia** (☎ 800/435–5622). For more information on reservation services, *see* Contacts and Resources *in* Vancouver Island A to Z, *below*.

VISITOR INFORMATION

Super, Natural British Columbia (☎ 800/435–5622, ✇). **Tourism Victoria** (✉ 812 Wharf St., ☎ 250/953–2033).

VANCOUVER ISLAND

The largest island on Canada's west coast, Vancouver Island stretches 564 km (350 mi) from Victoria in the south to Cape Scott in the north. A ridge of mountains, blanketed in spruce, cedar, and Douglas fir, crowns the island's center, providing opportunities for skiing, climbing, and hiking. Mining, logging, and tourism are the important island industries, although tourism—especially ecotourism—has become increasingly important in recent years.

Outside Victoria and Nanaimo, most towns on the island are so small as to be dwarfed by the surrounding wilderness. However, many have a unique charm, from pretty Victorian Chemainus to such isolated fishing villages as Bamfield and growing eco-tourism centers including Tofino.

Sooke

⑰ *42 km (26 mi) west of Victoria on Hwy. 14.*

The village of Sooke provides a peaceful seaside escape, with rugged beaches, hiking trails through the surrounding rain forest, and views of Washington's Olympic Mountains across the Strait of Juan de Fuca. **East Sooke Regional Park,** on the east side of the harbor, has more than 3,500 acres of beaches, hiking trails, and wildflower-dotted meadows. A popular hiking and biking route, the **Galloping Goose Regional Trail** (☎ 250/478–3344) is a former railway line that runs all the way to Victoria. The **Sooke Potholes** (✉ end of Sooke River Rd., off Hwy. 14), along the Galloping Goose Regional Trail, are a series of swimming holes carved out of the sandstone by the Sooke River.

The **Sooke Region Museum and Visitor Information Centre** displays Salish and Nootka crafts and artifacts from 19th-century Sooke. ⊠ *2070 Phillips Rd., Box 774, V0S 1N0,* ☎ *250/642–6351,* FAX *250/642–7089.* ☞ *Donations accepted.* ⊙ *July–Aug., daily 9–6; Sept.–June, daily 9–5.*

OFF THE BEATEN PATH

JUAN DE FUCA PROVINCIAL PARK – This park between the Jordan River and Port Renfrew has campsites and a long series of beaches, including Botanical Beach with its amazing tidal pools. The **Juan de Fuca Marine Trail** is a tough 47-km (30-mi) hike set up as an alternative to the overly popular West Coast Trail (☞ Pacific Rim National Park Reserve, *below*) that begins at China Beach, just west of the Jordan River. ⊠ *Hwy. 14,* ☎ *250/391–2300,* ☞ *Free, $5 a night for camping.*

Dining and Lodging

$$ ✕ **Seventeen Mile House.** Originally built as a hotel, this 1894 house is a study in turn-of-the-century island architecture. This is a good place for pub fare, a beer, or fresh local seafood on the road between Sooke and Victoria. Low-cost rooms, with a do-it-yourself breakfast, are also available here. ⊠ *5126 Sooke Rd.,* ☎ *250/642–5942. MC, V.*

$$$$ ✕▥ **Sooke Harbour House.** People (including incognito movie stars)
★ who are discerning about their R&R are drawn to this 1929 oceanfront clapboard inn with its elegant yet relaxed ambience and one of Canada's finest dining rooms. Dining here is an adventure: the cuisine is organic, seasonal, and uniquely Canadian, and makes the most of the local bounty. The menu changes daily, the seafood is just-caught fresh, and much of the produce—including herbs, mushrooms, and edible flowers—is grown on the property. The inn is also home to one of Canada's leading wine cellars. The guest rooms, each with a sitting area and fireplace, are individually decorated (some with fish, bird, or seaside themes) and photo-shoot perfect; only one doesn't have ocean views. The Victor Newman Longhouse and Thunderbird rooms display impressive First Nations art, and the bi-level Blue Heron Room has a summer-cottage feel, with a private deck overlooking the ocean. Breakfast (delivered to your room) is included in the room rates year-round; lunch (which can be a picnic lunch) is included May through October and on weekends the rest of the year. ⊠ *1528 Whiffen Spit Rd., V0S 1N0,* ☎ *250/642–3421 or 800/889–9688,* FAX *250/642–6988. 28 rooms. Restaurant, in-room data ports, refrigerators, room service, massage, hiking, snorkeling, kayaking, piano, laundry service, business services, meeting room. AE, DC, MC, V.* ☜

$$–$$$ ▥ **Markham House Bed & Breakfast.** Owners Sally and Lyall Markham make you feel welcome in this Tudor house set amid extensive grounds that include a trout pond, a putting green, and walking trails. The bedrooms have comfy mattresses with feather beds and are decorated with family pieces, including paintings of and by Lyall's relatives. The Garden Suite, which has a double Jacuzzi, and the Country Room are spacious; the Green Room is cozy but small and its bathroom is down the hall. Tucked away in the woods is the country-style Honeysuckle Cottage, a favorite for romantics. Its private deck has a barbecue and a hot tub, and there's a small kitchenette inside—but breakfast (which is delicious) can be delivered to the door. Despite its Victoria address, the Markham House is closer to Sooke. ⊠ *1853 Connie Rd., off Hwy. 14, Victoria V9C 4C2,* ☎ *250/642–7542 or 888/256–6888,* FAX *250/642–7538. 2 rooms, 1 suite, 1 cabin. In-room VCRs (some). AE, DC, MC, V.* ☜

$$–$$$ 🏨 **Point No Point.** Here's a place for your inner Robinson Crusoe. Twenty-two cabins sit on the edge of a cliff, overlooking a mile of sandy private beach and the open Pacific. The one- and two-bedroom cabins, in single, duplex, and quad units, range from rustic to romantic. Seven newer cabins have tall windows, water views, and hot tubs; the older, less expensive cabins are basic, with the original 1960s furniture (pets are allowed in two of these). Every unit has a kitchen, a fireplace or woodstove, and a deck. The lodge restaurant serves lunch, afternoon tea, and dinner from a seafood-oriented menu. Each table has a pair of binoculars for spotting whales and ships on the open sea. ✉ *1505 West Coast Rd., 15 mi west of Sooke, V0S 1N0,* ☎ *250/646–2020,* ſᴀx *250/646–2294. 22 cabins. Restaurant, no-smoking rooms, hiking. AE, MC, V. Restaurant closed for dinner Mon.–Tues.; check for winter closures.*

Shopping
At the **Blue Raven Gallery** (✉ 1971 Kaltasin Rd., ☎ 250/881–0528), Victor and Carey Newman, a father-and-son team of Kwakiutl and Salish artists, display traditional and modern prints, masks, and jewelry. January through March, the shop is open only by appointment.

Duncan

🔟⓼   *60 km (37 mi) north of Victoria on the Trans-Canada Hwy., or Hwy. 1.*

★ ℃   Duncan is nicknamed City of Totems for the many totem poles that dot the small community. The **Cowichan Native Village,** covering 6 acres on the banks of the tree-lined Cowichan River, is one of Canada's leading First Nations cultural and educational facilities. You can see the work (including a stunning whaling canoe diorama) of some of the Northwest's most renowned artists in a lofty longhouse-style gallery, learn about the history of the Cowichan people during a multimedia show, and sample traditional foods at the Riverwalk Café. You can also watch artisans at work in the world's largest carving house and even try your hand at carving on a visitors' pole. Craft demonstrations and performances take place in summer. ✉ *200 Cowichan Way,* ☎ *250/746–8119 or 877/746–8119.* 🎟 *$10.* ☉ *Daily 9–5; café closed Nov.–Apr.* ✎

The **British Columbia Forest Discovery Centre,** more a park than a museum, spans some 100 acres, combining indoor and outdoor exhibits that focus on the history of forestry in the province. In the summer you can ride an original steam locomotive around the property. The *Forest Renewal B.C.* exhibition has a theater, computer games, aquariums, and hands-on displays about the province's ecosystems. There are also nature trails on the property. ✉ *2892 Drinkwater Rd. (Trans-Canada Hwy.),* ☎ *250/715–1113,* ſᴀx *250/715–1170.* 🎟 *$8.* ☉ *May–early Sept., daily 10–6; early Sept.–Apr.; call for seasonal hrs.*

Shopping
Duncan is the home of Cowichan wool sweaters, hand-knit by the Cowichan people. Sweaters are available at the **Cowichan Native Village** (☞ *above*) and from **Hill's Indian Crafts** (☎ 250/746–6731), on the main highway, about 1½ km (1 mi) south of Duncan.

Chemainus

★ ⓽   *25 km (16 mi) north of Duncan.*

Chemainus is known for the bold epic murals that decorate its townscape, as well as for its beautifully restored Victorian homes. Once dependent on the lumber industry, the small community began to revitalize itself in the early 1980s when its mill closed down. Since then, the town has brought in international artists to paint more than 30 murals depicting local historical events around town. Footprints on the sidewalk lead you on a self-guided tour of the murals. Restaurants, shops, tearooms, coffee bars, art galleries, a mini-train line, several B&Bs, and antiques dealers have helped to create one of the prettiest little towns on Vancouver Island. The **Chemainus Dinner Theatre** (⊠ 9737 Chemainus Rd., ☎ 250/246–9820 or 800/565–7738) presents family-oriented fare along with dinner.

Dining and Lodging

$$–$$$$ ✕ **The Waterford Restaurant.** French-trained chef Dwayne Maslen and his wife Linda run this tiny restaurant tucked into a historic house near the center of town. Some highlights on the French-influenced menu are the scallop and prawns Provençal, breast of chicken stuffed with scallop-and-smoked-salmon mousse, and roast local venison with a currant demi-glace. ⊠ 9875 Maple St., ☎ 250/246–1046. AE, MC, V. Closed Mon.

$$–$$$ ✕ **Hummingbird Tea House.** A husband-and-wife team runs this little two-room café, which offers casual soup, salad, and sandwich lunches as well as more-elaborate dinners, including a popular warm goat-cheese salad starter, and entrées such as fillet of sole stuffed with crab and scallops. Personal touches, such as the organic flowers decorating each plate, make this a popular stop. ⊠ 9893 Maple St., ☎ 250/246–2290. AE, V. Oct.–May closed Tues. and no dinner Wed.

$$$$ 🏨 **Castlebury Inn.** This medieval-theme castle–cottage is a good place to act out your Camelot fantasies. From the royal-purple velveteen duvet and two-sided fireplace to the vaulted ceiling, 18th-century church window, frescoed walls, and suit of armor (salvaged from the Addams Family film set), the apartment-size suite is decorated in a delightfully theatrical style. A double soaking tub, TV with VCR, CD player, and a kitchen with a microwave and dishwasher are nods to the modern world, and stairs climb to a little Juliette balcony with views over the town and sea. (A second suite was planned at press time.) Breakfast is delivered to the door in a basket. You can also have medieval-theme dinners with costumed waiters and a harpist by advance arrangement. ⊠ 9910 Croft St., V0R 1K0, ☎ 240/246–9228, FAX 250/246–2909. 1 suite. AE, MC, V. ✍

$$ 🏨 **Bird Song Cottage.** This whimsical white and lavender Victorian cot-
★   tage, an easy walk from the beach and town, has been playfully decorated with antiques and collectibles, including a grand piano, a Celtic harp, and Victorian hats. A full breakfast (often with piano accompaniment) is served on the sunporch. The Nightingale room has a private garden and a claw-foot tub, and the other two rooms have baths with showers; every room has a window seat. ⊠ 9909 Maple St., Box 1432, V0R 1K0, ☎ 250/246–9910, FAX 250/246–2909. 3 rooms. AE, MC, V. ✍

Nanaimo

⓴   25 km (16 mi) north of Chemainus, 110 km (68 mi) northwest of Victoria.

Nanaimo is the primary commercial and transport link for the mid-island, with direct ferry service to the mainland. The **Nanaimo District Museum** (⊠ 100 Cameron Rd., ☎ 250/753–1821) has exhibits on the local First Nations' culture and the region's coal-mining history, as well as a variety of interesting temporary exhibits. May through September the museum is open 9–5 daily; the rest of the year it's open Tuesday through Saturday 9–5. Admission is $2.

From Nanaimo, you can take a 10-minute ferry ride (☎ 250/753–5141) in the summer to **Newcastle Island,** a provincial park where you can camp, picnic, bike, walk trails leading past old mines and quarries, and catch glimpses of deer, rabbits, and eagles.

Dining and Lodging

$$$–$$$$ ✕ **The Grotto.** The owners of this offbeat seafood and sushi place near the Departure Bay ferry terminal have been adding to their supply of nautical paraphernalia since 1960. Inside and out, the place looks like a sea shanty, full of driftwood, fishing floats, and weathered pillars borrowed from a dock. The five-page menu has enough options to keep everyone happy. Try the sushi, charred tuna, teriyaki spareribs, Cajun pasta, or Dungeness crab. ⊠ *1511 Stewart Ave.,* ☎ *250/753–3303. AE, MC, V. Closed Mon. No lunch.*

$$$ ✕ **Mahle House.** Much of the innovative Pacific Northwest cuisine served
★ at this cozy 1904 farmhouse is raised on site or in the neighborhood. Highlights on the seasonal menu include different versions of rabbit, venison, mussels, and salmon, as well as good vegetarian options. On Wednesday night, you can try the Adventure Dining Experience: for $27 you get five courses chosen by the chef, and your dinner companions (up to a party of four) each get something different. Mahle House is about 12 km (7 mi) south of Nanaimo. ⊠ *2104 Hemer Rd., at Cedar Rd.,* ☎ *250/722–3621. AE, MC, V. Closed Mon.–Tues. and first half of Jan. No lunch.*

$$–$$$ ✕ **Dar Lebanon.** From the outside, this restaurant near the harbor looks like the top floor of a historic house. Inside, the look is more night-at-the-casbah, with plaster arches, fringed light fixtures, and embroidered tablecloths. The food is Lebanese but takes its inspiration from both sides of the Mediterranean. Try the starter of tiger prawns in mustard, orange, cilantro, and garlic sauce; or, as a main course, kibbee, a sort of patty of lean beef mixed with cracked wheat and basil, and stuffed with ground walnuts and pomegranate juice. The menu also has such traditional items as stuffed grape leaves, tabbouleh, and moussaka, and plenty of vegetarian options. ⊠ *347 Wesley St.,* ☎ *250/ 755–9150. AE, MC, V. Closed Sun. Jan.–Feb.*

$$ ✕ **Crow and Gate Neighbourhood Pub.** With its low beams, weathered furniture, and pub paraphernalia, the Crow and Gate is probably the most authentic-looking British-style pub in the province. Set in acres of lawns on a country road about 15 km (9 mi) south of Nanaimo, the pub serves the expected pot pies, ploughman's lunches, and roast beef with Yorkshire pudding, as well as such local items as Fanny Bay oysters. The bar stocks both British and local brews, including hard-to-find Vancouver Island microbrews and estate cider. From Highway 1 between Ladysmith and Nanaimo, follow the signs for Yellow Point Lodge, then the signs for the pub. ⊠ *2313 Yellow Point Rd., Ladysmith,* ☎ *250/722–3731. Reservations not accepted. AE, MC, V.*

$$–$$$ ☷ **Yellow Point Lodge.** Since the '30s, this lodge on a spit of land 24
★ km (15 mi) south of Nanaimo has been a kind of adults-only summer camp. Everything's included, from the use of kayaks, bicycles, and tennis courts to the three full meals and snacks served communally in the dining room. Accommodations range from comfortable lodge rooms to cozy cottages with minirefrigerators and bed frames made with logs; there are also some very basic summer-only cabins with no running water and a shared bathhouse. The main lodge, with its great stone fireplace and ocean views, is a wonderful place to unwind; you can also stroll the resort's 165 acres, lounge on its secluded beaches, or take a tour on the owner's cutter. Guests must be over 14. ⊠ *3700 Yellow Point Rd., Ladysmith V9G 1E8,* ☎ *250/245–7422,* ℻ *250/245–7411. 9 lodge rooms, 25 rooms with no running water, 10 units in shared*

cabins, 12 private cabins. Dining room, saltwater pool, outdoor hot tub, sauna, 2 tennis courts, badminton, jogging, volleyball, boating, mountain bikes, meeting rooms. AE, MC, V. AP. ⊛

$$ 🏨 **Coast Bastion Inn Nanaimo.** This convenient business hotel downtown overlooks the harbor. The rooms are large and modern, and all have water views. Corner rooms on the 7th floor and up are larger and have sitting areas and panoramic ocean views. ⊠ *11 Bastion St., V9R 2Z9,* ☎ *250/753–6601,* 𝖥𝖠𝖷 *250/753–4155. 171 rooms, 4 suites. Restaurant, lounge, no-smoking floor, room service, hot tub, sauna, exercise room, laundry service, business services, meeting rooms. AE, D, DC, MC, V.* ⊛

Outdoor Activities and Sports

GOLF

Fairwinds Golf and Country Club (⊠ 3730 Fairwinds Dr., Nanoose Bay, ☎ 250/468–7666 or 888/781–2777) is an 18-hole, par-71 course that's open all year. Green fees are about $50.

KAYAKING

Kayak rentals and one- to six-day guided sea-kayak expeditions are offered by **Wild Heart Adventure Tours** (⊠ 2774 Barnes Rd., ☎ 250/722–3683, 𝖥𝖠𝖷 250/722–2175).

Gabriola Island

3½ nautical mi (20-min ferry ride) east of Nanaimo.

You can stay overnight on rustic, rural Gabriola Island. The island has several B&Bs, beaches, and parks. **BC Ferries** (☎ 250/386–3431; 888/223–3779 in British Columbia) runs car and passenger service from Nanaimo.

Port Alberni

❷ *80 km (50 mi) northwest of Nanaimo, 195 km (121 mi) northwest of Victoria.*

Port Alberni is a pulp- and sawmill town and a stopover on the way to Ucluelet and Tofino on the west coast. The salmon-rich waters attract anglers. The town's old industrial waterfront, at the foot of Argyle Street, has been revitalized into **Alberni Quay,** an attractive waterfront shopping area. The **Alberni Valley Museum** (⊠ 4255 Wallace St., ☎ 250/723–2181) features First Nations cultural exhibits as well as local industrial history and a folk-art collection. It's open 10–5 Tues.–Sat., with late hours (until 8) Thurs. Admission is by donation. From May 20 to September 30, a 1929 **Baldwin Steam Locomotive** (☎ 250/723–2181) leaves several times a day (Thurs.–Mon.) from the railway station at the foot of Argyle Street for a scenic 40-minute ride along the waterfront. The round-trip fare is $11. The Baldwin Steam Locomotive terminates at the **McLean Mill National Historic Site** (⊠ 5633 Smith Rd., off Beaver Creek Rd., ☎ 250/723–2181), a restored 1925 lumber camp, complete with bunkhouses, a cookhouse, a blacksmith's forge, and much of the original steam-driven sawmill equipment. Costumed staff and equipment demonstrations bring the site to life. It's open daily May 20–Sept. 30, 10–dusk. Admission is $6. The **Port Alberni Tourist Infocentre** (⊠ Port Alberni Hwy. and Johnston St., ☎ 250/724–6535) has area information.

From Port Alberni, you can take a breathtaking trip to Bamfield aboard the **Lady Rose,** a Scottish ship built in 1937, or, on the newer **M.V. Francis Barkley,** to the Broken Group Islands or Ucluelet (☞ Getting Around by Boat *in* Vancouver Island A to Z, *below*).

About 13 km (8 mi) west of town on Highway 4 is **Sproat Lake Provincial Park,** with a swimming beach and trails leading to ancient petroglyphs. Sproat Lake is also home to the only two Martin Mars water bombers still in existence. Originally World War II troop carriers, they are now used to fight forest fires. The park is open sunrise to sunset and is free.

Lodging

$$ 🏨 **Cedar Wood Lodge.** Built in 1998, this clapboard lodge is set on 2 acres of gardens. The rooms, most of which can sleep four, are decorated in rich greens and burgundies, with attractive art-deco furniture, gas fireplaces, and whirlpool tubs. The comfortable lounge has a pool table and leather couches set around a fireplace. Guests also have access to swimming, canoeing, and fishing in the river across the road. ✉ *5895 River Rd. (Hwy. 4), V9Y 6Z5,* ☎ *250/724–6800 or 877/314–6800,* ☏ *250/724–6887. 8 rooms. Breakfast room, in-room data ports, no-smoking rooms, fishing, billiards, meeting room. AE, MC, V. CP.* 🐾

Bamfield

🟤 *100 km (62 mi) southwest of Port Alberni by gravel road.*

In Bamfield, a remote village of about 500, the seaside boardwalk affords an uninterrupted view of ships heading up the inlet to Port Alberni. The town is well equipped to handle overnight visitors. Bamfield is also a good base for fishing, boating trips to the Broken Group Islands, and hikes along the West Coast Trail (☞ Pacific Rim National Park Reserve, *below*). You can take a boat here from Port Alberni to protect your car from the gravel road.

Dining and Lodging

$$$ ✕🏨 **Eagle Nook Ocean Wilderness Resort.** This adult-oriented, wilder-
★ ness country inn, accessible only by sea or air, sits on a narrow strip of land in Barkley Sound. For all its blissful isolation, Eagle Nook offers highly civilized comforts. Every spacious room has a water view, and the lounge has leather chairs and the ambience of an English country inn. The dining room has a stone fireplace, floor-to-ceiling windows, and fine Pacific Northwest cuisine, which you can enjoy inside or alfresco. Hiking trails lace the woods, and many activities, including fishing, kayaking, and nature cruises, can be prebooked. Getting here—by floatplane or by the inn's own water taxi from Port Alberni (an extra $99 round-trip)—is a scenic adventure in its own right. There's a two-night minimum stay; prices are per person and include meals and nonguided activities. ✉ *Box 575, Port Alberni V9Y 7M9,* ☎ *250/723–1000 or 800/760–2777,* ☏ *250/723–6609. 23 rooms. Restaurant, lounge, no-smoking rooms, outdoor hot tub, sauna, exercise room, hiking, dock, boating, fishing, laundry service, meeting room, helipad. AE, MC, V. Closed Nov.–May. AP.* 🐾

Ucluelet

🟤 *100 km (62 mi) west of Port Alberni, 295 km (183 mi) northwest of Victoria.*

Ucluelet, which in the Nuchahnuth First Nations language means "safe landing place," is, along with Bamfield and Tofino, one of the towns serving Pacific Rim National Park Reserve (☞ *below*).

Various charter companies (☞ Outdoor Activities and Sports *and* Contacts and Resources *in* Vancouver Island A to Z, *below*) take boats to greet the 20,000 gray whales that pass close to Ucluelet on their migration to the Bering Sea every March and April. The **Pacific Rim Whale Festival,** a month-long event, has sprung up (in Tofino, too) to welcome the whales each spring. **The Ucluelet Chamber of Commerce** (☎ 250/726–4641) has information.

Visitors increasingly are coming in the off-season to watch the dramatic winter storms that pound the coast here. **Amphitrite Point Lighthouse** (✉ end of Coast Guard Rd.), which has a panoramic view of the beach, is the starting point for the **Wild Pacific Trail**, a level, part-board-walk, wheelchair-accessible path along the coast and through the rain forest. When completed (in about 2003), the trail is to link Ucluelet to Long Beach in Pacific Rim National Park Reserve.

Dining and Lodging

$$$–$$$$ ✕ **Kingfisher Restaurant.** You can spot eagles, seals, otters, and, on a good day, the village's one kingfisher through the picture windows at this cozy little restaurant on Ucluelet inlet. Even without the wildlife, the views over the outlying islands are striking, and the seafood, including local oysters, Dungeness crab, and baby shrimp, comes straight from the docks daily. ✉ 168 Fraser La., ☎ 250/726–3463. MC, V.

$$–$$$ ✕ **Matterson House.** In a tiny 1931 cottage with just seven tables and an outdoor deck in summer, husband-and-wife team Sandy and Jennifer Clark serve up generous portions of seafood, burgers, pasta, and filling standards such as prime rib and veal cutlets. It's simple food, prepared well with fresh local ingredients; everything, including soups, desserts, and the wonderful bread, is homemade. The wine list has local island wines unavailable elsewhere and worth trying. Matterson House is also a good breakfast stop. ✉ 1682 Peninsula Rd., ☎ 250/726–2200. MC, V. Closed part of Nov.

$$$–$$$$ 🏠 **Reef Point Adventure Station.** This resort on Ucluelet's harbor resembles a west coast fishing village of the early 1900s. The whole woodsy complex is built on posts and linked by raised boardwalks and bridges that run through the rain forest. The accommodation options are a 20-room lodge and beachfront cabins. At press time, much of Reef Point was still under construction. Shops, a restaurant, a pub, and a 100-room hotel were planned for 2001; call ahead to confirm details and prices. ✉ 131 Seabridge Way, Box 730, V0R 3A0, ☎ 250/726–2700; 888/594–7333 in British Columbia, ℻ 250/726–2701. 20 rooms, 10 cottages. Spa, boating. AE, DC, MC, V.

$$$–$$$$ 🏠 **A Snug Harbour Inn.** Set on a cliff above the Pacific, this couples-oriented B&B offers some of the most dramatic views anywhere. The rooms, all with fireplaces, private balconies or decks, whirlpool baths, and ocean views, are decorated in a highly individual style. The Sawadee room reflects hosts Skip and Denise Rowland's time in Thailand, and the Lighthouse room winds up three levels for great views. Eagles nest nearby, and trails through the woods lead to the seaside. Full breakfast is included. ✉ 460 Marine Dr., Box 367, V0R 3A0, ☎ 250/726–2686 or 888/936–5222, ℻ 250/726–2685. 4 rooms. Breakfast room, outdoor hot tub, hiking, helipad. MC, V. 🐾

$$$ 🏠 **Tauca Lea by the Sea.** This complex of blue-stained cedar lodges is on a small island on Ucluelet Inlet, but is walking distance to the village (a road connects the island). Hand-crafted furniture and terra-cotta tiles decorate the suites, which also have ocean-view balconies, kitchens, soaking tubs, sofa beds, and gas fireplaces. A boardwalk around the property leads to a sheltered viewpoint for spotting eagles, sea lions, and bears across the inlet. At press time, plans were in place for a marina-view restaurant, an espresso bar, a First Nations art gallery, and an Aveda spa. ✉ 1971 Harbour Crescent, V0R 3A0, ☎ 250/726–4625 or 800/979–9303. 10 1-bedroom and 17 2-bedroom suites. In-room

data ports, boating, fishing, coin laundry, laundry service, business services, meeting room. AE, DC, MC, V.

$–$$$ 🏨 **Canadian Princess Fishing Resort.** If vintage ships are to your liking, you may want to book a cabin on this converted 230-ft, steam-powered survey ship, which has comfortable but hardly opulent staterooms. Each has one to four berths, and all share bathrooms. Larger than the ship cabins, the resort's deluxe shoreside rooms have more-contemporary furnishings; a few have fireplaces. This unique resort appeals to nature enthusiasts and anglers, and whale-watching can be arranged. The Stewart Room Restaurant is open to nonguests; the specialty is (no surprise) seafood. ⊠ *Boat Basin, 1943 Peninsula Rd., Box 939, V0R 3A0,* ☎ *250/726–7771 or 800/663–7090,* FAX *250/726–7121. 46 shoreside rooms, 30 shipboard sleeping units without bath. Restaurant, 2 bars, boating, fishing. AE, DC, MC, V. Closed late Sept.–early Mar.*

Outdoor Activities and Sports

Most Ucluelet operators offer whale-watching, fishing, or cruising options. The **Canadian Princess Fishing Resort** (☎ 250/726–7771 or 800/663–7090) has 10 comfortable fishing and whale-watching boats with heated cabins and bathrooms. **Subtidal Adventures** (☎ 250/726–7336 or 877/444–1134) specializes in whale-watching and nature tours; there's a choice of an inflatable Zodiac or a 36-ft former coast-guard rescue boat. Some other local operators include **Island West Fishing Resort** (☎ 250/726–7515), **Jamie's Whaling Station** (☎ 250/726–7444), and **Quest Charters** (☎ 250/726–7532).

A great way to learn about the area's ecosystems is on a guided walk or hike with **Long Beach Nature** tours (☎ 250/726–7099). Led by a naturalist and biologist, the day trips range from easy to challenging, and include looks at intertidal life, wildflowers, and the rain forest, as well as bird-watching and photography-oriented walks.

Tofino

★ ㉔ *42 km (26 mi) northwest of Ucluelet, 337 km (209 mi) northwest of Victoria.*

The end of the road makes a great stage—and Tofino is certainly that. On a narrow peninsula just beyond the north end of the Pacific Rim National Park Reserve (☞ *below*), this is as far west as you can go on Vancouver Island by paved road. One look at the pounding Pacific surf and the old-growth forest along the shoreline convinces many people that they've reached not just the end of the road but the end of the earth.

Tofino's tiny number of year-round residents know what they like and have made what could have been a tourist trap into a funky little town with several art galleries, an excellent bookstore, sociable cafés, and plenty of opportunity to get out to the surrounding wilds—to see the old-growth forests of Meares Island, the natural hot springs at Hot Springs Cove, the long stretches of beach, and, of course, the whales and other wildlife. At the **Tofino Botanical Gardens** (☎ 250/725–1237), about 2 km (1 mi) south of the village on the Pacific Rim Highway, trails wind through displays of indigenous plant life. There's also a café on site; it's open 9 AM–10 PM. The gardens close at dusk, and admission is $8. Tofino has plenty of accommodations and campsites in and around town, and a full-service spa at The Wickaninnish Inn, but advance reservations are highly recommended if you're visiting Tofino in the summertime.

Dining and Lodging

$$$-$$$$ ✕ **The Schooner Restaurant.** You can't miss this 1930s-era red clapboard building in central Tofino—it's the one with the schooner sticking out the back; the front half of the boat takes up a chunk of the cozy rooms. The menu changes every two weeks or so. Try, if they're available, the smoked-duck salad; the Halibut Bombay, a halibut fillet stuffed with brie, pine nuts, crab, and shrimp in an apple–brandy cream sauce; the charbroiled seafood platter; or any of the daily oyster or pasta specials. The lunch menu includes sandwiches, burgers, and pastas. ✉ *331 Campbell St.,* ☎ *250/725–3444. AE, MC, V. No lunch Dec.–Feb.*

$$-$$$$ ✕ **Raincoast Café.** Local seafood treated creatively with Asian and Mediterranean techniques and a good selection of vegetarian dishes are the draws at this intimate central Tofino restaurant. Try, for example, the salad of baby greens, smoked wild salmon, and goat cheese, or a starter of seafood in Thai red curry with pomegranate seeds and coconut threads. Entrées include a west coast cioppino (a seafood stew) in chardonnay broth and an ahi tuna steak with a Japanese plum-wine coulis. The decor is minimalist and candlelit, with peekaboo sea views. ✉ *101–120 4th St.,* ☎ *250/725–2215. AE, MC, V.*

$$$$ ✕🏨 **The Wickaninnish Inn.** Set on a rocky promontory above Chester-
★ man Beach, with open ocean on three sides and old-growth forest as a backdrop, this three-story weathered cedar building is a comfortable place to enjoy the area's dramatic wilderness scenery, summer or winter. The inn, 5 km (3 mi) south of Tofino, is no-smoking and every spacious room has a sitting area, an ocean view, and its own balcony, fireplace, and soaking tub. The staff takes very good care of guests, and the full-service Ancient Cedars Spa (also open to nonguests) adds to the pampering. The glass-enclosed Pointe Restaurant offers 240° views of the crashing surf and is renowned in Canada for its Pacific Northwest cuisine; the kitchen makes the most of such local delicacies as oysters, gooseneck barnacles, wild mushrooms, Dungeness crab, and Pacific salmon. ✉ *Osprey La. at Chesterman Beach, Box 250, V0R 2Z0,* ☎ *250/725–3100 or 800/333–4604,* 🖷 *250/725–3110. 46 rooms. Restaurant, lounge, in-room data ports, minibars, room service, massage, spa, steam room, hiking, beach, fishing, laundry service, meeting room. AE, DC, MC, V.* ⊗

$$$$ 🏨 **Clayoquot Wilderness Resorts.** This luxury wilderness retreat offers two options: a floating lodge moored in Clayoquot Sound, a Unesco Biosphere Reserve 25 minutes by water taxi from Tofino, or high-style camping on the edge of Strathcona Provincial Park. The lodge is moored next to its own 127-acre wilderness backyard, with lakes, extensive hiking trails, and acres of old-growth forest. Guests can enjoy fishing, whale-watching, kayaking, horseback riding, hiking, and nature cruises, as well as the restaurant's fine Pacific Northwest cuisine. The comfortable rooms all have water or forest views and private decks. The rates are per person and include all meals and water-taxi pickup from Tofino. The tents at Wilderness Outpost, a safari-style camp on Bedwell River—a pristine area 9 km (6 mi) from Tofino by boat—sit on wooden platforms and come with king-size beds, Persian-style carpets, wood stoves, Adirondack furniture, and porches overlooking the water. Campers can enjoy a hot tub, a sauna, and elegant cuisine served on china and crystal. The activities at the Outpost, including sailing, canoeing, kayaking, horseback riding, mountain biking, hiking, and fishing, are included in the rates, as are all meals and water-taxi pickup from Tofino. A two-night minimum stay applies for both the lodge and the camp. ✉ *Box 130, V0R 2Z0,* ☎ *250/726–8235 or 888/333–5405,* 🖷 *250/726–8558. 16 rooms; 5 tents. Lodge: restaurant, lounge, outdoor hot tub, sauna, spa, exercise room, horseback*

riding, boating, dock, meeting room, helipad. AE, MC, V. AP. Lodge closed Dec.–Feb.; Outpost closed Oct.–Apr. ✥

$$–$$$$ ⌂ **Middle Beach Lodge.** A longtime favorite on the beach 3 km (2 mi) south of Tofino has a choice of two lodges. The Lodge at the Beach, a wooden, adults-only building on the forest edge, has basic rooms (no phones or TVs), some with sea views, and a path down to the beach. The newer (1996) Headlands complex, made with recycled timber and perched on an oceanfront bluff, offers larger, more luxurious rooms, some with fireplaces and ocean-view balconies, and family-size cabins with kitchenettes and fireplaces. Each lodge has a common room with a floor-to-ceiling stone fireplace and ocean views. A third building, with six more suites, was planned for 2001. In July and August dinner is available Wednesday through Sunday; the rest of the year it's served only on Saturday. Smoking isn't allowed on the premises. ⊠ *400 McKenzie Beach Rd., Box 100, V0R 2Z0,* ☎ *250/725–2900,* 𝔽𝔸𝕏 *250/725–2901. 35 rooms, 4 suites, 19 cabins. Dining room, beach, coin laundry, meeting rooms. AE, MC, V. CP.* ✥

$$–$$$ ⌂ **Chesterman Beach Bed and Breakfast.** The front yard of this small, rustic, West Coast cedar B&B on the beach is the rolling ocean surf. The self-contained two-bedroom suite in the main house (with sauna, gas fireplace, and kitchen) and the Lookout room, with its gas fireplace and private ocean-view balcony, are both romantic and cozy. The self-sufficient one-bedroom Garden Cottage has a secluded garden, a large deck, a kitchen, and a fireplace; it's a good option for families. ⊠ *1345 Chesterman Beach Rd., Box 72, V0R 2Z0,* ☎ *250/725–3726,* 𝔽𝔸𝕏 *250/725–3706. 1 room, 2 suites. No-smoking rooms, beach. MC, V. CP.* ✥

$$ ⌂ **Inn at Tough City.** The owners of this inn, on Tofino Harbour scoured the province for such nifty recyclables as stained-glass windows and vintage advertising paraphernalia and added First Nations artwork to create a fun and funky ambience in the lobby and common rooms. The name is derived from Tofino's old nickname, from the days before roads, when life was fairly rough here. It certainly isn't anymore: the guest rooms, decorated in rich, bold colors, have stained-glass windows, hardwood floors, antiques, covered decks or balconies, and down duvets. Six of them have striking views over Tofino Harbour and Clayoquot Sound; several have fireplaces and soaking tubs. The main floor has a cozy common room with leather sofas and a wood stove, and a wraparound veranda. ⊠ *350 Main St., V0R 2Z0,* ☎ *250/725–2021 or 877/725–2021,* 𝔽𝔸𝕏 *250/725–2088. 8 rooms. No-smoking rooms. AE, MC, V.* ✥

$$ ⌂ **Red Crow Guest House.** On the sheltered side of the Tofino peninsula, about 2 km (1 mi) south of the village, sits this Cape Cod–style house amid 17 acres of cedar and hemlock. Two large rooms underneath the main part of the house open onto a covered veranda and a private pebble beach, offering stunning east-facing views over island-dotted Clayoquot Sound. Decorated with family heirlooms and First Nations art, each of the large comfortable rooms has a king bed, wood stove, coffeemaker, and breakfast table. A lavish breakfast of home-baked goodies is delivered to your door. A rustic cedar cottage in the woods has a full kitchen and sleeps six. ⊠ *1084 Pacific Rim Hwy., Box 37, V0R 2Z0,* ☎ 𝔽𝔸𝕏 *250/725–2275. 2 rooms, 1 cottage. Refrigerators. V.* ✥

$ ⌂ **Paddlers' Inn.** This multiple-business inn on the waterfront in the center of Tofino covers all the bases. Downstairs, an espresso bar and bookstore overlook a kayaking outlet. Upstairs, five clean, fresh rooms have Scandinavian furniture and futons but no phones or TVs. The rooms share two bathrooms and a kitchen. The inn is completely no-smoking. ⊠ *320 Main St., Box 620, V0R 2Z0,* ☎ *250/725–4222 or 800/*

863–4664, ℻ 250/725–2070. 5 rooms without bath. Café, boating. MC, V. Closed Nov.–Feb. CP. ⌘

$ 📺 **Whalers on the Point Guesthouse (Hostelling International Tofino).** On Tofino Harbour, this modern seaside hostel has pretty much everything a budget traveler could want; there's a game room and TV lounge, a shared kitchen, living room, dining room, and patio overlooking the bay, and even surfboard storage and Internet access. Accommodation is available in private rooms and dorms. ✉ 81 West St., Box 296, V0R 2Z0, ☎ 250/725–3443, ℻ 250/725–3463. 7 rooms, 3 with bath; 15 4-bed dorms. Sauna, bicycles, coin laundry. MC, V. ⌘

Outdoor Activities and Sports

FISHING

Local charter companies include **Chinook Charters** (☎ 250/725–3431 or 800/665–3646) and **Weigh West Marine Resort** (☎ 250/725–3277 or 800/665–8922).

GOLF

Long Beach Golf Course (✉ Pacific Rim Hwy., ☎ 250/725–3332) is a 9-hole, par-36 course.

KAYAKING

Remote Passages Sea Kayaking (✉ 71 Wharf St., ☎ 250/725–3330 or 800/666–9833) has guided day and evening paddles; no experience is necessary. **Tofino Sea-Kayaking Company** (✉ 320 Main St., ☎ 250/725–4222 or 800/863–4664) rents kayaks and runs a kayaking school and wilderness kayaking trips.

SURFING

Tofino, despite the chilling waters, is a popular place to surf. **Live to Surf** (✉ 1180 Pacific Rim Hwy., ☎ 250/725–4464) rents boards and wetsuits.

WHALE-WATCHING AND MARINE EXCURSIONS

Between March and May, gray whales migrate along the coast here; resident grays can be seen anytime between May and November. Humpback whales, sea otters, and other wildlife are increasingly seen in the area. Most whale-watching operators also offer boat trips to Meares Island, with its stands of old-growth forest, and Hot Springs Cove, where you can soak in natural rock pools.

Jamie's Whaling Station (✉ 606 Campbell St., ☎ 250/725–3919, 800/667–9913 in Canada) is one of the most established operators on the coast and has both Zodiacs and more comfortable 65-ft tour boats. **Remote Passages Marine Excursions** (✉ 71 Wharf St., ☎ 250/725–3330 or 800/666–9833), a well-established operator, offers whale-watching and other wildlife-viewing trips with an ecological focus. The **Whale Centre** (✉ 411 Campbell St., ☎ 250/725–2132) has a museum with a 40-ft whale skeleton you can study while waiting for your boat. **Chinook Charters** (✉ 450 Campbell St., ☎ 250/725–3431 or 800/665–3646) offers guided fishing charters and whale-watching and Hot Springs Cove trips. **Sea Trek Tours and Expeditions** (☎ 250/725–4412 or 800/811–9155) runs whale- and bear-watching and harbor tours and day trips to Hot Spring Cove and Meares Island.

Shopping

The magnificent **Eagle Aerie Gallery** (✉ 350 Campbell St., ☎ 250/725–3235) houses a collection of prints, paintings, and carvings by the renowned native artist Roy Henry Vickers in a traditional longhouse. **House of Himwitsa** (✉ 300 Main St., ☎ 250/725–2017) sells native crafts, jewelry, and clothing. The complex also has a seafood restaurant and lodge rooms. **Islandfolk Gallery** (✉ 120 4th St., ☎ 250/725–

3130) sells the work of Tofino wildlife artist Mark Hobson and other local artists. Photographs, paintings, carvings, pottery, and jewelry by local artists are available at **Reflecting Spirit Gallery** (✉ 411 Campbell St., ☎ 250/725–2472), which also runs a children's art program in the summer. **Wildside Booksellers** (✉ 320 Main St., ☎ 250/725–4222) has an extensive selection of books and an espresso bar.

Pacific Rim National Park Reserve

★ ㉕ *105 km (63 mi) west of Port Alberni, 9 km (5 mi) south of Tofino.*

This national park (✉ 2185 Ocean Terrace Rd., Box 280, Ucluelet V0R 3A0, ☎ 250/726–7721, FAX 250/726–4720, ✍) has some of Canada's most stunning coastal and rain-forest scenery, abundant wildlife, and a unique marine environment. It comprises three separate areas— Long Beach, the Broken Group Islands, and the West Coast Trail—for a combined area of 123,431 acres and stretches 130 km (81 mi) along Vancouver Island's West Coast. The **Park Information Centre** (2 km, or 1 mi, north of the Tofino–Ucluelet junction on Hwy. 4, ☎ 250/726– 4212) is open daily mid-June to mid-September, 9:30–5. Park-use fees apply in all sections of the park.

The **Long Beach** unit gets its name from a 16-km (10-mi) strip of hard-packed sand strewn with driftwood, shells, and the occasional Japanese glass fishing float. Long Beach is the most accessible part of the park, and roads can get busy in summer. People come in the off-season to watch winter storms and to see migrating whales in early spring. An $8 daily group pass, available from dispensers in the parking lots, admits up to 10 people in one vehicle for a day and includes admission to the Wickaninnish Centre.

A first stop for many visitors, the **Wickaninnish Centre** (✉ Hwy. 4, ☎ 250/726–4701 for center; 250/726–7706 for restaurant) is the park's visitor and interpretive center, right on the ocean edge about 16 km (10 mi) north of Ucluelet. It's a great place to learn about the wilderness; theater programs and exhibits provide information about the park's marine ecology and rain-forest environment. Open daily mid-March to mid-October, 10:30–6, the center is also a good lunch stop—it was originally an inn, and its restaurant still serves up hearty seafood lunches and dinners (until 9 PM). Park information is available here when the Park Information Centre is closed.

The 100-plus islands of the **Broken Group Islands** can be reached only by boat. Many commercial charter tours are available from Ucluelet, at the southern end of Long Beach, and from Tofino, Bamfield, and Port Alberni. The islands and their waters are alive with sea lions, seals, and whales. The inner waters near Gibraltar, Jacques, and Hand islands offer protection and good boating conditions, but go with a guide if it's your first trip.

The third element of the park, the **West Coast Trail,** runs along the coast from Bamfield to Port Renfrew. This extremely rugged 75-km (47-mi) trail is for experienced hikers. It can be traveled only on foot, takes an average of six days to complete, and is open May through September. The park controls the number of people allowed on the trail, so it's best to reserve a spot. A number of fees apply: $25 for a reservation (paid when you book); $70 in park-use fees; and $25 in ferry fares. Reservations can be made, up to three months in advance, with Super, Natural British Columbia (☞ Visitor Information *in* Vancouver Island A to Z, *below*) from March through September.

En Route   Heading back to the east coast from Port Alberni, stop at **Cathedral Grove** in MacMillan Provincial Park on Highway 4. Walking trails lead past Douglas fir trees and western red cedars, some as much as 800 years old. Their remarkable height creates a spiritual effect, as though you were gazing at a cathedral ceiling.

Parksville

❷ *47 km (29 mi) east of Port Alberni, 38 km (24 mi) northwest of Nanaimo, 72 km (45 mi) southeast of Courtenay, 154 km (95 mi) north of Victoria.*

Parksville is one of the primary resort areas on the eastern side of the island; lodges and waterfront motels cater to families, campers, and boaters. In **Rathtrevor Beach Provincial Park** (✉ off Hwy. 19, ☎ 250/954–4600), 2 km (1 mi) south of Parksville, high tide brings ashore the warmest ocean water in British Columbia. It's a good place for a swim.

OFF THE   **COOMBS** – If you're traveling from Parksville to Port Alberni, it's worth
BEATEN PATH   taking the quieter Highway 4A past this odd little village, best known for
               the goats grazing on the grass-covered roof of its Old Country Market.
               Also worth a stop is **Butterfly World** (✉ 1080 Winchester Rd., ☎ 250/
               248–7026), where you can wander through an atrium filled with hun-
               dreds of free-flying butterflies. It's open March and October daily 10–4
               and April through September daily 10–5. Admission is $6.50.

Lodging

$$–$$$ 🏨 **Tigh-Na-Mara Resort.** About 2 km (1 mi) south of Parksville on High-
way 19 is this family-oriented resort set on 22 forested seaside acres. The beach, with its warm water and wide tidal flats, is just right for the bucket-and-spade brigade, as are the playgrounds, playhouse, and extensive children's programs. The log-construction accommodations include a three-story lodge high over the water (a winding pathway leads down to the beach), a more basic inland lodge, and several one-and two-bedroom cabins in the woods. All ocean-side units have fireplaces and decks with expansive views over Craig Bay; some have whirlpool tubs. ✉ *1095 East Island Hwy., V9P 2E5,* ☎ *250/248–2072 or 800/663–7373,* FAX *250/248–4140. 101 rooms, 41 cabins. Restaurant, lounge, in-room data ports, kitchenettes, no-smoking floors, refrigerators, indoor-outdoor pool, hot tub, massage, steam room, horseshoes, Ping-Pong, volleyball, beach, fishing, bicycles, children's programs (ages 4–12), playground, coin laundry, convention center, travel services, car rental. AE, DC, MC, V.* 🐾

Outdoor Activities and Sports

Morningstar Golf Course (✉ 525 Lowry's Rd., ☎ 250/248–8161) is an 18-hole, par-72 course that's open all year.

Qualicum Beach

❷ *10 km (6 mi) north of Parksville.*

Qualicum Beach is known largely for its salmon fishing and opportunities for beachcombing. The **Old School House Gallery and Art Centre** (✉ 122 Fern Rd. W, ☎ 250/752–6133) shows and sells the work of local artists and artisans.

Spelunking tours for all levels are offered April–October at **Horne Lake Caves Provincial Park** (☎ 250/248–7829). Prices start at $15 for a 1½-hour tour. The turn off for the park, from Highway 19, is 18 km (11 mi) north of Qualicum Beach. From the turnoff it's another 13 km (8 mi).

En Route Between Qualicum Beach and the twin cities of Courtenay and Comox is tiny Buckley Bay, where BC Ferries (☞ Getting Around *in* Vancouver Island A to Z, *below*) leave for **Denman Island,** with connecting service to **Hornby Island.** Both these pretty rural islands have crafts shops, cafés, walking trails, and accommodations; Hornby is best known for its long, sandy beaches.

Courtenay and Comox

㉘ *220 km (136 mi) northwest of Victoria, 17 nautical mi west of Powell River, 57 km (34 mi) northwest of Qualicum Beach; Comox is 6 km (4 mi) east of Courtenay.*

Courtenay and Comox are commercial towns that also provide a base for Mt. Washington skiers. In Courtenay you can catch the **Esquimalt & Nanaimo** small-gauge railway to Nanaimo, Victoria, and other South Island stops (☞ Getting Around *in* Vancouver Island A to Z, *below*).

Dinosaur fans will love the **Courtenay and District Museum and Paleontology Centre** (✉ 207 Fourth St., Courtenay, ☎ 250/334–3611), British Columbia's leading paleontology center. It's home to the reconstructed skeleton of a 13-m (43-ft) Elasmasour—a dinosaur-era sea creature found in the Comox Valley. The museum also has some interesting First Nations and pioneer artifacts, and arranges fossil-hunting day trips in the area. Admission is $3. The museum is open June through August daily 10–4:30, closed Sun.–Mon. the rest of the year.

The **Comox Airforce Museum** (☎ 250/339–8162), at Canadian Forces Base Comox in Lazo, about 1 km (½ mi) north of Comox, has an interesting collection of air-force memorabilia and historic aircraft in the airpark next door. It's open Wednesday through Sunday 10–4 June through August; weekends and holidays 10–4 the rest of the year. Admission is by donation. At the **Filberg Heritage Lodge and Park** (✉ 61 Filberg Rd., Comox, ☎ 250/339–2715), you can stroll around 9 acres of beautifully landscaped waterfront grounds and tour the rustic 1929 lodge. The lodge is open 11–5, daily June through August and Friday through Sunday in May and September. In summer, a separate petting zoo and seaside teahouse are also open. Admission to the gardens, which are open dawn to dusk all year, is free. Admission to the lodge is $1.

Dining and Lodging

$$–$$$
★ ✗ **Old House Restaurant.** This riverside restaurant set among gardens (though also overlooking a pulp mill across the way) provides casual dining in a restored 1938 house with cedar beams, four stone fireplaces, and a patio for dining. People flock here for the West Coast home-style cuisine—pastas, salads, and sandwiches, along with fancier, more innovative dishes (seafood stir-fry, peppered Fanny Bay oysters)—and the fresh daily specials. ✉ *1760 Riverside La., Courtenay,* ☎ *250/338–5406. AE, DC, MC, V.*

$$–$$$
★ 🏨 **Kingfisher Oceanside Resort and Spa.** Soothing is the word to describe this seaside resort 10 minutes south of Courtenay. Thirty-two new beachfront units, all with decks or patios, kitchenettes, gas fireplaces, and expansive ocean views, are decorated in soft sea blues and greens. A full-service spa (also open to nonguests) offers the works, including beauty treatments, aromatherapy, hydrotherapy, and massage (for two, if you like). The steam room looks like a mermaid's cave, and the exercise room has an ocean view. The original, lower-price rooms, set a little farther back from the water, are also modern and spacious, and some have kitchens. Suites have in-room data ports and VCRs. ✉ *4330 S. Island Hwy., R.R. 6, Site 672, C-1, Courtenay V9N 8H9,* ☎

250/338–1323 or 800/663–7929, FAX 250/338–0058. 28 rooms, 32 suites. Restaurant, lounge, no-smoking floor, room service, pool, outdoor hot tub, sauna, tennis court, beach, boating, fishing, bicycles, baby-sitting, playground, laundry service, business services, meeting rooms. AE, D, DC, MC, V. ✏

$ 🏠 **Greystone Manor.** This 1918 house about 3 km (2 mi) south of Courtenay has a lovingly tended 1½-acre English garden and views over Comox Bay, where seals are often visible. Inside, the original hardwood floors, period furnishings, and a woodstove make things cozy. Two of the prettily decorated rooms have baths with showers; the third has a claw-foot tub in a room across the hall. The hosts, Mike and Maureen Shipton, from Bath, England, serve a full hot breakfast, which is included in the rates. ✉ 4014 Haas Rd., R.R. 6, Site 684, C-2, Courtenay V9N 8H9, ☎ 250/338–1422. 3 rooms. Breakfast room, piano. MC, V. ✏

Outdoor Activities and Sports

GOLF

The 18-hole, par-72 course at the **Crown Isle Golf Resort & Golf Community** (✉ 399 Clubhouse Dr., off Ryan Rd., Courtenay, ☎ 250/703–5000 or 800/378–6811) is, at 7,024 yards, the longest course on Vancouver Island. The resort also has on-site accommodation and a lavish club house. It's one of several courses in the area.

SKIING

Mt. Washington Alpine Resort (✉ Box 3069, Strathcona Park Way, Courtenay, ☎ 250/338–1386; 888/231–1499 for lodging reservations), 30 km (18 mi) from Courtenay, with 50 downhill runs, a 1,657-ft vertical drop, five chairlifts, and an elevation of 5,200 ft, is the island's largest ski area. The resort also has 40 km (25 mi) of track-set cross-country trails, a snowboard park, snow-tubing chutes, and, in summer, miles of hiking trails accessible by chairlift. The resort has a good selection of restaurants, shops, and hotel, condo, and B&B accommodations.

Campbell River

🔵 **29**   50 km (31 mi) north of Courtenay and Comox, 155 km (96 mi) northwest of Nanaimo, 270 km (167 mi) northwest of Victoria.

Campbell River draws people who want to fish; some of the biggest salmon ever caught on a line have been landed just off the coast here. Cutthroat trout are also plentiful in the river.

The primary access to Strathcona Provincial Park (☞ below) is on Highway 28 west from town. Other recreational activities include diving in Discovery Passage, where a battleship has been sunk; kayaking; or taking a summer whale-watching tour. For information, contact **Campbell River Visitor Information Centre** (✉ 1235 Shoppers Row, Box 400, V9W 5B6, ☎ 250/287–4636).

The **Haig-Brown House** (✉ 2250 Campbell River Rd., ☎ 250/286–6646), the preserved home of conservationist and writer Roderick Haig-Brown, is set in 2 acres of formal gardens surrounded by 20 acres of trail-laced woods. The center runs seminars and workshops on topics ranging from conservation to writing, and also offers B&B rooms.

Dining and Lodging

$$ ✕ **Royal Coachman Neighbourhood Pub.** Informal, blackboard-menu restaurants like this one dot the landscape of the island. The menu, which changes daily, is surprisingly daring for what is essentially a high-end pub, and the inn draws crowds nightly, especially Tuesday and Sat-

urday (prime-rib nights). Come early for both lunch and dinner to avoid a wait. ⊠ *84 Dogwood St.,* ☎ *250/286–0231. AE, MC, V.*

$$–$$$$ 🔟 **Painter's Lodge.** Bob Hope, John Wayne, and their fishing buddies came to this lodge overlooking Discovery Passage to catch big Tyee (spring salmon) in the 1940s and '50s. The attractive cedar complex now draws nature-oriented visitors and whale-watchers as well as anglers; the resort's own fleet runs guided fishing and nature cruises. The 15 lodge rooms and the rooms, suites, and one- to three-bedroom cabins spread around the property all have balconies or patios, and some have kitchens, fireplaces, and whirlpool baths. The owner, the Oak Bay Marine Group, also runs a water taxi to Painter's sister resort, April Point Lodge, on Quadra Island (☞ *below*), where you can kayak or explore biking and hiking trails. Painter's Lodge is 8 km (5 mi) north of Campbell River. ⊠ *1625 McDonald Rd., Box 460, V9W 5C1,* ☎ *250/286–1102 or 800/663–7090,* FAX *250/286–0158. 90 rooms, 4 cabins. Restaurant, lounge, pub, pool, 2 outdoor hot tubs, 2 tennis courts, exercise room, fishing, bicycles, playground, meeting rooms. AE, D, DC, MC, V. Closed mid-Oct.–mid-Mar.* 🐾

Outdoor Activities and Sports

Storey Creek Golf Club (⊠ 300 McGimpsey Rd., ☎ 250/923–3673) is an 18-hole, par-72 course 20 minutes south of Campbell River.

Quadra Island

③⓪ *10 minutes by ferry from Campbell River.*

Quadra is a thickly forested island, rich with wildlife and laced with hiking trails. The **Kwagiulth Museum and Cultural Centre** (⊠ 34 Weway Rd., ☎ 250/285–3733) in Cape Mudge Village houses a collection of potlatch (ceremonial feast) regalia and historical photos. The museum is open daily year-round; admission is $3.

Dining and Lodging

$$ ✕🔟 **Tsa-Kwa-Luten Lodge.** Authentic Pacific Coast native food and cultural activities are highlights of this resort operated by members of the Cape Mudge First Nations band. The main lodge, on a high bluff amid 1,100 acres of forest, is striking, with a lofty foyer built in the style of a longhouse. The guest rooms, decorated with modern furniture and Kwagiulth artwork, all have balconies or patios overlooking Discovery Passage; many also have fireplaces or lofts. Three two-bedroom beachfront cottages have gas fireplaces, whirlpool baths, kitchenettes, and private verandas. A four-bedroom guest house is great for groups. You can visit nearby petroglyphs, kayak, bike, hike, fish, dive, snorkel, take a whale-watching cruise, or even try archery here. The restaurant, serving traditional Kwagiulth cuisine, is open to nonguests by reservation. ⊠ *Lighthouse Rd., Box 460, Quathiaski Cove V0P 1N0,* ☎ *250/285–2042 or 800/665–7745,* FAX *250/285–2532. 30 rooms, 4 cottages. Restaurant, lounge, no-smoking rooms, outdoor hot tub, sauna, archery, boccie, exercise room, boating, fishing, mountain bikes, laundry service, business services, meeting rooms. AE, DC, MC, V.* 🐾

$$–$$$ 🔟 **April Point Lodge and Fishing Resort.** This former fishing lodge, spread across a point and surrounded by forest, is now a family-oriented ecotourism getaway, with whale- and bird-watching, kayaking, hiking, and saltwater fishing available. The accommodations include lodge rooms and suites, many with fireplaces, and guest houses with kitchens, fireplaces, and sundecks. Guests have access, via free water taxi, to the pool, hot tubs, tennis courts, and fitness center at Painter's Lodge (☞ *above*), near Campbell River. ⊠ *900 Quathiaski Cove, Box 248, Quadra Island V0P 1N0,* ☎ *250/285–2222 or 800/663–7090,* FAX *250/285–2411. 46 rooms, 8 guest houses. Restaurant, lounge, picnic area, sushi bar, no-smoking rooms,* *hiking, dock, boating, bicycles, baby-sitting, meeting rooms, helipad. AE, D, DC, MC, V. Closed Nov.–Mar.* 🐿

Strathcona Provincial Park

★ ③ *40 km (25 mi) west of Campbell River.*

The largest provincial park on Vancouver Island, Strathcona Provincial Park (☎ 250/954–4600) encompasses **Mt. Golden Hinde,** at 7,220 ft the island's highest mountain, and **Della Falls,** Canada's highest waterfall, reaching 1,440 ft. This strikingly scenic wilderness park's lakes and 161 campsites attract summer canoeists, hikers, anglers, and campers. The main access is by Highway 28 from Campbell River; Mt. Washington ski area, also in the park, can be reached by roads out of Courtenay (☞ *above*).

Lodging

$–$$ 🏨 **Strathcona Park Lodge and Outdoor Education Centre.** A privately owned lakefront resort on the outskirts of Strathcona Provincial Park, the center has reasonably priced lodge rooms, lakefront cabins, and a variety of outdoor adventure programs—including rock-climbing, canoeing, kayaking, and sailing—available to the public in summer. It's about 45 km (28 mi) west of Highway 19. ✉ *Box 2160, Campbell River V9W 5C5,* ☎ *250/286–3122,* FAX *250/286–6010. 38 rooms, 10 cabins. Restaurant, hiking, boating, fishing, children's programs (ages 6–18), meeting rooms. MC, V. Lodge and restaurant closed Nov.–Apr.; cabins available year-round.* 🐿

Johnstone Strait

East side of Vancouver Island, roughly between Campbell River and Telegraph Cove.

Pods of resident orcas live year-round in the Inside Passage and around Vancouver Island; in Robson Bight they like rubbing against the soft pebble beaches. Whales are most often seen during the salmon runs of July, August, and September. Because of their presence, Robson Bight has been made into an ecological reserve: whales there must not be disturbed by human observers. Some of the island's best whale-watching tours, however, are conducted nearby, out of **Alert Bay** and **Telegraph Cove,** a village built on pilings over water.

There are other things to do in the area. From **Port McNeill,** a 30-minute ferry ride will take you to Alert Bay, where you can see the First Nations artifacts at the **U'mista Cultural Centre** (☎ 250/974–5403), or to **Sointula** to visit the remains of a Finnish Utopian community.

Outdoor Activities and Sports

KAYAKING

North Island Kayak (☎ 250/949–7707 or 877/949–7707), at Alder Bay Resort on the way to Telegraph Cove and several other locations, rents canoes and kayaks and runs guided paddles.

WHALE-WATCHING

Most trips run from June through October. **Robson Bight Charters** (☎ 250/282–3833, 800/658–0022 in British Columbia) in Sayward offers full-day whale- and bear-watching expeditions. **Stubbs Island Whale Watching** (☎ 250/928–3185 or 800/665–3066) in Telegraph Cove offers four-hour whale-watching trips.

Port Hardy

32 *238 km (148 mi) northwest of Campbell River, 499 km (309 mi) northwest of Victoria, 274 nautical mi southeast of Prince Rupert.*

Port Hardy is the departure and arrival point for BC Ferries' (☞ Getting Around *in* Vancouver Island A to Z, *below*) year-round trips through the scenic Inside Passage to and from Prince Rupert, the coastal port serving the Queen Charlotte Islands, and, in summer, to Bella Coola and other small communities along the midcoast. (For more information about these areas, *see* Chapter 4.) In summer Port Hardy can be crowded, so book your accommodations early. Ferry reservations for the trip between Port Hardy and Prince Rupert or Bella Coola should also be made well in advance. **North Island Transportation** (☎ 250/949–6300) runs a shuttle bus between most Port Hardy hotels and the ferry terminal. The fare is $5.25.

OFF THE BEATEN PATH | **CAPE SCOTT PROVINCIAL PARK** – At the northern tip of Vancouver Island, 67 km (42 mi) north of Port Hardy, Cape Scott Provincial Park (☎ 250/954–4600) is a wilderness camping region suitable for well-equipped and experienced hikers.

Lodging

$$ 🏨 **Glen Lyon Inn.** Eagles can often be spotted scouting the water for fish to prey on from this modern hotel next to the marina on Hardy Bay. Completely refurbished in 2000, all rooms have full ocean views; most have balconies, microwaves, and refrigerators. Some of the suites have whirlpool tubs and fireplaces and several units have kitchenettes. The inn is one of the closest to the ferry terminal, 7 km (4 mi) away. Fishing and whale-watching charters can be arranged from here. ✉ 6435 Hardy Bay Rd., Box 103, V0N 2P0, ☎ 250/949–7115 or 877/949–7115, ℻ 250/949–7415. 37 rooms, 7 suites. Restaurant, pub, in-room data ports, no-smoking rooms, refrigerators, exercise room, coin laundry, meeting room. AE, MC, V. ⌖

$$ 🏨 **Quarterdeck Inn and Marine Resort.** All rooms have water views at this new hotel, opened in 1999 on Port Hardy's waterfront. The bright, spacious rooms have modern decor and rich colors; some have kitchenettes. One room has a fireplace and a whirlpool tub. Salmon fishing, day hikes, and whale-watching can be arranged from the hotel, which is a 10-minute drive from the ferry terminal. ✉ 6555 Hardy Bay Rd., Box 910, V0N 2P0, ☎ 250/902–0455 or 877/902–0459, ℻ 250/902–0454. 39 rooms, 1 suite. Pub, in-room data ports, no-smoking floor, hot tub, exercise room, marina, meeting room. AE, D, DC, MC, V. CP. ⌖

Vancouver Island A to Z

Arriving and Departing

BY BUS

Greyhound (☎ 604/482–8747 or 800/661–8747) serves Nanaimo from Vancouver (☞ By Ferry, *below*). **Pacific Coach Lines** (☎ 250/385–4411 in Victoria, 604/662–8074 in Vancouver, 800/661–1725 elsewhere) operates daily connecting service between Victoria and Vancouver on BC Ferries (☞ By Ferry, *below*).

BY FERRY

BC Ferries (☎ 250/386–3431, 888/223–3779 in British Columbia outside Victoria; for vehicle reservations, 604/444–2890 from outside B.C., 888/724–5223 in province) provides frequent, year-round passenger and vehicle service to Vancouver Island: a 1½-hour crossing from Tsawwassen (about an hour's drive south of Vancouver) to Swartz Bay (a 30-minute drive north of Victoria); a two-hour crossing from Tsawwassen to Duke Point, 15 km (9 mi) south of Nanaimo; and a 1½-hour crossing from Horseshoe Bay (a 30-minute drive north of Vancouver) to Departure Bay, 3 km (2 mi) north of Nanaimo. Vehicle reservations can be made for any of these routes; a $15 reservation fee applies. You can also make reservations on BC Ferries' Web site (www.bcferries.com), which has up-to-date fare and schedule information on all routes.

B.C. Ferries also links Comox with Powell River on the Sunshine Coast (☞ Chapter 4), though reservations cannot be made for this route. For information about other B.C. Ferries routes, including travel between Port Hardy and Bella Coola or Prince Rupert, *see* British Columbia A to Z *in* Chapter 4.

BY PLANE

Vancouver Island is served by Victoria International Airport (☞ Victoria A to Z, *above*). There are domestic airports in most cities. **Air B.C.** (☎ 604/688–5515; 888/247–2262 in British Columbia outside Vancouver and Victoria), operated by Air Canada, is the dominant carrier. **Kenmore Air Harbour** (☎ 425/486–1257 or 800/543–9595) offers direct daily flights from Seattle to Victoria year-round, and has summer service from Seattle to Nanaimo, Campbell River, and Port McNeill. **North Vancouver Air** (☎ 604/278–1608 or 800/228–6608) links Victoria, Tofino, and Comox with Vancouver. **Northwest Seaplanes** (☎ 800/690–0086) offers summer floatplane service between Seattle and Tofino, Campbell River, and Port Hardy.

Getting Around

BY BOAT AND FERRY

BC Ferries (☎ 250/386–3431; 888/223–3779 in British Columbia outside Victoria) provides year-round passenger and vehicle service to most of the inhabited islands off Vancouver Island's east coast.

Lady Rose Marine Services (☎ 250/723–8313; 800/663–7192 for reservations Apr.–Sept.) takes passengers on packet freighters from Port Alberni to Vancouver Island's west coast. The M.V. *Lady Rose,* a Scottish ship built in 1937, makes the 4½-hour trip to Bamfield at 8 AM Tuesday, Thursday, and Saturday year-round. The round-trip fare is $40. The newer M.V. *Francis Barkley* sails from Port Alberni to the Broken Group Islands and Ucluelet at 8 AM Monday, Wednesday, and Friday between early June and late September. The round-trip fare is $50 to Ucluelet, $40 to the Broken Group Islands. Both ships leave from **Argyle Pier** (✉ 5425 Argyle St., Port Alberni).

The **M.V. Uchuck** (☎ 250/283–2515 or 250/283–2325), a 100-passenger coastal packet freighter, sails from Gold River, 100 km (62 mi) west of Campbell River at the end of Highway 28, to a number of isolated west coast settlements. Day trips ($40–$45 per person) and overnight trips ($310 per couple, including one night's bed and breakfast) are available all year. Reservations (and good sea legs) are essential.

BY BUS

Laidlaw Coach Lines (☎ 250/385–4411; 800/318–0818 in British Columbia; 800/663–8390 from the U.S.) serves most towns on Vancouver Island. **The Link** (☎ 250/726–7779) runs a scheduled shuttle-bus service along the island's west coast, serving Ucluelet, Tofino, Tofino Airport, and the Pacific Rim National Park Reserve.

BY CAR

Highway 17 connects the Swartz Bay ferry terminal on the Saanich Peninsula with downtown Victoria. The **Trans-Canada Highway** (Highway

1) runs from Victoria to Nanaimo. The **Island Highway** (Highway 19) connects Nanaimo to Port Hardy. Most of the way between Nanaimo and Courtenay, Highway 19 is a new freeway. (Highway 19A, the old road, runs parallel. It's a slower, seaside option.) The freeway is being extended to Campbell River. **Highway 14** connects Victoria to Sooke and Port Renfrew on the west coast. **Highway 4** crosses the island from Parksville to Tofino and Pacific Rim National Park Reserve.

Major roads on Vancouver Island, and most secondary roads, are paved and well engineered. Many wilderness and park access roads are unpaved. Inquire locally about logging activity before using logging or forestry service roads. **B.C. Highways** (☎ 900/565–4997) has 24-hour highway reports; the toll call is 75¢ a minute.

BY TRAIN

VIA Rail's **Esquimalt & Nanaimo Rail Liner** (☎ 800/561–8630 in Canada, 800/561–3949 in the U.S.) serves Duncan, Chemainus, Nanaimo, and Courtenay from Victoria's **VIA Rail Station** (✉ 450 Pandora Ave.), at the east end of the Johnson Street Bridge.

Contacts and Resources

B&B AND LODGING RESERVATION AGENCIES

Reservations for lodging anywhere in the province can be made through **Super, Natural British Columbia**'s reservation service (☎ 800/435–5622). From March through October, the provincial government runs a toll-free **Campground Reservation Line** (☎ 800/689–9025).

Best Canadian Bed and Breakfast Network (✉ 1064 Balfour Ave., Vancouver V6H 1X1, ☎ 604/738–7207, FAX 604/732–4998) can book B&Bs across the province, including Vancouver Island. **Garden City B&B Reservation Service** (✉ 660 Jones Terr., Victoria V8Z 2L7, ☎ 250/479–1986, FAX 250/479–9999) can book B&B accommodations throughout Vancouver Island. The **Gourmet Trail** books packages at five of the province's finest inns (☞ Guided Tours, *below*).

CAR RENTAL

Most major agencies, including **Avis, Budget, Hertz,** and **National Tilden** serve cities throughout the island (☞ Car Rental *in* Smart Travel Tips A to Z).

EMERGENCIES

Ambulance, fire, poison control, police (☎ 911).

Guided Tours

The **Gourmet Trail** (✉ 304–1913 Sooke Rd., Victoria V9B 1V9, ☎ 250/478–9505 or 800/970–7722) offers self-drive and all-inclusive escorted tours linking five hotels and country inns on Vancouver Island and Salt Spring Island famous for their cuisine. **Island Outings** (☎ 250/642–4469 or 888/345–4469) conducts day-long artisan and winery tours around southern Vancouver Island. **Pride of Victoria Cruises and Tours** (1175 Beach Dr., Victoria V8S 2N2, ☎ 250/592–3474 or 800/668–7758) offers day trips from Victoria to Salt Spring Island, the San Juan Islands, and Chemainus on a 45-ft catamaran. Experts from the **Royal British Columbia Museum** (☎ 250/356–5877) lead day trips to study Vancouver Island's natural and cultural history.

Outdoor Activities and Sports

For other outdoor-adventure operators, also *see* the listings under individual towns.

FISHING

Separate licenses are required for saltwater and freshwater fishing in British Columbia. Both are available at sporting-goods stores, government agency offices, and most fishing lodges and charter-boat companies in the province. A one-day license for nonresidents costs $15 for freshwater fishing, $7.50 for saltwater fishing, and $14 for saltwater salmon fishing. For information about saltwater-fishing regulations, contact **Fisheries and Oceans Canada** (☎ 604/666–2828), or pick up a free *Sport Fishing Guide,* available at most tourist-information centers. **Super, Natural British Columbia** (☎ 800/435–5622) has a brochure o freshwater fishing.

GOLF

Vancouver Island's mild climate allows most golf courses to stay open all year. Green fees are about $30–$60, and usually include a cart.

Golf Central (☎ 250/380–4653) offers a transportation and booking service for golfers in southern Vancouver Island. For advance tee-time bookings at courses in Victoria or Parksville, you can try **Last Minute Golf** (☎ 604/878–1833 or 800/684–6344). **West Coast Golf Shuttle** (☎ 888/599–6800) offers hotel and golfing packages on Vancouver Island.

HIKING

B.C. Parks (⌧ Box 9398, Stn. Prov. Govt., Victoria V8W 9M9, ☎ 250/387–4557 or 250/387–5002) offers detailed information.

Island Outings (☎ 250/642–4469 or 888/345–4469) runs full- and half-day guided hikes in the wilderness areas of southern Vancouver Island. **Nature Calls Eco-Tours** (☎ 250/361–4453 or 877/361–4453) offers a four-day trek on the Juan de Fuca Marine Trail, as well as day hikes in southern Vancouver Island.

KAYAKING

Several companies offer multiday sea-kayaking trips to the coastal areas of Vancouver Island. Some of the excursions are suitable for beginners, and many trips offer an excellent chance to view orcas. **Canadian Outback Adventure Company** (☎ 604/921–7250 or 800/565–8735) schedules three- to six-day sea-kayaking trips to Johnstone Strait for beginner and intermediate paddlers. **Ecosummer Expeditions** (☎ 250/674–0102 or 800/465–8884) runs multiday paddles to Johnstone Strait. **Gabriola Cycle and Kayak** (☎ 250/247–8277) offers sea-kayaking trips to the Broken Group Islands and other areas off the west coast of Vancouver Island, as well as to Johnstone Strait. **Ocean West** (☎ 604/898–4979 or 800/660–0051) has three- to six-day paddling, camping, and orca-watching trips in Johnstone Strait. **Go Green Eco Adventures** (☎ 250/336–8706 or 888/324–7336) gives kayaking, backpacking, and sightseeing tours in several regions on Vancouver Island.

VISITOR INFORMATION

Comox Valley Visitor Infocentre (⌧ 2040 /ckuffe Ave., Courtenay, ☎ 250/334–3234). **Port Hardy Visitor Information Centre** (⌧ 7520 Market St., Port Hardy, ☎ 250/949–7622). **Super, Natural British Columbia** (☎ 800/435–5622). **Tourism Vancouver Island** (⌧ 203–335 Wesley St., Nanaimo V9R 2T5, ☎ 250/754–3500).

4 BRITISH COLUMBIA

From rugged mountains to lush inland valleys, from northern woodlands to lakeside vineyards and forested islands, this western province has an abundance of natural beauty. There are plenty of opportunities for wildlife viewing, as well as for skiing, golfing, fishing, hiking, and kayaking—or you can simply relax in a peaceful country inn. Your visit may take you to First Nations villages, luxurious ski resorts, historic towns, and isolated islands.

Revised by Sue
Kernaghan

BRITISH COLUMBIA, CANADA'S WESTERNMOST province, harbors Pacific beaches, verdant islands, year-round skiing, and world-class fishing—a wealth of outdoor action and beauty. The people of the province are a similarly heterogeneous mix: descendants of the original Native American peoples and 19th-century British, European, and Asian settlers, and more-recent immigrants from all corners of the earth.

Canada's third-largest province (only Québec and Ontario are bigger), British Columbia occupies almost 10% of Canada's total surface area, stretching from the Pacific Ocean eastward to the province of Alberta, and from the U.S. border north to the Yukon and Northwest Territories. It spans more than 360,000 square mi, making it larger than every American state except Alaska.

British Columbia's appeal as a vacation destination stems from its status as the most spectacular part of the nation, with abundant coastal scenery and stretches of snowcapped peaks. Outdoor enthusiasts have gravitated here for sports including fishing, golfing, kayaking, rafting, and skiing.

Most of British Columbia's population clusters in two coastal cities. Vancouver (☞ Chapter 2) is an international city whose relaxed lifestyle is spiced by a varied cultural scene embracing large ethnic communities. Victoria (☞ Chapter 3), the provincial capital on Vancouver Island, is a smaller, more subdued town of 19th-century brick and well-tended gardens, although it, too, has undergone an international metamorphosis in recent years.

One of the most dramatic recent changes in British Columbia has been in the status of the province's native, or First Nations, peoples—the Haida, Kwakiutl, Nootka, Salish, and others—who occupied the land for more than 12,000 years before the first Europeans arrived. In 1998 and 1999, two ground-breaking treaties, signed with the Nisga'a people in the north and the Sechelt people in the south, heralded a new era of native self-government in the province. At the same time, there has been a resurgence in First Nations culture throughout the region, evident in art galleries, restaurants, and a growing number of cultural centers and re-created villages. Another recent change has been a decline in the province's traditional industries of forestry, fishing, and mining, and an increasing reliance on tourism.

Pleasures and Pastimes

Dining

Although Vancouver and Victoria have the most varied and cosmopolitan cuisine in British Columbia, some excellent restaurants in smaller towns, particularly Whistler, and several fine country inns have helped to define a local cuisine based on the best of regional fare, including seafood, lamb, organic produce, and increasingly good wine. Attire is generally casual in the region. Smoking is banned in all public places in the Gulf Islands, including restaurants and bars.

CATEGORY	COST*
$$$$	over $35
$$$	$25–$35
$$	$15–$25
$	under $15

*per person, in Canadian dollars, for a three-course meal, excluding drinks, service, and 7% GST

Lodging

Accommodations range from bed-and-breakfasts and rustic cabins to deluxe chain hotels, country inns, and remote fishing lodges. In the cities you'll find an abundance of lodgings, but outside the major centers, especially in summer, it's a good idea to reserve ahead, even for campsites. In winter, many backcountry resorts close, and city hotels drop prices by as much as 50%. Most small inns and B&Bs in the province ban smoking indoors; and virtually all hotels offer no-smoking rooms.

CATEGORY	COST*
$$$$	over $250
$$$	$170–$250
$$	$90–$170
$	under $90

All prices are for a standard double room, excluding 10% provincial accommodation tax and 7% GST, in Canadian dollars.

🐢 *following the text of a review is your signal that the property has a Web site, where you will find details and, usually, images; for a link, visit www.fodors.com/urls.*

Outdoor Activities and Sports

CANOEING AND KAYAKING

The Inside Passage, Queen Charlotte Strait, the Strait of Georgia, and the other island-dotted straits and sounds that border the mainland provide fairly protected sea-going from Washington State to the Alaskan border, with numerous marine parks to explore along the way. BC Ferries' Discovery Coast Passage service gives kayakers direct access to the channels and islands of the midcoast (☞ Getting Around by Ferry *in* British Columbia A to Z, *below*). Two favorites for canoeing are the Powell Forest Canoe Route, an 80-km (50-mi) circuit of seven lakes, and Bowron Lake Park, in the Cariboo region.

FISHING

Miles of coastline and thousands of lakes, rivers, and streams bring more than 750,000 anglers to British Columbia each year. The waters of the province hold 74 species of fish (25 of them sport fish), including Chinook salmon and rainbow trout.

GOLF

There are more than 230 golf courses in British Columbia, and the number is growing. The province is now an official golf destination of both the Canadian and American PGA tours. The topography here tends to be mountainous and forested, and many courses have fine views as well as treacherous approaches to greens.

HIKING

Virtually all of British Columbia's provincial parks have fine hiking-trail networks and many ski resorts keep their chairlifts running throughout the summer to help hikers reach alpine trail networks. Heli-hiking is also very popular here; helicopters deliver hikers to high alpine meadows and verdant mountaintops.

RAFTING

A wide range of rafting trips is available on the many beautiful rivers lacing British Columbia, including the Adams, Chilcotin, Chilliwack, Fraser, and Thompson.

SKIING AND SNOWBOARDING

With more than half the province higher than 4,200 ft above sea level, new downhill areas are constantly opening. More than 60 resorts in the province have downhill skiing and snowboarding facilities. Most of these resorts also have groomed cross-country (Nordic) ski trails, and many of the provincial parks have cross-country trails as well.

Native Culture

Before the arrival of Europeans, the lush landscapes of the Pacific Northwest gave rise to one of the richest and most artistically prolific cultures on the continent. There have long been archaeological sights and museums, but newer sights, including the re-created villages at 'Ksan, near Hazelton, and Secwepemc, in Kamloops, are run by First Nations people and offer ways to share a living culture through music, dance, and food.

Exploring British Columbia

Most of British Columbia's population huddles in a region known as the Lower Mainland, in and around Vancouver in the southwest corner of the province. In the mountains about two hours north of Vancouver is the international resort town of Whistler. Beyond the Lower Mainland, three highways and a rail line climb over the Coast Mountains to the rolling high plateau that forms the central interior. To the north are the Cariboo ranch country and, beyond that, the vast, sparsely inhabited northern half of the province. To the east are the Okanagan and Shuswap valleys, which hold the province's fruit- and wine-growing region and its lake district. Farther east are the mountainous Kootenays and the foothills of the Rockies.

The southernmost stretch of coastline just north of Vancouver, called the Sunshine Coast, is popular with boaters, artists, and summer vacationers. Farther north is a roadless, fjord-cut wilderness leading to the mist-shrouded Haida Gwaii, or Queen Charlotte Islands—home to the Haida people and to old-growth forest. The gentler, more pastoral Gulf Islands, in Georgia Strait just west of Vancouver, have long attracted escapists of every kind.

The North Coast and the Queen Charlotte Islands can be wet year-round. The interior is drier, with greater extremes, including hot summers and reliably snowy winters. Temperatures here drop below freezing in winter and sometimes reach 90°F in summer.

When you travel by car, keep in mind that more than three-quarters of British Columbia is mountainous terrain. Many areas, including the North Coast, have no roads at all and are accessible only by air or sea.

Numbers in the text correspond to numbers in the margin and on the Southern British Columbia map.

Great Itineraries

British Columbia is about the size of Western Europe, with as much geographical variety and substantially fewer roads. The good news is that many great sights, stunning scenery, and even wilderness lie within a few days' tour of Vancouver or the U.S. border.

IF YOU HAVE 3 DAYS

One option, offering stunning mountain and ocean scenery, is to take the Coast Mountain Circle tour, driving north from Vancouver along the scenic Seas to Sky Highway to 🏨 **Squamish** ② and the resort town of 🏨 **Whistler** ③, then over the scenic Duffy Lake Road to the gold-rush town of **Lillooet** ④. You can then return to Vancouver through the steep gorges of the Fraser Canyon, with stops at Hell's Gate on the Fraser River in **Hope** ⑤ and at the 🏨 **Harrison Hot Springs** ⑥.

An alternative is to take a ferry out to one of the Gulf Islands—🏨 **Galiano** ⑪, 🏨 **Mayne** ⑫, or 🏨 **Salt Spring** ⑬—to stay at a romantic country inn for a night. Or, also by ferry, take a brief tour of the Sunshine Coast: **Gibsons Landing** ⑦, **Sechelt** ⑧, **Powell River** ⑨, and **Lund** ⑩.

IF YOU HAVE 6 DAYS

A longer trip allows time to explore the interior of the province. Start with a one- or two-day trip over the mountains either via ☷ **Whistler** ③ and **Lillooet** ④ or through the Fraser Canyon, or even by the quicker, if less scenic, Coquihalla Highway. Days 3 through 5 can be spent making a loop through the High Country and the Okanagan Valley. You can make stops in ☷ **Kamloops** ㉒ to fish or visit the Secwepemc Native Heritage Museum, in **Vernon** ㉔ to enjoy the O'Keefe Historic Ranch, or in ☷ **Kelowna** ㉕, **Summerland and Peachland** ㉖, ☷ **Penticton** ㉗, or ☷ **Osoyoos** ㉘ to relax at a beach or tour the vineyards. Any of these towns is fine for your overnights.

IF YOU HAVE 10 DAYS

A 10-day trip gives you time to see Vancouver Island (☞ Chapter 3), and then to cruise the breathtaking **Inside Passage** ⑭ from Port Hardy, on the northern tip of Vancouver Island, to ☷ **Prince Rupert** ⑯, where you can catch another ferry to see the old-growth forest and abandoned Haida villages of the ☷ **Queen Charlotte Islands (Haida Gwaii)** ⑰. From Port Hardy you could also take the scenic **Discovery Coast Passage** ⑮ to Bella Coola. Then complete the circle back to Vancouver by air, ferry, road, or—from Prince Rupert—train.

If you have more time or if you're traveling to or from the Rockies, try to make time for **Nelson** ㉙ and the Kootenays—one of the most beautiful, but least visited, parts of southern British Columbia.

When to Tour British Columbia

The Gulf Islands and the Sunshine Coast are enjoyable anytime, but there are fewer ferries and more rain between September and May, and many tourist facilities close in winter.

The interior of the province—the Cariboo, High Country, Okanagan Valley, and Kootenays—can be tough to get to in winter, but more ski resorts are making it worth the effort. Spring and fall, with their blossoms and harvest and wine festivals, are attractive, peaceful times to travel; summer is a great time for most of the interior, although the Okanagan Valley can get hot and crowded in July and August.

COAST MOUNTAIN CIRCLE

A stunning sampler of mainland British Columbia, a drive into the Coast Mountains from Vancouver follows the Sea to Sky Highway (Highway 99) past fjordlike Howe Sound, the town of Squamish, and Whistler Resort and then continues on a quiet back road to the goldrush town of Lillooet. From Lillooet, it's possible to continue into the High Country or to return to Vancouver on Highways 12 and 1 through the gorges of the Fraser Canyon, stopping for a soak at the spa town of Harrison Hot Springs on the way. This is a scenic two- to three-day drive; the roads are good but are best avoided in snow past Whistler. A BC Rail line also cuts a dramatic swath through the mountains from North Vancouver to Lillooet, on its way north to Prince George.

Horseshoe Bay

❶ *20 km (12 mi) north of Vancouver; 100 km (62 mi) south of Whistler.*

Tucked into a cove under the coast mountains, this little community is best known as a ferry hub. From here you can catch ferries to Nanaimo on Vancouver Island (☞ Chapter 3), Langdale on the Sun-

Southern British Columbia

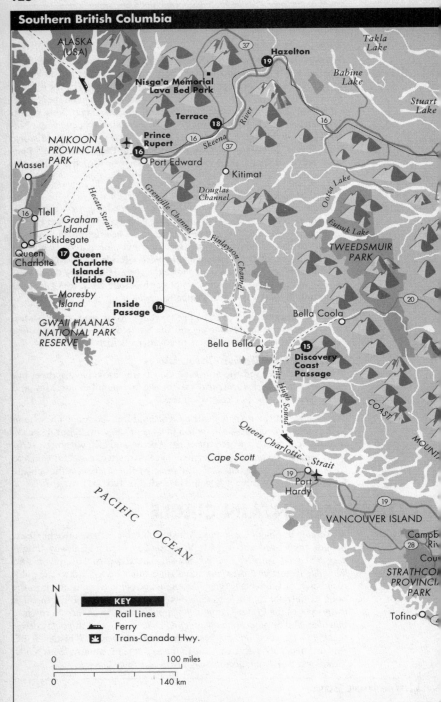

ALASKA (USA)

Takla Lake

37

Hazelton 19

Babine Lake

Stuart Lake

Nisga'a Memorial Lava Bed Park

Terrace 18

Skeena River

37

16

NAIKOON PROVINCIAL PARK

Prince Rupert 16

16

Port Edward

Kitimat

Ootsa Lake

Eutsuk Lake

Masset

Hecate Strait

Grenville Channel

Douglas Channel

Finlayson Channel

TWEEDSMUIR PARK

16 Tlell

Graham Island

Skidegate

Queen Charlotte

17 **Queen Charlotte Islands (Haida Gwaii)**

Moresby Island

GWAII HAANAS NATIONAL PARK RESERVE

Inside Passage 14

Bella Coola

20

Bella Bella

15 **Discovery Coast Passage**

Fitz Hugh Sound

COAST

Queen Charlotte Strait

MOUNT

Cape Scott

19 Port Hardy

VANCOUVER ISLAND

19

Campbell River

28

Cou

STRATHCONA PROVINCIAL PARK

PACIFIC OCEAN

Tofino

N

KEY
— Rail Lines
⛴ Ferry
🍁 Trans-Canada Hwy.

0   100 miles
0   140 km

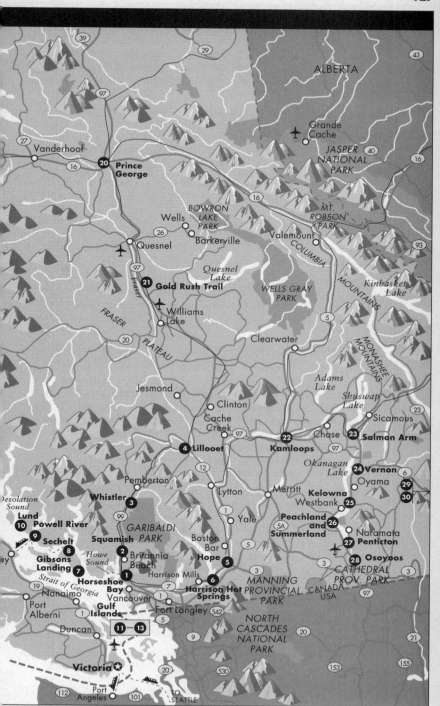

ALBERTA

39

29

97

Grande
Cache

JASPER
NATIONAL
PARK

43

40

16

27 Vanderhoof

16

**20 Prince
George**

16

MT.
ROBSON
PARK

Wells

BOWRON
LAKE
PARK

26

Barkerville

Valemount

COLUMBIA

93

Quesnel

97

Quesnel
Lake

Kinbasket
Lake

21 Gold Rush Trail

WELLS GRAY
PARK

MOUNTAINS

Williams
Lake

5

MONASHEE
MOUNTAINS

FRASER

20

PLATEAU

Clearwater

Adams
Lake

Shuswap
Lake

Jesmond

Clinton

Sicamous

23

Cache
Creek

97

Chase

23 Salmon Arm

4 Lillooet

22 Kamloops

97

12

Okanagan
Lake

24 Vernon

6

Pemberton

Lytton

Merritt

Kelowna

Oyama

29

Whistler

1

Yale

Westbank

25

30

3

99

**Peachland
and
Summerland**

26

Naramata

10 Lund

Powell River

GARIBALDI
PARK

Boston
Bar

5A

27 Penticton

Desolation
Sound

9 **Sechelt**

8

Squamish

Howe
Sound

2 Britannia
Beach

5

28 Osoyoos

CATHEDRAL
PROV. PARK

3

**Gibsons
Landing** 7

Harrison Mills

Hope

3

CANADA
USA

97

**Horseshoe
Bay** 1

5

MANNING
PROVINCIAL
PARK

3

19 Nanaimo

Vancouver

7

6

**Harrison Hot
Springs**

**Gulf
Islands**

1

Fort Langley

542

Port
Alberni

1

5

9

NORTH
CASCADES
NATIONAL
PARK

20

21

Duncan

11 — 13

153

155

Victoria

20

530

112

Port
Angeles

101

TO
SEATTLE

Strait of Georgia

shine Coast (☞ *below*), and tiny Bowen Island, a rural retreat 30 minutes across the sound that has pubs, B&Bs, craft shops, and even a winery. Horseshoe Bay is served by **West Vancouver Blue Buses** (✉ ☎ 604/985–7777), which provides direct service from downtown Vancouver. Near Horseshoe Bay, off Marine Drive, is **Whytecliff Marine Park,** with a swimming beach, picnic sites, and a rocky little island that's connected to the mainland at low tide.

From Horseshoe Bay, Highway 99 (the Sea to Sky Highway) becomes one of B.C.'s most scenic roads, climbing into the mountains along the edge of Howe Sound. Most people on this road are eager to reach the resort town of Whistler (☞ *below*), two hours to the north. A number of sights along the way are worth a stop, however.

At the **B.C. Museum of Mining,** once the largest copper mine in the British Empire and now a national historic site, knowledgeable staff offer guided tours of old mine workings and a chance to pan for gold. The museum is about an hour north of Vancouver. ✉ *Hwy. 99, Britannia Beach,* ☎ *604/896–2233; 604/688–8735 in Vancouver.* 🔄 *$9.50.* ☺ *Early May–June and Sept.–mid-Oct.; Wed.–Sun. 10–4:30; July–Aug., daily 10–4:30; mid-Oct.–Apr. prebooked group tours only.*

En Route   Just south of the town of Squamish is **Shannon Falls,** which at 1,105 ft is Canada's third-highest waterfall. You can see it from the highway, or follow a short trail through the woods for a closer look.

Squamish

❷ *67 km (42 mi) north of Vancouver; 58 km (36 mi) south of Whistler.*

Squamish, or "mother of the winds" in the local First Nations language, has long languished in the shadow of Whistler Resort up the highway. However, outdoors enthusiasts recently have begun to discover its possibilities. The big winds that gave the area its name make it an excellent windsurfing spot. Diving in Howe Sound, kayaking on the sea and in nearby rivers, and hiking are also drawing visitors here. The **Stawamus Chief,** an enormous rock face on the edge of Highway 99, is the world's second-largest granite monolith (after the Rock of Gibraltar). It attracts rock climbers from all over.

In December and January, one of the world's largest concentrations of bald eagles gathers at the **Brackendale Eagle Reserve** (Government Rd. off Hwy. 99, Brackendale, ☎ no phone), about 14 km (8 mi) north of Squamish. The reserve is open dawn to dusk; admission is free. You can watch the eagles from the banks of the Squamish River, off Government Road in Brackendale; another option is to spot the birds from a raft on the Cheakamus River. **Canadian Outback Adventures** (☎ 604/921–7250 or 800/565–8735) offers eagle rafting trips on the Cheakamus River, as does the **Sunwolf Outdoor Centre** (☞ Dining and Lodging, *below*). The Brackendale Eagle Festival, with music and art events, has sprung up around the annual eagle count, held in January. For more information, contact the **Brackendale Art Gallery** (☎ 604/898–3333).

At the **West Coast Railway Heritage Park,** about a 10-minute drive north of downtown Squamish, you can explore more than 50 vintage railway cars and locomotives and take a ride on a miniature railway. ✉ *39645 Government Rd.,* ☎ *604/898–9336.* 🔄 *$4.50.* ☺ *Daily 10–5.*

For a flight-seeing tour (by plane or helicopter) over nearby glaciers, a picnic on a glacier, heli-hiking, heli-rafting, or other helicopter-based adventures, contact **Glacier Air Tours** (☎ 604/898–9016 or 800/265–0088).

Dining and Lodging

$$–$$$ ✕ **Klahanie Road House.** A fixture on Highway 99 since the 1970s, this roadhouse across from Shannon Falls (☞ Horseshoe Bay, *above*) has recently been remade, with lunch and dinner menus of Pacific Northwest comfort food, and an ambience the owners call "seriously casual." Starters include steamed mussels and pan-fried oysters; main dishes range from updated diner food to more substantial meals such as wild-mushroom risotto, grilled yellow-fin tuna, and roast chicken breast stuffed with spinach and ricotta cheese. Tables by the window or on the outdoor terrace offer striking views of the mountains and the falls. The roadhouse is also open for breakfast. ⊠ *Shannon Falls, Hwy. 99 (5 km, or 3 mi, south of Squamish),* ☎ *604/892–5312. MC, V.*

$$
★ ✕🖸 **Howe Sound Inn & Brewing Company.** This modern cedar country inn near Squamish town center and the Royal Hudson train station covers all the bases. The fireplace in the cozy post-and-beam brew pub is a great place to relax after a day of hiking or rafting. You can also watch climbers tackling Stawamus Chief from the pub's patio, have a go at the inn's own mini climbing wall, or take a brewery tour. The elegantly rustic restaurant serves Pacific Northwest cuisine, breads from the in-house bakery (try the ale-and-cheddar bread), and cuisine featuring the inn's ales. The rooms upstairs have furniture made of reclaimed fir and fluffy down duvets; most have striking views of Stawamus Chief or the Tantalus Mountains. ⊠ *37801 Cleveland Ave., Box 978, V0N 3G0,* ☎ *604/892–2603 or 800/919–2537,* 🖷 *604/892–2631. 20 rooms. Restaurant, pub, fans, in-room data ports, sauna, billiards, business services, meeting rooms. AE, MC, V.* ✍

$$ 🖸 **Sunwolf Outdoor Centre.** A highlight of this former fishing lodge on the banks of the Cheakamus River, 10 km (6 mi) north of Squamish, is its rafting and adventure center. The rafting center specializes in class 4 (very fast) whitewater trips, but also offers peaceful floats on slow-moving water. Sunwolf's cabins, tucked in the woods on the 5½-acre property, are attractive and modern, with fir floors, four-poster beds, hand-crafted pine furniture, gas fireplaces, and vaulted ceilings; the cozy lodge has fireplaces and an outdoor deck. In December and January, this is a prime spot for viewing one of the world's largest gatherings of bald eagles. ⊠ *70002 Squamish Valley Rd., Box 244, Brackendale V0N 1H0,* ☎ *604/898–1537,* 🖷 *604/898–1634. 10 cabins. Café, kitchenettes, badminton, croquet, volleyball, boating, meeting rooms. MC, V.* ✍

Outdoor Activities and Sports

Squamish is a major rock-climbing destination, and also a popular spot for hiking, diving, trail riding, sailing, rafting, and kayaking. You can book any of these activities through the **Garibaldi Eco-Adventure Centre** (⊠ Hwy. 99, ☎ 604/892–2088 or 888/684–8828), across from Shannon Falls, 5 km (3 mi) south of Squamish.

The challenging 18-hole, par-72 course (open early March–late October) at **Furry Creek Golf and Country Club** (⊠ Hwy. 99, Furry Creek, ☎ 604/922–9576 or 888/922–9462), south of Squamish, has striking ocean views and a green fee that ranges from $80 to $95 and includes a mandatory cart. The **Squamish Valley Golf & Country Club** (⊠ 2458 Mamquam Rd., ☎ 604/898–9691 or 888/349–3688) is an 18-hole, par-72 course close to town.

En Route Between Squamish and Whistler on Highway 99 is the 231-ft-high **Brandywine Falls.** A short trail through the woods takes you to a viewing platform for striking views of the falls.

Whistler

★ ❸ *120 km (74 mi) north of Vancouver; 58 km (36 mi) north of Squamish.*

Whistler and Blackcomb mountains, part of the Whistler Resort, are the two largest ski mountains in North America and are consistently ranked as the No. 1 or 2 ski destinations on the continent. They offer winter and summer glacier skiing, the longest vertical drop in North America, and one of the most advanced lift systems in the world. Whistler has also grown in popularity as a summer destination, with a range of outdoor activities and events.

At the base of Whistler and Blackcomb mountains are Whistler Village, Village North (also called Marketplace), and Upper Village—a rapidly expanding, interconnected community of lodgings, restaurants, pubs, gift shops, and boutiques. Locals generally refer to the entire area as Whistler Village. With dozens of hotels and condos within a five-minute walk of the mountains, the site is frenzied with activity. Culinary options in the resort range from burgers to French food, Japanese fare to deli cuisine; nightly entertainment runs the gamut from sophisticated piano bars to casual pubs.

Whistler Village is a pedestrian-only community. Anywhere you want to go within the resort is at most five minutes away, and parking lots are just outside the village. The bases of Whistler and Blackcomb mountains are also just at the village edge; in fact, you can ski right into the lower level of the Chateau Whistler Hotel.

In winter, the village buzzes with skiers and snowboarders from all over the world; in summer the pace is more relaxed, as the focus shifts to cycling, hiking, and boating around the Whistler Valley.

Dining

Dining at Whistler is informal; casual dress is appropriate everywhere. Many restaurants close for a week or two between late October and late November. In the winter and summer, you'll need dinner reservations in all but the fast-food joints.

$$$$ ✕ **Bearfoot Bistro.** The cutesy name belies the elegance of this highly rated two-part bistro. The 75-seat dining room has a warm Latin feel with tall leather chairs, dark wood, and live jazz several nights a week. Menu items available in the restaurant include a starter of seared duck foie gras with a rhubarb compote, and main dishes such as pheasant breast stuffed with wild-mushroom mousseline, and herb-crusted striped bass fillet. The wild caribou is a house specialty; try it when it's available. The wine bar's menu is simpler and less expensive. It features such items as grilled Pacific salmon with lemon sauce, and penne with mussels, calamari, and baby shrimp. Guests in either section can sample from the highly rated 1,100-label wine cellar. ✉ *4121 Village Green,* ☎ *604/932–3433. Reservations essential in the dining room, not accepted in the wine bar. AE, D, DC, MC, V. No lunch.*

$$$$ ✕ **Val d'Isère.** Chef-owner Roland Pfaff satisfies a skier's craving for fine French food with traditional dishes from his native Alsace and with Gallic takes on Canadian produce. Some specialties served in this elegant but welcoming room overlooking the Town Plaza are Dungeness crab ravioli with smoked-salmon cream sauce, braised duck legs with roast figs, and rabbit rillette in phyllo pastry. ✉ *4314 Main St.,* ☎ *604/932–4666. Reservations essential. AE, DC, MC, V. No lunch Nov.–May.*

$$$–$$$$ ✕ **Araxi.** Golden walls, terra-cotta tiles, antiques, and original artwork help create an elegant ambience at one of Whistler's most established restaurants. The chefs here work closely with farmers in the Pemberton Valley (just up the road) who produce vegetables and herbs ex-

clusively for Araxi's French and Italian menu. The chef here also makes good use of local sheep's brie, goat cheeses, and trout as well as ostrich, salmon, scallops, and venison from the province. Breads and pastries are made in-house each morning. The menu changes seasonally, but highlights that have appeared in the past include alder-smoked B.C. arctic char with a saffron and oyster-mushroom sauce, and braised Fraser Valley rabbit. Wine lovers take note: there's a 12,000-bottle, international inventory and a full-time sommelier. A heated patio is open in the summer, and the lounge is a popular après-ski spot. ⊠ *4222 Village Square,* ☎ *604/932–4540. Reservations essential. AE, MC, V. No lunch Oct.–May.*

$$$–$$$$ ✕ **Il Caminetto di Umberto.** Owner Umberto Menghi offers homestyle Italian cooking in a relaxed atmosphere. Il Caminetto has an urban, Florentine style with warm gold walls and terra-cotta tiles. It's known for its grilled veal chops, osso buco, and game dishes. Sister restaurant Trattoria di Umberto (☞ *below*) is more casual and slightly less expensive. ⊠ *4242 Village Stroll,* ☎ *604/932–4442. Reservations essential. AE, DC, MC, V. No lunch.*

$$$–$$$$ ✕ **La Rúa.** One of the brightest lights on the Whistler dining scene is on the ground floor of Le Chamois (☞ Lodging, *below*). Reddish flagstone floors and sponge-painted walls, a wine cellar behind a wrought-iron door, modern oil paintings, and sconce lighting give the restaurant an intimate, Mediterranean ambience. Favorites from the Continental menu include charred rare tuna, loin of deer, rack of lamb, and grilled ostrich fillet with fettucine Stroganoff and marsala sauce. ⊠ *4557 Blackcomb Way,* ☎ *604/932–5011. Reservations essential. AE, DC, MC, V. No lunch.*

$$$–$$$$ ✕ **Wildflower.** The main dining room of Chateau Whistler (☞ Lodging, *below*) is decorated with antique birdhouses and artifacts from a demolished church in Québec and has a rustic, comfortable feel. Its huge windows overlook the ski slopes. The à la carte menu focuses on creative dishes starring fresh, often organic, Pacific Northwest fare. Also popular are the daily breakfast buffets, which are especially lavish Sunday. ⊠ *4599 Chateau Blvd.,* ☎ *604/938–2033. Reservations essential. AE, D, DC, MC, V. No lunch some days in spring and fall; call to check.*

$$–$$$$ ✕ **The Brewhouse.** Whistler's first brew pub serves up six of its own ales and lagers, with such names as Big Wolf Bitter and Dirty Miner Stout, in a cozy setting in Village North. The restaurant's open kitchen serves wood-oven pizza, rotisserie prime rib, and spit-roast chicken; the casual pub on the same premises has pool tables, TV screens, and some creative pub grub. ⊠ *4355 Blackcomb Way,* ☎ *604/905–2739. AE, MC, V.*

$$–$$$$ ✕ **Zeuski's.** This friendly taverna in Village North brings big portions of tasty Greek fare to Whistler. Wall murals of the Greek islands surround candlelit tables, helping create a Mediterranean atmosphere. There's also a patio for alfresco dining. It's hard to pass on the spanakopita, souvlaki, and other standards, but the house special, *kotapoulo* (chicken breast rolled in pistachios and roasted), is not to be missed, nor is the tender, delicately herb-battered calamari. ⊠ *4314 Main St.,* ☎ *604/932–6009. Reservations essential. AE, DC, MC, V.*

$$$ ✕ **Trattoria di Umberto.** Owned by Umberto Menghi, who also owns Il Caminetto di Umberto (☞ *above*), this relaxed restaurant specializes in such Tuscan countryside dishes as risotto with smoked goose, asparagus, and wild mushrooms; and cioppino with saffron, local seafood, and vegetables. ⊠ *Mountainside Lodge, 4417 Sundial Pl.,* ☎ *604/932–5858. Reservations essential. AE, DC, MC, V.*

Lodging

Lodgings, including B&B inns, pensions, and hundreds of time-share condos, can be booked through **Whistler Central Reservations** (☎ 604/932–4222; 604/664–5625 in Vancouver; 800/944–7853 in the U.S. and Canada).

Price categories are based on January-to-April ski-season rates; rates are somewhat higher during Christmas and spring break and can be slightly lower in the summer. Many Whistler lodgings require minimum stays, especially during the Christmas season. Also be aware that Whistler Village has some serious nightlife. If peace and quiet are important to you, ask for a room away from the main pedestrian thoroughfares or consider staying in one of Whistler's residential neighborhoods outside the village.

$$$$ 🏨 **Chateau Whistler Resort.** This family-friendly fortress just steps
★   from the Blackcomb ski lifts is a self-contained, ski-in, ski-out resort-within-a-resort, with its own shopping arcade, golf course, and spa. The marvelous lobby is filled with rustic Canadiana, handmade Mennonite rugs, a grand stone fireplace, and enticing overstuffed sofas. The standard rooms are comfortably furnished and of average size, decorated in burgundies and turquoises, and all have mountain views. Rooms and suites on the Entrée Gold floors have fireplaces, whirlpool tubs, and their own concierge and private lounge. ⊠ *4599 Chateau Blvd., V0N 1B4,* ☎ *604/938–8000 or 800/606–8244,* 🆆 *604/938–2099. 502 rooms, 56 suites. 2 restaurants, lobby lounge, air-conditioning, in-room safes, minibars, no-smoking rooms, room service, indoor-outdoor pool, pool, beauty salon, indoor and outdoor hot tub, sauna, spa, steam room, 18-hole golf course, 3 tennis courts, health club, ski shop, ski storage, shops, baby-sitting, coin laundry, dry cleaning, concierge, concierge floor, convention center, parking (fee). AE, D, DC, MC, V.* 🐾

$$$$ 🏨 **Delta Whistler Resort.** The resort, at the base of Whistler and Blackcomb mountains and across the road from the Whistler Golf Course, is a large complex with shopping, dining, and fitness amenities. Rooms are very generous in size (almost every room easily sleeps four). Many rooms have fireplaces, whirlpool baths, balconies, and kitchens; some suites have private saunas. The Delta chain also owns the Delta Whistler Village Suites, an all-suites hotel, in Village North. ⊠ *4050 Whistler Way, V0N 1B4,* ☎ *604/932–1982 or 800/515–4050,* 🆆 *604/932–7332. 264 rooms, 24 suites. Restaurant, sports bar, in-room data ports, minibars, no-smoking floors, room service, pool, indoor and outdoor hot tubs, massage, steam room, 2 tennis courts, exercise room, ski shop, ski storage, shops, baby-sitting, coin laundry, concierge, business services, meeting rooms. AE, DC, MC, V.* 🐾

$$$–$$$$ 🏨 **Pan Pacific Lodge.** This eight-story lodge is tucked at the base of both mountains, just steps from either the Whistler or Blackcomb gondola. Accommodation choices include studios with pull-down queen beds and one- and two-bedroom units, all with kitchens, balconies, gas fireplaces, and tall windows that make the most of the mountain or valley views. The guest rooms, done in light colors and an attractive, modern, slightly Art Deco style, are all no-smoking. In the evenings, there's excellent Irish cuisine and live traditional music at the Dubh Linn Gate Pub downstairs. ⊠ *4320 Sundial Crescent, V0N 1B4,* ☎ *604/905–2999,* 🆆 *604/905–2995. 76 suites, 45 studios. Pub, in-room data ports, in-room safes, room service, pool, outdoor hot tub, exercise room, steam room, ski shop, ski storage, coin laundry, meeting rooms. AE, DC, MC, V.* 🐾

$$$ ⌂ **Chalet Luise.** As traditionally alpine inside as out, Chalet Luise features carved wood furnishings, big sofas, and a gas fireplace in the cozy guest lounge. A hot tub in a whimsical gazebo on the patio is also a great place to unwind. The snug guest rooms have hand-crafted pine furniture and Laura Ashley fabrics, and are phone- and TV-free. One of the two romantic rooms with bay windows and gas fireplaces is large enough to sleep three people. Attention is paid to details: Robes and slippers are on hand for guests, a wooden crib above a staircase to the hot tub holds rolled towels, while a hallway en route to the sauna is lined with racks for ski clothing to be warmed by a wood stove. The chalet has a five-night minimum stay between December and May, and a two-night minimum in summer. ⌂ *7461 Ambassador Crescent, Box 352, V0N 1B0,* ☎ *604/932–4187 or 800/665–1998,* ℻ *604/938– 1531. 8 rooms. Breakfast room, outdoor hot tub, sauna, ski storage, coin laundry, free parking. MC, V. www.chaletluise.com.*

$$$ ⌂ **Durlacher Hof.** Custom fir woodwork and doors, exposed ceiling beams, a *kachelofen* (traditional farmhouse fireplace-oven), and antler chandeliers hung over fir benches and tables carry out the rustic European theme of this fancy Tyrolean inn a few minutes' walk outside the village. The bedrooms, done with Ralph Lauren decor, contain more custom-crafted furniture but no phones or TVs to disturb the peace. Four upgraded rooms are very spacious and have such added amenities as whirlpool tubs; smaller rooms have showers rather than tubs. A hearty European breakfast and afternoon tea are included in the tariff, and occasional dinners are also available at this no-smoking inn. Durlacher Hof has a five-day minimum-stay requirement during the January-to-March ski season. ⌂ *7055 Nesters Rd., Box 1125, V0N 1B0,* ☎ *604/932–1924,* ℻ *604/938–1980. 8 rooms. Breakfast room, massage, outdoor hot tub, sauna, ski storage, free parking. MC, V.* 🐾

$$ ⌂ **Edgewater Lodge.** This modern cedar lodge lies along glacier-fed Green Lake on 45 acres of private forested land, about 3 km (2 mi) north of the village. All rooms have private entrances, TVs, phones, and expansive water and mountain views. A bit removed from Whistler's ski slopes and nightlife, Edgewater is perfectly placed for peace, quiet, and the resort's myriad other activities. Biking, hiking, and cross-country ski trails run past the lodge, and the Nicklaus North Golf Course is nearby. The Whistler Outdoor Experience (☞ Boating *in* Outdoor Activities and Sports, *below*) runs an activity center here, offering fishing, hiking, canoeing, kayaking, and trail rides in summer, and snowshoeing, sleigh rides, and cross-country skiing in winter; these activities are also available to nonguests. Breakfast is included in the rates at this no-smoking inn, and highly rated evening meals are also available. ⌂ *8841 Hwy. 99, Box 369, V0N 1B0,* ☎ *604/932–0688 or 888/870– 9065,* ℻ *604/932–0686. 6 rooms, 6 suites. Restaurant, bar, outdoor hot tub, meeting room, free parking. AE, MC, V. CP.* 🐾

$ ⌂ **Hostelling International Whistler.** One of the nicest hostels in Canada is also the cheapest sleep in the area. Beds in men's or women's four-bunk dorms, a shared kitchen, and a game room with a pool table and fireplace make up the basic accommodations of this no-smoking hostel overlooking Alta Lake. The hostel is next to the swimming beach at Rainbow Park and is 7 km (4 mi) by road, or 4 km (2½ mi) by footpath, from the village. About five Buslink buses a day serve the hostel from Whistler Village, and BC Rail will make a request stop here. ⌂ *5678 Alta Lake Rd., V0N 1B0,* ☎ *604/932–5492,* ℻ *604/932–4687. 32 beds in 7 dorms, 1 private room (no bath). Sauna, boating, ski storage, free parking. MC, V.* 🐾

Outdoor Activities and Sports

The best first stop for any Whistler outdoor activity is the **Whistler Activity and Information Center** (⌂ 4010 Whistler Way, ☎ 604/932–2394) in the conference center at the edge of the village, where you can book activities and pick up hiking and biking maps.

Adjacent to the Whistler area is the 78,000-acre **Garibaldi Provincial Park** (⌂ off Hwy. 99, ☎ 604/898–3678), with dense mountainous forests splashed with hospitable lakes and streams.

BOATING

Canoe and kayak rentals are available at Alta Lake at both Lakeside Park and Wayside Park. A spot that's perfect for canoeing is the River of Golden Dreams, which connects Alta Lake with Green Lake. For guided canoeing and kayaking trips as well as sailing and rafting, call **Whistler Outdoor Experience** (⌂ 8841 Hwy. 99, ☎ 604/932–3389 or 877/386–1888) at the Edgewater Lodge on Green Lake.

FISHING

All five of the lakes around Whistler are stocked with trout. **Whistler Backcountry Adventures** (☎ 604/932–3474) or **Whistler Fishing Guides** (☎ 604/932–4267) will take care of anything you need—equipment, guides, and transportation. **Whistler River Adventures** (☎ 604/932–3532 or 888/932–3532) offers guided fishing trips on rivers in the area.

GOLF

Golf season in Whistler runs from May through October; green fees range from $80–$185.

Chateau Whistler Golf Club (⌂ 4612 Blackcomb Way, ☎ 604/938–2092 or 877/938–2092) has an excellent 18-hole, par-72 course designed by Robert Trent Jones II. The **Nicklaus North Golf Course** (⌂ 8080 Nicklaus North Blvd., ☎ 604/938–9898 or 800/386–9898) is a challenging 18-hole, par-71 course designed by Jack Nicklaus. Arnold Palmer designed the 18-hole, par-72 championship course at the **Whistler Golf Club** (⌂ 4010 Whistler Way, ☎ 604/932–3280 or 800/376–1777).

HIKING

In summer, Whistler and Blackcomb's ski lifts whisk hikers up to the alpine, where marked trails are graded by difficulty. Pick up a map at the **Whistler Activity and Information Center** (☞ *above*) in the village. **Whistler Outdoor Experience** (☎ 604/932–3389 or 877/386–1888) offers guided hikes and nature walks.

HORSEBACK RIDING

Sea to Sky Stables (☎ 604/898–3908), south of Whistler, and **Whistler Outdoor Experience** (☎ 604/932–3389 or 877/386–1888) at Green Lake run trail rides.

INDOOR SPORTS

Alpenrock (⌂ 100–4295 Blackcomb Way, under the Holiday Inn, ☎ 604/938–0082), in the village, has bowling. You'll also find billiards and carnival games as well as a bar, a nightclub, and a family restaurant at this indoor entertainment emporium. **Meadow Park Sports Centre** (⌂ 8107 Camino Dr., ☎ 604/938–3133), about 6 km (4 mi) north of Whistler Village, has a six-lane pool, children's wading pool, hockey–ice-skating rink, hot tub, sauna, steam room, an exercise room, and two squash courts.

SKIING AND SNOW SPORTS

Cross-country skiing. The meandering trail around the Whistler Golf Course in the village is an ideal beginners' route. The 28 km (17 mi) of track-set trails that wind around scenic Lost Lake, Chateau Whistler

Golf Course, the Nicklaus North Golf Course, and Green Lake include routes suitable for all levels; 4 km (2½ mi) of trails around Lost Lake are lit for night skiing 4–10 each evening. Cross-country trail maps and equipment-rental information are available at the **Whistler Activity and Information Center** (☞ *above*) in the village.

Downhill skiing and snowboarding. The vertical drops and elevations at **Blackcomb and Whistler mountains** (☎ 604/932–3434 or 800/766–0449) are perhaps the most impressive features to skiers here. The resort covers 7,071 acres of skiable terrain in 12 alpine bowls and on three glaciers, and has more than 200 marked trails. It is served by the most advanced high-speed lift system on the continent. Blackcomb has a 5,280-ft vertical drop, North America's longest, although Whistler comes in second, with a 5,020-ft drop. The top elevation is 7,494 ft on Blackcomb and 7,160 ft on Whistler. Blackcomb and Whistler receive an average of 360 inches of snow a year. Blackcomb is open June to early August for summer glacier skiing.

Whistler/Blackcomb Ski and Snowboard School (☎ 604/932–3434 or 800/766–0449) has lessons for skiers of all levels. Equipment rentals are available at the **Whistler Gondola Base** (☎ 604/905–2252) and at several outlets in the village. The **Mountain Adventure Centre** (☎ 604/905–2295) in the Pan Pacific Hotel rents high-performance gear and lets you swap equipment during the day. It also has two alpine locations and one at Blackcomb Day Lodge. For a primer on the ski facilities here, drop by the free **Whistler Welcome Night** (☎ 604/932–3434 or 800/766–0449), held at 6:30 every Sunday evening during the ski season at the base of the village gondolas. First-timers at Whistler, whether beginners or experienced skiers or snowboarders, may want to try **Ski or Ride Esprit** (☎ 604/932–3434 or 800/766–0449). Run by the resort, these three- to four-day programs combine ski or snowboarding lessons, après-ski activities, and an insider's guide to the mountains.

Heli-skiing. Whistler Heli-Skiing (☎ 604/932–4105 or 888/435–4754) has guided day trips with up to three glacier runs, or 8,000 to 10,000 ft of skiing, for intermediate to expert skiers; the cost is about $475.

Other activities. Whistler has plenty of snow options for nonskiing days. **Blackcomb Snowmobiling** (☎ 604/932–8484) runs guided snowmobile trips into the backcountry. **Cougar Mountain Adventures** (☎ 604/932–4086) has dogsled trips as well as snowmobiling and snowshoeing. **Outdoor Adventures@Whistler** (☎ 604/932–0647) can take you for walks in the deep powder on snowshoes. **Whistler Outdoor Experience** (☎ 604/932–3389 or 877/386–1888) runs romantic horse-drawn sleigh rides as well as snowshoeing and cross-country ski trips.

Whistler A to Z

ARRIVING AND DEPARTING

By Bus. Greyhound Lines of Canada (☎ 604/482–8747 or 800/661–8747) has service to Whistler from the downtown Vancouver depot (✉ 1150 Station St.) every few hours. **Perimeter Whistler Express** (☎ 604/266–5386 in Vancouver; 604/905–0041 in Whistler) has daily service from Vancouver International Airport to Whistler (the coaches leave every two hours from 9:30 AM to 11:30 PM in the ski season, with slightly fewer trips in the summer). Perimeter has a ticket booth at domestic arrivals Level 2 and one at the airport's international receiving lounge. The fare is around $49 one-way; reservations are highly recommended.

By Car. Whistler is 120 km (74 mi), or 2½ hours, north of Vancouver on winding Highway 99, the Sea to Sky Highway. **LimoJet Gold** (☎ 604/273–1331) runs a limousine service from Vancouver Airport to Whistler. With **Vancouver All-Terrain Adventures** (✉ ☎ 604/434–

2278 or 888/754–5601) you can charter a four-wheel drive Suburban from the Vancouver airport or Downtown Vancouver to Whistler. The vehicles travel regardless of the weather, and can stop for sightseeing along the way. The cost is $278 one-way or $498 round-trip for up to 7 passengers.

By Train. BC Rail (☎ 604/631–3500; 800/339–8752 in British Columbia; 800/663–8238 from outside British Columbia) has daily service from the North Vancouver BC Rail Station to Whistler. It also offers day trips to points north of Whistler that are accessible only by rail. The BC Rail station is about a 30-minute drive from downtown Vancouver; a shuttle links the Vancouver bus depot and the train terminal in summer.

GETTING AROUND

Streets in Whistler Village, Village North, and Upper Village are all pedestrian-only; pay parking is available on the village outskirts. Whistler Municipality operates a free **public transit system** (☎ 604/932–4020) that loops throughout the village, and paid public transit serves the whole valley; call for information and schedules. For a cab, call **Sea to Sky Taxi** (☎ 604/932–3333).

CONTACTS AND RESOURCES

Car Rental. Budget Rent-A-Car (☎ 604/932–1236). **Thrifty Car Rental** (☎ 604/938–0302 or 800/367–2277).

Emergencies. Ambulance, poison control, police (☎ 911).

Guided Tours. Blackcomb Helicopters (☎ 604/938–1700 or 800/330–4354) flies year-round flightseeing tours over Whistler's stunning mountains and glaciers. In summer, it offers heli-hiking, -fishing, -picnics, and even heli-weddings. Several companies, including **Outdoor Adventures@Whistler** (☎ 604/932–0647) and **Whistler ATV Tours** (☎ 604/932–6681), have guided rides through the backcountry on all-terrain vehicles.

Glacier Transportation and Tours (☎ 604/932–7565 or 888/287–7488) runs day trips to Vancouver for guided city tours and also offers trips to see ice-hockey games in Vancouver. **West Coast City and Nature Sightseeing** (☎ 604/451–1600 in Vancouver) offers a sightseeing tour to Whistler that allows passengers to stay over and return on their date of choice to Vancouver. The tours run year-round; the cost is about $57.

Visitor Information. A provincial government **Travel Infocentre** (☎ 604/932–5528) is on Highway 99 about 4 km (2½ mi) south of Whistler; it's open daily. The **Whistler Activity and Information Center** (✉ 4010 Whistler Way, ☎ 604/932–2394) runs an information booth in Whistler Village at the front door of the conference center; it's open year-round, daily 9–5. Contact the **Whistler Resort Association** (✉ 4010 Whistler Way, ☎ 604/932–4222; 604/664–5625 in Vancouver; 800/944–7853 in the U.S. and Canada, FAX 604/938–5758, ✉).

Lillooet

❹ *131 km (81 mi) northeast of Whistler.*

Beyond Whistler, Highway 99 is much less traveled as it makes its way past lakes and glaciers, through the Mount Currie First Nations reserve, and over the mountains to Lillooet.

The arid gullies and Wild West landscape around Lillooet may come as a surprise after the greenery of the coast and mountains. During the 1850s and 1860s this was Mile Zero of the Cariboo Wagon Road, which took prospectors to the gold fields. There are several motels in Lillooet and a BC Rail station.

Hope

5 *153 km (95 mi) south of Lillooet; 150 km (93 mi) east of Vancouver.*

Hope is the only sizeable town on Highway 1 between Vancouver and the province's interior; it's also the point where the scenery changes suddenly from the steep gorges of the Fraser Canyon to wide flat farmland of the Fraser Valley. If you're traveling into the interior from Vancouver, you have a choice of three routes here: Highway 1 through the Fraser Canyon, the Coquihalla (Highway 5), and Highway 3. Highway 1, the Trans-Canada Highway, follows the Fraser River as it cuts its way from the High Country through the Coast Mountains to Vancouver; the deepest, most dramatic cut is the 38-km (24-mi) gorge between Yale and Boston Bar, north of Hope, where the road and rail line cling to the hillside high above the water. Highway 5 is a fast, high-altitude toll road, and Highway 3 is a quiet back road through Manning Park.

You'll find plenty of facilities for overnight stays in Hope.

At the **Coquihalla Canyon Recreation Area** (☎ 604/824–2300), 6 km (4 mi) northeast of Hope off Highway 5, you can walk through the abandoned tunnels of the old Kettle Valley Railway and catch spectacular views of the Coquihalla Gorge. The tunnels are open dawn to dusk April through mid-October, weather permitting.

At **Hell's Gate,** about 40 km (23 mi) south of Lytton, an airtram (cable car) carries passengers across the foaming canyon above the fishways, where millions of sockeye salmon fight their way upriver to spawning grounds. The lower airtram terminal has displays on the life cycle of the salmon, a fudge factory, a gift shop, and a restaurant. ⊠ *Hell's Gate Airtram, Exit 170 off Hwy. 1,* ☎ *604/867–9277.* ☎ *$10.* ☉ *Apr. and Oct., daily 10–4; May–June and Sept., daily 9–5; July–Aug., daily 9–6.*

The Hope **Visitor InfoCentre** (⊠ 919 Water Ave., off Hwy. 1, ☎ 604/869–2021) has details about area attractions.

En Route Following Highway 3 east to Princeton and Penticton, you'll pass through **Manning Provincial Park,** which has campgrounds, hiking trails, swimming, boating, and trail rides, in addition to downhill and cross-country skiing in the winter. Also on Highway 3 are the year-round **visitor center** (☎ 250/840–8836) and **Manning Park Resort** (☎ 250/840–8822), which includes a restaurant.

Harrison Hot Springs

6 *128 km (79 mi) northeast of Vancouver.*

The small resort community of Harrison Hot Springs lies at the southern tip of picturesque Harrison Lake, off Highway 7 in the Fraser Valley. Mountains surround the 64-km-long (40-mi-long) lake, which is ringed by pretty beaches. Besides the hot springs, boating, windsurfing, and swimming are popular here.

A striking 60-m-high (200-ft-high) waterfall is the main attraction at **Bridal Veil Falls Provincial Park** (⊠ off Hwy. 1 about 15 km, or 9 mi, southeast of Harrison Hot Springs, ☎ 604/824–2300), ☉ open dawn to dusk. A short path through the forest leads to a viewing platform.

The **Harrison Public Pool,** across from the beach in Harrison Hot Springs, is an indoor hot spring–fed pool. ⊠ *224 Esplanade,* ☎ *604/ 796–2244.* ⚏ *$7.* ☼ *Daily 9–9.*

☟ **Kilby Historic Store and Farm,** a 20-minute drive west of Harrison Hot Springs, re-creates a rural British Columbian store and farm of the 1920s with some original buildings and some replicas, farm animals, and 1920s-style home cooking in the **Harrison River Tearoom.** ⊠ *215 Kilby Rd. (off Hwy. 7), Harrison Mills,* ☎ *604/796–9576.* ⚏ *$5.* ☼ *June–Oct., Thurs.–Mon. 11–5; call for off-season hrs.*

Minter Gardens, 8 km (5 mi) southwest of Harrison Hot Springs, is a 27-acre compound with 11 beautifully presented theme gardens (Chinese, English, and rose, for example), playgrounds, and a giant evergreen maze. ⊠ *Exit 135 off Hwy. 1, 52892 Bunker Rd., Rosedale,* ☎ *604/794– 7191 or 888/646–8377.* ⚏ *$11.* ☼ *Apr.–mid-Oct., daily 9–dusk.*

Dining and Lodging

$$–$$$ ✕🛏 **Harrison Hot Springs Resort.** A fixture on Harrison Lake since 1926, the hotel originally was set up to take advantage of the hot springs and lakeside location, and it still does; there are several indoor and outdoor hot-springs–fed pools and a marina offering a range of watersports, including sturgeon-fishing charters and lake cruises. Rooms in the original building are decorated with Laura Ashley linens and brass beds, and breakfast is delivered to the door. Those in the three newer extensions have contemporary decor; most have patios or balconies and those on the north side have striking views over the lake and nearby glacier-topped mountains. The Copper Room restaurant serves beautifully prepared, locally sourced, Continental cuisine in a vast room. Try the veal medallions with Stilton and blueberry cream, or the rack of lamb with basil–Grand Marnier sauce. The Copper Room is one of the few places in the province still offering dining and dancing. A four-piece swing band plays for guests Tuesday through Sunday on the large lit dance floor. The resort's Lakeside Restaurant is a good spot for Sunday brunch. ⊠ *100 Esplanade, V0M 1K0,* ☎ *604/796–2244 or 800/663–2266,* ℻ *604/796–3682. 302 rooms, 11 cottages. 2 restaurants, coffee bar, lounge, no-smoking floors, room service, indoor lap pool, pool, wading pool, massage, mineral baths, saunas, 9-hole golf course, 2 tennis courts, exercise room, jogging, volleyball, dock, water park, boating, waterskiing, fishing, bicycles, shops, playground, laundry service, convention center. AE, D, DC, MC, V.* ⚐

Outdoor Activities and Sports

The **Hemlock Valley Resort** (⊠ Hemlock Valley Rd., off Hwy. 7, Agassiz, ☎ 604/797–4411; 800/665–7080 for snow report), 40 km (24 mi) northwest of Harrison Hot Springs, is a small, family-oriented ski resort with three chairlifts, 19 runs, and a vertical rise of 1,200 ft. You can also try cross-country skiing and snow tubing here.

En Route From Harrison Hot Springs, two routes lead back to Vancouver. Highway 7 is a scenic back road along the north side of the Fraser River. Highway 1 is the faster, main highway. On Highway 1, you'll pass the turnoff to **Fort Langley National Historic Site,** a restored 1850s Hudson's Bay trading post about an hour west of Harrison Hot Springs. ⊠ *23433 Mavis St., Fort Langley,* ☎ *604/513–4777.* ⚏ *$4.50.* ☼ *Mar.– Oct., daily 10–5.*

SUNSHINE COAST

The stretch of mainland coast north of Vancouver, backed by mountains and accessible only by sea or air (☞ Getting Around *in* British

Columbia A to Z, *below*), is so deeply cut with fjords that it has the look and feel of an island—or rather, two islands. The Sechelt Peninsula to the south has long been popular with artists, writers, and Vancouver weekenders. The Malaspina Peninsula, a ferry ride across Jervis Inlet to the north, is wilder and more densely forested; it is focused on the pulp-mill town of Powell River. Highway 101, the one paved road running the length of the coast, forms the last (or the first) 139 km (86 mi) of the Pan-American Highway, connecting the village of Lund, British Columbia, to Puerto Mont, Chile, 24,000 km (14,880 mi) away.

The coast is a bit sunnier than the more exposed coastline to the north (hence its name), and its many provincial parks, marinas, lakes, and walking trails are popular with outdoorspeople and families, though not, as yet, with mass tourism or luxury-resort developers. The Sunshine Coast remains one of the quieter, more affordable places to travel in southern British Columbia.

Gibsons Landing

❼ *5 km (3 mi) plus 12 nautical mi northwest of Vancouver.*

The first stop on the Sunshine Coast, just 5 km (3 mi) north of the Langdale ferry terminal, Gibsons Landing (often just called Gibsons) is an attractive seaside town that's best known as the location of *The Beachcombers,* a long-running Canadian television show about life on the B.C. coast. Though most of the region's best scenery is farther north, Gibsons is worth a stop for its shops, B&Bs, restaurants, attractive waterfront, and fishing-village air.

Elphinstone Pioneer Museum (⊠ 716 Winn Rd., ☎ 604/886–8232) has an eclectic collection of First Nations and pioneer artifacts. ☉ It's open mid-June to Labor Day, Tuesday through Saturday 10:30–4:30, by donation. Call for winter hours. The **Sunshine Coast Maritime Museum** (⊠ Molly's Lane, on the waterfront, ☎ 604/886–4114) showcases the region's seafaring history. Gibsons' **Tourist InfoCentre** (⊠ 668 Sunnycrest Rd., ☎ 604/886–2325) in the Sunnycrest Mall, off Highway 101, has maps and information about the area.

About 15 minutes north of Gibsons on Highway 101 is the 1930s-era village of **Roberts Creek**; there's a public beach a short stroll from the village.

Dining and Lodging

$$$–$$$$ ✗ **The Creekhouse.** This little house set amid gardens in Roberts Creek, 15 minutes north of Gibsons Landing, serves classic French cuisine with a touch of Italian. The menu changes seasonally, but there are always good lamb and fresh local seafood options. Hardwood floors, white tablecloths, a fireplace, and patios overlooking the garden create a casual, cozy ambience; many guests like to stroll down to the beach between courses. ⊠ 1041 Roberts Creek Rd., Roberts Creek, ☎ 604/885–9321. *Reservations essential. MC, V. Closed Mon.–Wed. No lunch.*

$$ ✗ **Gumboot Garden Café.** Everyone knows everyone else at this funky, kid-friendly, village-center café in Roberts Creek. The place is so well known that the sign outside reads simply CAFÉ. The mostly vegetarian menu features homemade soup, bread, sauces, and desserts, and, where possible, local and organic ingredients. There's a garden in summer, a fireplace in winter, gum boots (rubber boots) by the door, and an environment that, especially on rainy days, makes it tempting to just hang out. Try the eggs, sausage, and granola breakfasts; the burritos, burgers, and homemade soups on offer at lunch; or the candlelit dinners featuring pizza, pasta, seafood, and vegetarian dishes. ⊠ 1057 Roberts Creek Rd., Roberts Creek, ☎ 604/885–4216. MC, V. No dinner Sun.–Wed.

$$–$$$ ✕🏨 **Bonniebrook Lodge.** For a romantic place to spend the night, consider this seaside lodge 5 km (3 mi) north of Gibsons. The rooms and suites in the original 1922 building are freshly done in a Victorian style and each has a private deck and a whirlpool tub for two. Three rooms in a 1998 addition have fireplaces, VCRs, minirefrigerators, and whirlpool baths for two. Chez Philippe ($$$–$$$$), a fine French restaurant in the lodge, is open to the public for dinner; the $28 four-course set menu is an excellent value. A full breakfast is included at this no-smoking inn. ✉ *Foot of Gower Point Rd., R.R. 5, 1532 Ocean-beach Esplanade, V0N 1V5,* ☎ *604/886–2887 or 877/290–9916; 604/886–2188 for dinner reservations,* FAX *604/886–8853. 5 rooms, 2 suites. Beach, camping. AE, DC, MC, V. Restaurant closed Tues.–Thurs. mid-Sept.–mid-May and all of Jan. No lunch.* 🐾

$$ 🏨 **Country Cottage.** Loragene and Philip Gaulin have lovingly decorated two private, adult-oriented cottages in the delightfully 1930s-vintage village of Roberts Creek, about 9 km (6 mi) north of Gibsons Landing. Rose Cottage is tiny and romantic, with a woodstove and antique sideboard. Cedar Lodge, the farm's former barn, is a feast of woodsy Canadiana, from its stone fireplace to its handmade Arts and Crafts furniture. Both have cooking facilities, and a full hot breakfast, delivered to the rooms, is included in the rate at this no-smoking B&B. ✉ *1183 Roberts Creek Rd., Box 183, Roberts Creek V0N 2W0,* ☎ *604/885–7448. 2 cottages. No credit cards.*

$ 🏨 **Marina House Bed & Breakfast.** From the street, this seaside home near Ganges' town center looks like an ordinary house; from the beach side though, it's a striking bright yellow, three-story 1931 heritage house. The rooms (one with a bath across the hall) are small, phone- and TV-free, and prettily decorated with Victorian antiques. Molly's Room has a spectacular view over Shoal Channel and Keats Island. The lounge, the porch, and the breakfast room also overlook the sea. The town is a few minutes stroll along the beach. ✉ *546 Marine Dr., Box 1696, V0N 1V0,* ☎ *604/886–7888 or 888/568–6688. 3 rooms. Library, beach. MC, V. Full breakfast.* 🐾

Outdoor Activities and Sports

Sunshine Coast Golf & Country Club (✉ 3206 Hwy. 101, Roberts Creek, ☎ 604/885–9212 or 800/667–5022) is an 18-hole, par-71 course with tree-lined fairways and mountain and ocean views.

Sechelt

8 *37 km (23 mi) plus 12 nautical mi northwest of Vancouver.*

Sechelt, the largest town on the scenic peninsula of the same name, suffers a bit from sprawl but has several interesting shops and restaurants. It's home to many artists and writers as well as a strong First Nations community, the Sechelt Nation. If you're in Sechelt in mid-August, you can catch readings by internationally acclaimed Canadian writers at the **Sunshine Coast Festival of the Written Arts** (✉ ☎ 604/885–9631 or 800/565–9631), held at Sechelt's Rockwood Centre.

House of Hewhiwus (✉ 5555 Hwy. 101, ☎ 604/885–4592) includes a small First Nations museum and a gift shop–art gallery. **Porpoise Bay Provincial Park** (☎ 604/898–3678), north of Sechelt on Sechelt Inlet, has a sandy swimming beach, as does **Davis Bay,** south of Sechelt on Georgia Strait. Sechelt's **Visitor Information Centre** (✉ Trail Bay Mall, 45–5755 Cowrie St., ☎ 604/885–0662) has maps and information about the area.

The best scenery on the coast is to the north of Sechelt, around and beyond the little marinas of Madiera Park, Garden Bay, and Irvine's

Landing, collectively known as Pender Harbour. Here Highway 101 winds past forests, mountains, and a delightful confusion of freshwater lakes and ocean inlets.

You can experience a dramatic natural sight at **Skookumchuk Narrows Provincial Park** (✉ Egmont Rd. off Hwy. 101, ☎ 604/898–3678), 5 km (3 mi) inland from the Earls Cove ferry terminal and 45 km (28 mi) northwest of Sechelt. A 4-km (2½-mi) walk through the forest comes out at a viewpoint where, at the turn of the tide, seawater churning through the narrow channel creates one of the world's fastest tidal rapids. Tide tables are posted at the trailhead and at the **Pender Harbour Info Centre** (☎ 604/883–2561) in Madiera Park.

Princess Louisa Inlet is a narrow fjord at the top of Jervis Inlet; more than 60 waterfalls tumble down its steep walls. The fjord is accessible only by boat, and a number of local companies, including **Sunshine Coast Tours** (☎ 604/886–7033 or 800/870–9055), offer summer day trips.

Dining and Lodging

$-$$ ✕🏠 **Ruby Lake Resort.** The Cogrossi family from Milan chose this unlikely looking spot—a seaside cabin resort just off Highway 101—to settle and, coincidentally, for cooking up some of the best Italian food ($$-$$$$) in the area. Diners come from up and down the coast for Aldo Cogrossi's Lobster Michelangelo, wild boar, and pasta dishes, as well as salads from the resort's own organic garden, and seafood specials based on what's fresh at the docks that day. The resort also has five duplex cabins that overlook a lagoon and bird sanctuary. The cabins, accessed by a floating bridge over the lagoon, all have fresh modern decor; all are no-smoking. ✉ Hwy. 101 (R. R. 1, C65, S15), Madeira Park, V0N 2H0, ☎ 604/883–2269 or 800/717–6611. 5 rooms, 5 suites. Restaurant, kitchenettes, lake, massage, hiking, boating, fishing. MC, V. Late Dec.– mid-Mar. CP. ☜

$-$$ 🏠 **Sundowner Inn.** An atmospheric, family-run budget hotel, this 1929 clapboard building perched on a hill overlooking Garden Bay was once a mission hospital. The rooms are basic, with 1950s furniture, but the setting is stunning. You can take a boat trip to Princess Louisa Inlet and Desolation Sound, or a hiking, cycling, or kayaking tour from here, or join in the occasional dinner-theater and murder-mystery weekends. Garden Bay is 8 km (5 mi) off Highway 101, 30 km (19 mi) north of Sechelt. ✉ 4339 Garden Bay Rd., Box 113, Garden Bay V0N 1S0, ☎ 604/883–9676 or 888/288–8780, FAX 604/883–9886. 10 rooms, 7 with bath. Restaurant, fans, outdoor hot tub, dock, boating, fishing, bicycles, chapel, meeting rooms. AE, MC, V. Closed weekdays mid-Oct.–Mar. 1. ☜

Outdoor Activities and Sports

Pender Harbour and the Sechelt Inlet are spectacular diving spots, especially in the winter, when the water is clearest. An artificial reef has been formed by a scuttled navy ship off Kunechin Point in Sechelt Inlet. Local guides and outfitters include the **Diving Locker** (✉ 5659 Dolphin St., Sechelt, ☎ 604/885–9830).

Powell River

❾   70 km (43 mi) plus 12 nautical mi by ferry northwest of Sechelt, 121 km (75 mi) plus 12½ nautical mi northwest of Vancouver, 17 nautical mi (75-min ferry ride) east across Strait of Georgia from Comox on Vancouver Island.

The main town on the Malaspina Peninsula, Powell River was established around a pulp-and-paper mill in 1912, and the forestry industry continues to have a strong presence in the area. The town has several

B&Bs and restaurants, as well as a park with oceanfront camping and RV hookups. The **Powell River Townsite,** one of the oldest functioning mill towns in the province, is a national historic site.

Renowned as a year-round salmon-fishing destination, Powell River also has 30 regional lakes with exceptional trout fishing and is becoming increasingly popular as a winter scuba-diving destination. The **Inland Lake Site and Trail System**—12 km (8 mi) inland from Powell River— is a 13-km-long (8-mi-long) hiking and biking trail around Inland Lake that's accessible to people who use wheelchairs. It's possible to hike parts of the **Sunshine Coast Trail,** a partially completed trail that eventually is to run the entire 180-km (112-mi) length of the Malaspina Peninsula. Nearby, the 80-km (50-mi) **Powell Forest Canoe Route** and **Desolation Sound Marine Park** attract boaters.

The **Powell River Visitors Bureau** (✉ 4690 Marine Ave., ☎ 604/485–4701) has information about the many activities and hiking trails in the area.

OFF THE BEATEN PATH   **TEXADA ISLAND** – From Powell River, **BC Ferries** (☎ 888/223–3779) sails to this rustic, forested island that has accommodation, hiking trails, and campsites.

Lodging

$ 🏨 **Old Court House Inn and Hostel.** The views over the neighboring pulp mill are less than inspiring, but inside, this nicely refurbished historic courthouse offers the best lodging value in town. Private rooms, some with private bathrooms and all with TVs, are decorated in an early 20th-century style (some with antiques), and go for under $50 a night. Two dorm rooms are also available at $15 a person, and a shared kitchen is available to all guests in this no-smoking inn. ✉ *6243 Walnut St., V8A 4K4,* ☎ *604/483–4000,* FAX *604/483–4089. 8 rooms, 6 with bath; 2 dorm rooms (one with 4 beds; one with 2 beds). Café, refrigerators, baby-sitting. MC, V.* 🐾

Sports and Outdoor Activities

CANOEING AND KAYAKING

Powell River Sea Kayaks (☎ 604/485–2144) and **Wolfson Creek Adventures** (✉ ☎ 604/487–1699) offer rentals and tours.

DIVING

Sunken ships, red coral, wolf eels, some of the world's largest octopi, and—especially in winter—uncommonly clear water, make Powell River one of Canada's leading scuba-diving spots. Local outfitters include **Don's Dive Shop** (☎ 604/485–6969).

Lund

🔟 *27 km (17 mi) north of Powell River.*

Founded by the Swedish Thulin brothers in 1889, the historic boardwalked village of Lund marks the end (or start) of the Pan-American Highway. Lund is the nearest village to **Desolation Sound,** British Columbia's largest marine park and a major draw for boaters and kayakers. **Good Diving and Kayaking** (☎ 604/483–3223) can arrange diving, kayaking, and canoeing trips and rentals. You can catch a water taxi (☎ 604/483–9749) from here to **Savary Island,** and its white-sand beaches.

Dining

$$–$$$ ✕ **The Laughing Oyster.** All the seats at this pretty, blue two-tiered restaurant five minutes from Lund have stunning views over Okeover Arm (especially those on the outdoor deck). Though vegetarian and poul-

try dishes are on offer, the focus here is on local seafood. Try the laughing oysters—these are steam shucked and broiled with artichokes, olives, sun-dried tomatoes, capiscum, and feta cheese. The west-coast seafood harvest includes salmon fillet, red snapper, oysters, prawns, and scallops. A selection of lighter bistro meals includes sautéed salmon, snapper, and shrimp on salad; and chicken breast and scallops baked with wine, herbs, cream, and Asiago cheese. Boaters can tie up at the restaurant dock. ⊠ *10052 Malaspina Rd., Powell River,* ☎ *604/483–9775. Reservations essential. AE, MC, V.*

THE GULF ISLANDS

Of the hundreds of islands sprinkled across Georgia Strait between Vancouver Island and the mainland, the most popular and accessible are Galiano, Mayne, and Salt Spring. A temperate climate (warmer, with half the rainfall of Vancouver), white shell beaches, rolling pasturelands, and virgin forests are common to all, but each island has its unique flavor. Marine birds are numerous, and there is unusual vegetation such as arbutus trees (also known as madrones, a leafy evergreen with red peeling bark) and Garry oaks. Writers, artists, craftspeople, weekend cottagers, and retirees take full advantage of the undeveloped islands.

These islands are rustic (only Salt Spring has a bank machine) but not undiscovered; they are popular escapes from Vancouver and Victoria, and in summer it's a good idea to reserve accommodations. If you're bringing a car from mainland British Columbia, ferry reservations are highly recommended, and required on some of the busier sailings (☞ Getting Around *in* British Columbia A to Z, *below*).

Galiano Island

❶ *20 nautical mi (almost 2 hrs by ferry due to interisland stops) from Swartz Bay (32 km, or 20 mi, north of Victoria), 13 nautical mi (a 50-min ferry ride) from Tsawwassen (39 km, or 24 mi, south of Vancouver).*

Galiano's long, unbroken eastern shoreline is perfect for leisurely beach walks, and the numerous coves and inlets along the western coast make it a prime area for kayaking.

Biological studies show that the straits between Vancouver Island and the mainland of British Columbia are home to the largest variety of marine life in North America. The frigid waters offer superb visibility, especially in winter. Alcala Point, Porlier Pass, and Active Pass are top locations for scuba diving.

Montague Harbour Provincial Marine Park (Montague Park Rd. off Montague Rd., ☎ 250/391–2300) has camping and boating facilities. Galiano has miles of trails through Douglas-fir forest that beg for exploration by foot or bike. Hikers can climb to the top of **Mt. Galiano** for a view of the Olympic Mountains in Washington or trek the length of **Bodega Ridge.** The best spots to view Active Pass and the surrounding islands are **Bluffs Park** and **Bellhouse Park**; these are also good for picnicking and bird-watching. Anglers head to the point at Bellhouse Park to spin cast for salmon from shore, or they go by boat to Porlier Pass and Trincomali Channel.

Go Galiano (☎ 250/539–0202) offers year-round taxi, bus, ferry pickup, and sightseeing services on Galiano Island. In summer, **Dionisio Express** (☎ 250/539–3109) runs a boat service to Dionisio Marine Park, on Galiano's northwestern tip, which doesn't have road access.

Dining and Lodging

$$–$$$ ✕▥ **Woodstone Country Inn.** You'll find this serene inn at the edge of
★ a forest overlooking a meadow that's fantastic for bird-watching. Tall
windows bring the pastoral setting into spacious bedrooms decorated
in green and rose. All the rooms have fireplaces, and most have patios
and oversize soaking tubs. A hearty gourmet breakfast and afternoon
tea are included in the room rates. Woodstone's elegant restaurant serves
French-influenced Pacific Northwest fare, such as yam soup with
toasted almonds or herb-crusted rack of lamb with pear–tomato chutney and mustard-seed sauce. Guests and nonguests can have four-
course dinners here by advance reservation. ⊠ *Georgeson Bay Rd.,
R.R. 1, V0N 1P0,* ☎ *250/539–2022 or 888/339–2022,* ℻ *250/539–
5198. 12 rooms. Restaurant, hiking, piano, library, meeting room. AE,
MC, V. Closed Dec.–Jan.* ◈

$$–$$$ ▥ **Bellhouse Inn.** Modeled on an English manor house, this historic
★ red-and-white clapboard inn sits on six seaside acres of farmland next
to Bellhouse Park. The interior is decorated in a simple 19th-century
country style, with numerous antiques including an 1860 farmhouse
table where breakfast is served. The peaceful lounge and library has a
big fireplace and picture windows overlooking the ocean; on the table
are binoculars for spotting whales and bald eagles in Active Pass. The
Kingfisher room has soft green walls, a jet tub, and French doors
opening onto a balcony with a full water view. The Eagle room also
has a balcony, with a forest and ocean view, as well as a soaking tub
and the original hardwood floor. The Heron room is the largest, with
both a single bed and an 1860s double brass bed. The inn, all no-smoking, is adult-oriented, but two 1960s self-contained two-bedroom cottages on site are a good choice for families. The owner can also take
guests out on his 22-ft cruiser in the summertime. ⊠ *29 Farmhouse
Rd., Box 16, Site 4, V0N 1P0,* ☎ *250/539–5667 or 800/970–7464,*
℻ *250/539–5316. 3 rooms, 2 cottages. Breakfast room, croquet, hiking, beach. MC, V. CP.* ◈

$–$$ ▥ **Sutil Lodge.** Family photos from the 1920s and Art Deco furnish-
★ ings re-create a sense of lodge life in an earlier era at this 1929 bungalow set on 20 wooded acres on Montague Bay. The simple guest rooms
have throw rugs on dark hardwood floors and beds tucked under
window nooks. The kayak center on the property attracts folks from
around the world (rentals and guided trips are available). A full breakfast, served in the lodge's old dance hall, and afternoon tea are included
in the room rate at this friendly, no-smoking inn. ⊠ *637 Southwind
Rd., V0N 1P0,* ☎ *250/539–2930 or 888/539–2930,* ℻ *250/539–
5390. 7 rooms share 3 baths. Breakfast room, hiking. AE, MC, V. Closed
Oct.–Mar. CP.* ◈

Outdoor Activities and Sports

BIKING

Biking is a fun way to explore the island's miles of trails. Bike rentals
are available from **Galiano Bicycle** (⊠ 36 Burrill Rd., ☎ 250/539–9906),
within walking distance of the Sturdies Bay ferry terminal.

DIVING

For dive charters, contact **Galiano Diving** (☎ 250/539–3109). **Lead-
foot Diving & Water Sports** (☎ 250/539–5341 or 888/609–6924) rents
paddleboats and offers harbor tours as well as dive charters.

FISHING

B.C. Fisherman's Unique Tours (☎ 250/539–2278 or 800/304–1389)
runs fishing and sightseeing charters.

The **Galiano Golf and Country Club** (⊠ 24 St. Andrew Crescent, ☎ 250/539–5533) is a 9-hole, par-32 course in a forest clearing.

Galiano Island Sea Kayaking (☎ 250/539–2930 or 888/539–2930) has rentals and tours; it also offers catamaran cruises. **Gulf Islands Kayaking** (☎ 250/539–2442) has equipment rentals and guided kayak tours.

Mayne Island

⑫ *28 nautical mi from Swartz Bay (32 km, or 20 mi, north of Victoria), 22 nautical mi from Tsawwassen (39 km, or 24 mi, south of Vancouver).*

Middens of clam and oyster shells give evidence that tiny Mayne Island—only 21 square km (8 square mi)—was inhabited as early as 5,000 years ago. It later became the stopover point for miners headed from Victoria to the gold fields of the Fraser River and Barkerville. By the mid-1800s it had developed into the communal center of the inhabited Gulf Islands, with the first school, post office, police lockup, church, and hotel. Farm tracts and orchards established in the 1930s and 1940s and worked by Japanese farmers until their internment during World War II continue to thrive today. Mayne's mild hills and wonderful scenery make it great territory for a vigorous bike ride.

Mount Parke was declared a wilderness park in 1989. A 45-minute hike leads to the highest point on the island and a stunning view of the mainland and other gulf islands.

The small town of **Miners Bay** is home to **Plumper Pass Lockup,** built in 1896 as a jail but now a minuscule museum (open July to Labor Day, Friday to Monday 11–3) chronicling the island's history. You could also stop for a drink at the seaside **Springwater Lodge,** one of the oldest hotels in the province. From Miners Bay head north on Georgina Point Road to **St. Mary Magdalene Church,** a pretty stone chapel built in 1898. Across the road, a stairway leads down to the beach.

Active Pass Lighthouse, at the end of Georgina Point Road, is part of **Georgina Point Heritage Park.** It was built in 1855 and still signals ships into the busy waterway. The grassy grounds are great for picnicking. There's a pebble beach for beachcombing at shallow (and therefore warmer) **Campbell Bay.**

Dining and Lodging

$$–$$$$
★ ✕🏠 **Oceanwood Country Inn.** This Tudor-style house on 10 forested acres overlooking Navy Channel has English Country decor throughout. Fireplaces, French doors that open onto ocean-view balconies, and whirlpool baths make several rooms deluxe. The waterfront restaurant serves four-course table d'hôte dinners of outstanding regional cuisine, such as pan-seared Fraser Valley turkey breast and potato-crusted sea bass. Room rates include afternoon tea and breakfast. ⊠ *630 Dinner Bay Rd., Mayne Island V0N 2J0,* ☎ *250/539–5074,* 𝖥𝖠𝖷 *250/539–3002. 12 rooms. Restaurant, hot tub, sauna, hiking, jogging, bicycles, library, meeting room. MC, V. Closed late Nov.–Mar. 1. CP.* ✑

$$
🏠 **A Coachhouse on Oyster Bay.** Owner Brian Johnston designed this 1991 grey clapboard waterfront house in the style of a turn-of-the-20th-century carriage house. All three rooms are elegant, with bold colors, hardwood floors, private entrances, gas fireplaces, and views of Active Pass and Oyster Bay. The Laundau Room, in a former hayloft above the barn, is the most decadent option, with a four-poster bed and a private hot tub on the deck overlooking the ocean. You can swim in the warm shallow bay next to the property, watch seals and eagles from

the gazebo on the shoreline, or soak in the hot tub on the ocean's edge. Full breakfast is included in the room rate. ⊠ *511 Bayview Dr., Mayne Island V0N 2J0,* ☎ *250/539–3368 or 888/629–6322,* ℻ *250/539–2236. 3 rooms. Breakfast room, fans, outdoor hot tub, beach, boating, bicycles, piano. MC, V.* ✍

Outdoor Activities and Sports

Bay View Bike Rentals (⊠ 764 Steward Rd., Miners Bay, ☎ 250/539–2924) rents bicycles. For kayak rentals, try **Mayne Island Kayaking** (⊠ 359 Maple Dr., Seal Beach, Miners Bay, ☎ 250/539–2667).

Salt Spring Island

🔢 *28 nautical mi from Swartz Bay (32 km, or 20 mi, north of Victoria), 22 nautical mi from Tsawwassen (39 km, or 24 mi, south of Vancouver).*

Named for the saltwater springs at its north end, Salt Spring is the largest and most developed of the Gulf Islands. Among its first nonnative settlers were black Americans who came here to escape slavery in the 1850s. The agrarian tradition they and other immigrants established remains strong (a Fall Fair has been held every September since 1896), but tourism and art now support the local economy.

Ganges, a pedestrian-oriented seaside village about 6 km (4 mi) from the Long Harbour ferry terminal, is the main commercial center for the island's 10,000 residents. It has dozens of smart boutiques, galleries, and restaurants. **Mouat's Trading Company** (⊠ Fulford–Ganges Rd., ☎ 250/537–5593), built in 1912, was the original village general store. It's now a hardware store but still houses a display of historical photographs.

Dozens of working **artists' studios** are open to the public here; pick up a studio tour map at the **Visitor Information Centre** (⊠ 121 Lower Ganges Rd., ☎ 250/537–5252).

At the south end of the island, where the ferries from Victoria arrive, is the tiny village of **Fulford,** which has two cafés, a kayaking outlet, and several offbeat boutiques. Ferries from Crofton, on Vancouver Island, arrive at **Vesuvius,** an even smaller village than Fulford, with a seaside pub, a swimming beach, and craft studios, on the west side of the island.

St. Mary Lake, on North End Road, and **Cusheon Lake,** south of Ganges, are the best bets for warm-water swimming.

Near the center of Salt Spring, the summit of **Mt. Maxwell Provincial Park** (⊠ Mt. Maxwell Rd., off Fulford–Ganges Rd.) has spectacular views of south Salt Spring, Vancouver Island, and other Gulf Islands. The last portion of the drive is steep, winding, and unpaved.

Ruckle Provincial Park (⊠ Beaver Point Rd., ☎ 250/391–2300) is the site of an 1872 homestead and extensive fields still farmed by the Ruckle family. The park also has seaside camping and picnic spots, 11 km (7 mi) of coastline, a beach, and 8 km (5 mi) of trails leading to rocky headlands.

For more information about hiking trails, beach access, and historic sites on the island, pick up a copy of the Salt Spring Out-of-Doors Map, available at Salt Spring bookstores and the Ganges Visitor Information Centre.

There is no public transportation on Salt Spring. For a cab, call **Silver Shadow Taxi** (☎ 250/537–3030). Car, truck, and scooter rentals are available in Ganges through **Heritage Car and Truck Rental** (☎ 250/

Salt Spring Island

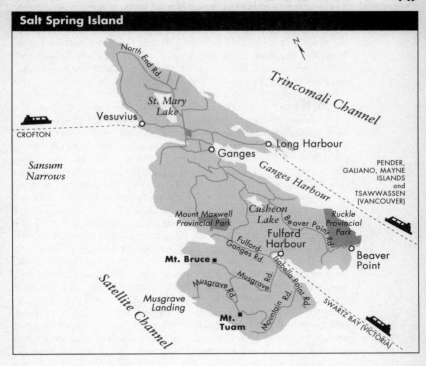

537–4225) and **Budget Rent-a-Car** (☎ 250/537–9100), both at the head of Ganges Harbour. A tiny passenger ferry, the **Queen of de Nile** (☎ no phone) runs passengers from Moby's Marine Pub (☞ *below*) and Ganges Marina to Ganges town center.

Dining and Lodging

The **Visitor Information Centre** (☞ *above*) can direct you to many of Salt Spring's lodging options.

$$$$ ✕ **House Piccolo.** This intimate nine-table restaurant, in a little blue-and-white house in Ganges Village, serves beautifully prepared and presented European food. Appetizers feature classics from the chef-owner's native Finland such as gravlax and herring; the warm, local goat cheese with island smoked salmon, and the scallop-and-king-prawn brochette are also excellent. Favorite main courses include venison with a juniper-and-rowanberry demi-glace, and fillet of beef tenderloin with gorgonzola sauce. For dessert, there's homemade ice cream, lingonberry crepes with vodka, and chocolate terrine Finlandia—which is rich, delicious, and worth ordering for the artistic presentation alone. The 200-item wine list is among the best on the islands and includes many hard-to-find vintages. The indoor tables are cozy and candlelit; the outdoor patio is a pleasant summer dining spot. ⊠ *108 Hereford Ave., Ganges,* ☎ *250/537–1844. Reservations essential. AE, DC, MC, V. No lunch.*

$$–$$$ ✕ **Moby's Marine Pub.** Big portions of great food such as warm salmon or scallop salad and lamb burgers, a harborside deck, a cozy room with fireplaces, and Sunday evening jazz make this friendly, no-smoking pub a favorite among visitors and islanders alike. ⊠ *124 Upper Ganges Rd.,* ☎ *250/537–5559. Reservations not accepted. MC, V.*

$–$$ ✕ **The Treehouse Café.** This tiny 1927 cottage, dwarfed by the sprawling plum tree in its yard, has been a fixture on the Ganges waterfront for generations. Now it's a funky café that serves wholesome breakfasts, and rich homemade soups, hefty sandwiches, salads, and chili the rest of the day. There are only three tables tucked into the cottage; most guests opt for a rustic table under the tree outside. That's also where people gather to hear local musicians most summer evenings. ✉ *106 Purvis La. (next to Mouat's Trading Company),* ☎ *250/537–5379. Reservations not accepted. MC, V. No dinner Oct.–June.*

$$$$ ✕▥ **Hastings House.** The centerpiece of this luxurious 25-acre seaside farm estate is a 1940 country house, built, convincingly, in the style of an 11th-century Sussex manor. Guest quarters are in the manor, in beautifully renovated buildings around the property (including one in an original Hudson's Bay trading post), or in a 1999 addition on a hill overlooking Ganges Harbour. Rooms are furnished with antiques and locally crafted woodwork in an English Country theme and all have fireplaces (gas or wood) or woodstoves. Accommodations in the older buildings are quieter; the newer hillside units have expansive views, but are closer to the main road. In-room spa services are available and the inn provides transportation to and from the floatplane dock and ferry terminals, and to most island activities, including kayaking, golf, and fishing. Room rates include a full breakfast and afternoon tea. Five-course prix-fixe dinners in the manor house are open to the public (reservations essential); the excellent cuisine features local lamb, seafood, and herbs and produce from the inn's own gardens. Typical entrées include peppered venison medallions and grilled leg of local lamb. A jacket is required in the formal dining room but not in the more casual lower-floor dining area, or on the covered patio. ✉ *160 Upper Ganges Rd., V8K 2S2,* ☎ *250/537–2362 or 800/661–9255,* 🅵🅰🆇 *250/537–5333. 3 rooms, 14 suites. Restaurant, in-room data ports, minibars, no-smoking rooms, massage, boccie, croquet, mountain bikes, dry cleaning, laundry service, business services, meeting rooms. AE, MC, V. Closed Jan.–early Mar.* ✍

$$$ ▥ **Anne's Oceanfront Hideaway.** Perched on a steep slope above the sea 6 km (4 mi) north of the Vesuvius ferry terminal, this modern waterfront home has panoramic ocean views, a cozy library, a sitting room, an elevator, and two covered verandas. A lavish hot breakfast is included in the price, and one room is wheelchair accessible. Every room has a hydromassage tub; three have private balconies. The Douglas Fir and Garry Oak rooms have the best views. Luxurious details—including morning coffee in the rooms, robes, and a welcoming bottle of wine—make this a comfortable place to unwind. ✉ *168 Simson Rd., V8K 1E2,* ☎ *250/537–0851 or 888/474–2663,* 🅵🅰🆇 *250/537–0861. 4 rooms. Breakfast room, air-conditioning, outdoor hot tub, boating, bicycles, library. AE, MC, V.* ✍

$$$ ▥ **Beach House on Sunset.** The sunsets are stunning from this Mediterranean-style house set on a waterfront slope 5 km (3 mi) north of the Vesuvius ferry terminal. Three upstairs rooms in the B&B have private entrances and balconies with sea views; one has French doors, a fireplace, a claw-foot tub, and a private deck with an outdoor shower. A one-bedroom cedar cottage with a wraparound porch and a kitchen sits over the boathouse at water's edge. Extras include down comforters, terry robes, slippers, fruit platters, decanters of sherry, early morning coffee delivered to the room, and a bountiful breakfast. You can also arrange boat charters and kayak tours here. ✉ *930 Sunset Dr., V8K 1E6,* ☎ *250/537–2879,* 🅵🅰🆇 *250/537–4747. 3 rooms, 1 cottage. Breakfast room, boating. MC, V. Closed Dec.–Feb.* ✍

$$$ ⊞ **Old Farmhouse Bed and Breakfast.** A registered historic property built in 1894, this delightful white saltbox farmhouse sits in a quiet 3-acre meadow near St. Mary Lake. The style of the main house is echoed in the four-room guest wing added in 1989, which has country-comfortable guest rooms furnished with pine bedsteads, down comforters, hardwood floors, and wicker chairs. Each has a private balcony or patio. The breakfasts of fresh baked goods and hot entrées such as smoked-salmon soufflé are legendary. ⊠ *1077 North End Rd., V8K 1L9,* ☎ *250/537–4113,* FAX *250/537–4969. 4 rooms. Breakfast room, boating. MC, V. Closed Nov.–Feb.* ⚭

$$–$$$ ⊞ **Beddis House.** Emily Beddis and her family built this white clapboard farmhouse overlooking Trincomali Channel in 1900. The original farmhouse is still home to a guest parlor and breakfast room (though with modern decor); a separate 1995 coach house, built in the same style, has three spacious guest rooms. Done in modern country pine with a sprinkling of antiques, all rooms have wood stoves, clawfoot tubs, and a private ocean-view deck or balcony. The Rose Bower room is the most romantic option: it takes up most of the top floor and has a four-poster king bed and a sofa, as well as views over both the sea and the garden. Guests can stroll in the 1¼-acre garden or step down to the inn's white clamshell beach. Local outfitters will deliver kayaks to the property, too. Beddis House is about a 15-minute drive from Ganges, and, like most Salt Spring B&Bs, it's completely no-smoking. ⊠ *131 Miles Ave., V8K 2E1,* ☎ *250/537–1028,* FAX *250/537–9888. 3 rooms. Breakfast room, fans, beach. MC, V. Closed late Dec.–early Jan.* ⚭

$ ⊞ **Salt Spring Island Hostel.** In the 10 forested acres behind this hostel near Cusheon Lake are three canvas teepees and two comfortable furnished treehouses (sleeping rooms without bathrooms) wrapped around trees and reached by a ladder or a staircase. Inside, the freshly decorated hostel also has two private rooms, two small dorms with six to eight beds, a shared kitchen, and a cozy common room with a fireplace. The hostel is about 5 km (3 mi) from Ganges, and a 25-minute walk from either an ocean beach or a swimming lake. You can rent bicycles and scooters here, and the friendly owners can arrange kayaking, sailing, and a range of other activities. This no-smoking, Hostelling International facility is very popular—reservations are highly recommended. *640 Cusheon Lake Rd., V8K 2C2,* ☎ *250/537–4149. 2 rooms, 1 with bath; 2 treehouses; 3 teepees; 2 dorms with 6–8 beds. Bicycles. MC. Closed Nov.–Mar. 1.* ⚭

Nightlife and the Arts

You can catch a live theater production at **Artspring** (⊠ 100 Jackson Ave., ☎ 250/537–2125), a theater and gallery complex in Ganges. Artspring is the main venus for the **Salt Spring Festival of the Arts,** a festival of international music, theater, and dance, held in July. **Moby's Marine Pub** (☞ Dining and Lodging, *above*), in Ganges, and **The Fulford Inn,** (⊠ 2661 Fulford-Ganges Rd., ☎ 250/653–4432), in Fulford, often feature local musicians. See the local weeklies, the *Driftwood* or the *Barnacle,* or the Information Centre in Ganges, for listings.

Outdoor Activities and Sports

Cycling and kayaking are the main activities on Salt Spring, and operators tend to double up. **Island Escapades** (⊠ 163 Fulford-Ganges Rd., Ganges, ☎ 250/537–2537 or 888/529–2567) offers kayaking, sailing, hiking, and climbing tours, in addition to outdoor adventure programs for children and teens. For kayaking trips, lessons, and rentals, as well as bike rentals and repairs, try **Salt Spring Kayak and Cycle** (⊠ 2923 Fulford-Ganges Rd., Fulford, ☎ 250/653–4222), on the wharf at Fulford. **Salt Spring Marine Rentals** (⊠ at the head of Ganges Harbour, ☎ 250/537–9100) has fishing, sailing, and diving charters, as well as nature cruises, and powerboat, kayak, bicycle, and scooter rentals. A source for kayak rentals, tours, and lessons is **Sea Otter Kayaking** (⊠ 149 Lower Ganges Rd., on Ganges Harbour at foot of Rainbow Rd., Ganges, ☎ 250/537–5678 or 877/537–5678).

GOLF

Blackburn Meadows Golf Club (⊠ 269 Blackburn Rd., ☎ 250/537–1707) and **Salt Spring Island Golf and Country Club** (⊠ 805 Lower Ganges Rd., ☎ 250/537–2121) are both pleasant 9-hole courses. For something a bit different, try the **Frisbee Golf Course**(⊠ end of Seaview Ave., Ganges)in Mouat Park.

Shopping

Mahon Hall in Ganges is the site of **ArtCraft,** a summer-long arts-and-crafts sale featuring the work of more than 200 artisans.

The island's biggest arts-and-crafts gallery, **Coastal Currents Gallery** (⊠ 133 Hereford Ave., Ganges, ☎ 250/537–0070), occupies a historic house and is filled with the work of local artisans. Everything at Ganges' **Market in the Park,** held in Centennial Park every Saturday April through October, has been made, baked, or grown on the island. Fresh produce, seafood, crafts, clothing, candles, toys, home-canned items, and more are on offer.

NORTH COAST

Gateway to Alaska and the Yukon, this vast, rugged region is marked by soaring, snowcapped mountain ranges, scenic fjords, primordial islands, and towering rain forests. Once the center of a vast trading network, the mid- and north coasts are home to First Nations peoples who have lived here for 10,000 years and to more-recent immigrants drawn by the natural resources of fur, fish, and forest. The region is thin on roads, but you can travel by ferry, sailboat, cruise ship, plane, or kayak to explore the ancient native villages of the coast and the Queen Charlotte Islands (☞ Getting Around *in* British Columbia A to Z, *below*). The climate of this mist-shrouded coast is among the wettest in the world; winters are a time for torrential rains, summers are damp, and rain gear is essential year-round.

Inside Passage

★ ⑭ *507 km (314 mi), or 274 nautical mi, between Port Hardy on northern Vancouver Island and Prince Rupert.*

The Inside Passage, a sheltered marine highway, follows a series of natural channels behind protective islands along the green-and-blue-shaded British Columbia coast. The undisturbed landscape of rising mountains and humpbacked islands has a striking, prehistoric look. You can take a ferry cruise along the Inside Passage or see it on one of the more expensive luxury liners that sail along the British Columbia coast from Vancouver to Alaska.

The comfortable *Queen of the North* ferry carries up to 700 passengers and 120 vehicles, and has cabins, food services, and a licensed lounge on board. Between mid-May and mid-October, sailings are direct and take 15 hours, almost entirely in daylight, to make the trip from Port Hardy on Vancouver Island to Prince Rupert (or vice versa). Sailings are less frequent and longer during the rest of the year, as the ferry makes more stops along the way. Reservations are required for vehicles and recommended for foot passengers. It's also a good idea to reserve hotel accommodations at Port Hardy and Prince Rupert. ⊠ BC Ferries, *1112 Fort St., Victoria V8V 4V2, ☎ 250/386–3431 in Victoria and*

*outside British Columbia; 888/223–3779 elsewhere in British Columbia.
⊠ One-way summer passage for a car and driver $324; $106 for each
adult passenger; $43–$65 for a day cabin; $117 for an overnight cabin.
Discounts available May–mid-June and Sept.–mid-Oct. ⊙ Mid-May–
mid-Oct. departing on alternate days from Port Hardy and Prince Rupert at 7:30 AM, arriving 10:30 PM. Mid-Oct.–Feb., once weekly; Mar.–
mid-May, twice weekly.* ✍

Discovery Coast Passage

★ ⓯ *258 km (160 mi), or 138 nautical mi, between Port Hardy on northern Vancouver Island and Bella Coola.*

This BC Ferries service travels up the Inside Passage to the First Nations community of Bella Bella and then turns up Dean Channel to the
mainland town of Bella Coola. The scenery is stunning, and the route
allows passengers to visit communities along the way, including Namu,
Shearwater, Klemtu, and Ocean Falls. It also provides an alternative
route into the Cariboo region, via Highway 20 from Bella Coola to
Williams Lake. Lodging at ports of call varies from luxury fishing lodges
to rough camping, but it is limited and must be booked in advance.

The ***Queen of Chilliwack,*** carrying up to 375 passengers and 115 vehicles, takes from 17 to 33 hours (depending on the number of stops)
to make the trip from Port Hardy on Vancouver Island to Bella Coola.
Reservations are required for vehicles and advised for foot passengers.
Cabins are not available. ⊠ *BC Ferries, 1112 Fort St., Victoria V8V
4V2,* ☎ *250/386–3431 in Victoria and outside British Columbia; 888/
223–3779 elsewhere in British Columbia.* ⊠ *One-way fares between
Port Hardy and Bella Coola are approximately $110 for a passenger,
$220 for a vehicle.* ⊙ *Mid-June–mid-Sept., departing Port Hardy on
Tues., Thurs., and Sat.; leaving Bella Coola on Mon., Wed., and Fri.*

Prince Rupert

⓰ *1,502 km (931 mi) by highway and 750 km (465 mi) by air northwest
of Vancouver; 15 hrs by ferry northwest of Port Hardy on Vancouver
Island.*

The fishing and logging town of Prince Rupert is the largest town on
the North Coast. It's the final stop on the BC Ferries route through
the Inside Passage, as well as the home base for ferries to the Queen
Charlotte Islands and a port of call for Alaska ferries. The ferry terminal is about 2 km (1 mi) from town; in summer, a downtown shuttle bus meets each ferry.

Cow Bay is a historic waterfront area a 10-minute walk from downtown and close to the Museum of Northern British Columbia (☞
below). Originally the town's fishing hub, it's recently been revitalized
with attractive shops, galleries, and restaurants.

The **Museum of Northern British Columbia** in a newish longhouse-style
facility on the waterfront, has one of the province's finest collections
of coastal First Nations art, with some artifacts that date back 10,000
years. Artisans work on totem poles in the carving shed, and in summer the museum runs walking tours of the town and a 2½-hour boat
tour of the harbor and Metlakatla native village. Prince Rupert's **Visitor Info Centre** (☎ 250/624–5637 or 800/667–1994) is on site, and
the museum also operates the **Kwinista Railway Museum,** a five-
minute walk away on the waterfront. ⊠ *100 1st Ave. W,* ☎ *250/624–
3207.* ⊠ *$5.* ⊙ *Sept.–May, Mon.–Sat. 9–5; June–Aug., Mon.–Sat. 9–
8, Sun. 9–5.*

The **North Pacific Cannery Village Museum** in Port Edward, 20 km (12 mi) south of Prince Rupert, is the oldest salmon cannery on the west coast. You can tour the cannery and managers' houses, where interpretive displays about the canning process and village life are set up. The old mess hall is now a café, and there's a B&B in the old bunk house. You can also take a boat tour of historic sites on the Skeena River from here. ⊠ *Off Hwy. 16, Port Edward,* ☎ *250/628–3538.* ☜ *May–mid-Oct. $6.75; mid-Oct.–May by donation.* ⊙ *May–mid.-Oct., daily 9–6 with three tours a day; mid-Oct.–May, daily 9–5 (no tours).*

Dining and Lodging

$$–$$$ ✕⊞ **Crest Hotel.** Warm and modern, the Crest is close to the train station, the museum, and the town's main shopping areas, but stands on a bluff overlooking the harbor. Many rooms have striking water views, and some have minibars and whirlpool baths. The restaurant, pleasantly decorated with brass rails and beam ceilings, has a view of the waterfront and specializes in seafood, particularly salmon. You can also book cruises and fishing charters from here. ⊠ *222 1st Ave. W, V8J 3P6,* ☎ *250/624–6771 or 800/663–8150,* ℻ *250/627-7666. 101 rooms, 1 suite. Restaurant, coffee shop, lounge, in-room data ports, no-smoking floor, room service, outdoor hot tub, steam room, exercise room, fishing, baby-sitting, laundry service, business services, meeting rooms. AE, D, DC, MC, V.* ☜

$$ ⊞ **Highliner Inn.** This modern high-rise near the waterfront is conveniently situated in the downtown shopping district. Most of the spacious, modern rooms will sleep four. The ones with balconies and water views are the most attractive. ⊠ *815 1st Ave. W, V8J 1B3,* ☎ *250/624–9060 or 800/668–3115,* ℻ *250/627-7759. 94 rooms. Restaurant, pub, no-smoking floor, room service, beauty salon, coin laundry, business services, meeting rooms. AE, D, DC, MC, V.* ☜

Outdoor Activities and Sports

Eco-Treks Adventures (⊠ 203 Cow Bay, ☎ 250/624–8311) has kayak rentals and kayaking tours (one- and multiday) of nearby fjords and islands. Tours include trips to view ancient petroglyphs and pictographs, visits to the edge of the nearby Khutzeymateen grizzly-bear sanctuary, and whale-watching excursions.

Shopping

Arts and crafts by local and regional artists are for sale at **Studio 9** (⊠ 105–515 3rd Ave. W, ☎ 250/624–2366). The historic **Cow Bay** area (☞ *above*) on the waterfront has a number of interesting shops.

Queen Charlotte Islands (Haida Gwaii)

★ ⑰ *93 nautical mi southwest of Prince Rupert, 367 nautical mi northwest of Port Hardy.*

The Queen Charlotte Islands, or Haida Gwaii ("Islands of the People"), have been called the Canadian Galápagos. Their long isolation off the province's North Coast has given rise to subspecies of wildlife found nowhere else in the world. The islands are also the preserve of the Haida people, who make up half the population. Their vibrant culture is undergoing a renaissance, evident throughout the islands.

Most of the islands' 6,000 permanent residents live on Graham Island—the northernmost and largest of the group of 150 islands—where 108 km (65 mi) of paved road connects the town of Queen Charlotte in the south to Masset in the north. Moresby Island, to the south, is the second largest of the islands and is largely taken up by the Gwaii Haanas National Park Reserve (☞ *below*), an ecological reserve with restricted access. The wildlife (including bears, eagles, and otters), old-growth forest, and stunning scenery make the islands a nature lover's delight, and kayaking enthusiasts from around the world are drawn to waterways here. The islands have most services, including banking, grocery stores, and a range of accommodation and campsites, though public transportation isn't available. It's a good idea to reserve your accommodation before arriving on the islands.

Three **Visitor Information Centres** (✉ 3220 Wharf St., Queen Charlotte, ☎ 250/559–8316; ✉ 1 Airport Rd., in the airport terminal, Sandspit, ☎ 250/637–5362; ✉ Hwy. 16, Masset, ☎ 250/626–3982) are open during the summer. For information about the islands' ancient Haida villages, contact the **Haida Gwaii Watchmen** (✉ Museum Rd., Skidegate, ☎ 250/559–8225).

The 1,470-square-km (570-square-mi) **Gwaii Haanas National Park Reserve/Haida Heritage Site,** managed jointly by the government of Canada and the Council of the Haida Nation, protects a vast tract of wilderness, unique species of flora and fauna, and many historic and cultural sites including **Nan Sdins,** a UNESCO World Heritage Site that contains some of the finest heraldic poles found anywhere. The reserve is on Moresby Island and numerous smaller islands at the southern end of the archipelago. The protected area, accessible only by air or sea, is both ecologically and culturally sensitive. One way to visit—and highly recommended for those unfamiliar with wilderness travel—is with a licensed operator. Gwaii Haanas has a list, or *see* Outdoor Activities and Sports, *below*. To visit on your own (without a licensed operator), you must make a reservation, register for each trip, and attend a mandatory orientation session. ✉ *Parks Canada, Box 37, Queen Charlotte V0T 1S0,* ☎ *250/559–8818; 800/435–5622 for information pack and reservations,* FAX *250/559–8366.*

On the southern end of Graham Island, the **Haida Gwaii Museum** has an impressive display of Haida totem poles, masks, and carvings of silver and argillite (hard black slate). A gift shop sells Haida art, and a natural-history exhibit gives interesting background on the wildlife of the islands. ✉ *2nd Beach Rd., Skidegate,* ☎ *250/559–4643.* 🎟 *$3.* ☉ *June–Aug., daily 10–5; May and Sept., weekdays 10–noon and 1–5, Sat. 1–5; Oct.–Apr., Mon. and Wed.–Fri. 10–noon and 1–5, Sat. 1–5.*

Naikoon Provincial Park (☎ 250/557–4390), in the northeast corner of Graham Island, preserves a large section of unique wilderness with dramatic sand dunes, pine and cedar forests, lakes, and wildlife. A 5-km (3-mi) (3½–4-hour) walk leads from the Tlell Picnic Site to East Beach and onto the wreck of a 1928 logging vessel, the *Pesuta.* At the north end of the park, a climb up 400-ft Tow Hill gives the best views of McIntyre Bay. A 20-km (12-mi) hike along the Fife Trail will take you from the Tow Hill parking lot to East Beach. The park also has two drive-in campgrounds.

Lodging
Accommodation is available in Sandspit, the village of Queen Charlotte, Tlell, Port Clements, and Masset. Reservations are recommended. **Super, Natural British Columbia** (☎ 888/435–5622) can be of assistance. The islands also have numerous campgrounds.

$ 🏠 **Alaska View Lodge.** On a clear day, you can see the mountains of Alaska from the large front deck of this B&B, 13 km (8 mi) east of Masset. A 10-km-long (6-mi-long) sandy beach borders the lodge on one side and woods on the other. Eagles are a familiar sight, and in winter you can often catch glimpses of the northern lights. There's also a golf course nearby. Every room in this no-smoking B&B has two queen beds. Full breakfast is included. ✉ *Tow Hill Rd., Box 227, Masset V0*

1M0, ☎ 250/626–3333 or 800/661–0019, FAX 250/626–3303. 4 rooms, 2 with bath. Breakfast room, hiking, beach. MC, V. 🐾

$ 🏠 **Spruce Point Lodge.** This cedar-sided building, encircled by a balcony, is right on the beach, about 5½ km (3½ mi) from the ferry terminal at Skidegate. Like many other Queen Charlotte accommodations, it has pine furnishings and a rustic, down-home feel. A Continental breakfast, delivered to your room, is included. Three rooms have kitchenettes. ✉ 609 6th Ave., Box 735, Queen Charlotte V0T 1S0, ☎ FAX 250/559–8234. 7 rooms. Boating, fishing. MC, V. CP. 🐾

Outdoor Activities and Sports

GUIDED TOURS

Bluewater Adventures (☎ 604/980–3800 or 888/877–1770, FAX 604/980–1800) has eight- and nine-day sailboat tours around the Charlottes; trips start and end in Sandspit. Vancouver-based **Ecosummer Expeditions** (☎ 250/674–0102 or 800/465–8884, FAX 250/674–2197) runs kayak and sailing tours of the islands. **Queen Charlotte Adventures** (☎ 250/559–8990 or 800/668–4288, FAX 250/559–8983) leads multiday kayak, power-boat, fishing, luxury-yacht, and llama-trekking tours around the islands.

Parks Canada, Gwaii Haanas (☎ 250/559–8818) has a list of tour companies licensed to operate in Gwaii Haanas.

KAYAKING

Moresby Explorers (✉ 469 Alliford Bay Rd., Sandspit, ☎ 250/637–2215 or 800/806–7633) in Sandspit is a source for kayak rentals, kayak transport, and guided Zodiac tours.

Shopping

The Haida carve valuable figurines from argillite, a variety of hard, black slate. Other island specialties are silk-screen prints and silver jewelry. A number of shops in Queen Charlotte City are on **3rd Avenue.** In Old Massett, at the islands' north end, try **Haida Arts and Jewellery** (✉ 387 Eagle Rd., ☎ 250/626–5560). The **Haida Gwaii Museum** (☞ above) has an excellent gift shop.

THE CARIBOO AND THE NORTH

This is British Columbia's wild west, a vast, thinly populated region stretching from the snow peaks and dense forests of the north to the rolling, arid ranching country of the south. The Cariboo covers an area roughly bordered by Bella Coola on the west, Lillooet in the south, Wells Gray Park on the east, and Prince George in the north. In the 19th century, thousands came here looking for—and finding—gold. Those times are remembered throughout the region, most vividly at the re-created gold-rush town of Barkerville. You can still pan for gold here, but these days visitors are more likely to come for ranch holidays, horseback riding, fly-fishing, mountain biking, and cross-country skiing.

Terrace

⑱ 138 km (86 mi) east of Prince Rupert on Hwy. 16, 577 km (346 mi) northwest of Prince George, 1,355 km (813 mi) northwest of Vancouver.

Traveling into the mountainous interior from Prince Rupert, both Highway 16 and the railway line follow the wide Skeena River. The route is strikingly scenic as it passes under snow-capped mountain peaks and past cascading waterfalls. Terrace, the first town en route, is a logging town and the major commercial center for the Skeena Valley. The region is also home to the Kitsumkaum and Kitselas peoples, whose art and heritage is evident throughout the region.

Ferry Island Municipal Park in the Skeena River on the east side of town, and accessed by bridges, has a campground, picnic sites, and hiking trails. **Heritage Park** (⊠ 4113 Sparks St., ☎ 250/635–4546) is a re-created turn-of-the-20th-century village, with costumed guides and many original buildings. It's open Tuesday through Saturday in the summer months.

A 15-minute drive south of Terrace on Highway 37 is the hot-springs complex at **Mt. Layton Resort** (☎ 250/798–2214), which includes a swimming pool, slides, and hot-springs–fed pools. About 100 km (62 mi) north of Terrace, partly by gravel road, is the **Nisga'a Memorial Lava Bed Park** (☎ 250/798–2277), the site of Canada's most recent volcanic eruption (more than 250 years ago).

About 35 km (21 mi) northwest of Terrace, off Highway 16, is the ski resort at **Shames Mountain** (☎ 250/635–3773 or 800/663–7754), with a vertical rise of 497 m (1,640 ft), a double chairlift, and 17 trails (open for hiking in summer). The resort also lays claim to the most accumulated snow of any North American ski hill. Anglers flock to the **Skeena River** and its tributaries for some of the richest sport fishing in the province (a 92-lb. king salmon, said to be a world-record catch, was caught just west of Terrace).

For more information about these and other attractions in the region, contact the **Terrace Travel Info Centre** (⊠ 4511 Keith Ave., or Hwy. 16, ☎ 250/635–0832 or 800/499–1637).

Hazelton

⑲ *293 km (182 mi) northeast of Prince Rupert, 439 km (272 mi) northwest of Prince George, 1,217 km (755 mi) northwest of Vancouver.*

Hazelton is rich in the culture of the Gitxsan and Wet'suwet'en peoples. ★**'Ksan Historical Village and Museum,** about a 15-minute drive from New Hazelton, is a re-created Gitxsan village. The elaborately painted community of seven longhouses is a replica of the one that stood on the site when the first European explorers arrived in the 19th century. The carving shed, often used by 'Ksan artists, is open to the public, and three other longhouses can be visited: one displays modern masks and robes, another has song-and-dance performances on Friday evenings in summer, and the third exhibits both original items and copies of tools, household goods, and artifacts from before the time of European contact. A restaurant serves traditional Gitxsan food. ⊠ *Hwy. 62,* ☎ *250/842–5544 or 877/842–5518.* ⊡ *$2; $8 with tour.* ☉ *Apr. 15–Sept. 30, daily 9–6 (optional tours on the half hour); Oct.–Apr. 14 museum and gift shop only, weekdays 9–5.* ✍

OFF THE BEATEN PATH | **FORT ST. JAMES NATIONAL HISTORIC PARK** – This park, 62 km (38 mi) north of Vanderhoof on Highway 27, is the former Hudson's Bay Company fur-trading post on the south shore of Stuart Lake and the oldest continually inhabited European settlement west of the Rockies. Careful restoration of the original buildings, costumed staff, and a self-guided audio tour help visitors experience life as a fur trader in 1896. ☎ 250/996–7191. ⊡ $4. ☉ Mid-May–late Sept., daily 9–5; off-season tours by advance reservation.

Prince George

⑳ *440 mi (273 mi) southeast of Hazelton, 721 km (447 mi) east of Prince Rupert, 786 km (487 mi) north of Vancouver.*

At the crossroads of two railways and two highways, Prince George has grown to become the capital of northern British Columbia and the third-largest city in the province. In Ft. George Park, you can visit the **Fraser–Ft. George Regional Museum** to see the fine collection of artifacts illustrating local history; it includes a hands-on gallery for children and a virtual-reality theater. ✉ *333 Gorse St.,* ☎ *250/562–1612.* ✉ *$6.50.* ◷ *May–Sept., daily 10–5; Oct.–Apr., Wed.–Sun. noon–5.*

A collection of photos, rail cars, and logging and sawmill equipment at the **Prince George Railway and Forestry Museum** traces the history of the town and the region from the arrival of the railroad. ✉ *850 River Rd., next to Cottonwood Park,* ☎ *250/563–7351.* ✉ *$4.50.* ◷ *May–Oct., daily 10–5.*

Tourism Prince George (✉ 1198 Victoria St., ☎ 250/562–3700 or 800/668–7646) has information about sights in the area.

Lodging

$$ 🏨 **Coast Inn of the North.** This centrally located, nine-story, full-service hotel has a striking rosewood lobby with a brass fireplace, and connects to a retail concourse with a range of high-end shops. The standard rooms have two double beds; the premium rooms are corner units with balconies; and the suites have fireplaces and large balconies. ✉ *770 Brunswick St., V2L 2C2,* ☎ *250/563–0121 or 800/663–1144,* ℻ *250/563–1948. 148 rooms, 2 suites. 2 restaurants, coffee shop, lounge, pub, in-room data ports, air-conditioning, no-smoking floor, indoor pool, beauty salon, hot tub, sauna, exercise room, shops, meeting rooms, travel services. AE, DC, MC, V.* ✑

Shopping

The **Prince George Native Art Gallery** (✉ 1600 3rd Ave., ☎ 250/614–7726) sells traditional and contemporary works, including carvings, sculpture, jewelry, and literature.

Gold Rush Trail

㉑ *Begins at Prince George and ends at Lillooet, 170 km (105 mi) west of Kamloops, 131 km (81 mi) northeast of Whistler.*

From Prince George, Highway 97 heads south toward Kamloops and the Okanagan Valley, following the 640-km (397-mi) Gold Rush Trail, along which frontiersmen traveled in search of gold in the 19th and early 20th centuries. The trail goes through Quesnel, Williams Lake, Wells, Barkerville, Cache Creek, and along the Fraser Canyon. Many communities have historic sites that help tell the story of the gold-rush era. The **Cariboo, Chilcotin, Coast Tourism Association** (✉ 118A N. First Ave., Williams Lake V2G 1Y8, ☎ 250/392–2226 or 800/663–5885, ℻ 250/392–2838) has information about the trail.

★ The most vivid re-creation of the gold rush is at **Barkerville Historic Town,** 80 km (50 mi) east of Quesnel on Highway 26. Once the biggest town west of Chicago and north of San Francisco, it is now a provincial historic site with more than 120 restored and reconstructed buildings. Actors in period costume, merchants vending 19th-century goods, stagecoach rides, and live musical revues capture the town's heyday. The town is open year-round, but most of the theatrical fun happens in summer. There are B&Bs in Barkerville and a campground nearby. ✉ *Hwy. 26, Barkerville,* ☎ *250/994–3302.* ✉ *Mid-May–mid-Sept., $7.50 for a 2-day pass; free in winter.* ◷ *Daily 8–8.* ✑

Bowron Lake Provincial Park (✉ end of Hwy. 26), 30 km (19 mi) east of Barkerville by gravel road, has a 116-km (72-mi) chain of rivers, lakes, and portages that make up a popular canoe route. Canoeists must reserve ahead (☎ 800/435–5622) and pay a fee of $50 per person.

Lodging

$$$$ 🏨 **Echo Valley Ranch Resort.** At the base of Mt. Bowman, 50 km (31 mi) northwest of Clinton, this adult-oriented ranch makes the most of its scenic setting. Included in the rates are a range of activities and three fine Continental meals using the ranch's own organic produce. You can indulge in spa and beauty treatments or hike, bike, fish, or ride. Tennessee Walker horses and experienced Cariboo cowboys take riders on day and overnight trips. White-water rafting, flightseeing, and staying at a First Nations teepee village can be arranged, too. Winter activities include snowshoeing, cross-country skiing, sleigh rides, and ice fishing. A three-night minimum stay is required at this no-smoking inn. ⌧ *Box 16, Jesmond V0K 1K0,* ☎ *250/459–2386 or 800/253–8831,* ℻ *250/459–0086. 20 rooms, 3 cabins. Dining room, indoor pool, lakes, outdoor hot tub, massage, sauna, steam room, hiking, horseback riding, fishing, bicycles, cross-country skiing, sleigh rides, recreation room, business services, meeting rooms. MC, V. AP.* 🐾

$–$$ 🏨 **Wells Hotel.** This faithfully refurbished 1930s hotel makes a good base for visiting nearby Barkerville (8 km, or 5 mi, away) and the Bowron Lake canoeing area and for accessing the 80 km (50 mi) of hiking, biking, and cross-country ski trails nearby. Rooms are simple, comfortable, and freshly decorated; in keeping with the historic theme, they don't have phones or TVs. Wells is 74 km (46 mi) east of Quesnel on Highway 26; the hotel can arrange pickups from Quesnel. An on-site casino is planned for 2001. The hotel is no-smoking. ⌧ *2341 Pooley St., Box 39, Wells V0K 2R0,* ☎ *250/994–3427 or 800/860–2299,* ℻ *250/994–3494. 16 rooms, 9 with bath. Restaurant, pub, hiking, meeting rooms. AE, MC, V. CP.* 🐾

THE HIGH COUNTRY AND THE OKANAGAN VALLEY

South-central British Columbia (often simply called the "Interior" by Vancouverites) encompasses the high arid plateau between the Coast Mountains on the west and the Monashees on the east. The Okanagan Valley, five hours east of Vancouver by car, or one hour by air, contains the interior's largest concentration of people. The region's sandy lake beaches and hot, dry climate have long made it a family holiday magnet for Vancouverites and Albertans, and rooms and campsites can be hard to come by in summer.

The Okanagan Valley is also the fruit-growing capital of Canada and a major wine-producing area. Many of the region's more than 45 wineries are in scenic spots and they welcome visitors with tastings, tours, and restaurants. The Wine Museum in Kelowna, and the B.C. Wine Information Centre in Penticton (☞ *below*) can help you create a winery tour and can provide details about annual wine festivals.

Throughout the Okanagan you'll see depictions of a smiling green lizard that looks a bit like the Loch Ness Monster without the tartan cap. This is Ogopogo, a harmless, shy, and probably mythical creature said to live in Okanagan Lake.

Kamloops

㉒   *355 km (220 mi) northeast of Vancouver, 163 km (101 mi) northwest of Kelowna.*

Virtually all roads meet at Kamloops, the High Country's sprawling transport hub. From here, highways fan out to Vancouver, the Okanagan, the Cariboo, and Jasper in the Rockies. Kamloops is also the closest town to Sun Peaks, one of the province's leading ski resorts.

The **Secwepemc Museum and Heritage Park,** a reconstructed village set on a traditional gathering site, interprets and celebrates the culture and lifestyle of the Shuswap people, who have lived in this area for thousands of years. Displays include winter houses and summer lodges; the museum holds recorded oral history, photographs, artifacts, and artwork. ⊠ *202–355 Yellowhead Hwy.,* ☎ *250/828–9801.* 🖃 *$6.* ☉ *June–Sept. 7, weekdays 8:30–8, weekends 10–6; Sept. 8–May, weekdays 8:30–4:30.*

OFF THE   **WELLS GRAY PROVINCIAL PARK –** This park is a vast wilderness area with
BEATEN PATH great canoeing, fishing, and hiking. About 120 km (74 mi) north of Kamloops on Highway 5 is Clearwater, the major access point to Wells Gray. There's a visitor information center (☎ 250/674–2646 or 250/851–3000) at the junction of Highway 5 and the Clearwater Valley Road.

Lodging

$$ 🏠 **Woody Life Village.** This complex has modern duplex log cabins and a lodge with such unwoodsy amenities as an indoor pool and an exercise room. You also have access to the fishing and boating at Lac Le Jeune resort, a five-minute drive away. Woody Life is 25 km (16 mi) south of Kamloops, just off Highway 5. ⊠ *Lac le Jeune Rd. (650 Victoria St., V2C 2B4),* ☎ *250/374–3833 or 800/561–5253,* 🄵🄰🄷 *250/372–8755. 30 rooms. Dining room, kitchenettes, indoor pool, hot tub, sauna, exercise room. AE, DC, MC, V. Closed Nov.–mid-Apr.* 🐾

Outdoor Activities and Sports

GOLF

Rivershore Golf Links (⊠ 330 Rivershore Dr., ☎ 250/573–4211) is an 18-hole, par-72 course designed by Robert Trent Jones Sr. It's about 20 km (12 mi) east of Kamloops on Highway 1. There's an 18-hole course at **Sun Peaks Resort** (☞ *below*).

SKIING

With a 2,953-ft vertical drop and one of the largest snowboard parks in North America, **Sun Peaks Resort** (⊠ 50 Creekside Way, Sun Peaks, ☎ 250/578–7222 or 800/807–3257), 53 km (33 mi) north of Kamloops, has developed into a leading ski resort, with many hotels, restaurants, an outdoor ice rink, and a golf course. It has 64 downhill runs, five chairlifts, and 12 groomed and tracked cross-country trails.

Salmon Arm

➋➌   *108 km (67 mi) east of Kamloops, 106 km (66 mi) north of Kelowna.*

Salmon Arm is the commercial center of the Shuswap (named for Shuswap Lake), a greener and less visited region than the Okanagan to the south. From Sicamous, 27 km (16 mi) northeast of Salmon Arm, you can take a summer (May to October) day trip on Shuswap Lake on the ***Phoebe Anne*** (☎ 250/836–2220), a mini-paddlewheeler.

Roderick Haig-Brown Provincial Park (⊠ off Hwy. 1 at Squilax, ☎ 250/851–3000) is where thousands of salmon come to spawn in the Adams River in late September and October; the park is about 40 km (25 mi) northwest of Salmon Arm.

Dining and Lodging

$$ ✕🏨 **Quaaout Lodge Resort.** Owned by the Little Shuswap First Nations band, this modern cedar hotel on Little Shuswap Lake provides an opportunity to experience the culture of interior native peoples. Some of the well-appointed rooms have fireplaces and whirlpool baths for two set under windows overlooking the lake; the restaurant serves native cuisine. The lodge has a ceremonial sweat lodge and a traditional *kekuli,* or winter shelter, as well as a sandy beach and trails through hundreds of acres of forested land. The hotel is 43 km (27 mi) northwest of Salmon Arm. ⊠ *Off Hwy. 1, Box 1215, Chase V0E 1M0,* ☎ *250/679–3090 or 800/663–4303,* 𝖥𝖠𝖷 *250/679–3039. 72 rooms. Restaurant, indoor pool, hot tub, steam room, exercise room, horseback riding, jogging, dock, boating, fishing, bicycles, meeting rooms. AE, MC, V.* ✎

Outdoor Activities and Sports

Sicamous on Shuswap Lake is a mecca for houseboat holidays. Several operators, including **Three Buoys** (☎ 250/836–2403 or 800/663–2333) and **Twin Anchors** (☎ 250/836–2450 or 800/663–4026), rent fully equipped floating homes that are a fun way to explore the lake.

Vernon

㉔ *117 km (73 mi) southeast of Kamloops.*

Because Vernon has no public access to Okanagan Lake, it's less of a tourist draw than other towns in the area. Nearby are two other lakes and the all-season, gaslight era–theme village resort atop Silver Star Mountain.

The 50-acre **Historic O'Keefe Ranch** provides a window on 19th-century cattle-ranch life. Among the many restored ranch buildings are a mansion, a church, a working blacksmith's shop, and a general store. The restaurant serves ranchers' fare. ⊠ *9380 Hwy. 97, 12 km (8 mi) north of Vernon,* ☎ *250/542–7868.* 🎫 *$6.* ☉ *May–mid-Oct., daily 9–5; tours by appointment rest of yr.*

Kalamalka Lake Provincial Park (⊠ Kidston Rd., ☎ 250/494–6500) has warm-water beaches and some of the most scenic viewpoints and hiking trails in the region.

From the Vernon train station you can take a six-hour round-trip to Kelowna on the vintage **Okanagan Valley Wine Train** (☞ Kelowna, *below*).

Outdoor Activities and Sports

GOLF

Predator Ridge Golf Resort (⊠ 360 Commonage Rd., ☎ 250/542–3436) is a 27-hole facility, with a 36 par on each nine. It's about 15 km (9 mi) south of Vernon on Highway 97.

SKIING

Silver Star Mountain Resort (⊠ Silver Star Rd., Silver Star Mountain, ☎ 250/542–0224 or 800/663–4431 for reservations), 22 km (13 mi) east of Vernon, has five chairlifts and two T-bars, a vertical drop of 2,500 ft, 85 runs, and night skiing. The resort also has 35 km (22 mi) of groomed, track-set cross-country trails, as well as hiking and mountain-biking trails open in the summer. The resort's Victorian gaslight-themed village has several hotels, restaurants, and shops, many of which are open all year.

Kelowna

㉕ *46 km (29 mi) south of Vernon, 68 km (42 mi) north of Penticton.*

The largest town in the Okanagan Valley, Kelowna (pop. 97,000), on the edge of Okanagan Lake, makes a good base for exploring the region's beaches, ski hills, wineries, and golf courses. Although its edges are looking untidily urban these days, the town still has an attractive, walkable core and a restful beachside park.

The city is at the heart of British Columbia's wine and fruit-growing district. The **Wine Museum** (⊠ 1304 Ellis St., ☎ 250/868–0441) set in a historic packinghouse, has wine-making exhibits, as well as a wine shop, and information about touring local wineries. Admission is free; the museum is open Monday through Saturday 10–5, Sunday noon–5. The **British Columbia Orchard Museum** ⊠ 1304 Ellis St., ☎ 250/763–0433), in the same building as the Wine Museum, has displays about the area's other critical industry.

On the **Okanagan Valley Wine Train** (⊠ 600 Recreation Ave., ☎ 250/712–9888 or 888/674–8725), you can take a six-hour day trip to Vernon along Kalamalka Lake and taste wines on board. The 1950s vintage train runs Wednesday through Sunday between late June and October.

The **Father Pandosy Mission** (⊠ 3685 Benvoulin Rd., ☎ 250/860–8369) the first European settlement in central British Columbia, was founded here by Oblate missionaries in 1859. The 4-acre site is home to four original mission buildings made of log (including a tiny chapel), as well as a farmhouse and settler's cabin. The buildings, furnished to look as they did in the late 19th century, are open for viewing (Easter to mid-October, daily 8–8; as weather permits during the rest of the year). Donations are accepted.

The **Kelowna Art Gallery** (⊠ 1315 Water St., ☎ 250/762–2226) is an elegant public art gallery with a variety of local and international exhibits. It's open Tuesday through Saturday 10–5 (until 9 Thursday) and Sunday 1–5.

For many Canadians, the Okanagan means apples, and much of the valley is still planted with orchards. One of the largest and oldest (it dates to 1904) is the **Kelowna Land & Orchard Company,** which you can tour on foot or on a tractor-drawn hay ride. The farm animals, including llamas and alpacas, are a hit with kids; a teahouse serves lunch, dinner, and snacks on a patio with a lake view. ⊠ *3002 Dunster Rd. (8 km, or 5 mi, east of Kelowna),* ☎ *250/763–1091.* 🎫 *$5.25.* ⊙ *Tours: May–June and Oct., daily at 10 and 1; July–Sept., daily at 10, 1, and 3. Teahouse: May–Oct., daily 8–8.*

Dining and Lodging

Many local wineries also have excellent restaurants.

$$$$ ✕ **De Montreuil Restaurant.** This cozy downtown restaurant makes the most of the regional bounty, serving dishes—such as quenelles of Okanagan goat cheese, duck breast with raspberry and shallot confit, and rack of lamb with rosemary, garlic, and mint—that the owners (two local brothers) have dubbed Cascadian cuisine. The menu, priced by the number of courses rather than by the dish, encourages experimentation; the warm yellow decor encourages lingering. ⊠ *368 Bernard Ave.,* ☎ *250/860–5508. AE, DC, MC, V. No lunch weekends.*

$$–$$$$ ✕ **Guisachan House Restaurant.** Once the summer home of Lord Aberdeen, a former Governor General of Canada, this 1891 house set in 2½ acres of gardens is now an attractive restaurant. White cane chairs, pink tablecloths, period furniture, and seating on the broad, glassed-in veranda re-create a Victorian summertime ambience. Chef Georg Rieder, originally from Germany, offers a lengthy menu that features several varieties of schnitzel, risottos, pastas, and seafood, as well as bison, local venison, and such Asian-influenced dishes as Szechuan pork tenderloin and rack of lamb with honey and coriander. A four-course lunch for under $9 is an especially good value. ☒ *1060 Cameron Ave.,* ☎ *250/862–9368. AE, DC, MC, V. No dinner Mon.–Wed.*

$$$ 🏨 **Grand Okanagan Lakefront Resort and Conference Centre.** On the shore of Okanagan Lake, this full-service resort hotel is a five-minute stroll from downtown Kelowna, though the on-site services—which include a health club and spa, a casino, an Internet café, boat rentals, and a waterfront park—mean virtually everything is here. Most of the standard rooms and suites are spacious, with balconies, sitting areas, and attractive modern decor (the north tower is newer than the south tower). About half the rooms have views over the lake and the surrounding hills. The two-bedroom waterfront condo suites are a good option for families: they come with two full bathrooms, full kitchens, washer/dryers, gas fireplaces, and whirlpool baths. ☒ *1310 Water St., V1Y 9P3,* ☎ *250/763–4500 or 800/465–4651,* 🆁🅰🆇 *250/763–4565. 255 rooms, 75 suites. 4 restaurants, café, lounge, pub, air-conditioning, in-room data ports, no-smoking floor, room service, indoor-outdoor pool, pool, beauty salon, indoor and outdoor hot tubs, sauna, spa, exercise room, boating, dock, mountain bikes, casino, baby-sitting, laundry service, concierge, business services, convention center, travel services. AE, DC, MC, V.* ✎

$$$ 🏨 **Lake Okanagan Resort.** This self-contained, kid-friendly resort 16 km (10 mi) from Kelowna spreads across a 300-acre hill on the undeveloped west side of Okanagan Lake. The attractive modern units, decorated with rich colors and pine furniture, range from one-bedroom suites in the main hotel to three-bedroom chalets. All have lake views and kitchens or kitchenettes, and most have balconies or decks. Activities, including golf and tennis, are plentiful, and a resort shuttle scoots guests up and down the hillside. ☒ *2751 Westside Rd., V1Z 3T1,* ☎ *250/ 769–3511 or 800/663–3273,* 🆁🅰🆇 *250/769–6665. 113 suites and chalets. Restaurant, bar, café, air-conditioning, kitchenettes, 2 pools, indoor and outdoor hot tubs, massage, sauna, 9-hole golf course, 7 tennis courts, exercise room, hiking, horseback riding, beach, dock, boating, jet skiing, waterskiing, video games, children's programs (ages 6–16), playground, coin laundry, meeting rooms, helipad. AE, DC, MC, V.* ✎

$$$ 🏨 **Manteo Resort Waterfront Hotel & Villas.** Kelowna's newest resort opened on the shore of Okanagan Lake in spring 2000. Accommodation choices include rooms and suites in the Tuscan-style main building (some with kitchenettes, all with balconies) and two- and three-bedroom villas with complete kitchens.The villas are especially attractive, with gas fireplaces, terra-cotta tiles, high ceilings, and private patios. The resort makes the most of its waterfront location with two marinas, a swimming beach, and a lakeside boardwalk. The resort's restaurant, the Wild Apple Grill, serves Pacific Northwest cuisine inside and on its big lakeside patio. Smoking isn't allowed indoors here. ☒ *3766 Lakeshore Rd., V1W 3L4,* ☎ *250/860–1031 or 800/ 445–5255,* 🆁🅰🆇 *250/860–1041. 48 rooms, 30 suites, 24 villas. Restaurant, coffee shop, lounge, air-conditioning, in-room data ports, kitchenettes (some), room service, 1 indoor and 1 outdoor pool, indoor and outdoor hot tubs, massage, sauna, steam room, putting green, tennis court, exercise room, beach, water park, boating, marina, parasailing, waterskiing, billiards, cinema, baby-sitting, children's programs (ages 3-10), playground, dry cleaning, laundry service, concierge, business services, meeting rooms. AE, DC, MC, V.* ✎

Outdoor Activities and Sports

BIKING AND HIKING

Bikers and hikers can try the rail bed of the **Kettle Valley Railway** between Penticton and Kelowna. The **Visitors Bureau for Kelowna** (☎ 250/861–1515) can provide maps and information.

GOLF

Gallagher's Canyon Golf and Country Club (✉ 4320 Gallagher's Dr. W, ☎ 250/861–4240), about 15 km (9 mi) southeast of Kelowna, has an 18-hole, par-72 course and a 9-hole, par-32 course; green fees for the 18-hole course are $85 in the high season. Surrounded by orchards (golfers can pick fruit as they play), **Harvest Golf Club** (✉ 2725 KLO Rd., ☎ 250/862–3103 or 800/257–8577) has 18 holes and is a par-72 course. Green fees in the high season are $80. **The Harvest Dining Room** (☎ (250/862–3177)), in the clubhouse, has lake views and is open to nongolfers for dinner. The **Okanagan Golf Club** (✉ 3200 Via Centrale, ☎ 250/765–5955 or 800/898–2449) has two 18-hole, par-72 courses with Okanagan Valley views. High-season green fees are $80 for the Quail Course, a challenging hillside course with tight tree-lined fairways, and $85 for the newer Jack Nicklaus Group–designed Bear Course, which is more forgiving.

SKIING

Big White Ski Resort (✉ Big White Rd., off Hwy. 33, about 1 hr east of Kelowna, ☎ 250/765–3101; 800/663–2772 for accommodation reservations) is an affordable, family-oriented resort with excellent day care and children's programs, a ski school, a good mix of runs, and up-to-date lift equipment that includes a new gondola and four high-speed quad chairs. Ski guides will take you out on the mountain for a half day at no charge. You can ski or walk anywhere in the compact village, which has several restaurants and a total of 9,000 beds in a variety of hotels, condos, bed-and-breakfasts, and hostels. The resort, which is expanding rapidly, has 12 lifts, more than 100 runs on 2,165 acres of skiable terrain, a vertical drop of 2,550 ft, average annual snowfall of more than 24 ft, and night skiing five nights a week. You'll also find three snowboard parks and 25 km (15 mi) of cross-country trails, as well as snowmobiling, snowshoeing, ice-skating, horse-drawn sleigh rides, snow tubing, and even dog sledding.

Wineries

Kelowna is at the heart of British Columbia's wine country. Virtually all of the region's wineries offer tastings and tours throughout the summer and during the Okanagan Wine Festivals held each April and October; several have restaurants and most also have wine shops open year-round. The tours are usually free, though some wineries charge for tastings. The Wine Museum (☞ *above*) can help you create a winery tour and can provide details about annual wine festivals. Several local operators will act as guides and designated drivers. **Okanagan Limousine** (☎ 250/717–5466 or 877/295–9373) offers nonnarrated chauffeur-driven tours of the wine area. **Okanagan Wine Country Tours** (☎ 250/868–9463) gives narrated wine-country tours to small groups.

British Columbia's oldest winery, and still one of the largest, **Calona Vineyards** (✉ 1125 Richter St., ☎ 250/762–9144 or 888/246–4472) is in central Kelowna, walking distance from most hotels, and offers free tours and tastings. Call for tour times.

Cedar Creek Estate Winery (✉ 5445 Lakeshore Rd., ☎ 250/764–8866 or 800/730–9463), south of Kelowna on the east side of the lake, has a scenic waterside location with picnic areas. Tours are given daily mid-May to mid-October; call for times.

On a hilltop overlooking Okanagan Lake, **Mission Hill Winery** was rebuilt in 2000 to look, as the owner describes it, like "a combination of monastery, Tuscan hill village, and French winery," complete with a vaulted cellar blasted from volcanic rock and a 12-story bell tower. Tours include a video presentation and tastings; snacks and wine by the glass are served on the patio, and an outdoor amphitheater hosts music and theater events on summer evenings. ⊠ *1730 Mission Hill Rd., Westbank,* ☎ *250/768–7611 or 800/957–9911.* ⊙ *July–Aug., daily 9–7 with tours 10–5; June and Sept., daily 9–6 with tours at 11, 1, and 3; Oct.–May, daily 9–5 with tours on weekends at 11, 1, and 3.*

Quails' Gate Estate Winery (⊠ 3303 Boucherie Rd., ☎ 250/769–4451 or 800/420–9463), on the edge of Okanagan Lake, gives tours daily from late April to the middle of October. It has a wine shop in a 19th-century log home and a patio restaurant with views of the vineyard and lake (open for lunch and dinner April to mid-October).

Summerhill Estate Winery (⊠ 4870 Chute Lake Rd., ☎ 250/764–8000 or 800/667–3538), south of Kelowna on the east side of the lake, is an organic producer best known for its sparkling and ice wines. What tends to startle visitors, though, is the four-story-high replica of the Great Pyramid at Cheops; it's used to age and store sparkling wine. There's also a wine shop, and a restaurant with a lake-view veranda overlooking Okanagan Lake that serves lunch daily, as well as a preserved settler's cabin, and a re-created First Nations earth house. Call for tour times.

Summerland and Peachland

㉖ *Summerland: 52 km (31 mi) south of Kelowna; Peachland: 25 km (15 mi) southwest of Kelowna.*

Between Kelowna and Penticton, Highway 97 winds its way along the west side of Okanagan Lake, past vineyards, orchards, fruit stands, small lake-side resorts, and some of the prettiest lake and hill scenery in the region.

At Summerland, you can ride the historic **Kettle Valley Steam Railway** (⊠ 18404 Bathville Rd., ☎ 250/494–8422 or 877/494–8424 in British Columbia), which has trips along 10 km (6 mi) of a 1915 rail line between late May and October.

WINERIES

Hainle Vineyards Estate Winery (⊠ 5355 Trepanier Bench Rd., Peachland, ☎ 250/767–2525 or 800/767–3109), British Columbia's first organic winery and also the first to make ice wines, is a small producer open for tastings (though not tours). The **Amphora Bistro** ($$) on site has lovely lake views and lunches that highlight seasonal and organic ingredients. Try the cracked-grain salad with herbs, toasted seeds, and dried fruit in a peach vinaigrette, or the polenta pizza with caramelized onions, smoked tomato sauce, smoked salmon, olives, and Asiago cheese. The bistro is open for lunch Thursday through Sunday from early April to mid-October.

Tours are given daily from late April until the middle of October at **Sumac Ridge Estate Winery** (⊠ 17403 Hwy. 97 N, Summerland, ☎ 250/494–0451), but you can taste or buy wines here all year. The winery's **Cellar Door Bistro** ($$–$$$; ☎ 250/494–3316) serves lunches and dinners of imaginative local cuisine. It's closed Sunday and Monday and from mid-October until late April.

Penticton

❷ *16 km (10 mi south of Summerland, 395 km (245 mi) east of Vancouver.*

Penticton, with its long sandy beach backed by pink motels and cruising pickup trucks, is a nostalgia-inducing family-holiday spot. The arid hills around town are full of orchards, vineyards, and small farms. The **S.S. Sicamous** (⌧ 1099 Lakeshore Dr. W, ☎ 250/492–0403), a paddlewheeler moored at the lakeside, is now a museum.

The **B.C. Wine Information Centre** (⌧ 888 Westminster Ave. W, ☎ 250/490–2006) will help you plan a self-drive winery tour and can provide details about the annual wine festivals, held in spring and fall. It also stocks more than 300 local wines. The **Penticton Visitors Information Centre** (⌧ 888 Westminster Ave. W, ☎ 250/493–4055 or 800/663–5052), in the same building as the B.C. Wine Information Centre, has information about other activities in the area.

Dining and Lodging

$$$$ ✕ **Country Squire.** Plan to spend the evening if you book a meal at this rambling country house in Naramata, 10 km (6 mi) north of Penticton. Diners are asked to choose one of seven or eight main courses when they reserve their table; the chef then designs a five-course meal around it. The options change each evening but have included various treatments of sea bass, duck breast, ostrich, venison, and rack of lamb. There's only one sitting per evening, so lingering over the meal—even taking a stroll along the lake between courses—is very much the thing to do. The wine cellar has hundreds of local and imported labels, and a notable selection of hard-to-find vintages from smaller Okanagan vineyards. ⌧ *3950 First St., Naramata,* ☎ *250/496–5416. Reservations essential. MC, V. No lunch; no dinner Mon.–Wed.*

$$$–$$$$ ✕ **Granny Bogner's.** Chef and owner Peter Hebel's hearty traditional European recipes are featured in this homey restaurant, set in a 1915 house full of antique furniture and fresh flowers. The poached salmon and roast duckling dishes are favorites here, and the wine list has a good local and imported selection. ⌧ *302 Eckhardt Ave. W,* ☎ *250/493–2711. Reservations essential. AE, MC, V. Closed Mon. and Jan. No lunch.*

$$–$$$ ▦ **Penticton Lakeside Resort and Conference Centre.** On the shore of Okanagan Lake, this modern resort hotel is within walking distance of Penticton's beachfront and town center. The rooms have fairly standard modern decor, but all are spacious and have large balconies and either a lake or a mountain view. The facilities include a full-size health club, a casino, a private beach, and a lakeside outdoor café. ⌧ *21 Lakeshore Dr. W, V2A 7M5,* ☎ *250/493–8221 or 800/663–9400,* ℻ *250/493–0607. 197 rooms, 7 suites. Restaurant, bar, in-room data ports, no-smoking floor, room service, indoor pool, beauty salon, hot tub, aerobics, health club, beach, dock, shop, casino, baby-sitting, children's programs, dry cleaning, concierge, convention center. AE, D, DC, MC, V.* ✆

$$ ▦ **God's Mountain Crest Chalet.** This Mediterranean-style villa sits on 100 acres of empty, arid hilltop overlooking Skaha Lake, 4 km (2½ mi) south of Penticton. Inside, an eccentrically sumptuous mix of plush cushions, couches, lush fabrics, European antiques, and theatrical props decorates the three common living rooms. The broad patio, a poolside bar and gazebo, and two guest suites have expansive lake views. Each suite, done in light colors and pretty fabrics, has a living room and kitchenette. A lavish hot breakfast buffet is included in the rates, and the European hosts can also provide evening meals. ⌧ *4898 Lakeside Rd.,*

V2A 8W4, ☎ FAX *250/490–4800. 6 suites. Dining room, pool, outdoor hot tub, hiking, meeting room, helipad. MC, V. Closed Nov.–Feb.* ✍

Outdoor Activities and Sports

For downhill skiing, **Apex Mountain Resort** (✉ Apex Mountain Rd. off Green Mountain Rd., ☎ 250/292–8222 or 877/777–2739; 250/ 292–8256 for accommodations) has 60 trails, two chairlifts, a vertical drop of 2,000 ft, and a peak elevation of 7,187 ft. The resort, known for its intimate ambience and soft powder snow, also has night skiing as well as cross-country trails, a snow-tube park, and snowmobile and dogsled tours. Apex is 32 km (19 mi) northwest of Penticton. The resort village has restaurants, bars, shops, ski rentals, a ski school, and children's programs. A full-service hotel, **The Coast Inn at Apex** (☎ 800/387–2739), and a variety of condos and cabins for summer and winter rentals are available.

Wineries

You can wander around the lakeside **Lake Breeze Vineyards** (✉ 930 Sammet Rd., Naramata, ☎ 250/496–5659), one of the region's most attractively located wineries. Tours are given May–October daily and by appointment during the rest of the year. The **Patio Restaurant** ($$) is open daily for lunch July through September; mid-April through June it's open for lunch Wednesday through Sunday.

Osoyoos

㉘ *58 km (36 mi) south of Penticton.*

South of Penticton between the southern tip of Lake Okanagan and the U.S. border, Highway 97 runs along a chain of lakes: Skaha, Vaseaux, and Osoyoos, and through Canada's only desert. The area's hot dry climate makes it a prime wine-producing area; there are several wineries in the area and most offer tours and tastings. For more information, contact the B.C. Wine Information Centre in Penticton (☞ *above*). Accommodation is available in Osoyoos and other towns in the area.

THE KOOTENAYS

Tucked between Highways 1 and 3, along which most travelers rush to and from the Rockies, the Kootenays are an idyllic backwater of mountains, lakes, natural hot springs, ghost towns, and prettily preserved Victorian villages. Kootenay Lake and Lower Arrow Lake define the region. A century ago this area was booming because of the discovery of silver in the hills, and with the prospectors came vestiges of European society: stately homes, an elegant paddlewheeler, and the town of Nelson, built in respectable Victorian brick. These days the Kootenays are filled with fine restaurants, historic country inns, a wealth of opportunities for hiking, fishing, boating, and skiing, and some of the best scenery in the province.

Nelson

★ **㉙** *321 km (199 mi) east of Penticton, 657 km (407 mi) east of Vancouver.*

Bypassed a little by history, this city of 10,000, with its Victorian architecture, lake and mountain setting, and college-town ambience, is one of the most attractive towns in British Columbia. Nelson has a wealth of crafts shops and coffee bars, several B&Bs, a youth hostel, and a restored 1906 streetcar running along the lakeshore. The **Visitor Info Centre** (✉ 225 Hall St., ☎ 250/352–3433) can direct you on a self-guided tour of the town's art and crafts galleries and its more than 355 historic buildings.

About 45 km (30 mi) north of Nelson is **Ainsworth Hot Springs Resort** (⌧ Hwy. 31, Ainsworth Hot Springs, ☎ 250/229–4212 or 800/668–1171), where you can stroll through a network of caves and plunge into hot and cold spring-fed pools.

OFF THE
BEATEN PATH

KASLO – On the west side of Kootenay Lake, heading north from Nelson on Highway 31, is this very pretty village. An 1898 sternwheeler, the S.S. *Moyie* (☎ 250/353–2525), is moored on the lakeshore, its interior restored to *Titanic*-era opulence. It's open mid-May to mid-October for tours. If you head west from Kaslo on scenic, winding Highway 31A, you'll pass a number of 19th-century silver-mining towns. Most were abandoned when the ore ran out, but **Sandon**, off Highway 31A, is enjoying a resurgence as a historic site, with several shops and a visitor center. **Silversmith Tours** (☎ 250/358–2247) gives tours daily in the summer and by appointment in the off-season.

Dining and Lodging

$$–$$$ ★ ✕ **All Season's Café.** Tucked into an alley between Baker and Victoria streets, this former family cottage serves innovative cuisine that its owners have dubbed (because people kept asking) Left Coast Inland Cuisine. In practice, this means a seasonally changing menu that uses fresh, local, often organic produce and lists lots of vegetarian creations. Among the good choices are the baked goat-cheese soufflé on greens with maple-walnut vinaigrette and the seared salmon, scallops, and prawns with summer-squash risotto. ⌧ *620 Herridge La.,* ☎ *250/352–0101. MC, V. No lunch Mon.–Sat.*

$$–$$$ ✕ **Fiddler's Green.** Imaginative Northwest cuisine featuring local organic produce and an exclusively B.C. wine list is featured in this ivy-covered 1920s country house, about 10 km (6 mi) north of Nelson. Dinner is served in the main dining room, in any of three smaller rooms (two have fireplaces), or in the garden in summer. Highlights on the seasonally changing menu have included a salmon and prawn cake appetizer; Angus New York steak served with gorgonzola butter; and grilled-scallop and smoked-salmon ravioli. Everything, from the pasta to the smoked salmon, is prepared in house. ⌧ *2710 Lower Six Mile Rd.,* ☎ *250/825–4466. MC, V. No lunch.*

$–$$ ★ 🏨 **Willow Point Lodge.** About 6 km (4 mi) north of Nelson, this three-story 1920 country inn is perched on 3½ acres of forested mountainside. The views from the broad, covered veranda and most of the rooms take in Kootenay Lake, the Selkirk Mountains, and the inn's own extensive gardens. The rooms are beautifully decorated; a favorite is the Oak Room, with its big stone fireplace, red velvet bed canopy, and a private entrance. One room has a detached bath. A lavish breakfast is included in the rate, and trails lead from the property to waterfalls nearby. A cedar gazebo in the garden is popular for weddings or peaceful meditation. ⌧ *2211 Taylor Dr. (R.R. 1, S-21, C-31), V1L 5P4,* ☎ *250/825–9411 or 800/949–2211,* 𝔽𝔸𝕏 *250/825–3432. 6 rooms. Breakfast room, outdoor hot tub, hiking. MC, V.* 🐾

$ 🏨 **Emory House Bed and Breakfast.** This 1926 Arts-and-Crafts house near downtown Nelson is attractive and uncluttered, with hardwood floors, antique furniture, local art, and views of Kootenay Lake from the sunroom and one of the guest rooms. Guests can share the cozy sitting room, which has a fireplace, with the three resident cats. A lavish breakfast with fresh baked goods and a choice of entrées is included in the rates at this no-smoking B&B. ⌧ *811 Vernon St., V1L 4G3,* ☎

FAX *250/352–7007. 4 rooms, 2 with bath. Breakfast room, air-conditioning. MC, V.* 😊

Outdoor Activities and Sports

HIKING

Kokanee Creek Provincial Park and Kokanee Glacier Provincial Park (☏ 250/422–4200 for both), north of Nelson off Highway 3A, have extensive trail networks. Kokanee Creek also has lake swimming, picnic sites, and nearby boat rentals.

SKIING

Red Mountain Resorts (✉ 1000 Red Mountain Rd., Rossland, ☏ 250/362–7384 or 800/663–0105), about an hour southwest of Nelson, spans two mountains and three mountain faces, and has 83 marked runs, five lifts, and a vertical drop of 2,900 ft as well as cross-country ski trails. Accommodation, ski rental, and ski lessons are also available. **Whitewater Ski and Winter Resort** (✉ Whitewater Ski Rd., off Hwy. 6, ☏ 250/354–4944 or 800/666–9420), about 10 km (6 mi) south of Nelson, has 38 runs, three lifts, a 1,300-ft vertical drop, and plenty of powder skiing. Ski rentals and lessons are available, though the resort doesn't offer lodging.

Crawford Bay

③⓪ *40 km (25 mi) northeast of Nelson, including ferry ride.*

This peaceful backwater has pretty pastoral scenery framed by snow-capped mountains. On the east side of Kootenay Lake, Crawford Bay can be accessed by a scenic, 45-minute free **car ferry** (☏ 250/229–4215) from Balfour, north of Nelson. By car, it's off Highway 3 on Route 3A.

Lodging

$–$$ 🏨 **Wedgwood Manor.** Built for the daughter of the famous china mag-
★ nate, this 1909 country manor with a wide veranda has been restored to its Edwardian beauty. The rooms are elegant: two have whirlpool baths, and several have canopy beds and their original fine woodwork. Much of the 50-acre estate is forested, walking trails lead through the woods, and the Purcell Mountains form a striking backdrop to croquet games on the lawn. A full breakfast, included in the rates, is served by the fire in the breakfast room. ✉ *16002 Crawford Creek Rd., Box 135, V0B 1E0,* ☏ FAX *250/227–9233 or 800/862–0022. 6 rooms. Breakfast room, badminton, croquet, hiking. MC, V. Closed mid-Oct.–early Apr.* 😊

Outdoor Activities and Sports

The 18-hole, par-72 **Kokanee Springs Golf Resort** (✉ 16082 Woolgar Rd., ☏ 250/227–9226 or 800/979–7999) is one of western Canada's most scenic courses, with views of Kokanee Glacier, accommodations, and a restaurant.

BRITISH COLUMBIA A TO Z

Arriving and Departing

By Bus

Greyhound Lines (☏ 604/482–8747 or 800/661–8747) connects destinations throughout British Columbia with cities and towns all along the Pacific Northwest Coast.

By Car

Driving time from Seattle to Vancouver is about three hours by I–5 and Highway 99. From other Canadian regions, three main routes lead into

British Columbia: through Sparwood, in the south, Highway 3; from Jasper and Banff, in the central region, Highways 1 and 5; and through Dawson Creek, in the north, Highways 2 and 97.

By Ferry

For information about ferry service from Vancouver Island, *see* Vancouver Island A to Z *in* Chapter 3.

By Plane

British Columbia is served by Vancouver International Airport (☞ Vancouver A to Z *in* Chapter 2). There are domestic airports in most cities. **Air Canada** and **Canadian Airlines International** (☞ Air Travel *in* Smart Travel Tips) had been the two dominant carriers and were in the process of merging at press time. **Northwest Seaplanes** (☎ 800/690–0086) offers summer floatplane service between Seattle and fishing lodges in the Inside Passage.

Getting Around

By Bus

Greyhound Lines of Canada (☎ 604/482–8747 or 800/661–8747) serves most towns in British Columbia.

Malaspina Coach Lines (☎ 877/227–8287) has routes from Vancouver to towns on the Sunshine Coast. **Sunshine Coast Transit** (☎ 604/885–3234) serves towns between Langdale and Halfmoon Bay on the Sunshine Coast.

By Car

Major roads in British Columbia, and most secondary roads, are paved and well engineered, although snow tires and chains are needed for winter travel. Many wilderness and park access roads are unpaved, and there are no roads on the mainland coast once you leave the populated areas of the southwest corner near Vancouver. Inquire locally about logging activity before using logging or forestry service roads. **B.C. Highways** (☎ 900/565–4997, 75¢ a minute) has 24-hour highway reports.

Highway 99, also known as the Sea to Sky Highway, connects Vancouver to Whistler and continues to Lillooet in the interior. The **Trans-Canada Highway** (Highway 1) connects Vancouver with Kamloops and points east via the Fraser Canyon. The **Coquihalla Highway** (Highway 5), a toll road ($10 for cars and vans) linking Hope and Kamloops, is the fastest route to the interior. **Highway 101,** the Pan-American Highway, serves the Sunshine Coast from Langdale to Lund.

By Ferry

THE SUNSHINE COAST

BC Ferries (☎ 250/386–3431 in Victoria and outside British Columbia; 888/223–3779 from elsewhere in British Columbia) provides passenger and vehicle service between Horseshoe Bay north of Vancouver and Langdale on the Sunshine Coast; Earls Cove to Saltery Bay (these towns are about halfway up the coast); and Powell River on the coast to Comox on Vancouver Island. These routes cannot be reserved. If you're planning to combine travel to the Sunshine Coast and Vancouver Island, ask BC Ferries about discount packages.

Pender Harbour Ferries (☎ 604/883–0083) runs summer-only passenger services between Garden Bay, Madeira Park, and Irvine's Landing.

GULF ISLANDS

BC Ferries (☎ 250/386–3431 in Victoria and outside British Columbia; 888/223–3779 from elsewhere in British Columbia) provides service to Galiano, Mayne, Pender, Saturna, and Salt Spring islands from

Tsawwassen (vehicle reservations recommended, and required on some sailings) and from Swartz Bay, on Vancouver Island (reservations not accepted). Salt Spring Island can also be reached from Crofton on Vancouver Island. The Northern Gulf Islands, including Gabriola, Denman, Hornby, Quadra and Cortes Islands, can be reached from ports on Vancouver Island. For more information on ferry travel from Vancouver Island, *see* Vancouver Island A to Z *in* Chapter 3.

Gulf Islands Water Taxi (☎ 250/537–2510) runs passengers and bicycles between Salt Spring, Mayne, and Galiano islands Wednesday through Saturday from June 1 through Labor Day.

THE INSIDE PASSAGE
BC Ferries (☎ 250/386–3431 in Victoria and outside British Columbia; 888/223–3779 from elsewhere in British Columbia) sails along the Inside Passage from Port Hardy to Prince Rupert (year-round) and from Port Hardy to Bella Coola (summer only). Reservations are required for vehicles and recommended for foot passengers.

QUEEN CHARLOTTE ISLANDS
The **Queen of Prince Rupert** (☎ 250/386–3431 in Victoria; 888/223–3779 elsewhere in British Columbia), a BC Ferries ship, sails six times a week from late May through September (three times a week the rest of the year). The crossing from Prince Rupert to Skidegate, near Queen Charlotte on Graham Island, takes about seven hours. Schedules vary and vehicle reservations are required. BC Ferries also connects Skidegate Landing to Alliford Bay on Moresby Island (near the airport at Sandspit). Access to smaller islands is by boat or air; plans should be made in advance through a travel agent.

By Plane
Air B.C., Canadian Airlines, and WestJet serve towns around the province (☞ Air Travel *in* Smart Travel Tips for phone numbers).

GULF ISLANDS
Harbour Air Ltd. (☎ 604/688–1277 in Vancouver; 250/385–2203 in Victoria; 800/665–0212 from elsewhere) provides regular service from Victoria, Nanaimo, and Vancouver to Salt Spring, Thetis, Mayne, Saturna, Galiano, and South Pender islands. **Pacific Spirit Air** (☎ 800/665–2359) provides scheduled floatplane service from Vancouver Harbour and Vancouver International Airport to all southern Gulf Islands.

QUEEN CHARLOTTE ISLANDS
Harbour Air Ltd. (☎ 250/627–1341 or 800/689–4234) runs scheduled floatplanes between Sandspit, Masset, Queen Charlotte City, and Prince Rupert year-round.

By Train
BC Rail (☎ 800/339–8752 in British Columbia; 800/663–8238 from outside British Columbia) operates the **Cariboo Prospector,** a year-round scheduled service between North Vancouver and Prince George, with service to Whistler, Lillooet, Williams Lake, Quesnel, and many smaller centers in the Cariboo region. BC Rail also offers accommodation, golf, and spa packages for stops en route, and can arrange circle tours of the province by linking with VIA Rail (☞ *below*) and with BC Ferries' Inside Passage service. BC Rail also operates the **Royal Hudson Steam Train,** a vintage locomotive that runs between North Vancouver and Squamish (☞ Vancouver A to Z *in* Chapter 2). The **BC Rail station** (✉ 1311 W. 1st St., North Vancouver) is about a 30-minute drive from downtown Vancouver; a shuttle links the Vancouver bus depot and the train terminal between early June and late October.

Rocky Mountaineer RailTours (☎ 604/606–7200 or 800/665–7245) is a luxury, catered train tour that travels across British Columbia from Vancouver to Jasper (in Alberta), and from Vancouver to Calgary via Banff. **VIA Rail** (☎ 800/561–8630 in Canada, 800/561–3949 in the U.S.) provides service between Vancouver and Jasper (in Alberta), and from Prince Rupert to Jasper via Prince George.

Contacts and Resources

B&B and Lodging Reservation Agencies

Reservations for lodging anywhere in the province can be made through **Super, Natural British Columbia**'s reservation service (☎ 888/435–5622). From March through October, the provincial government runs a toll-free **Campground Reservation Line** (☎ 800/689–9025).

Best Canadian Bed and Breakfast Network (✉ 1064 Balfour Ave., Vancouver V6H 1X1, ☎ 604/738–7207) can book B&Bs across the province. **Gulf Islands B&B Reservation Service** (☎ 888/539–2930) can book about 150 Gulf Island B&Bs and holiday homes.

Car Rentals

Most major agencies, including **Avis, Budget, Enterprise, National Tilden,** and **Hertz** serve cities in the province (☞ Car Rentals *in* Smart Travel Tips).

Emergencies

Ambulance, fire, poison control, police (☎ 911). A few outlying areas do not have 911 service. If you don't get immediate response, dial 0.

Guided Tours

Town listings also have information about cruises, outfitters, and tour operators, including whale-watching tours.

CRUISES

Bluewater Adventures (☎ 604/980–3800 or 888/877–1770) has multiday natural-history sailboat cruises to the Queen Charlotte Islands, Vancouver Island, and the Inside Passage. **Canadian Gulf Island Kayak and Catamaran Cruises** (☎ 250/539–2930 or 888/539–2930) will pick up and drop off at any of the Southern Gulf Islands (Salt Spring, Galiano, Pender, or Mayne) for a day of sailing or kayaking among the islands. You can cruise the Queen Charlotte Islands and the Inside Passage on a sailboat with **Ecosummer Expeditions** (☎ 250/674–0102 or 800/465–8884). **Silver Challenger Marine Eco Tours** (☎ 604/943–3343 or 877/943–3343) can take small groups around the Gulf Islands on a commercial fishing boat. The boat stops at deserted beaches and islets where you can harvest shellfish; on-board chefs then prepare meals with your catch.

ORIENTATION

Gray Line of Vancouver (☎ 604/879–3363 or 800/667–0882) has tours from Vancouver to Whistler. **Pacific Spirit Tours** (☎ 604/683–0209 or 888/286–8722) offers a variety of guided and self-guided coach, train, and ferry tours around the province, including trips to Whistler, the Sunshine Coast, Vancouver Island, the Cariboo, and the Okanagan Wine country.

Hospitals

British Columbia has hospitals in many towns: **Kelowna General Hospital** (✉ 2268 Pandosy St., ☎ 250/862–4000); **Lady Minto Hospital** (☎ 250/538–4800) in Ganges on Salt Spring Island; **Prince George Regional Hospital** (✉ 2000 15th Ave., ☎ 250/565–2000; 250/565–2444 for emergencies); in Kamloops, **Royal Inland Hospital** (✉ 311 Columbia St., ☎ 250/374–5111).

Outdoor Activities and Sports

For other outdoor-adventure operators, also *see* the listings under individual towns.

FISHING

Separate licenses are required for saltwater and freshwater fishing in British Columbia. Both are available at sporting-goods stores, government-agency offices, and most fishing lodges and charter boat companies in the province. A one-day license for nonresidents costs $15 for freshwater fishing, $7.50 for saltwater fishing, and $14 for saltwater salmon fishing. For information about saltwater-fishing regulations, contact **Fisheries and Oceans Canada** (☎ 604/666–2828) or pick up a free *Sport Fishing Guide,* available at most tourist-information centers.

GOLF

There are golf courses in all regions of the province, though Whistler and the Okanagan are the most popular destinations. Most courses are open April to mid-October, with green fees ranging from about $30 to $100, including a cart. Whistler courses, usually open May to late September, are pricier, with green fees of $125 to $185.

For advance tee-time bookings at any of 60 courses in British Columbia, call **Last Minute Golf** (☎ 604/878–1833 or 800/684–6344). The company matches golfers and courses, sometimes at substantial green-fee discounts. **West Coast Golf Shuttle** (☎ 888/599–6800) offers hotel and golfing packages for Whistler and the Okanagan.

HIKING

B.C. Parks (✉ Box 9398, Stn. Prov. Govt., Victoria V8W 9M9, ☎ 250/387–4557 or 250/387–5002) offers detailed information.

KAYAKING

The **Canadian Outback Adventure Company** (☎ 604/921–7250 or 800/565–8735) schedules sea-kayaking trips to Desolation Sound and the Gulf Islands. **Ecosummer Expeditions** (☎ 250/674–0102 or 800/465–8884) and **Gabriola Cycle and Kayak Tours** (☎ 250/247–8277) run multiday paddles to the Queen Charlottes, the Inside Passage, and other parts of the coast. **Ocean West** (☎ 604/898–4979 or 800/660–0051) offers multiday camping and kayaking tours to the Gulf Islands and Desolation Sound.

MULTIACTIVITY

Fresh Tracks Canada (☎ 604/737–8743 or 800/667–4744) has 55 different outdoor-adventure trips, including hiking, kayaking, river-rafting, and sailing adventures, all over the province and Canada.

RAFTING

The following companies provide options from lazy half-day floats to exhilarating white-water journeys of up to a week: **Canadian Outback Adventure Company** (☞ Kayaking, *above*), **Canadian River Expeditions** (☎ 604/938–6651 or 800/898–7238), **Fraser River Raft Expeditions Ltd.** (☎ 604/863–2336 or 800/363–7238), and **Hyak Wilderness Adventures** (☎ 604/734–8622 or 800/663–7238). **Whistler River Adventures** (☎ 604/932–3532 or 888/932–3532) offers both river-rafting and jet-boating trips on rivers near Whistler.

SKIING

For cross-country and downhill ski-area information, *see* listings under individual towns. For information about helicopter and snowcat skiing, contact the **B.C. Helicopter and Snowcat Skiing Operators Association** (☎ 250/542–9020).

Visitor Information

For information about the province, contact **Super, Natural British Columbia** (☎ 888/435–5622, ✍).

The principal regional tourist offices are as follows: **Cariboo, Chilcotin, Coast Tourism Association** (✉ 118A North First Ave., Williams Lake V2G 1Y8, ☎ 250/392–2226 or 800/663–5885); **Northern British Columbia Tourism Association** (✉ Smithers Airport Service Rd., Box 1030, Smithers V0J 2N0, ☎ 250/847–5227 or 800/663–8843, FAX 250/847–4321), for information on the Queen Charlotte Islands and northern British Columbia; **Northern Rockies, Alaska Highway Tourism Association** (✉ 9923 96th Ave., Box 6850, Fort St. John V1J 4J3, ☎ 250/785–2544 or 888/785–2544) for information on northeastern British Columbia; **Thompson Okanagan Tourism Association** (✉ 1332 Water St., Kelowna V1Y 9P4, ☎ 250/860–5999 or 800/567–2275); **Vancouver, Coast & Mountains Tourism Region** (✉ 250–1508 W. 2nd Ave., Vancouver V6J 1H2, ☎ 604/739–0823 or 800/667–3306) for information about the Coast Mountain Circle and the Sunshine Coast.

Galiano Island Visitor Information Centre (✉ Box 73, Galiano V0N 1P0, ☎ FAX 250/539–2233) and the **Salt Spring Island Visitor Information Centre** (✉ 121 Lower Ganges Rd., Ganges V8K 2T1, ☎ 250/537–5252) provide information on the Gulf Islands.

The **Prince Rupert Infocentre** (✉ 100 1st Ave. W, Box 669, Prince Rupert V8J 3S1, ☎ 250/624–5637 or 800/667–1994) has information about that town. For information on the Queen Charlotte Islands, contact the **Queen Charlotte Visitor Information Centre** (✉ Box 819, Queen Charlotte V0T 1S0, ☎ 250/559–8316) in Queen Charlotte. For information about Prince George, contact **Tourism Prince George** (✉ 1198 Victoria St., V2L 2L2, ☎ 250/562–3700 or 800/668–7646).

INDEX

Icons and Symbols

★ Our special recommen-
  dations
✕ Restaurant
🏠 Lodging establishment
✕🏠 Lodging establishment
  whose restaurant war-
  rants a special trip
🦆 Good for kids (rubber
  duck)
☞ Sends you to another
  section of the guide for
  more information
✉ Address
☎ Telephone number
🕐 Opening and closing
  times
💰 Admission prices
🖎 Sends you to
  www.fodors.com/urls
  for up-to-date links to
  the property's Web site

Numbers in white and black
circles ③❸ that appear on the
maps, in the margins, and
within the tours correspond to
one another.

A

Abigail's Hotel🏠, 92
Active Pass Lighthouse, 145
Admiral Motel🏠, 93
Aerie🏠, 90–91
Ainsworth Hot Springs
  Resort, 166
Air tours, 74
Air travel
  British Columbia, 168, 169
  Vancouver, 72
  Vancouver Island, 118
  Victoria, 98
Alaska View Lodge🏠, 153–154
Alberni Valley Museum, 104
Alert Bay, 116
Allegro Café✕, 46–47
All Season's Café✕, 166
Amphitrite Point Lighthouse,
  106
Amphora Bistro✕, 163
Amusement parks, 26, 31
Anne's Oceanfront Hideaway
  🏠, 148
April Point Lodge and Fishing
  Resort🏠, 115–116
Aquariums, 27
Aqua Riva✕, 42
Araxi✕, 130–131
Art Gallery of Greater
  Victoria, 83

B

Bacchus✕, 44
Baldwin Steam Locomotive,
  104
Bamfield, 105
Barb's Place✕, 90
Barclay Hotel🏠, 60
Bard on the Beach, 8
Barkerville Historic Town,
  156
Basketball, 69
B.C. Museum of Mining, 128
B.C. Sports Hall of Fame and
  Museum, 37
B.C. Wine Information
  Centre, 164
Beaches, 26, 32, 65–66
Beach House at Dundarave
  Pier✕, 50
Beach House on Sunset🏠,
  148
Beacon Hill Park, 85
Beaconsfield Inn🏠, 92
Bearfoot Bistro✕, 130
Bed-and-breakfasts
  British Columbia, 170
  Vancouver, 74
  Vancouver Island, 119
Beddis House🏠, 149
Bellhouse Inn🏠, 144
Bellhouse Park, 143
Bengal Lounge✕, 89
Bicycling
  Galiano Island, 144
  Kelowna, 162
  Salt Spring Island, 149–150
  tours, 74
  Vancouver, 66, 74
Bird Song Cottage🏠, 102
Bird-watching, 28
Bishop's✕, 50
Bloedel Conservatory, 35
Blue Crab Bar and Grill ✕,
  90
Bluffs Park, 143
Boating
  Vancouver, 66
  Victoria, 96
  Whistler, 134
Boat tours, 75
Boat travel
  Victoria, 97–98
Boleto at Ecco Il Panne ✕, 48
Bonniebrook Lodge✕🏠, 140
Books on Vancouver and
  British Columbia, 6–7
Borgo Antico✕, 46
Bowron Lake Provincial Park,
  156–157
Brackendale Eagle Reserve,
  28, 128
Brandywine Falls, 129
Bread Garden Bakery, Café &
  Espresso Bar ✕, 39, 41, 48
Brewhouse✕, 131

Bridal Veil Falls Provincial
  Park, 137–138
Bridges✕, 50
British Columbia, 122
  Cariboo and the North, 154–
    157
  Coast Mountain circle, 125–
    138
  emergencies, 170
  First Nations culture, 124
  Gulf Islands, 143–150, 168–
    169
  High Country and Okanagan
    Valley, 157–165
  Kootenays, 165–167
  North Coast, 150–154
  price categories, 121, 122
  Sunshine Coast, 138–143, 168
British Columbia Forest
  Discovery Centre, 101
British Columbia Golf
  Museum, 34
British Columbia Orchard
  Museum, 160
Brix✕, 42–43
Broken Group Islands, 111
Buchan Hotel🏠, 60
Bus travel
  British Columbia, 167, 168
  Vancouver, 71, 73
  Vancouver Island, 117, 118
  Victoria, 98
  Whistler, 135
Butchart Gardens, 85
Butterfly World, 112
Byrnes Block, 21

C

C✕, 47
Cafe Brio✕, 89
Café de Paris✕, 44
Caffé de Medici✕, 45
Calona Vineyards, 162
Camille's✕, 88
Campbell River, 114–115
Canada Day, 8
Canada Place, 16
Canadian Craft Museum, 16
Canadian International
  Dragon Boat Festival, 8
Canadian Princess Fishing
  Resort🏠, 107
Cannery✕, 52
Canoeing
  British Columbia, 123
  Powell River, 142
  Vancouver Island, 80
Capers✕, 48
Cape Scott Provincial Park,
  117
Capilano River Regional
  Park, 38
Capilano Suspension Bridge
  and Park, 38
Cariboo, 154–157

Carol Ships, *8*
Carr, Emily, *85–86*
Car rentals
British Columbia, 170
Vancouver, 74
Vancouver Island, 119
Victoria, 98
Whistler, 136
Car travel
British Columbia, 167–168
Vancouver, 71, 73
Vancouver Island, 118–119
Whistler, 135–136
Cassis✕, *88*
Castlebury Inn🏨, *102*
Cathedral Grove, *112*
Cedar Creek Estate Winery, *162–163*
Cedar Wood Lodge🏨, *105*
Cellar Door Bistro✕, *163*
Chalet Luise🏨, *133*
Charles H. Scott Gallery, *30*
Chartwell✕, *41*
Chateau Victoria🏨, *93*
Chateau Whistler Resort 🏨, *132*
Chemainus, *101–102*
Cherry Bank🏨, *94*
Chesterman Beach Bed and Breakfast🏨, *109*
Children's attractions
Duncan, 101
Harrison Hot Springs, 138
Kelowna, 160
Vancouver, 16, 18, 26, 27, 31, 32–33, 37, 38, 39
Victoria, 85, 86, 87
Chinese Cultural Centre Museum and Archives, *21*
Chinese Freemasons Building, *21*
Chinese Times Building, *21*
Chiyoda✕, *46*
Christ Church Cathedral, *16*
Churches
Mayne Island, 145
Vancouver, 16
Cin Cin✕, *45*
Clarion Hotel Grand Pacific 🏨, *92*
Clayoquot Wilderness Resorts🏨, *108–109*
Cleveland Dam, *38*
Climbing/mountaineering, *xxiv*
Squamish, 129
Clock, steam-powered, *22*
CN IMAX Theatre, *16*
Coachhouse on Oyster Bay 🏨, *145–146*
Coast Bastion Inn Nanaimo 🏨, *104*
Coast Harbourside Hotel and Marina🏨, *91*
Coast Inn of the North 🏨, *156*
Coast Mountain circle, *125–138*
Comox, *113–114*

Comox Airforce Museum, *113*
Consulates, *74*
Coombs, *112*
Coquihalla Canyon Recreation Area, *137*
Country Cottage🏨, *140*
Country Squire✕, *164*
Courtenay, *113–114, 120*
Courtenay and District Museum and Paleontology Centre, *113*
Cowichan Native Village, *101*
Craigdarroch Castle, *85*
Crawford Bay, *167*
Creekhouse✕, *139*
Crest Hotel✕🏨, *152*
Crow and Gate Neighbourhood Pub✕, *103*
Cruises, *170*
Crystal Garden Conservation Centre, *85*
Cusheon Lake, *146*

D

Dams, *38*
Dar Lebanon✕, *103*
Davis Bay, *140*
Days Inn🏨, *59*
Delilah's✕, *43*
Della Falls, *116*
Delta Pacific Resort & Conference Center🏨, *58*
Delta Pinnacle🏨, *56–57*
Delta Vancouver Suites 🏨, *57*
Delta Whistler Resort🏨, *132*
De Montreuil Restaurant ✕, *160*
Denman Island, *113*
Desolation Sound, *142*
Discovery Coast Passage, *151*
Diving. ☞ Scuba diving
Dr. Sun Yat-Sen Classical Chinese Garden, *21–22*
Don Mee's✕, *88*
Dragon boat festivals, *8*
Du Maurier International Jazz Festival, *8*
Duncan, *101*
Durlacher Hof🏨, *133*

E

Eagle Nook Ocean Wilderness Resort✕🏨, *105*
Eagles, *28, 128*
Earl's✕, *41, 48*
East Sooke Regional Park, *99*
Echo Valley Ranch Resort 🏨, *157*
Ecotourism
Vancouver, 75
Edgewater Lodge🏨, *133*
Elphinstone Pioneer Museum, *139*
Emergencies
British Columbia, 170
Vancouver, 74

Vancouver Island, 119
Victoria, 98, 99
Whistler, 136
Emily Carr House, *85–86*
Emily Carr Institute of Art and Design, *30*
Emory House Bed and Breakfast🏨, *166–167*
Empress🏨, *86, 91*
Empress Room✕, *88–89*
English Bay Inn🏨, *58*
Esquimalt & Nanaimo railway, *113*
Ezogiku Noodle Cafe✕, *46*

F

Fairmont Vancouver Airport Hotel🏨, *57*
Father Pandosy Mission, *160*
Ferry Island Municipal Park, *155*
Ferry travel
British Columbia, 168–169
Discovery Coast Passage, 151
Inside Passage, 150–151
Vancouver, 71–72, 73
Vancouver Island, 117–118
Victoria, 98
Festivals and seasonal events, *8–9*
Fiddler's Green✕, *166*
Filberg Heritage Lodge and Park, *113*
First Nations culture
Alert Bay, 116
British Columbia, 124
Duncan, 101
Hazelton, 155
Prince Rupert, 151
Quadra Island, 115
Queen Charlotte Islands, 152–153
Sechelt, 140
Sooke, 100
tours, 75
Vancouver, 26–27, 34, 39
Vancouver Island, 80
Victoria, 86, 87
Fisgard Lighthouse, *86*
Fish House in Stanley Park ✕, *47*
Fishing
British Columbia, 123, 171
Galiano Island, 144
museum on, 30
Powell River, 142
Terrace, 155
Tofino, 110
Vancouver, 66
Vancouver Island, 80, 119–120
Whistler, 134
Five Sails✕, *41*
Fleuri✕, *42*
Folk Music Festival, *8*
Football, *69*
Fort Langley National Historic Site, *138*
Fort Rodd Hill, *86*

Fort St. James National
  Historic Park, 155
Four Seasons⛺, 53–54
Fraser-Ft. George Regional
  Museum, 156
Fulford, 146

G

Gabriola Island, 104
Galiano Island, 143–145, 172
Ganges, 146, 170
Gardens
 Harrison Hot Springs, 138
 Tofino, 107
 Vancouver, 21–22, 35
 Victoria, 85, 86
Gate of Harmonious Interest,
  85
George C. Reifel Migratory
  Bird Sanctuary, 28
Georgina Point Heritage
  Park, 145
Gibsons Landing, 139–140
Glacier tours
 Squamish, 128–129
 Whistler, 136
Glen Lyon Inn⛺, 117
God's Mountain Crest Chalet
  ⛺, 164–165
Gold Rush Trail, 156–157
Golf
 British Columbia, 123, 171
 Campbell River, 115
 Courtenay, 114
 Crawford Bay, 167
 Galiano Island, 145
 Kamloops, 158
 Kelowna, 162
 museum on, 34
 Nanaimo, 104
 Parksville, 112
 Salt Spring Island, 150
 Squamish, 129
 Tofino, 110
 Vancouver, 66–67
 Vancouver Island, 120
 Vernon, 159
 Victoria, 96
 Whistler, 134
Gordon MacMillan Southam
  Observatory, 32–33
Grand King Seafood✕, 48
Grand Okanagan Lakefront
  Resort and Conference
  Centre⛺, 161
Granny Bogner's✕, 164
Granville Island Brewing, 30
Granville Island Hotel ⛺, 58
Granville Island Museums, 30
Granville Island Public
  Market, 30–31
Granville Island Water Park,
  31
Great Canadian Family
  Picnic, 8
Greystone Manor⛺, 114
Griffin's✕, 43
Grotto✕, 103
Grouse Mountain, 39

Guisachan House Restaurant
  ✕, 160–161
Gulf Islands, 143–150, 168–
  169
Gumboat Garden Café ✕,
  139
Gwaii Haanas National Park
  Reserve/Haida Heritage
  Site, 153

H

Habibi's✕, 52
Haida Gwaii, 152–154
Haida Gwaii Museum, 153
Haig-Brown House, 114
Hainle Vineyards Estate
  Winery, 163
Harrison Hot Springs, 137–138
Harrison Hot Springs Resort
  ✕⛺, 138
Harrison River Tearoom ✕, 138
Hastings House✕⛺, 148
Hastings Mill Museum, 34
Haterleigh Heritage Inn ⛺, 92
Hatley Castle, 86
Hazelton, 155
Helicopter travel, 98
Hell's Gate, 137
Helmcken House, 86
Herald Street Caffe✕, 89
Heritage Park, 155
Highliner Inn⛺, 152
Hiking
 British Columbia, 123, 171
 Kelowna, 162
 Nelson, 167
 tours, 75–76
 Ucluelet, 107
 Vancouver, 67, 75–76
 Vancouver Island, 80, 120
 Victoria, 96
 Whistler, 134
Historic O'Keefe Ranch, 159
Hiwus Feast House, 39
Hockey, 69
Holland House Inn⛺, 93–94
Hon's Wun-Tun House✕, 41
Hope, 137
Hornby Island, 113
Horne Lake Caves Provincial
  Park, 112
Horseback riding, 134
Horseshoe Bay, 125, 128
Hostelling International
  Tofino⛺, 110
Hostelling International
  Vancouver⛺, 60
Hostelling International
  Victoria⛺, 94
Hostelling International
  Whistler⛺, 133
Hotel Europe, 22
Hotel Vancouver⛺, 16, 54
Houseboat holidays, 159
House of Hewhiwus, 140
House Piccolo✕, 147
Howe Sound Inn & Brewing
  Company✕⛺, 129

H.R. MacMillan Space Centre,
  32–33
Humboldt House⛺, 91
Hummingbird Tea House✕,
  102

I

Icewine festivals, 8
Icons and symbols, 53, 79,
  123, 173. ☞ Also Web sites
Il Caminetto di Umberto ✕,
  131
Il Giardino di Umberto ✕, 45
Il Terrazzo✕, 89–90
Imperial Chinese Seafood ✕,
  41
Incendio✕, 47
Inland Lake Site and Trail
  System, 142
Inn at Tough City⛺, 109
Inside Passage, 150–151, 169

J

Jewel of India✕, 45
Joe Fortes Seafood and Chop
  House✕, 47
Jogging, 68
Johnstone Strait, 116
Juan de Fuca Provincial Park,
  100

K

Kalamalka Lake Provincial
  Park, 159
Kamloops, 157–158, 170
Kaslo, 166
Kayaking
 British Columbia, 123, 171
 Galiano Island, 145
 Johnstone Strait, 116
 Nanaimo, 104
 Powell River, 142
 Prince Rupert, 152
 Queen Charlotte Islands, 154
 Salt Spring Island, 149–150
 Tofino, 110
 Vancouver, 68
 Vancouver Island, 80, 120
Kelowna, 160–163, 170
Kelowna Art Gallery, 160
Kelowna Land & Orchard
  Company, 160
Kettle Valley Steam Railway,
  163
Kids' Market, 31
Kilby Historic Store and
  Farm, 138
Kingfisher Oceanside Resort
  and Spa⛺, 113–114
Kingfisher Restaurant✕, 106
Kingston⛺, 60
Kirin Mandarin Restaurant
  ✕, 41
Kirin Seafood Restaurant ✕,
  48
Kitsilano Beach, 32
Klahanie Road House✕, 129
Kootenays, 165–167

'Ksan Historical Village and Museum, *155*
Kwagiulth Museum and Cultural Centre, *115*
Kwinista Railway Museum, *151*

L

Lake Breeze Vineyards, *165*
Lake Okanagan Resort🏨, *161*
Langtry🏨, *59*
La Rúa✕, *131*
Laughing Oyster✕, *142–143*
Laurel Point Inn🏨, *92*
Lava beds, *155*
Le Crocodile✕, *44*
Le Gavroche✕, *44*
Le Petit Saigon✕, *90*
Lighthouses
Mayne Island, *145*
Ucluelet, *106*
Victoria, *86*
Liliget Feast House✕, *47*
Lillooet, *136–137*
Listel Vancouver🏨, *57*
Loggers Sports Festival, *8–9*
Long Beach, *111*
Lookout at Harbour Centre, *16, 18*
Lord Stanley Suites on the Park🏨, *59*
Lumbermen's Arch, *26*
Lumière✕, *51*
Lund, *142–143*
Lynn Canyon Park, *39*

M

Mahle House✕, *103*
Manning Provincial Park, *137*
Manteo Resort Waterfront Hotel & Villas🏨, *161*
Marina House Bed & Breakfast🏨, *140*
Marina Restaurant✕, *90*
Marine Building, *18*
Maritime Museum of British Columbia, *86*
Markham House Bed & Breakfast🏨, *100*
Matterson House✕, *106*
Mayne Island, *145–146*
McLean Mill National Historic Site, *104*
Metropolitan Hotel🏨, *54*
Middle Beach Lodge🏨, *109*
Miners Bay, *145*
Miniature Railway and Children's Farmyard, *26*
Miniature World, *86*
Minter Gardens, *138*
Misaki✕, *46*
Missionary settlements, *160*
Mission Hill Winery, *163*
Moby's Marine Pub✕, *147*
Model Ships Museum, *30*
Model Trains Museum, *30*

Montague Harbour Provincial Marine Park, *143*
Mouat's Trading Company, *146*
Mt. Galiano, *143*
Mt. Golden Hinde, *116*
Mt. Layton Resort, *155*
Mt. Maxwell Provincial Park, *146*
Mount Parke, *145*
Moyie (sternwheeler) *166*
Mulberry Manor🏨, *94*
Murals, *101–102*
Museum of Anthropology, *34–35*
Museum of Northern British Columbia, *151*

N

Naam Restaurant✕, *53*
Naikoon Provincial Park, *153*
Nanaimo, *102–104, 120*
Nanaimo District Museum, *102*
Nan Sdins, *153*
National and provincial parks
Cariboo, *156–157*
Coast Mountain circle, *137–138*
Fodor's Choice, *5*
Gulf Islands, *143, 146*
Okanagan Valley, *158, 159*
Queen Charlotte Islands, *153*
Sunshine Coast, *140, 141*
Vancouver Island, *100, 103, 105, 111, 112, 116, 117*
Nelson, *165–167*
Net Loft, *31*
Newcastle Island, *103*
900 West✕, *42*
Nine O'Clock Gun, *26*
Nisga'a Memorial Lava Bed Park, *155*
Nitobe Memorial Garden, *35*
North Coast, *150–154*
North Pacific Cannery Village Museum, *152*

O

Oak Bay Beach Hotel & Marine Resort🏨, *93*
Observatories, *32–33*
O Canada House🏨, *58–59*
Ocean Pointe Resort Hotel and Spa🏨, *91–92*
Oceanwood Country Inn✕🏨, *145*
Okanagan Fall Wine Festival, *9*
Okanagan Icewine Festival, *8*
Okanagan Valley, *157–165*
Okanagan Valley Wine Train, *160*
Old Court House Inn and Hostel🏨, *142*
Old Farmhouse Bed and Breakfast🏨, *149*

Old House Restaurant✕, *113*
Old School House Gallery and Art Centre, *112*
Orchards, *160*
Oritalia✕, *43–44*
Osoyoos, *165*

P

Pacific Mineral Museum, *18*
Pacific Rim National Park Reserve, *111–112*
Pacific Rim Whale Festival, *8*
Paddlers' Inn🏨, *109–110*
Painter's Lodge🏨, *115*
Pan Pacific Hotel🏨, *54*
Pan Pacific Lodge🏨, *132*
Parks. *Also National and provincial parks*
Galiano Island, *143*
Terrace, *155*
Vancouver, *22–24, 26–27, 35, 38, 39*
Victoria, *85*
Parksville, *112*
Parliament Building, *86–87*
Pastis✕, *51*
Patio Restaurant✕, *165*
Peachland, *163*
Penticton, *164–165*
Penticton Lakeside Resort and Conference Centre 🏨, *164*
Pharmacies
Vancouver, *77*
Victoria, *99*
Piccolo Mondo Ristorante ✕, *46*
Plane travel. ☞ Air travel
Planet Veg✕, *53*
Plumper Pass Lockup, *145*
Point Ellice House, *87*
Point No Point🏨, *101*
Polar Bear Swims, *8*
Porpoise Bay Provincial Park, *140*
Port Alberni, *104–105*
Port Hardy, *117, 120*
Powell River, *141–142*
Price categories
British Columbia, *121, 122*
Vancouver dining, *39*
Vancouver lodging, *53*
Victoria and Vancouver Island, *79*
Prince George, *155–156, 170, 172*
Prince George Railway and Forestry Museum, *156*
Prince Rupert, *151–152, 172*
Princess Louisa Inlet, *141*
Prior House Bed & Breakfast Inn🏨, *93*
Prospect Point, *26*
Prospect Point Café ✕, *26*
Provincial parks. ☞ National and provincial parks

Q

Quaaout Lodge Resort×⌧, 159
Quadra Island, 115–116
Quails' Gate Estate Winery, 163
Qualicum Beach, 112–113
Quarterdeck Inn and Marine Resort⌧, 117
Quattro on Fourth×, 51
Queen Charlotte Islands, 152–154, 169, 172
Queen Elizabeth Park, 35
Queen of Chilliwack (ferry) 151
Queen of the North (ferry) 150–151

R

Rafting
British Columbia, 123, 171
Vancouver, 68
Railroads
Courtenay, 113
Kelowna, 160
Port Alberni, 104
Squamish, 128
Summerland, 163
Vancouver, 37
Raincity Grill×, 42
Raincoast Café×, 108
Raintree at the Landing ×, 43
Ranches, 159
Rasputin×, 52
Re-Bar Modern Food×, 90
Red Crow Guest House⌧, 109
Reef Point Adventure Station⌧, 106
Restored historic sites
Barkerville, 156
Harrison Hot Springs, 138
Hazelton, 155
Kamloops, 158
Port Alberni, 104
Salt Spring Island, 146
Vernon, 159
River Run Cottages⌧, 59
Roberts Creek, 139
Roderick Haig-Brown Provincial Park, 158
Rodney's Oyster House×, 48
Roedde House Museum, 18
Roundhouse, 37
Royal British Columbia Museum, 87
Royal Coachman Neighbourhood Pub×, 114–115
Royal London Wax Museum, 87
Ruby Lake Resort×⌧, 141
Ruckle Provincial Park, 146

S

St. Ann's Academy, 87
St. Ann's Schoolhouse, 86
St. Mary Lake, 146

St. Mary Magdalene Church, 145
Salmon Arm, 158–159
Salmon hatcheries, 38
Salmon House on the Hill ×, 52–53
Salt Spring Island, 146–150, 172
Salt Spring Island Hostel ⌧, 149
Sam Kee Building, 22
Sandon, 166
Savary Island, 142
Schoolhouses, 86, 87
Schooner Restaurant×, 108
Science World, 37
Scuba diving
Galiano Island, 144
Powell River, 142
Sechelt, 141
Seasons in the Park×, 51
Sechelt, 140–141
Second Beach, 26
Secwepemc Museum and Heritage Park, 158
Seventeen Mile House×, 100
Shames Mountain, 155
Shannon Falls, 128
Sheraton Suites Le Soleil ⌧, 54, 56
Ships, historic, 164, 166
Siam Thai×, 90
Sicamous (paddlewheeler) 164
Sinclair Centre, 18
Siwash Rock, 26
Skeena River, 155
Skiing
British Columbia, 123–124, 171
competitions, 8
Courtenay, 114
Harrison Hot Springs, 138
Kamloops, 158
Kelowna, 162
Nelson, 167
Penticton, 165
Terrace, 155
tours, xxviii
Vancouver, 68
Vernon, 159
Whistler, 134–135
Skookumchuck Narrows Provincial Park, 141
Skyride aerial tramway, 39
Snow sports
British Columbia, 123–124
Whistler, 134–135
Snug Harbour Inn⌧, 106
Sointula, 116
Sooke, 99–101
Sooke Harbour House×⌧, 100
Sooke Region Museum and Visitor Information Centre, 100
Spinnakers Guest House ⌧, 94
Sport Fishing Museum, 30

Sproat Lake Provincial Park, 105
Spruce Point Lodge⌧, 154
Squamish, 8, 128–129
Stanley Park, 22–24, 26–27, 28
Star Anise×, 50
Stawamus Chief rock face, 128
Steam-powered clock, 22
Stepho's Souvlaki×, 45
Strathcona Park Lodge and Outdoor Education Centre ⌧, 116
Strathcona Provincial Park, 116
Sumac Ridge Estate Winery, 163
Summerhill Estate Winery, 163
Summerland, 163
Sundowner Inn⌧, 141
Sunshine Coast, 138–143, 168
Sunshine Coast Festival of the Written Arts, 140
Sunshine Coast Maritime Museum, 139
Sun Sui Wah×, 50
Sunwolf Outdoor Centre ⌧, 129
Surfing, 110
Sutil Lodge⌧, 144
Sutton Place⌧, 56
Süze Lounge and Restaurant×, 89
Swans⌧, 94
Swiftsure International, 8
Sylvia Hotel⌧, 60
Symbols and icons, 53, 79, 123, 173. ☞ also Web sites
Symphony of Fire, 8

T

Tapastree×, 44
Tauca Lea by the Sea⌧, 106–107
Taxis
Vancouver, 74
Victoria, 98
Teahouse Restaurant×, 42
Tennis
Vancouver, 68
Terrace, 154–155
TerrifVic Jazz Party, 8
Texada Island, 142
Thunderbird Park, 86
Tigh-Na-Mara Resort⌧, 112
Tofino, 107–111
Tofino Botanical Gardens, 107
Tojo's×, 52
Topanga Café×, 53
Totem poles
Duncan, 101
Vancouver, 26–27
Tour operators
British Columbia, 170
Vancouver, 74–77

Vancouver Island, 119
Victoria, 98–99
Whistler, 136
Train tours, 76
Train travel. ☞ Also
Railroads
British Columbia, 169–170
Vancouver, 72–73
Vancouver Island, 119
Whistler, 136
Trattoria di Umberto✕, 131
Treehouse Café✕, 148
Tsa-Kwa-Luten Lodge✕☲, 115

U

Ucluelet, 105–107
U'mistra Cultural Centre, 116
University of British Columbia
Botanical Garden, 35
Urban Fare✕, 37
Utopian communities, 116

V

Val d'Isère✕, 130
Vancouver
Chinatown, 19–22
consulates, 74
Downtown, 14–19
emergencies, 74
False Creek, 35–37
Gaoler's Mews, 22
Gastown, 19–22
Granville Island, 27, 29–31
greater Vancouver, 33–35
Kitsilano, 31–33
Library Square, 37
North Vancouver, 37–39
Plaza of Nations, 37
price categories, 39, 53
Robson Square, 18
Robson Street, 18
Stanley Park, 22–24, 26–27, 28
Yaletown, 35–37
Vancouver Aquarium Marine
Science Centre, 27
Vancouver Art Gallery, 19
Vancouver Convention and
Exhibition Centre, 16
Vancouver Fringe Festival, 9
Vancouver International
Children's Festival, 8
Vancouver International
Comedy Festival, 8

Vancouver International Film
Festival, 9
Vancouver International
Writers Festival, 9
Vancouver Island. ☞ Also
Victoria
emergencies, 119
price categories, 79
Vancouver Maritime Museum,
33
Vancouver Museum, 33
Vancouver Playhouse
International Wine Festival,
8
Vancouver Police Centennial
Museum, 22
Vancouver Tourist Info
Centre, 19
VanDusen Botanical Garden,
35
Vernon, 159
Vesuvius, 146
Victoria
Bastion Square, 83
Chinatown, 85
emergencies, 98, 99
Market Square, 86
price categories, 79
Victoria Bug Zoo, 87–88
Victoria Day, 8
Victorian Restaurant✕, 88
Victoria Regent☲, 93
Videos on Vancouver and
British Columbia, 6–7
Vij's✕, 51
Villa del Lupo✕, 46
Visitor information
British Columbia, 172
Vancouver, 77
Vancouver Island, 120
Victoria, 88, 99
Whistler, 136

W

Walking tours
Vancouver, 76–77
Waterfalls
British Columbia, 128, 129,
137–138
Vancouver Island, 116
Waterford Restaurant✕, 102
Waterfront☲, 57
Waterfront Station, 19
Water Street Café✕, 43

Wedgewood Hotel☲, 57–58
Wedgwood Manor☲, 167
Wells Gray Provincial Park,
158
Wells Hotel☲, 157
West Coast Railway Heritage
Park, 128
West End Guest House☲, 59
Westin Bayshore Resort and
Marina☲, 56
Westin Grand Vancouver ☲,
56
Whalers on the Point
Guesthouse☲, 110
Whale-watching
Johnstone Strait, 116
Tofino, 110
Ucluelet, 107
Vancouver Island, 80
Victoria, 96
Whistler
emergencies, 136
Whistler Summer Festivals, 8
Whytecliff Marine Park, 128
Wickaninnish Centre, 111
Wickaninnish Inn✕☲, 108
Wildflower✕, 131
Wildlife preserves
Squamish, 128
Vancouver area, 28
Victoria, 85
William Tell✕, 43
Willow Point Lodge☲, 166
Windsurfing, 68
Wine Museum, 160
Wineries
Kelowna, 162–163
Penticton, 165
Summerland and Peachland,
163
Woodstone Country Inn✕☲,
144
Woody Life Village☲, 158

Y

Yachting events, 8
Yellow Point Lodge☲, 103–
104
YWCA Hotel/Residence☲,
60–61

Z

Zeuski's✕, 131
Zoos, 87–88